Management, Organizations and Contemporary Social Theory

T0332043

Social theorists speculate about large-scale social questions, asking of any phenomenon, how is it possible? This book addresses how various social theories contribute key insights into the nature of organizations and management.

The cast of characters to be found in this book have had a transcendental impact, including on the practices of the management and organization disciplines. For students, however, engaging with social theory in a conversation that is much broader and potentially richer than those that may have been previously encountered is not at first easy. The question is where to begin: this book provides answers.

Drawing on research from international contributors, this valuable textbook is an essential resource for students and introduces key social theories and theorists making them accessible to a management audience. The chapters include objectives and end-of-chapter reflective questions, as well as a glossary for readers grappling with new terms.

Stewart Clegg is Distinguished Professor in Management at UTS Business School and a Visiting Professor at Nova School of Business and Economics, Lisbon, Portugal. The central focus of his theoretical work has always been on power relations, enabling him to write on many diverse and ubiquitous topics – as power relations are everywhere. He is the co-author of two widely used textbooks and a prolific contributor to leading journals in the fields of organization studies, political power and management.

Miguel Pina e Cunha is the Fundação Amélia de Mello Professor of Leadership and a member of the Leadership for Impact Center at Nova School of Business and Economics, Lisbon, Portugal. His research deals with the surprising (paradox, improvisation, serendipity, zemblanity, vicious circles) and the extreme (positive organizing, genocide). He recently co-authored *Positive Organizational Behaviour* (Routledge, 2019).

Management, Organizations and Contemporary Social Theory

Edited by Stewart Clegg and
Miguel Pina e Cunha

Routledge
Taylor & Francis Group

LONDON AND NEW YORK

First published 2019
by Routledge
2 Park Square, Milton Park, Abingdon, Oxon OX14 4RN

and by Routledge
52 Vanderbilt Avenue, New York, NY 10017

Routledge is an imprint of the Taylor & Francis Group, an informa business

British Library Cataloguing-in-Publication Data
A catalogue record for this book is available from the British Library

Library of Congress Cataloging-in-Publication Data
Names: Clegg, Stewart, editor. | Cunha, Miguel Pina e, editor.
Title: Management, organizations and contemporary social theory/edited by Stewart Clegg and Miguel Pina e Cunha.
Description: 1 Edition. | New York: Routledge, 2019. | Includes bibliographical references and index.
Identifiers: LCCN 2019006224 (print) | LCCN 2019007805 (ebook) |
ISBN 9780429279591 (eBook) | ISBN 9780815365846 (hardback: alk. paper) |
ISBN 9780367233778 (pbk.: alk. paper) | ISBN 9780429279591 (ebk)
Subjects: LCSH: Management. | Organization.
Classification: LCC HD31.2 (ebook) | LCC HD31.2 .M363 2019 (print) |
DDC 302.3/5–dc23
LC record available at https://lccn.loc.gov/2019006224

ISBN: 978-0-815-36584-6 (hbk)
ISBN: 978-0-367-23377-8 (pbk)
ISBN: 978-0-429-27959-1 (ebk)

Typeset in Sabon
by Integra Software Services Pvt. Ltd.

Visit the eResource: www.routledge.com/9780367233778

MIX
Paper from
responsible sources
FSC   FSC™ C013985
www.fsc.org

Printed in the United Kingdom
by Henry Ling Limited

Contents

Contributors

Ira Chatterjee is a PhD student in the department of Management and Organization, at the Hanken School of Economics (Helsinki, Finland). Ira spent several years in industry, working for international companies, before entering academia. She studies social entrepreneurship and institutional theory and her current research examines the role of framing strategies on processes of social change. Ira has previously taught at the ICFAI Business School in India and the Etelä Tapiolan Lukio in Finland.

Stewart Clegg is Distinguished Professor in Management at UTS Business School. Before moving to UTS he was Reader at Griffith University (1976–1984), Professor at the University of New England (1985–1989), Professor at the University of St Andrews (1990–1993), and Foundation Professor at the University of Western Sydney (1993–1996). He holds a small number of Visiting Professorships at prestigious European universities and research centres. The central focus of his theoretical work has always been on power relations, enabling him to write on many diverse and ubiquitous topics – as power relations are everywhere! He is the co-author of two widely used textbooks: *Management & Organizations: An Introduction to Theory and Practice*, and *Strategy: Theory and Practice*, both published by Sage. He is also the co-editor of the *Handbook of Organization Studies, Handbook of Power* and *Handbook of Macro-Organizational Behavior*, all published by Sage. He is a prolific contributor to leading journals in the fields of organization studies, political power and management.

Cátia Miriam Costa is a researcher in the Centre for International Studies (ISCTE-IUL). She has a degree in International Relations from the Technical University of Lisbon and has a PhD in literature studies from the University of Évora. She is a member of Coopmar (an Iberian-American network on transatlantic culture and policy) and a member of OceanGov (a European network promoting sea-related sustainability research issues). She works on discourse analysis and international communication. She is conducting research on port cities and the colonial press in Africa, America and Asia. Before academia she worked in the private sector, public sector and the third sector. She is a columnist for the weekly *O Jornal Económico* and features regularly in television commentary.

Miguel Pina e Cunha is the Fundação Amélia de Mello Professor of Leadership and a member of the Leadership for Impact Center at Nova School of Business and Economics, Universidade Nova de Lisboa, Lisbon, Portugal. His research deals with the surprising (paradox, improvisation, serendipity, zemblanity, vicious circles) and the extreme (positive organizing, genocide). He recently co-authored *Positive Organizational Behaviour* (Routledge, 2019) and *Introduction to Theories of Organizational Resilience* (Elgar, 2019).

Xavier Deroy (PhD, HDR) is a Professor of Strategy and Organization Theory at NEOMA Business School. He is the Chairman of the Research Committee of NEOMA. He co-created and co-directed Masternova, a Specialized Master of Management in Bio-technologies, gathering jointly NEOMA and AGROPARIS-TECH. He is a member of LIRSA, a research laboratory of CNAM Paris and his research fields are critical studies, event theory applied to historical change of organizations, institutional change, ethics and organizational politics. He edited a book and co-authored books on event and organization theory, innovation and organizational history, organized a track about events and organizations during seven years for the EURAM conference, and published articles in journals such as *Organization Studies, Organization, Journal of Change Management* and *Management International.*

Frank den Hond is the Ehrnrooth Professor in Management and Organisation at Hanken School of Economics (Helsinki, Finland) and affiliated with the Vrije Universiteit (Amsterdam, the Netherlands). From 2013 to 2017, he was one of the Editors-in-Chief of *Organization Studies*. His research covers various topics in the broad area of business in society; he recently developed interests in partial organization and business ethics. Publications include articles in *Academy of Management Journal, Academy of Management Review, Business & Society, Journal of Business Ethics, Journal of Corporate Citizenship, Journal of Management Studies* and *Organization Studies*. He served the European Group for Organizational Studies (EGOS) as a board member and he was the main organizer of the 2008 EGOS Colloquium.

Edward Granter is a Senior Lecturer in Organizational Behaviour at the University of Birmingham, UK. His research interests lie in the intersections of Frankfurt School critical theory and the sociology of work and organization. He has written on the future of work (*Critical Social Theory and the End of Work*, Routledge, 2009) and the influence of critical theory on organization studies. Edward's empirical research on healthcare work and organization is reflected in co-authorship of *Deconstructing the Welfare State* (Routledge, 2016). He is co-editor of *The Sage Handbook of the Sociology of Work and Employment* (2015) and has written for various journals on topics such as the Global Financial Crisis (*Sociology*), corporate crime (*Competition & Change*) and extreme work (*Organization; Work, Employment and Society*). He teaches courses on organizational behaviour and critical analysis in management.

Charles Harvey is Professor of Business History and Management at Newcastle University Business School and Director of the Centre for Research on Entrepreneurship, Wealth and Philanthropy (REWP). He holds a PhD in International Business from the University of Bristol. He is author of numerous books and articles in the fields of strategy, leadership and management. His research focuses upon the historical processes that inform contemporary business practice, entrepreneurial philanthropy and the exercise of power by elite groups in society. His recent publications are in the *Academy of Management Review, Organization Studies, Organization, Human Relations* and the *Business History Review*.

Kate Kenny is Professor in Management and Organisation Studies at Queen's University Belfast. Her research focuses on power and identity in organizations, and whistle-blowing. She held a research fellowship at Cambridge University's Judge Business School from 2008–2016, and was an Edmond J. Safra Lab Fellow at Harvard University from 2013–2015. Professor Kenny's work has been published in *Organization Studies, Gender Work and Organizations, ephemera* and *Human Relations*, among other journals. Her books include *Understanding Identity and Organizations* (Sage, 2011, with A. Whittle and H. Willmott), and *Affect at Work: The Psychosocial and Organization Studies* (Palgrave, 2014, with M. Fotaki). Her forthcoming book on whistle-blowing will be published by Harvard University Press in 2019.

Jagat Kunwar is currently a lecturer at South-Eastern University of Applied Sciences, Kouvola, Finland. He is also a PhD student at the department of Management and Organization, Hanken School of Economics (Helsinki, Finland). As a lecturer at the South-Eastern University of Applied Sciences, he has taught a wide range of subjects including leadership, supply chain management, brand building and communication, and global marketing. As a doctoral researcher, his primary interests lie in the nexus of institutional theory and corporate governance. He has previous work experience in private businesses and non-governmental organizations.

Georg Loscher is a postdoctoral research fellow at the Chair of Human Resources Management and Organization Studies at the Bundeswehr University Munich, Germany. His research interests include practice theory, institutional complexity and professional service firms.

Alan McKinlay is Professor of HRM at Newcastle University Business School. He was awarded his doctorate by Nuffield College, Oxford University. His interests are the long-run dynamics of management and work organization as well as how to use Foucault to understand the evolution of management languages and practices. He is currently researching the emergence of industrial psychology in Britain after the Great War.

Mairi Maclean is Professor of International Business at the University of Bath, UK. She received her PhD from the University of St Andrews, Scotland. Her research interests include international business elites and elite power from a Bourdieusian perspective, entrepreneurial philanthropy and historical organization studies. She is currently working on an ESRC-funded project exploring the British interwar management movement. Recent publications include contributions to the *Academy of Management Review, Organization Studies, Human Relations, Organizational Research Methods* and the *Business History Review*.

Sandro Mendonça is Professor at the Department of Economics, ISCTE Business School. He is a German Marshall Fund Fellow and was a visiting scholar at King's College, London. In 2015 he was nominated 'European Young Leader' by the Friends of Europe Foundation. He has been a faculty member of SPRU, University of Sussex since 2016 and an invited professor at ISEG, University of

Lisbon since 2012. He teaches and supervises at the doctoral programmes of the Southern Medical University (Guanghzou) and the University of Electronic Science and Technology of China (Chengdu). His research and consultancy activities have mainly focused on innovation and industrial policy, and stretched to the fields of strategic foresight and conflict research. He is currently a member of the board of ANACOM, the national regulatory authority in Portugal for communications.

Frank Mueller is Professor of Strategy and Organisation at Newcastle University Business School. Before joining Newcastle University in 2012, Frank held a Chair in Management at St Andrews University. His overall research focus is on understanding organizational change as a discursive, political and strategic project under conditions of neo-liberalism and managerialism. Since 1991, he has published over 50 refereed journal articles and ten book chapters.

Alistair Mutch is Professor of Information and Learning at Nottingham Trent University. He has published widely in both organization studies and history. His *Religion and National Identity: Governing Scottish Presbyterianism in the Eighteenth Century* (Edinburgh, 2015) combined ideas drawn from the critical realist tradition with detailed archival work to suggest the importance of examining practices. He has continued this theme with work on institutional logics, notably in an article in *Academy of Management Review* (2018). He is working on a book on institutional logics drawing on the framework supplied by Margaret Archer, to be published by Routledge.

Damian O'Doherty is Professor of Management and Organization at the University of Manchester Alliance Manchester Business School where he is director of the Manchester Ethnography Network and co-director of the BEAM nuclear and social research network based at the Dalton Nuclear Research Institute also at the University of Manchester. His work focuses on how the on-going quest for organization *patterns* relations between social order and disorder and how new political imaginations and actions are forged out of these complex relations. In seeking answers to these questions he is influenced by the work of people like Jacques Derrida, Gilles Deleuze and Michel Foucault. In 2017 he published *Reconstructing Organization* based on two years of ethnographic research at the Manchester Airport Group in the UK. He also publishes regularly in *Organization Studies, Human Relations,* and *Organization* and has published in *Sociology, Sociological Review* and the *Journal of Cultural Economy.* He is now associate editor at *Organization* and former editor-in-chief of *Culture and Organization.* He is currently working ethnographically in the restaurant industry in Greater Manchester and in the nuclear industry in the UK, both of which are leading to the development of a research practice and 'ontological politics' in organization studies he is provisionally speculating might be called 'gaiagraphy'.

Eric Pezet is Professor in Management at Paris Nanterre University (France). He is co-founder of Paris Research in Norms Management and Law (PRIMAL) and co-editor-in-chief of *Personnel review.* He was co-founder and president of the French Association for the History of Management and Organizations (AHMO). He develops his research in a Foucauldian perspective and publishes in organization studies, management and organization history, and human resource management.

Dean Pierides is Lecturer in Business and Management at the University of Stirling, UK. He was awarded his BA from the University of Pennsylvania, and DipEd, MEd and PhD from the University of Melbourne. He was previously a visiting scholar at Copenhagen Business School and Lecturer in Organisations and Society at the University of Manchester. His research is about how organizations deal with uncertainty, with a focus on government agencies that are responsible for emergencies and disasters, whether natural, financial or otherwise.

Tiago Lima Quintanilha is a researcher at CIES-IUL – Centre for Research and Studies in Sociology (ISCTE-IUL). He was trained as a sociologist at ISCTE-IUL, has complemented those skills with a post-grad in Human Resources Management and is currently enrolled as a PhD candidate in Communication Sciences at ISCTE-IUL. His research interests include media studies, journalism and open science. He served as a researcher at the Portuguese media watch (OberCom) and acted as journal manager at the *OBS* Observatorio* from 2009 to 2017. He collaborated with the Research Centre in Economic and Organizational Sociology at the Lisbon School of Economics & Management, with the Portuguese regulatory authority for the Media (ERC) and with the Reuters Institute for the Study of Journalism on the project Digital News Report Portugal. In his research and consultancy career he has co-authored over 65 research reports, three books, 12 book chapters and nine peer-reviewed original scientific articles in topics ranging from radio innovation and newspaper industrial dynamics to digital advertising and the networked future of the European film sector. His work has been recognized by two academic merit-based scholarships and his doctoral research is supported by the Portuguese Foundation for Science and Technology (FCT).

David Seidl is a chaired Professor of Organization and Management at the University of Zurich and Research Associate at the Centre for Business Research (CBR) at the University of Cambridge. His research interests include strategy as practice, strategic change, standardization and the philosophy of science.

Graham Sewell is Professor of Management and Associate Dean, Research in the Faculty of Business & Economics, University of Melbourne. He received his BSc (hons) and PhD in urban planning from Cardiff University and has previously held appointments at the University of Manchester and Imperial College, London. He has also held visiting appointments at several institutions including UC Santa Cruz, UC Berkeley, and Pompeu Fabra, Barcelona. He is best known for his work on organizational surveillance.

Violetta Splitter is a Senior Research Associate at the Department of Business Administration at the University of Zurich. Her research interests include strategy as practice, participation in strategy, open strategy and the philosophy of science.

Robert van Krieken is Professor of Sociology at the University of Sydney, and Visiting Professor of Sociology at University College Dublin. Since 2015, he has been President of Research Committee 17, Sociology of Organizations, in the International Sociological Association. His research interests include the sociology of organizations, law, criminology, childhood, processes of civilization and decivilization, cultural genocide, and the history and sociology of celebrity, as well as contributing to the theoretical debates around the work of Elias, Foucault, Luhmann and Latour. In addition to journal articles in *Sociological Review, Sociology, British Journal of Sociology, Economy & Society, Journal of Sociology* and *Theory & Society,* his books include *Norbert Elias* (1998), *Celebrity and the Law* (2010, co-authored), *Celebrity Society* (2012) and *Sociology* (2016, 6th edition, co-authored). The second edition of *Celebrity Society: The Struggle for Attention* was published in 2018. He is especially interested in drawing on Weber, Foucault and Elias in understanding the ways in which social structures and dynamics are underpinned by particular organizational or institutional forms, how those forms of organization interweave with particular psychological dispositions, and how that interlinking of structure and habitus changes over time, using Weber's concepts of discipline and rationalisation, Foucault's account of discipline and government, and Elias's concepts of civilization and decivilization. Most recently he has extended Elias's account of 'court society' to analyse 'celebrity society', drawing out the linkages between the two in terms of their institutional structuring of interaction and habitus.

Andrea Whittle is Professor of Management and Organisation Studies at Newcastle University Business School. Before joining Newcastle University in 2013, Andrea held a Chair in Organisation Studies at Cardiff University. Her research is driven by a passion for understanding the role of language in business and management settings and is informed by theories and methodologies from the fields of discourse analysis, narrative, discursive psychology, ethnography, ethnomethodology and conversation analysis. She has studied the role of discourse across range of topic areas, including management consultants, identity and identification, branding, organizational change, technology, strategy and the Global Financial Crisis.

1 Management, organizations and contemporary social theory[1,2]

Stewart Clegg and Miguel Pina e Cunha

Exploring social theory

Social theorists speculate about large-scale social questions. A key focus is to ask of any phenomenon, how is it possible? The phenomena to which this question may be addressed include not only those that we may encounter in everyday life and practice, such as organizations and management; they also include explanation of these as a phenomenon. In this sense, what social theory addresses is how any social order or practices of ordering are possible. These practices thus include those constructing and those and that are constructed through these processes. For example, social theory is concerned with how prior theories of the social, in their explanations of important questions, such as the nature of power and social structure, gender and ethnicity, modernity and postmodernity, civilizations and their discontents, have been formulated in the past and require contemporary reformulating in analytic terms for present knowledges and times. Contemporary social theory laces through all the concerns of contemporary management and organization theory: it offers not so much theory *for* management or theory *for* organizations, but theory that is addressed not only to the social practices that constitute these theories but that also has implications for what these theories take for granted.

Management and organization theory are relatively recent areas of evolution in the social sciences; indeed, for the most part they evolved from earlier periods of embeddedness in broader social science areas such as sociology, history, economics or from engineering. The founders of these areas were people such as Adam Smith (1950; lived 1723–1790), a political economist and moral philosopher; Karl Marx (1976; lived 1818–1883), also a political economist as well as a philosopher; Max Weber (1978; lived 1864–1920), a legal scholar, economic historian and latterly a sociologist; and Frederick Taylor (1911; lived 1856–1915), not a scholar but a self-taught engineer.

As the fields of management and organization theory have subsequently developed, these disciplinary areas have become ever more specialized and those founders of the fields have largely faded from memory. Nonetheless, the big picture and large-scale theorizing that some of these figures engaged in (Taylor hardly counts in this calculus) has not faded away; there are many contemporary figures who approach larger questions of social, political, cultural and economic life, the power of whose thought has influenced broader theorizing about more specialized areas, including management and organization theory. Broadly speaking, those figures are recognized as social theorists because they have developed narrative and analytical frameworks that critically examine social phenomena. To say they do so 'critically' is the key: what they do not do is take for granted either how the field of knowledge has been constructed before them or accept the common-sense definitions of those phenomena that they are interested in.

What qualified a scholar to be considered a social theorist? Essentially, they are figures whose influence extends well beyond their home disciplines into the public sphere, combining the role of social theorist with that of being a public intellectual, someone that the educated non-specialist might come across, people whose ideas about the way that aspects of the world work have made a broad critical conceptual impact on that world: they make a difference as to how we see and think about our world. Making a difference is what great teachers do and we may say that the figures we have selected are all, through their books (and it is largely through books), figures who have made a significant difference to the way many others and we see the world. In this respect, they are heirs to the traditions that figures such as Marx, Smith or Weber initiated.

Let us consider Weber for a moment because he is an illustrative case of what makes a social theorist a social theorist. In management and organization theory, if he is remembered at all, it will most often be as classical theorist, concerned with bureaucracy. While this is not false it is hardly adequate: Weber was a major intellectual figure in debates about methodology, the origins of capitalism, the comparative study of major world religions, the ethics of vocation, economic history, the conditions of industrial workers, public administration and much else besides. What most management and organization theory know of him is very little. Consequently, what most students in these areas learn is even less. We may take from this founding example of Max Weber that social theorists are wide-ranging in their concerns; concerned with major intellectual debates that have contemporary relevance; concerned with delineating elaborated and coherent theory about the matters that debate encompasses and that they do so in such a way that they offer potential guidance to many substantive fields of knowledge.

Management and organization studies constitute a flow of knowledge fed by many streams, not all of them deemed social theory but nonetheless significant. Cybernetics, for instance, especially the contributions of Herbert Simon (1996; 2013) (a scholar awarded the Sveriges Riksbank prize in honour of Alfred Nobel), has played an important role. It is appropriate to state that the reason for the exclusion of Simon (and of other important intellectual figures who greatly contributed to the development of organization theory, such as Gregory Bateson [2000]) is not due to idiosyncratic preferences but rather to the decision to focus on social theory-informed contributions.

Social theory, as distinct from management or organization theory, is a continent of possibilities composed of many fields, with distinct but different topographical features. Social theory is concerned with the continent, with the overarching embeddedness of the distinct topographies of the different regions, or disciplinary areas. The effects of considerable evolution, erosion and accretion will have shaped some aspects of these disciplinary areas; other areas may be more recent, less sedimented, still being shaped. Social theory has been a major factor in the shaping, forming and evolving of these more recent substantive disciplinary areas, such as management and organization studies. The role of social theory produces very different inflections. Consider the ranking of Weber and Foucault, for instance.[3] Comparing leading European production of disciplinary knowledge in the journal *Organization Studies* with that of the American journal *Administrative Science Quarterly*, Üsdiken and

Pasadeos (1995) demonstrated that while Weber and Foucault loomed large in citations in the European consciousness, Foucault did not receive citation and Weber barely registered in America in the top 100 citations. The findings in this work are updated in Üsdiken (2014), which finds that differences between North American and European scholarship are still evident, looking at a broader range of journals and a longer period of time. Üsdiken (2010), in a related article, notes that perhaps as a result of national education systems' evaluation exercises that tend to privilege US-based journals, 'wholesale adoption of US-based theories and research practices has also been expanding' (Üsdiken, 2010, p. 732). At the earlier stage there was a big difference but now American work is increasingly prevailing, re-framing European work through a combination of demographic density and intellectual hegemony through overwhelming command of the circuits of power – editorial and review functions in the key journals – that define legitimacy. Nonetheless, discernible differences remain. For the future, one should not think that building only on European intellectual traditions is the best way. Similar advances could (and should) be achieved by building also on other philosophical and social traditions developed outside of Europe, for instance from Chinese scholarship (Fei, 1939), from the critical pedagogy of Brazilian Paulo Freire (2018) or from indigenous perspectives such as Mbigi (2005; see Seremani & Clegg, 2015, on epistemological third spaces).

The disciplines, by convention, are textually composed networks: who gets cited where, when and how often defines the disciplinary field. One of the things that social theory can do is address how the texts of disciplinary scholarship and more everyday practices have been formed, shaped and used. Any such engagement is inherently critical in its questioning of existing institutions constituting the management and the organization of ourselves and those things with which we live and work, the norms and practices established, their constitution of and by power and other disciplinary practices, such as writing, culture, politics, selfhood and technology.

The focus on social theories is not to deny the existence or significance of more organization or management-oriented writers such as those who regularly appear in the pages of the leading journals in these fields. Such figures are clearly significant. However, their significance remains largely specific to the management and organizations field: Karl Weick (1995) or Kathleen Eisenhardt (1989), for instance, are clearly major figures in management and organizations but they are of less influence in terms of the development of broader social theories. While these figures are important, they are not the focus here.

Our cast of characters have had a more transcendental impact, including on the practices of the management and organization disciplines, yet they will rarely be encountered in the undergraduate curriculum. The more advanced curriculum, however, is another matter: here the concerns, at best, are less with techniques and their application and more with what these techniques and applications do as practices. To ask these questions is to, necessarily, engage with social theory, and in so doing the student is engaging in a conversation that is much broader and potentially richer than those that may have been previously encountered. Such conversations are not easy at first; one is entering into the domains of scholarship that are well established, legitimate but contested, broad reaching and widely engaged. The question is where to begin: this book provides answers.

There is a considerable gap between what is typically taught in undergraduate business subjects and what is expected from research students. While the former courses are oriented towards producing technically competent managers, accountants, etc., the latter is more concerned to contribute original knowledge to the disciplinary corpus. An obstacle in this respect is the absence of a bridging text that covers aspects of contemporary social theory relevant to the world of business and organizations. Without grounding in social theory, research students are unlikely to gain the knowledge, skills and sophistication that will see them publish in the top-tier journals. The intent of this book is to help students and their teachers in bridging this gap.

The cast of characters

As we have said, social theory is a rich and encyclopaedic domain. One must be selective. What guided the selectivity in this instance? The personal knowledge, particular enthusiasms and social networks of the editors framed a large part of it. We all have our favourites and those theorists that are represented here are some personal favourites, drawn from the stocks of knowledge that we use and deploy. Obviously, our knowledge is a form of 'bounded rationality'; it is framed by preferences, habits and theoretical orientations. We make no apologies for having these and being candid about them, for it is impossible to be exhaustive. No one can claim perfect knowledge or disinterest; hence our interests and our bounded knowledge frame the choices made. We had one implicit rule in making our choices, which was that the social theorists chosen should be ones with a relatively contemporary relevance and output. In practice, this means that they should have been writing in the period from the contemporary flowering of social theory from the 1960s to the present day.

The first chapter, written by Andrea Whittle and Frank Mueller, on 'ethnomethodology', explores the influence of Harold Garfinkel and the approach to studying social action known as ethnomethodology. The chapter explores the distinct approach to studying organizing 'as it happens' developed by ethnomethodologists. Ethnomethodology was regarded as a quite radical approach when it was first encountered in Garfinkel's work because of its very evident difference from the dominant social theory of mainstream structural-functionalism. Its opposition to much embedded intellectual capital did not endear it those whose capital it was. The dominant theory, with its stress on systems, their functional prerequisites and pattern variables, on the centrality of socialization and social order within the frame of a central value system, could not have been more antithetical to the social theory that ethnomethodology established. Where the former was top-down and emphasized social order, the latter was very much a theory that worked from the intricacies of how order was established provisionally and capable of being easily breached in scenes drawn from everyday life: from decision-making by jurors, presentations of self in critical performances of transgender identity, scenes drawn from shopping, counselling and so on. Order, instead of being a monolith that is obeyed by the many and disobeyed by the few who are deviant, is instead something that is co-constructed on the basis of many tacit assumptions, cues and conventions.

Garfinkel's ethnomethodology has been indirectly influential in an important strand of management and organization theory. Karl Weick's (1995) approach to sensemaking, developed from his earlier concern with *The Social Psychology of Organizing* (1969 edition, especially), clearly learnt a lot from ethnomethodology. Indeed, one of us on occasion has been known to refer to the sensemaking literature as ethnomethodology translated into management. That translation was not the extent of the use to which ethnomethodology was put.

Far from the Californian campuses where ethnomethodology first flourished, its influence was felt in Europe, especially in the *École Nationale Supérieure des Mines* in Paris, where, as Damian O'Doherty writes in the chapter on 'Actor-network theory: Michel Callon, Bruno Latour, John Law', the three main protagonists of the approach translated, in part, ideas from ethnomethodology into actor-network theory. Actor-network theory (ANT) has become one of the most popular reference points across many regions of the social sciences and beyond. Moreover, it has become one of the most important approaches to management and organization, being 'applied' or extended by many well-known figures in the field, such as John Hassard (Alcadipani & Hassard, 2010; Law and Hassard, 1999), Barbara Czarniawska and Tor Hernes (2005). Elements of the ANT approach have also been cited as an influence and synthesized by other branches of social theory. As with ethnomethodology, ANT starts from the actors and their doings rather than seeing them as 'cultural dopes' dominated by social systems that constrain them. One of the major innovations of ANT is to extend the notion of the actor, however. It is not only people that can exert social agency, that can act: actants, things that are non-human, such as technologies, as well as devices humble and smart and non-human beings, such as scallops, also have agency in ANT. In a nutshell, ANT's main contribution is to regard the 'social' as the partial and contingent outcome of specific actor-networks' construction and understanding of the things of everyday practices. These practices are situated: they take place in field trips, in laboratories, in the accounts that scientists write of their practices (which does not always coincide with what these scientists are observed as doing by ANT observers) and they involve not only many other actors in networks of action but also actants. The test tube must be sterile, the acid pure, the vacuum chamber pristine, for science to work. These humble material things are all actants. As it is in science so it is elsewhere: the lecturer depends on material actants such as computers, software such as PowerPoint, video projectors and even simpler things such as electric cables and connections. The agency that emerges is a collective and relational phenomenon in which the properties of both actants and actors form *assemblages* that are responsible for what is done.

Garfinkel's ideas not only influenced 1970s Parisian intellectuals such as Bruno Latour and Michel Callon, as well as the Englishman who worked closely with them, John Law; they also made headway in the hallowed halls of Cambridge, where a prolific social theorist, Anthony Giddens, had made a name for himself through numerous publications as the foremost interpreter of the sociological trinity of founding fathers, Karl Marx, Max Weber and Emile Durkheim (Giddens, 1973). Having done this, in 1976 he turned his imagination to establishing some *New Rules of Sociological Method*, in which a rich mix of philosophical and sociological resources were drawn on to produce what became known as structuration theory, a mix in which a little ethnomethodology was clearly discernible.

New Rules of Sociological Method marked a shift in direction in Giddens' preoccupations from classical to contemporary social theory. Ira Chatterjee, Jagat Kunwar and Frank den Hond, in their chapter 'Giddens and structuration theory', discuss some of the major works that followed. What characterized these works was a concern with the duality of structure as a set of social relations and institutions framing social action by human agency. The concern with the duality of structure was not uppermost in either ethnomethodology or ANT, even though the relationship between individual action and social structure had long been a central topic in social theory. Anthony Giddens sought to reconcile the opposition between structure and agency which existed between the older focus of structural functionalism and the newer foci of approaches such as ethnomethodology and other approaches that were less inclined to constitute structure a priori.

Giddens' structuration theory regarded structure and agency as mutually constitutive, not as a dualism but as a duality. As a coin has two faces but is indubitably one thing, so it was with social action, according to Giddens. Structure, in the form of institutions, rules and resources, influences social action but the traffic is clearly not one way. Human actors are capable of changing the social structures they inhabit; moreover, that they can do the things they do is in part attributable to those structures they inhabit that enable certain kinds of action, as well as constraining other kinds of action. Structures are simultaneously always being (re)constituted through the actions that unfold. There is, in other words, a dynamic relationship between individual action and social structure that is played out empirically in what actors do. Giddens' theory of structuration seeks to explain the motivations for actions, the choices – real and perceived – that are afforded as structural opportunities and constraints framing the interactions, doings and practices that unfold.

Giddens' theory of structuration is not the only contender in the arena of social theory that seeks to formulate the relationship between structure and agency. As Alistair Mutch discusses in the chapter 'Morphogenesis and reflexivity: Margaret Archer, critical realism and organizational analysis', Margaret Archer also paid considerable attention to these relationships. In this work she provides a framework for examining relationships between agency and structure that are applicable to organizations. Archer draws on a specific philosophical approach known as critical realism. Roy Bhaskar (1975) and Harré and Madden (1975) first developed the ideas of critical realism. Crucial to the position was that things in themselves have what Harré and Madden termed causal powers, a position that Bhaskar named as transcendental realism. That science was possible, argued Bhaskar, was only because scientists could contrive experiments in which the real, manipulable nature of things could be *actualized* to produce particular outcomes. Under the appropriate standing conditions, designed in the laboratory, the causal powers inhering in things could be revealed, argued Harré and Madden. As a philosophy of science this is quite distinct from the more usual claim that science consists of observing the relationship between cause and effect in terms of events that are coterminous variables. Instead, it proposes that certain causal mechanisms may inhere in the nature of things: for instance, iron will rust if exposed to the elements of air and water; causality may be genetic rather than eventful; it may be historical rather than coterminous. Whilst empiricism and positivism locate causal relationships at the level of coterminous events, critical realism locates them at the level of generative mechanisms rather than a coincident relation between dependent and independent variables.

Critical realism prescribes social scientific methods that seek to identify the generative mechanisms producing social events while recognizing that socially constructed structures are subject to more change than the phenomena of natural science. Human agency is enabled and constrained by social structures that they reproduce or transform. Social structures are designed and can be changed – a practice facilitated by the findings of social research. Archer terms this capability agential reflexivity.

Drawing on critical realism, Archer engages in significant dispute between critical realists and structuration theorists. The chapter explores the relationship between Archer's work and the theory of institutional logics, to argue for the greater value of Archer's less deterministic approach than that of the typical institutional logician.

Pierre Bourdieu, a sociologist, anthropologist, philosopher and public intellectual, conducted his original fieldwork amongst the Berber of North Africa but became an acute observer of the society in which he resided, that of post-war France. Bourdieu brought an eye for ethnographic detail and an appreciation of the social constructions of a world of significations, stratifications and symbolism that great anthropologists respect. As Mairi Maclean and Charles Harvey acknowledge in their chapter 'Pierre Bourdieu and elites: making the hidden visible', Bourdieu was able to reveal and make manifest the hidden mechanisms of social stratification that often remain invisible in organizational and social life. The facility to do this was, perhaps, nowhere better displayed than in his book, *Distinction: A Social Critique of the Judgement of Taste* (Bourdieu, 1984), a book which relentlessly examines the cultural mores of French, more especially Parisian, life. Bourdieu's major contributions were many: he outlined a theory of practice that clearly influenced Giddens as well as Schatzki; he played a major role in debates in the sociology of education but for Maclean and Harvey his major contribution for the study of organizations and management was in his analyses of elites, their power relations and how they reproduce their social domination. In their chapter Bourdieu's ideas and concepts are used to illustrate four specific areas of research. These are class domination and its relation to cultural reproduction in big business; the importance of reflexivity for social mobility; how entrepreneurial philanthropy legitimates wealth; how distinctions, based on subtle and cultivated displays of taste, serve to stratify and exercise power. Bourdieu's work makes available resources for analysis of the activities of elites in the global field of power as they enjoy their undoubted domination, sometimes subtly so, other times more overtly.

Bourdieu was one of the earliest social theorists of practices *per se*, in his book *Outline of a Theory of Practice* (Bourdieu, 1977). Practice became the central concept in the emerging critical realist view of social science, coming into sharp focus with the work of Theodore Schatzki, as Georg Loscher, Violetta Splitter and David Seidl discuss in the chapter 'Theodor Schatzki's theory and its implications for organization studies'. Practice, as an analytical category, has a long and distinguished pedigree, going back at least to analytical philosophy, especially Wittgenstein's (1968) *Philosophical Investigations*, with its central focus on language games as forms of practical being in the world. The chapter introduces the practice theory developed by Theodore Schatzki and highlights its implications for organization studies. In particular, it shows how his theory, a fecund source for the 'practice turn' in organization and management theory, contributes to an understanding of the micro-foundations of organizations, the embeddedness of organizations in their wider social context, especially that there are temporal and spatial dimensions to organizations. Schatzki bases his work on a critique of Bourdieu and Giddens, two prominent practice-oriented theorists (Schatzki, 1996) to develop a version known as *site ontology* (Schatzki, 2002) that offers a general theoretical apparatus for examining the relationship between human activity and the social. For Schatzki, there is just one level of social reality, such that no distinction should be made between micro and macro levels. All human activity and social phenomena are situated within intertwined practices and it is to the practices that constitute these that we should attend.

Bourdieu, as we have seen, began his research career as an anthropologist. So too did Mary Douglas, another influential source of organization and management theorizing, as Dean Pierides and Graham Sewell elaborate on in their contribution to the book, 'Mary Douglas and institutions'. In their chapter, they demonstrate how those many researchers that claim an interest in institutions and institutional theory should read and use the work of Mary Douglas. Douglas, as with other social theorists we have encountered, such as Giddens and Archer, saw one of the central problems of social theory to be the extent to which the structure of institutions and organizations determines the agency afforded to individuals. Douglas deals with institutions in a way that is quite distinctive from the latent structural functionalism that characterizes many institutional theories in the management and organization studies field. She does this by way of a framework termed Grid-and-Group, which allows her to develop critiques of rational agency and methodological individualism. Her concerns build on the anthropological tradition of Durkheim and Mauss (1963) and focus on the ways in which classifications are social conventions. Douglas extends their analysis of classifications to the modern world. What needs to be understood in any specific analysis is how a classificatory enterprise is matched with social requirements. In building this understanding, she draws on the work of the educational sociologist, Basil Bernstein, with his work on elaborated and restricted linguistic codes. These constitute different values, divisions of labour and social organization that are differently upheld depending on the culture that produced them as classification systems. In Douglas's work, as they explain, this is developed through the concepts of 'group' as the experience of a bounded social unit whose identity is expressed through ritual. Group is independent of what Douglas calls 'grid', which consists either of rules prioritizing the individual as a nodal point from which relations radiate or placing them within a cross-hatching of rules, distinctions and regulations. As they explain, this sets up three conditions: *group and grid*, in which boundaries and internal order are well established; *group not grid*, where boundaries are rigid but there is internal disarray, and *grid not group*, where ego-centred networks prevail. Students of Douglas were subsequently to use these distinctions to generate a complete theory of *Organizing and disorganizing* (Thompson, 2008), the implications of which have been largely neglected. Organizational scholars, Pierides and Sewell argue, could benefit greatly from exploring how Douglas's cultural theory can be used to investigate how membership of social entities such as organizations involves a consideration of actions that are more than the enactment of schemas or logics, as organization institutionalists tend to argue.

Several scholars have focused on what they see as the key characteristics of contemporary times; for both Luhmann and Castells, although in different ways, it is the central issue of communication and its networks. Cátia Miriam Costa, Tiago Lima Quintanilha and Sandro Mendonça address the work of Manuel Castells, who has written extensively about the 'network society'. While Luhmann was very much a systematic and Germanic theorist of systems as an ontological totality, Castells was both theoretically sophisticated and open to the empirically changing world he experienced, from the 'Events of May, 1968' in Paris, a proto-revolutionary context harking both backwards to a fading industrial capitalism and forwards to a world yet to come that the students on the streets would help prepare, if not make, one marked by the material revolutions of the information age.

Castells is a Catalonian, educated in France during the events of '68, a student of Alain Touraine, who was a major social theorist of post-industrial society (Touraine, 1971), who works in the United States but plays a global intellectual and policy-related role. Castells' central interest is in communication and access to information. Understanding how the social appropriation of information and communication technologies came to define the contemporary period is his central research theme. Castells' social theory provides intellectual tools with which to focus on the processes of structural transformation that have been transformational from the late '60s to the present day. Castells key object of analysis is the 'network society' (Castells, 1996; 2002; 2005; 2009; 2012). Networks are the defining media of power relations and communication in contemporary times; power relations are also central to Castells' (2009; see Clegg, 2010) work. Networks have no centre but they do have nodal points and these are increasingly subject to the control of a small number of global multinational companies, behemoths of the contemporary scene, many of them media organizations. Informationalism, the result of the complex interaction of technology and society that took shape from the 1970s, has served these behemoths well. Informationalism refers to the broad template of patterns and dynamics that define the Information Age, the successor to the modern times of industrial capitalism. The augmentation of human capacities for information processing and communication made possible by microelectronics, computing, software, the Internet and other revolutionary technologies has served these businesses well.

States are no longer the only major crucibles of power as networks become the prime locus for contemporary analyses of global power, laced as multiple, overlapping, open and socio-spatially interactive systems comprising interconnected nodes. Communication flows through these nodes have revolutionized since the development of digital technologies, creating the global network society in its interactions and exchanges with, as well as its marginalization of, already existing societal sites, cultures, organizations and institutions of various types. The nodes configure power relations. Power relations have a structural architecture, expressed in terms of spatial and temporal orderings, focused on the extraction and appropriation of value conceived in terms of various logics that are themselves an expression of power. Behind his theorizing is an irreducible commitment to the value and values of life itself as the ultimate value on which any form of human organization should be judged.

Castells is a major figure in global social science while Nikolas Luhmann is a major figure in German social science whose ideas, although influential in Scandinavia and Germany, were less so elsewhere until relatively recently. He is famous for his construction of a total and coherent theorizing of modern society as a system built around communication networks endowed with their own rules and codes, as Xavier Deroy explores in his chapter, 'Luhmann and organizations as social systems'. The system was the major device of Talcott Parsons' (2013) structural functionalism, with which Luhmann was deeply familiar but does not follow. For Parsons modern societies were unified and ordered by a central value system and commonly patterned variables that all sub-systems had to deal with as institutional questions. Luhmann sees disorder and differentiation as more characteristic of modern societies in which communication is embedded within many specific, differentiated and fragmented social systems, each with specific discursive codes, which makes coordination difficult. Communication that is framed intra-systemically in a society of many systems creates a fragmented society of social systems centred on their inherent practices but not necessarily capable of communicating easily across distinct systems. Each specific type of social system's communication is structured by their respective codes, elaborated within the system and by reference to the system. In this context, diverse communication networks have no centre but systematically make up the complexity of modern societies, a complexity that may generate unexpected social evolutions. For instance, an event such as a referendum can become the occasion for unanticipated social evolutions flowing from a single decision point that summarily condensed all systemic complexities into a single binaryism: a referendum such as Brexit is an event whose binaryism has generated enormous amounts of uncertainty unforeseen in advance.

Typically, it is organizations that constitute stable units in modern societies and are characterized by decisions, designed as communication operations that typically provide structures and rules communicated by organizations to their members to reduce unexpected decisions. However, risk is an inherent element of an organization's systemic functioning, based on communication operations. It arises when events occur that cannot be coded on the basis of precedent and rules, thus creating situations in which the structures and rules communicated by organizations to their members do not reduce unexpected decisions. A national referendum that is not bounded within existing organization systems (such as political parties or other organizations) poses such an event, as the United Kingdom experienced in the wake of the Brexit decision, from which it emerged decidedly less united. From Luhmann's perspective, risk is an inherent element of organizational systemic functioning based on communication operations, but because systems have reflexive capabilities, which he calls autopoiesis, meaning that they can reproduce, repair and maintain their functioning, risks can be a source of learning how to manage better.

Organizations reduce the risks associated with the contingency of their operations of communication and absorb uncertainty derived from these operations, through hierarchies, decision premises and membership. Hence, organizations can achieve a partial reduction of uncertainty, but uncertainty is everlasting if only because each new decision cannot be guaranteed to account for its interpretation on future occasions and for future events. Everlasting uncertainty is irreducible. Paradoxically, organizational decisions can also reintroduce unexpected and worrying social evolutions. With his social systems theory, Luhmann provides an approach in which events and contingency are at the centre of modern societies based on communication.

Luhmann, as a theorist of the system, might seem to be about as far from Foucault as one can possibly imagine, although in his early work, especially *The Archaeology of Knowledge* (1972), Foucault proved capable of producing a complex closed system of communication. Nonetheless, if not for this work, Michel Foucault is probably the most celebrated and famous of the social theorists discussed in this book. Foucault was a philosopher and historian of ideas whose empirical data were documentary materials, often archival. His overall concern was with different modalities of power, its variation in history and in society as constituted by discourse and practice. Foucault distinguishes between sovereign power and disciplinary power. The former expresses itself through ceremony, the latter through routines and knowledge production that is expressed as a form of disciplinary power that structures the individuals' dispositions and lifeworld. In the neoliberal age, however, it is knowledge about populations and human behaviours that supports a specific practice of government that Foucault calls governmentality.

Foucault, as with many of the social theorists discussed here, is not easily contained within any singular account of his work as a unity. As Alan McKinlay and Eric Pezet state in their chapter, 'Organizing Foucault: power, knowledge and governmentality', there are many Foucaults: in different periods in his career he focused on discourse and archaeology, discipline and genealogy, as well as towards the end of his life, ethics and identity. The focus of the chapter, however, as the title indicates, is on Foucault the theorist of power, which treats his ideas as they were constituted historically. The explicit concern with power in Foucault's work is elaborated in *Discipline and Punish* (1975), a book that begins by juxtaposing two historical documents. It begins with a contemporary account of the execution of Damiens, who attempted regicide on the King of France. Robert-François Damiens was a domestic servant whose attempted assassination of King Louis XV in 1757 culminated in his notorious and controversial public execution. He was the last person to be executed in France by drawing and quartering, a gruesome description of which forms the core of the documentary account. This account is immediately followed by the rules of a model prison for young offenders from 80 years later that consist of a detailed timetabling of the offenders' daily activities. As Foucault states, a public execution and a timetable each define a distinct penal style; each has a distinct modality of power. In the execution, power is wreaked on the body of the offender in a way that symbolically and ceremoniously represents retribution for the offence to the sovereign; in the prison, it is bureaucratically regulated. The execution represents ceremonial sovereign power; the timetable represents a productive, prosaic and everyday practice of disciplinary power.

The chapter explores the characteristics of sovereign power through analysis of lectures that Foucault gave at the College de France in 1973. Sovereign power belongs to a set of absolutist powers embedded in a historical epoch that is now past, but that does not mean that sovereign power died with the birth of modern republicanism and constitutional monarchy. It is still inscribed in those moments of high ceremony and ritual when an event such as an Apple product launch is orchestrated or a famous fashion designer launches their collection of *haute couture*. These are relatively special events, marked as such by ceremony and the positioning of the definer or CEO as sovereign over what they have displayed; however, while sovereign displays of power are rare and rather staged, disciplinary power is embedded in the routines of everyday work and life, much as the timetable. Disciplinary power is imbricated in the most mundane moments of everyday work and life; embedded in diverse forms of surveillance that make of us knowingly subjected subjects, a theme that is explored in the chapter through consideration of the madness of King George III and the subordination of sovereign power to tight management and close surveillance during his bouts of ill health that was embedded in a fusion of power over the patient with knowledge codifying courses of treatment of the illness. The new power/knowledge became institutionalized in the practices of the asylum.

These practices of the asylum, much as the practices of the prison, formed a distinct regime of disciplinary power/knowledge, that were themselves characteristic of many practices developing in distinct spheres: schools, factories, hospitals, asylums, all with their distinct but family-related modalities of disciplinary power/knowledge, the very model of which Foucault found in Bentham's recourse to panopticism. In the modern era, however, while these disciplinary practices are still very evident, the modalities of power have grown to incorporate forms of governmentality that manage people through their freedoms, as McKinlay and Pezet go on to articulate. The relevancies for an understanding of contemporary managing and organizing should be evident.

The relation between Foucault's oeuvre and that of critical theory has been frequently discussed, probably most thoroughly by Mitchel Dean (1994). Critical theory emerged from a particular place and time in history: it was initially developed by a group of German intellectuals in the inter-war period amidst the collapse of the Weimar Republic and the rise of fascism. Not all of them survived the latter, although several managed to escape the Holocaust that was to consume so many and arrived in the United States where they continued their work in a very different conjuncture. As Marxist intellectuals, they were confronted by a Europe traumatized by what seemed to be the failure of the Marxist project in the Soviet Union under the tyranny of Lenin and Stalin and the rise of fascist totalitarianism in Germany; in the United States they found a very different 'new world'. In Europe, as Edward Granter notes in his chapter 'The Frankfurt School and critical theory', they were confronted with what Max Horkheimer and Theodor Adorno (2002), a leading member of the Frankfurt School, referred to as barbarism, a world scarred by unemployment, economic crisis, militarization and a terrorist regime; arriving in America in 1937, they saw a country that despite the Depression of the earlier 1930s appeared by contrast to be a land of plenty.

In the United States they did not surrender their critical analysis of social order. As critical scholars they took nothing for granted but sought to understand forms of social ordering in terms of their human potential for emancipating human beings from oppression, whether material or cultural. Indeed, the focus on the latter came to characterize the critical theorists' concerns, perhaps best seen in Marcuse's (2013) *One Dimensional Man*, a trenchant critique of consumerist society and its satisfactions, that was quite influential in various student movements of the late 1960s. Other elements of critical theory have been adopted and adapted in organization analysis as Granter explains, often in terms of Adorno's (1973) conception of negative dialectics: a commitment to not taking for granted the ways in which powerful interests in the world represent its nature, essence and being; the necessity of opposing ways of thinking in which analysis and everyday life can become trapped in the repletion of mundanity without ever aspiring to transcend and improve its quality.

One area that the critical theorists have been, in turn, criticized for, is their lack of attention to certain facts that sustained the capitalism they critiqued:

> Frankfurt School critical theory, despite its seminal insights into the relationships between domination, modern society, and the opportunities for redemption through art as critique, is stunningly silent on racist theory, anti-imperialist resistance, and oppositional practice in the empire.
>
> (Said, 1993, p. 278)

Others with an interest in emancipation might have seen further areas in which blindness was apparent. One of these was feminism, a perspective that the relative gender blindness of the student movements inspired by critical theory did much to provoke. Other forms of social theory were to prove more useful in this respect. Judith Butler's particular interest is in gender classifications and an approach to them that is developed in part from Foucault, although she also shares a common interest with Douglas in the ways that classifications work. Kate Kenny, in her chapter 'Judith Butler and performativity', explores her approach to studying identification and subjection in organizations, focusing especially on her theory of performativity. Butler's work develops out of her commitments as a feminist, examining discourses of gender and sexuality and how these play out in social life, including how they interact with each other.

In theorizing new directions for understanding identification, Butler's work followed on directly from the examination of subjection to power that Foucault developed in his later work, *The History of Sexuality* (Foucault, 1979). Butler's approach to identification and subjection is conceptualized in terms of affective recognition, which describes how we are compelled, affectively and often without our knowledge or will, into subjection to powerful discourses. These ideas become particularly evident when we look at the ways in which gender emerges as a classificatory system of recognition; not only does such a system have importance for understanding socialization processes (Allen, 2013), but it is also important for organization studies, in particular for studies of identification and subjection and the role of power in such processes. The subject emerges through the positions available and afforded in language, outside of which one cannot exist. Those norms with which we identify compel us to seek recognition in their terms; to be considered as well as to consider oneself as a valid subject, one must be legitimized by the normative identities available. Power relations and their manifestations as normative categories dictate how subjects may be recognized. Our compulsion to be recognized can be productive in many cases and for example leads to the formation of solidarity groups, but it can also lead to discrimination and exclusion of those constituted as others. Affective recognition, it is concluded, is ultimately ambivalent because the power of norms is neither determined nor monolithic but is always open to being subverted: the engagement of structure and agency is never-ending.

Many of the theorists that we have considered thus far focus extensively on the duality of agency and structure. Norbert Elias, the subject of Robert van Krieken's chapter 'Norbert Elias and organizational analysis: towards process-figurational theory', does not dwell on dualities. Elias's approach to analysis is deeply grounded in mastery of historical materials. Being so embedded in historical documents, such as manuals of etiquette and manners, Elias can hardly fail to take a processual approach, one that van Krieken terms a 'process-figurational' approach. At times, Elias's approach might seem far from contemporary concerns: the history of the civilizing process, the emergences of courtly society and the transformation of its norms, detailed analysis of table manners and arrangements: these are distinctive themes seemingly far from contemporary concerns with management and organizations. Not so, suggests van Krieken: he has much to offer. There are links with Weber's rationalization thesis (which immediately draws links to Ritzer's [2004] McDonaldization thesis); the importance of self-censorship as an institutionalized mode of psychic control has echoes in Foucault (1975), as does his insistence on a relational conception of power. The concept of figuration covers similar ground to that staked out in actor-network theory. Elias was discussing habitus before Bourdieu (1977).

Elias's approach is both processual, that is historical and relational, focused on social relations rather than static entities, expressed in concepts that are invariably reifications. In this respect, he shares a preference with Karl Weick (1995) for verbs as gerunds rather than for nouns. Focusing on the gerund form of verbs immediately orients us to social action, rather than to social structure; structure becomes contingent on doing rather than being. That structure exists is always an accomplishment constituted in action. The apparent independence of social order and social structure from intentional human action is an appearance that much relational work sustains; the task of social research is to make this relational work not so much apparent as transparent. In doing so the figurations that sustain social relations and the structures they assume and presume become the matter for analysis. A central figuration of modern times, of course, is the notion of the organization and its management, and as van Krieken argues, it is through close attention to phenomena such as the emergence of norms of meetings, protocols, dress and control of emotionality that we can bring Elias's perspective to bear on analysis. Indeed, as he charts in the chapter, there have been many major contributions using Elias as a resource, although they seem not to have been incorporated into mainstream theorizing.

Norbert Elias shared some characteristics with another of our cast of characters: he was an involuntary outsider who adopted another country for his professional life. Elias, of Jewish descent, was born in Breslau in Germany in 1897. In the 1930s he was working under Karl Mannheim at the Institute of Sociology in the University of Frankfurt, which was closed down by the fascists in 1933. Sensing the future of things to come, Elias fled, initially to Paris, eventually to England, where he reconnected with Mannheim, to work with him at the London School of Economics before being interred as an enemy alien during part of the war. Later, he was to join the University of Leicester Sociology Department, in 1957, where he stayed until his retirement. It was only several years after his retirement that he became well known outside of Leicester, when his study *The Civilizing Process* (Elias, 1969) was published. It was a career whose trajectory one would be unlikely to find in present times.

The other involuntary outsider was Zygmunt Bauman, a Polish émigré sociologist who spent most of his career in England, working at the University of Leeds in Yorkshire. He left not because of the Nazis but as a result of a political purge by the communist authorities in his native Poland in 1968. Initially he went to live in Israel but after three years moved to England. His output of books was prodigious and in his later years they focused on the issue of what he termed 'liquid modernity'. For Bauman, the world of organizations was becoming ever more liquid, dissolving old structures, certainties and relations. Stewart Clegg and Miguel Pina e Cunha explore the contours of these liquid changes and their import for organization analysis in their chapter 'Liquefying modernity: Zygmunt Bauman as organization theorist', by discussing liquid selves, liquid organizations and liquid aesthetics, as three facets of Bauman's work with implications for organizations and management.

Applying the metaphor of liquid to organizations highlights practices in which investments in people are highly liquid and easily liquidated, with no long-term investment implications. As the chapter explores, there are ethical, political, identity and organizational consequences of increasing liquidity. Ethically, modern leaders are seen to be forever reassembling the pieces of their own identity as the liquid state changes. Politically, power relations become marked by a new lightness of synoptical power relations (Mathiesen, 1997 for the original reference; also see Lancione & Clegg, 2015) augmenting and supplementing more traditional panoptical power as we encounter it in Foucault's disciplinary power. In terms of identity, liquidity is marked by the immediateness of the self in the moment. Organizationally, liquidity predisposes its leaders to improvisation over heavy scripting as role prescriptions become more fluid and uncertain and events less predictable. The focus of the chapter is on how liquid modernity frames contemporary leadership. Managerial expertise in 'leadership' is increasingly seen as a practice of shared, dispersed and mutually constituted influence gained in successful steering of projects despite the irreducible contingency of unforeseen events. Rather as Luhmann sees the modern world as composed of systems of communication that are specific and differentiated, Bauman is equally sceptical about the capacity of any central control to steer events. Deregulation, individualization, weakened human bonds, increased fluidity of solidarities and the drift from normative regulation through common patterns of socialization to processes that are much more individuated are all key features of the liquid condition identified by Bauman. As such, as the chapter concludes, they leave social ordering increasingly at risk from the sirens of authoritarian populism. Populism, of course, is not the only risk of contemporary times: to populism one must add climate catastrophe as a phenomenon that social theory can address to inform management and organization studies.

Conclusion

None of the social theorists surveyed here would regard managing and organizing, management and organizations, as a self-contained space of explanation that needed no reference to larger social forces and their theorization. Instead, in their different ways, they saw the field as a terrain in which rival social theories produced coherent, if diverse, insights into these wider social forces and their effects.

The world is increasingly global as a result of digital affordances, yet major business organizations are increasingly centralized as a result of the monopolizing tendencies inherent in command of these affordances. Patterns of everyday life, commerce and administration are, in Bauman's terms, increasingly liquid for the many but they are also solidifying wealth and privilege for the few. In a world in which old certainties are dissolving as fast as new opportunities emerge it is no longer the case that any organization provides boundaries strong enough to keep the uncertainties at bay nor has managers wise enough to understand the framing, transcending and upsetting of assumptions of what is normal. In such times the questioning that various social theories offer becomes ever more relevant to how we understand and live our lives, how those lives are constituted by power relations that legitimate certain ideologies, norms, values, roles, rules, identities, beliefs, discourses, symbols, meaning systems and systems of domination. Organizing and managing is rooted in the assumptions of everyday life that these power relations sustain. They are the matrix of normalcy, a matrix that cannot be understood through just those terms that the matrix manufactures, sustains and reproduces. Social theories enable us to understand that the ideational citadels of knowledge need to be open to disruption just as much as are those material phenomena upon which they speculate. Social theories provide devices for disruption of extremely consequential discourses, such as management and organization theory: in the concluding chapter we invite you to explore these theories by posing an index of possibilities for future work informed by the social theories whose exploration awaits you, the reader.

Notes

1 Miguel Pina e Cunha acknowledges support by National Funds through FCT – Fundação para a Ciência e Tecnologia under the project Ref. UID/ECO/00124/2013 and by POR Lisboa under the project LISBOA-01-0145-FEDER-007722.
2 Thanks to Marco Berti and Chris Carter for advice on earlier drafts of this chapter.
3 Carter (2008) suggests that the ranking for Foucault is a 'curiously British story' of a French philosopher and historian of ideas being embraced by British business school scholars in a way that their French counterparts, on the whole, did not.

References

Adorno, T. (1973). *Negative dialectics*. London: Routledge & Kegan Paul.

Alcadipani, R., & Hassard, J. (2010). Actor-network theory, organizations and critique: Towards a politics of organizing. *Organization, 17*(4), 419–435.

Allen, A. (2013). *The politics of ourselves: Power, autonomy and gender in contemporary critical theory*. New York: Columbia University Press.

Bateson, G. (2000). *Steps to an ecology of mind: Collected essays in aanthropology, psychiatry, evolution, and epistemology*. Chicago, IL: University of Chicago Press.

Bhaskar, R. (1975). *A realist theory of science*. Leeds: Leeds Books.

Bourdieu, P. (1977). *Outline of a theory of practice*. Cambridge: Cambridge University Press.

Bourdieu, P. (1984). *Distinction: A social critique of the judgement of taste*. London: Routledge.

Carter, C. (2008). A curiously British story: Foucault goes to business school. *International Studies of Management and Organization, 38*(1), 13–29.

Castells, M. (1996) *The information age: Economy, society, and culture, Vol.1: The rise of the network society*. Chichester: John Wiley & Sons.

Castells, M. (2002). *The internet galaxy: Reflections on the internet, business and society*. Oxford: Oxford University Press.

Castells, M. (2005). The network society: From knowledge to policy. In M. Castells and G. Cardoso (eds) *The network society: From knowledge to policy* (pp. 3–21). Washington, DC: Brookings Institution Press.

Castells, M. (2009). *Communication power*. Oxford: Oxford University Press.

Castells, M. (2012). *Networks of outrage and hope: Social movements in the internet age*. Cambridge: Polity Press.

Clegg, S. R. (2010). Controlling communication and contesting conceptualization: Power in 21st century global society, a review of Manuel Castells' *Communication Power*, Oxford: Polity. *The Journal of Power, 3*(1), 142–145.

Czarniawska, B., & Hernes, T. (2005). *Actor-network theory and organizing*. Copenhagen: Copenhagen Business School Press.

Dean, M. (1994). *Foucault's methods and historical sociology*. London: Routledge.

Durkheim, É., & Mauss, M. (1963). *Primitive classification*. London: Cohen & West.

Eisenhardt, K. M. (1989). Building theories from case study research. *Academy of Management Review, 14*(4), 532–550.

Elias, N. (1969) *The civilizing process, Vol. I. The history of manners*. Oxford: Blackwell.

Fei, X. (1939). *Peasant life in china: A field study of country life in the Yangtze Valley*. London: Routledge & Kegan Paul.

Foucault, M. (1972). *The archaeology of knowledge*. New York: Pantheon.

Foucault, M. (1975). *Discipline and punish: The birth of the prison*. New York: Random House.

Foucault, M. (1979). *The history of sexuality Volume 1: An introduction*. London: Allen Lane.

Freire, P. (2018). *Pedagogy of the oppressed*. New York: Bloomsbury.

Giddens, A. (1973). *The class structure of the advanced societies*. London: Hutchinson.

Giddens, A. (1976). *New rules of sociological method: A positive critique of interpretative sociologies*. London: Hutchinson.

Harré, R, & Madden, E. H. (1975). *Causal powers: A theory of natural necessity*. Lanham, MD: Rowman & Littlefield.

Horkheimer, M., & Adorno, T. W. (2002). *Dialectic of enlightenment*. Palo Alto, CA: Stanford University Press.

Lancione, M., & Clegg, S. R. (2015). The lightness of management learning. *Management Learning*, *46*(3), 280–298.

Law, J., & Hassard, J. (1999). *Actor network theory and after*. Oxford: Blackwell.

Marcuse, H. (2013). *One-dimensional man: Studies in the ideology of advanced industrial society*. London: Routledge.

Marx, K. (1976). *Capital*, Vol. 1. London: NLB/Penguin.

Mathiesen, T. (1997). The viewer society: Michel Foucault's panopticon revisited. *Theoretical Criminology*, *1*(2), 215–234.

Mbigi, L. (2005). *Ubuntu: The spirit of African transformation management*. Randburg: Knowres.

Parsons, T. (2013). *The social system*. London: Routledge.

Ritzer, G. (2004). *The McDonaldization of society*. Newbury Park, CA: Pine Forge Press.

Said, E. (1993). *Culture and imperialism*. New York: Knopf.

Schatzki, T. R. (2002). *The site of the social: A philosophical account of the constitution of social life and change*. Philadelphia, PA: Penn State Press.

Schatzki, T. R. (1996). *Social practices – a Wittgensteinian approach to human activity and the social*. Cambridge, MA: Cambridge University Press.

Seremani, T. W., & Clegg, S. R. (2015). Postcolonialism, organization and management theory: The role of 'epistemological third spaces'. *Journal of Management Inquiry*, DOI: 10.1177/1056492615589973.

Simon, H. A. (1996). *The sciences of the artificial*. Boston, MA: MIT Press.

Simon, H. A. (2013). *Administrative behavior*. New York: Simon and Schuster.

Smith, A. (1950). *An inquiry into the nature and causes of the wealth of nations*. London: Methuen.

Taylor, F. W. (1911). *The principles of scientific management*. New York: Harper & Brothers.

Thompson, M. (2008). *Organising and disorganising: A dynamic and non-linear theory of institutional emergence and its implications*. Charmouth: Triarchy Press.

Touraine, A. (1971). *The post-industrial society. Tomorrow's social history: Classes, conflicts and culture in the programmed society*. New York: Random House.

Üsdiken, B. (2010). Between contending perspectives and logics: Organizational studies in Europe. *Organization Studies*, *31*(6), 715–735.

Üsdiken, B. (2014). Centres and peripheries: research styles and publication patterns in 'top' US journals and their European alternatives, 1960–2010. *Journal of Management Studies*, *51*(5), 764–789.

Üsdiken, B., & Pasadeos, Y. (1995). Organizational analysis in North America and Europe: A comparison of co-citation networks. *Organization Studies*, *16*(3), 503–526.

Weber, M. (1978). *Economy and society: An outline of interpretive sociology*. Berkeley, CA: University of California Press.

Weick, K. E. (1969). *The social psychology of organizing*. Boston, MA: Addison-Wesley.

Weick, K. E. (1995). *Sensemaking*. Thousand Oaks, CA: Sage.

Wittgenstein, L. (1968). *Philosophical investigations*. London: Macmillan.

2 Harold Garfinkel and ethnomethodology

Andrea Whittle and Frank Mueller

Chapter objectives

The chapter discusses:

- The emergence of ethnomethodology as a distinct paradigm of sociological inquiry
- The relationship between ethnomethodology and mainstream structural-functionalist sociology
- Some key concepts in ethnomethodology, including reflexivity, indexicality and the documentary method of interpretation
- The approach to studying organizing 'as it happens' that is adopted by ethnomethodologists
- An illustration of the ethnomethodological approach to studying organizations by Lawrence Wieder
- Reflections on the methodological concerns and requirements of an ethnomethodological approach to organization studies
- Directions of future research in business, management and organizational settings

Introduction

What is ethnomethodology? The term ethnomethodology can easily be misunderstood because it sounds like it might refer to a type of research methodology. Despite its name, ethnomethodology is not a methodology for doing research – although it does have implications for the methodology used and requires observation (and ideally if possible and practical some kind of recording) of naturally occurring social settings, for reasons we will go on to explain. 'Ethno' means 'people', 'race' or 'culture', and 'methodology' refers to the set of *methods* or *procedures* that competent members of the social group in question use to go about organizing themselves by producing a shared social reality that is factual and objective to them. Put simply, then, ethnomethodology is the study of the *practical methods through which members of a particular social group accomplish social organization.*

Ethnomethodology is a distinct paradigm of enquiry in social science because it does not seek to provide the kind of second-order social scientific theory of how social order is generated which is typically provided by other sociological theories. These theories typically attempt to identify the cause-and-effect relationships (or other kinds of dependencies) between different social variables (Button, 1991). Ethnomethodology does not view the academic sociologist as having a 'superior' (i.e. more sophisticated or complete) way of understanding and explaining the social world and hence, on this basis, seek to supplement or enhance members' own understandings and explanations with their own academic theories. 'Ethnomethodology doesn't fit in with other people's conception of sociology. It was never meant to.' (Sharrock, 1989, p. 661) For Garfinkel and Rawls (2002), 'the worldwide social science movement' uses formal-analytic sociological methods in order to study society, thereby ignoring 'the enacted, unmediated, directly and immediately witnessable details of immortal ordinary society' (p. 97). Ethnomethodology recognizes that the people they study are themselves sociologists. They are 'folk' sociologists (Wieder, 1974) or 'practical' sociologists (Benson & Hughes, 1983) who use their own common-sense knowledge of the social realm to constitute the social world through their interactions. For ethnomethodology, the work of the sociologist is not *inherently* different from the work of the member living their life in the everyday (Zimmerman & Pollner, 1970).

Ethnomethodologists are interested in explicating the methods used by these 'practical sociologists' they study because it is their social knowledge and reasoning that *constitute* the social reality used in real-world settings and is therefore *consequential* for what happens within them (Garfinkel, 1967). For example, if we want to understand how and why particular decisions get made in the criminal justice system, which have very real material consequences for those involved (who gets arrested and charged for a crime, or who gets sentenced or acquitted in court), we would first need to understand the forms of sensemaking and reasoning used in these settings to make these decisions. Early ethnomethodological studies of policing and judicial settings have done precisely this (Sudnow, 1965; Garfinkel, 1967, Chapter 4; Cicourel, 1968; Meehan, 1986; Pollner, 1987, Chapter 2). The point of an ethnomethodological study is not for the analyst to decide which version of social reality is 'real' and 'true' – something often referred to as 'ethnomethodological indifference' (Garfinkel & Rawls, 2002, 170). For example, if studying a courtroom and seeing the two different versions of reality put forward by the prosecution and defence, the aim would not be to decide which is 'correct' or evaluate whether the judge or jury got their decision 'right'. Rather, the point is to identify *how* (i.e. through what *methods*) a group of people (in this case judges and juries) produce what they take to be social reality (Travers & Manzo, 2016; Winiecki, 2008; Dingwall, 2000).

In this chapter we will first discuss ethnomethodology's approach to the study of social order. This is followed by a discussion of some core concepts in ethnomethodology, including indexicality, reflexivity and the documentary method of interpretation. We then discuss the implications of adopting an ethnomethodological approach to the study of management and organization for the kinds of research methods that can (and should) be used. We go on to give an illustration of how an ethnomethodological approach studies organization by discussing Lawrence Wieder's study of the 'convict code' in a halfway house for the rehabilitation of prisoners on release. Finally, we conclude by outlining some potential avenues for future studies in the management and organization field.

Harold Garfinkel

Harold Garfinkel was born on October 29, 1917 in Newark, New Jersey. His father, Abraham Garfinkel, was a furniture dealer and a member of the large Jewish community in Newark. In 1935, during the Great Depression, Harold studied business and accounting at the University of Newark and worked in his father's furniture business in the evenings (vom Lehn, 2016). According to Garfinkel, his study of accounting practices was more influential on his work on everyday accounts than the theories of L. Wittgenstein, C.W. Mills and K. Burke, some of his contemporaries (Rawls, 2002). Garfinkel went on to study an MA in sociology at the University of North Carolina in 1942. His dissertation examined the methods through which inter-racial and intra-racial homicides were managed by the court system (Llewellyn, 2014). Garfinkel's war service for the US Air Force saw him assigned to an army hospital and training soldiers in Miami Beach for combat duties, amongst other things training the troops to fight tanks with small arms fire (Llewellyn, 2014; vom Lehn, 2016). After the war he studied under Talcott Parsons and completed his PhD in 1952 at Harvard. With the help of Philip Selznick, Garfinkel got his Assistant Professorship at UCLA in 1954. In 1967, Garfinkel published the now-classic book *Studies in Ethnomethodology*, which led to contentious, sometimes hostile commentary and debate. Garfinkel spent the rest of his academic career at UCLA until his retirement in 1987. He died on April 21, 2011.

Ethnomethodology and the study of social order

Garfinkel was certainly one of the most original – and controversial – thinkers in sociology. The publication of his book in 1967, *Studies in Ethnomethodology*, divided academic opinion (Llewellyn, 2014). Ethnomethodology emerged as a critique of the structural-functionalist sociology of Talcott Parsons (Parsons, 1937; 1951) – under whom Garfinkel studied at Harvard University in the 1940s. Functionalism was first popularized by Emile Durkheim (1964 [1895]; 2008 [1912]) and sought to identify the social structures, variables and forces that are understood within the functionalist theory to create social order. The term 'social order' refers to any kind of cooperative, predictable and stable set of social relations that exhibit some kind of orderliness (Parsons, 1937). It could refer to the division of roles within a whole society or the more local orderliness of a line of people forming a queue (Sharrock, 1995, p. 4). Structural-functionalists see shared values as a kind of 'glue' that binds society together (Parsons, 1937; 1951). It is thought to ensure that people cooperate with each other because they have shared goals, roles, expectations and norms that can guide their behaviour, thereby generating social solidarity and helping to avoid social conflict. The internalization of common values, according to structural-functionalism, explains everything from the 'macro' social order of a class structure to the 'micro' social order of people forming an orderly queue to buy goods in a shop. Indeed, Durkheimian (1964 [1895]) functionalism had started with the idea that these shared values, norms and rules are pre-existing 'social facts' – they exist 'out there' in the social realm and have a constraining power over people's behaviour.

Ethnomethodology attempts to rethink the fundamental premise of functionalist and structural-functionalist sociology that was at the time, and still is, the mainstream explanation of social order. Ethnomethodology instead takes these supposedly external 'constraints' and treats them as endogenous accomplishments of knowledgeable members of a social group (Leiter, 1980; Handel, 1982; Button, 1991; Coulon, 1995; Francis & Hester, 2004; ten Have, 2004). In other words, what structural-functionalist sociologists take as pre-given external social 'facts' and 'forces' that make members of a social group 'orderly' and 'organized', ethnomethodology takes as things that people have to *produce* in an ongoing social process. Ethnomethodology is the term that the field's founding thinker Harold Garfinkel used to describe the study of 'the work of fact production *in flight*' (Garfinkel, 1967, p. 79, emphasis added).

From its inception, ethnomethodology was never a unified field (Maynard & Clayman, 1991). Even today it is best described as a splintered set of related sub-fields (Button, 1991). One of the most significant relationships is that between ethnomethodology (EM) and conversation analysis (CA), the latter field emerging from the work of Harvey Sacks. Some people use the term EM/CA to highlight this link (Llewellyn & Hindmarsh, 2010). Technically, ethnomethodology is not a 'social theory' in the traditional sense of the term because it also rejects the traditional ways of 'theorizing' about matters of social order and organization in mainstream social science (vom Lehn, 2016, p. 52). Rather than being regarded as a 'social theory', it is often regarded as a distinct *paradigm* of sociological inquiry in its own right. It is distinct because it seeks to 're-specify' the issues, topics and concepts of mainstream social science (Button, 1991).

Ethnomethodology 're-specifies' conventional sociological topics because it turns these (presumed to be) already existing, stable and external 'social facts' into a topic of enquiry in their own right. It asks *how* do people produce those so-called 'facts' through their practical actions, reasoning and inferences as they interact with each other. Sharrock and Anderson (1986) think that re-specification is one of the reasons why ethnomethodology was often received in hostile ways and marginalized by the mainstream community of sociologists because it enquires into the very thing that they treat as their foundation. In other words, ethnomethodology 'pulls the rug from under the feet' of functionalism by questioning the fact-like status of what they treated as the starting point of their analysis. Rather than presume that social facts exist 'out there' in the abstract realm we call 'society' (Durkheim, 1964 [1895]), ethnomethodology turns this into an empirical question and matter of enquiry and asks: how do these social facts get produced in each situation?

Core concepts in ethnomethodology: indexicality, reflexivity and the documentary method of interpretation

Like other approaches, ethnomethodology comes with its own conceptual vocabulary to describe how it views the social world. We will now explain some of the most important and well-used terms. The term *indexicality* originates in linguistics and, within linguistics, it is used to refer to certain words which mean different things depending on the context that they 'index' (think of how an index in the back of a book 'points to' a page location) (Bar-Hillel, 1954). The word 'they', for instance, derives its sense from a particular group that is being 'indexed' or 'pointed to' in that particular context. Ethnomethodology extends this by proposing that *any social action* – not just certain words but any utterance, any gesture, or indeed any kind of socially recognizable action – only 'makes sense' through inferences about what the action 'indexes' or 'points to' in that particular context.

Seeing someone contract one eyelid is a simple example: it can be taken to 'index' a (not socially meaningful) physical act of clearing one's eye of debris or, when done in a particular way by a particular person in a particular context, can be interpreted as 'indexing' a (more socially meaningful) 'wink' that serves to indicate that what is going on is a wind-up, or signal some in-joke, or making a flirtatious pass and so on (Ryle, 1990; Geertz, 1973/2000). Whilst mainstream sociologists 'have difficulty in understanding that order can arise from indexicality' (vom Lehn, 2016, p. 97), EM showed that *order only arises from indexicality*. Unlike for social theorists, for members of society, order cannot exist in the abstract.

The *documentary method of interpretation* refers to the circular process through which every 'appearance' of social action that we encounter is interpreted as 'documenting', 'indexing' or 'pointing to' an underlying pattern or 'typification'. The term typification is taken from the phenomenology of Schutz (1953). If we fail to supply a pattern that connects what we are seeing and hearing right now to the 'typical' social scene (i.e. what type of social actor we are interacting with, what their role might be, what their motives might be and so on), the interaction will be impossible. Without this typification, we simply could not make sense of what they might be doing and how we should interact with them. Social order would break down. As Sharrock and Anderson (1986: 57) state, 'being able to see what is really going on is an indispensable precondition of action, of being able to orient oneself within a social scene and to carry on its life'. For example, we are routinely and unproblematically able to interpret 'How are you?' as a simple greeting that needs to be responded to with something suitable like 'Fine thanks, how are you?' rather than a genuine enquiry into the status of our health, relationships, career, finances and so on because we use our common-sense knowledge of that utterance as 'documenting' or 'indexing' a typical greeting sequence (see Garfinkel, 1967, p. 44; see also Sacks, 1975).

We can think of the term *appearance* as referring to the 'here and now' immediate scene you have just encountered (e.g. seeing the contraction of an eyelid or hearing someone say 'how are you?') and the term *pattern* refers to how this appearance is connected to the 'larger social scene' (Leiter, 1980, p. 171). The term 'social scene' refers to our sense of something that is an enduring, typical and recurring aspect of the social world (like a norm, rule, role, motive, social type and so on). The term *reflexivity* refers to the practices of producing accounts that both describe and constitute a social scene for what it is. Sharrock and Anderson (1986) explain that reflexivity refers not to an academic virtue (e.g. being 'more reflexive' about how data were generated and the effect of the researcher on what was said) but rather describes a fundamental property of accountable action, namely that 'the describing of social activities is part and parcel of the activities so described' (p. 57). If you answer in the affirmative to the question 'was that a promise?' you not only describe your previous speech act; you hereby fully turned it into a promise and you acknowledged your accountability and created future accountability.

> Just as the accountant is accountable for his work, the everyday actor is accountable for her/his action. Everyday actions are accounts and accountable just like the inputting of data by accountants; they are 'observable-and-reportable' (Garfinkel, 1967, p. 1) actions that actors are accountable for, because they are visible as the producers of the action.
>
> (vom Lehn, 2016, p. 18)

Because Garfinkel proposes that all talk and actions are indexical, that is, they depend on the context or setting for their meaning, it also means that this talk and action are what make the setting or context what it is. Both elaborate each other. In an example discussed by Garfinkel and Wieder (1992), the category of the 'abandoned car' is constituted by members (in this case traffic wardens) via a distinction with the category 'illegally parked car'. There is typically not one clear attribute that would distinguish one from the other; rather, once a car has been classified as ready to be towed away, it is then and thereby constituted as 'abandoned'. Members' methods have created the category of the abandoned car, a category that would not exist without these methods. 'The descriptions of the social world [the accounts that we produce when we interact with each other] become, as soon as they have been uttered, constitutive parts of what they have described' (Coulon, 1995, p. 23). A traffic warden's description of 'abandoned' becomes part of the scene (the car subsequently gets towed away) in a way that is unlike an anthropologist's categorization of a tribe's practice as deviant will *remain an observer's category* and not become part of the scene.

Clegg (1975) gives a fascinating example of how a group of joiners on a building site he was studying invoked the 'inclemency rule'. The inclemency rule was written into their contracts and stated that joiners should not work in 'inclement weather'. There was no consistent definition of how bad the weather had to be before it was categorized as 'inclement'. The joiners invoked the inclement rule to down their tools and have a break whenever they determined that the weather was too bad to continue working. Clegg showed how the common-sense use of rules played out within the management–labour power relations on the building site. Ethnomethodological studies therefore have a very different approach to studying the role of formal rules and regulations in organizational life. The formal written contract of these joiners was not 'pushing and pulling' these men into compliance with the rules written in them. Ethnomethodology therefore shows 'the inadequacy of formal rules and official procedures for capturing the detailed work that is necessary to perform competently the tasks that each setting poses' (Maynard & Clayman, 1991, p. 405).

The appearance of stability and orderliness, in everyday life as well as formal organizations of various kinds, is therefore built from the continuous use of members' *common-sense knowledge* of what is happening and *common-sense reasoning* about what they should say or do next derived from their use of the documentary method of interpretation. Ethnomethodology seeks to identify what 'stocks of knowledge' and 'reasoning procedures' – or what Cicourel (1973, p. 52) alternatively calls 'interpretive procedures' – exist that make social organization possible. It 'does not ask "under what conditions would a person be caused to act?" (which is the standard question) but "under what conditions does an action become recognisable and its cause (if any) identifiable?"' (Sharrock, 1989, p. 663) It therefore asks: what are these interpretive procedures and how do people use them to get things done? In so doing, ethnomethodological studies are able to show how social order requires constant, albeit largely imperceptible and predominantly unconscious, effort and activity. Rawls (2008, p. 701) refers to the 'constant mutual orientation' to unfolding scenes of action as people seek, turn by turn and action by action, to make and display their sense of what is going on.

Research methods used in ethnomethodological studies

Doing an ethnomethodological study comes with some quite specific requirements for the types of research methods you should use, as well as particular procedures for data analysis. Ethnomethodological studies have a strong preference for the observation of *naturally occurring settings* or, in Garfinkel's (1988) formulation, 'locally produced naturally accountable' phenomena. What this means is that settings that are 'contrived', that is, set up purely for the purposes of generating data for the researcher (such as interviews, focus groups, experiments, questionnaire surveys), have little value because they do not give us the ability to recover the ethno-methods used to accomplish the organization of that setting we are interested in studying.[1] For example, if the setting in question was an organization you are studying, asking people about the organization in interviews or focus groups, setting up an experiment to replicate a situation that takes place in the organization, or designing a questionnaire survey to be distributed to people in the organization would all give you little insight relevant to the key ethnomethodological question: what are the ethno-methods through which members of that organization go about organizing themselves? To generate these insights, you would need to *observe* the members of the organization doing whatever job it is that they do: managing people, selling goods or services, coordinating logistics, collecting donations for charity and so on. If you are able to get some kind of video or audio recording of the people doing their work, this is even better. The use of recording technologies enables you to slow down the moment-by-moment unfolding of the interaction (including both turns at talk and non-verbal signals and movements) and subject it to repeated analysis by replaying the sequence and looking for the ethno-methods that people were using, often unconsciously and in the split-second reaction time of an interaction, to produce social order (Llewellyn & Hindmarsh, 2010).

When people see ethnomethodological studies of interviews, such as Zimmerman's (1969) analysis of interviews with welfare claimants or Llewellyn's (2010) study of job interviews, or ethnomethodological studies of the collection and analysis of statistics generated from surveys (see Gephart, 2006), the point we just made about using observation as the primary method can seem confusing and perhaps even contradictory. There is an important distinction to be made here. Ethnomethodological researchers are interested in *observing* how these research methods and instruments (the interview, the survey, the focus group, etc.) are generated and used by the people who perform them as part of their normal work. The researcher is not seeking *themselves* to interview or survey people *about* their work, thereby generating their own interview accounts and survey results. Rather, the researcher is trying to find out how people who use interviews and surveys – or any other research method for that matter – use those methods to produce social reality and generate social order in whatever setting they happen to work in. For example, this could include welfare claim assessors using interviews in the course of their work in a welfare agency (Zimmerman, 1969), managers using interviews to recruit candidates for a job vacancy (Llewellyn, 2010) or policy officials using survey statistics to formulate policy recommendations (Cicourel, 1968).

If it is the researcher asking the questions and conducting an 'interview' – such as Garfinkel's (1967, Chapter 5) interviews with Agnes, the intersexed person seeking sex change surgery, or Wieder's (1974) informal questioning of the parolees in the halfway house we will discuss in more detail below – this interview data are also treated in a distinct way. The interview accounts are not treated as giving access into *the reality*, such as the subjective thoughts, feelings, attitudes and values of the person being interviewed (Rapley, 2001). Rather, they are treated as opportunities to tease out the methods people use for answering questions and telling stories that construct their social reality, albeit to a researcher rather than as part of their normal working lives (ten Have, 2004, Chapter 4). For example, an interview account could be analysed for what membership categories are used or how accounts of social reality are produced as objective and factual (ten Have, 2004, p. 75), without assuming that those membership categories or accounts necessarily get produced in the same way in other settings. (This would be an empirical question to be examined by studying the categories and accounts produced in those other settings.) In this sense, interviews should be treated as accounts that can be collected by the researcher and added to other accounts collected as part of field research (Atkinson & Delamont, 2006).

Issues of sampling are also considered in a different way in ethnomethodological studies (ten Have, 2004). It does not matter whether the social group you are studying is large or small, formal or informal. It could be an entire profession, an occupational group, a firm or a small work team that is being studied. It does not matter whether you study all the people doing that work activity or just a handful of those people, depending on what access you managed to negotiate. The key thing is that the people in the social group share, recognize and employ similar 'methods' to do whatever they do together and that you have gathered a sufficient number of observations of their work practice to be able to identify what these common methods are. In Clegg's (1975) study of a Yorkshire building site, he simply spent enough time with enough workmen to be able to see and understand the 'pattern' through which the inclement weather rule was being invoked. Ethnomethodology is the study of social *practices*, not social *variables*, and issues of the demographic profile or roles or attitudes of the people you study simply do not enter the equation. If demographic categories enter the analysis (e.g. gender, class, ethnicity, religious belief), it is through the analysis of how they are invoked and made relevant within the interaction by the members themselves (see e.g. Llewellyn, 2011a; 2011b). The point of an ethnomethodological analysis is to identify what shared social practices (ethno-methods) are being used to generate social order as the people interact, not what variables are making people behave the way they are behaving. As ten Have (2004, p. 75, emphasis in original) explains, 'the interest is *not* in people as such, but in people as *members*, as competent practitioners, because ultimately ethnomethodology is interested in order-producing *practices*'.

As a basic methodological requirement, then, an ethnomethodological study needs to use observation of the setting to identify how a particular sequence of interaction is accomplished by observing it *as it unfolds in real-time*. It would also ideally be informed by deep immersion in the field site(s) to enable 'an embodied experience of the work in question' (Rawls, 2008, p. 711). Indeed, in carrying forth the ethnomethodological programme, 'researchers have ventured into a wide range of bureaucratic and occupational settings – e.g. classrooms, courtrooms, medical clinics, police departments, public welfare agencies, and elsewhere – to produce findings that are institutionally sensitive. These studies explicate the processes through which participants perform.' (Maynard & Clayman, 1991, p. 404)

Such deep immersion could mean *participant* observation and this could quite literally mean training to become competent in doing the work activity in question and then actually taking part in the activity with those you are studying (Lynch, Livingston & Garfinkel, 1983, p. 207). This *deep immersion* is particularly important in settings where the ethno-methods are more specialized and technical rather than 'common knowledge'. Ethnomethodologists sometimes refer to this as the 'unique adequacy requirement', in which the researcher must have 'adequate' mastery of the setting under study 'as a precondition for making ethnomethodological observations and descriptions' (Lynch, 1993, p. 274; see also Rawls, 2008; Rouncefield & Tolmie, 2011). However, some ethnomethodologists do not actively participate in the setting and just act as a 'fly on the wall', observing (and perhaps recording) the action as it unfolds. This works perfectly well if the researcher has a basic competence and 'adequate' mastery of the setting already. For example, Llewellyn (2011a; 2011b) did not need any special competence to study the selling of a charity magazine on the high street or people paying for admission to an art gallery.

As in Llewellyn's (2011a; 2011b) study, it is also possible to collect observational data without being there as a researcher, just setting up a camera or recording device (or using one that is already there, such as the CCTV already present in the setting or audio recordings already made in the setting) without being physically present. There are, of course, important matters of research ethics to be considered with any observational study, regardless of whether the researcher is present and whether recording technology is used. These include how to ensure informed consent and how to ensure confidentiality for those observed, if such confidentiality is important for avoiding any harm to your participants. Signed consent and confidentiality forms are sometimes not possible or practical in every setting, so alternatives ways of protecting those you study would need to be designed, such as displaying a sign notifying people that a study is underway and giving them the right to withdraw from the study or receive further information if they are unsure about giving their consent (Llewellyn, 2011a; 2011b), as well as giving details of how the data will be stored and used.

The way that data is analysed in an ethnomethodological study is also very different to the types of analysis found in other qualitative approaches, again indicating 'the fact there is a great gulf [which] typically divides ethnomethodologists from other sociologists' (Sharrock, 1989, p. 660). The researcher does not try to 'code' the data (i.e. the observations or recordings of people at work) using some kind of software package that enables disparate bits of data (e.g. extracts from interview transcripts, fieldnotes of observations, survey responses) to be grouped together into a 'code', later to be grouped together again into higher-order codes as part of the abstraction of general themes or patterns from the data. Rather, the data must be *kept within its interactional context* and the patterns looked for are *patterns in the interactional organization* of the work the people are doing.

There are two main ways in which cases (i.e. extracts of sequences of interaction) can be drawn out for analysis (ten Have, 2004). The first is single case analysis. An extended sequence of talk and interaction, one which is particularly important for that setting or particularly rare and stands out as different or unusual in some way (e.g. an exception to the norm, an unusual occurrence that had to be treated differently to normal occurrences), is transcribed and subject to turn-by-turn analysis to identify how social order was produced. The discovery of the optical pulsar, for example, was a one-time event and therefore suitable for a single case analysis (Garfinkel, Lynch & Livingston, 1981). The second is the creation of a 'collection' of cases. For example, the analyst could gather a collection of instances of people answering recruitment questions in an interview, instances of managers making recruitment selection decisions, instances of people making judgements about the welfare benefits that claimants should receive or people making policy recommendations on the basis of survey statistics. The analyst would use this collection of cases to identify the shared inferential practices (ethno-methods) those people used to get their work done.

Re-specifying organizations: the case of the convict code

It would be useful to look in more detail at one particular study to show how an ethnomethodological perspective takes a somewhat distinct approach to conceptualizing 'organizations' by re-specifying them as a product of members' interpretive procedures. Lawrence Wieder's (1974) study is particularly useful for a number of reasons. Not only has Wieder's study become renowned as a classic study in ethnomethodology and not only does his study involve a formal 'organization' (and hence is particularly relevant to students of management and organization studies); Wieder also directly contrasted his ethnomethodological perspective with more conventional social theory explanations to illustrate the difference between them. His work has also gone on to influence more recent ethnographies of deviant groups (see e.g. Jimerson & Oware, 2006).

Lawrence Wieder's (1974) book *Language and Social Reality: the Case of Telling the Convict Code* tells the story of his fieldwork in a 'halfway house': a place where recently paroled prisoners – in his case narcotic offenders – were sent to live for 'rehabilitation' before being released into the community. Wieder spent many months conducting non-participant observation in the halfway house. He informally interviewed the staff and residents about their behaviours and decisions, observed meetings of the various programmes and activities, attended staff meetings, and generally hung around in the communal areas hoping to learn about life in the organization from the perspective of the residents and staff.

Wieder's halfway house was a formal 'organization' with all its attendant matters of business to be accomplished. There was an official organizational *goal* – in this case the goal was the rehabilitation of narcotic offenders before being released into the community. There were formal *rules and policies* to be followed, such as rules about visitors, a night-time curfew, and an official schedule of therapy and employment skills training for rehabilitation purposes. There was also a clear *division of labour* and *distribution of roles* between staff, and between staff and residents. There were a range of *organizational decisions* to be made, such as where residents should be allowed to go and when they were permitted release. In other words, this was a type of organization that required managing and organizing just like any other organization, whether in the commercial, public or third sector, with its formal rules and structures as well as its informal sense of 'how we do things around here'.

Before starting his study, Wieder was well aware of the existing sociological and anthropological work that had been done on the so-called 'counter-cultures' that are presumed to govern communities of criminals and other such deviant groups.

Existing social theory explanations of deviant behaviour held that there exists a 'moral code' that deviants followed, with 'rules' or 'maxims' such as:

- Do not 'snitch' (i.e. inform on the deviant behaviour of other convicts)
- Do not 'cop out' (i.e. admit you have done something illegal)
- Show your loyalty to other convicts (e.g. by providing alibis or cover stories or sharing your drugs)
- Do not trust officials (e.g. police, prison guards, social workers)
- Do not be a 'kiss ass' (i.e. act friendly towards officials, participate in their rehab programmes)
- Do not be a 'sniveller' (i.e. complain to officials for better treatment)

The traditional social theory explanation for convict behaviour goes as follows: these 'rules' or 'maxims' of the convict code are deeply held norms and values that convicts have internalized through their socialization into the counter-culture and can therefore *explain* why convicts behave the way they do and *predict* how they will behave in a given situation. This traditional type of analysis is based on the idea popularized by the structural-functionalist sociology of Parsons (1937; 1951) that rules, norms and values are external 'social facts' which are understood to 'push' and 'pull' people to behave in particular ways and thereby create the social order that we see in front of us: a structured world of consistent patterns of behaviour that gives society and social groups their 'structured' form. The structural-functionalist explanation proposes that social order is generated by the 'rules', 'norms' and 'values' purported to emanate from institutions such as the state, the education system or religion – or in the case of counter-cultures reactions against them – which create a structured and ordered society.

Wieder's ethnomethodological analysis of the convict code can be contrasted with this traditional structural-functionalist analysis. Wieder was interested in the *methods* through which the convict code came to be experienced as external and constraining 'facts'. The code was not just something that convicts and other deviants talked about in interviews or reported in questionnaire surveys. The code was also something used by the residents and staff to interpret and explain their behaviour – both to themselves and to others. Wieder turned the analytic lens on himself and studied how he pieced together the various observations and interactions he experienced in the first days and weeks of his study, in order to assemble the idea of this 'convict code'. Using the notion of the convict code he had started to learn about from conversations with staff and residents, Wieder used the documentary method of interpretation (described earlier in this chapter) to make sense of what he experienced as a researcher – including what he saw (from his non-participant observations) and what people told him when he asked them questions (in his informal interviews).

For example, Wieder noticed that during the group therapy sessions, where chairs were assembled in a circle formation and participants asked to talk about their deviant behaviour and address its causes and propose solutions, residents would sit in an excessively slouched position (slouched so much that their necks would rest at the back of the chair), make little eye contact with the staff member, make side conversations and sometimes refuse to answer questions. Some didn't even attend, despite the sanctions in place for non-attendance. These 'appearances' he observed in group sessions he placed together in a 'pattern' by employing one of the maxims of the convict code, namely, 'do not be a kiss ass'. This process was reflexive because: 'the sense of the rules and the sense of the meaning of the patterns of behaviour are mutually elaborative. The code furnishes meaning for the behaviour, which, in turn, supplies the meaning of the code.' (Leiter, 1980, p. 198)

This insight has profound consequences for how the researcher uses their 'data' to produce a sociological 'theory'. It fundamentally questions the assumptions made in most traditional theories about causation – such as the idea that social facts (such as rules, norms or values) 'shape our action as individuals ... Social facts ... are external to individuals and have a reality of their own' (Giddens, 2009, p. 13; Durkheim, 1982 [1895]). In contrast, for ethnomethodology, social facts such as the 'convict code' (or indeed any other organizational 'variable' for that matter) are viewed as interpretive devices used by members rather than as causal agents: 'To be a causal agent ... the code must be capable of being defined and recognized independent of context' (Leiter, 1980). As Wieder showed, the convict code did not exist independent of its methodical use in context.

Staff members also used the convict code to make sense of events using the documentary method of interpretation. For example, when residents refused to give information about deviant behaviour of a fellow resident – such as breaking a curfew or being caught with drugs in their room – this 'appearance' was interpreted using the 'pattern' of the code by treating the refusal as motivated by the maxim 'do not snitch'. The staff therefore accepted this explanation and did not probe further, even though they probably could and should have done in order to investigate violations of the official rules. Wieder's analysis showed that the code was not only used retrospectively, to make sense of things that had already happened. It was also used *prospectively* as well. One of the residents, Pablo, asked to be released early on the grounds that a fellow convict who was about to join the halfway house suspected that he was a 'snitch' and therefore his life was in danger (retribution for 'snitches' was typically violent). Residents who gave other reasons for requests for early release, such as claiming to be experiencing racial harassment or having secured employment a distance away, were not granted their request. But Pablo was. The code was used as a reasoning procedure to anticipate future events that had not even happened yet. Similarly, official policies, such as policies on curfews and compulsory attendance at therapeutic meetings, were never put into practice on the grounds that they would be simply 'unrealistic', because the normative constraints of the code anticipated that residents would not comply. No such resistance or lack of compliance actually occurred, but it was anticipated because of their knowledge of the normative constraints of the code. Deviance from official organizational policies and orders was rendered 'reasonable' through the *reasoning procedures* provided by the code. Wieder's study therefore neatly demonstrates the use of the 'informal organization' (i.e. the convict code) as a scheme of interpretation for making sense of why aspects of the 'formal organization' (i.e. official policies) should not be implemented. The study also illustrates the *consequential* nature of 'telling the code'. Material consequences arose from its use. Certain residents were released (such as Pablo), while others were not. Certain policies were implemented and others were abandoned as a result of the code being employed as a scheme of interpretation.

To sum up, Wieder concluded that this so-called 'counter-culture' referred to by the term 'convict code' was not a stable and external set of facts and forces that somehow *caused* the residents to behave in a particular way. It was not a 'property' or 'attribute' of the social group. Rather, the convict code was in fact a scheme of interpretation that enabled staff, residents and observers such as Wieder to 'organize particular behaviours into coherent, classifiable types of behaviour' (Wieder, 1974, p. 166). What Wieder's study shows is that knowledge of the code enabled members to undertake the interpretive work of transforming each and every behaviour and utterance they encountered into the 'application of a rule', namely the rules of the convict code. The 'business' of this organization – namely rehabilitating narcotics offenders back into society after release from prison – was achieved (or at times abandoned) through this continuous sensemaking process.

Mainstream sociologists 'treat order as an aggregate result of individual action in a context of either structurally constrained or goal-oriented activity' (Rawls, 2008, p. 703). In contrast, Wieder showed that the norms and rules of the convict code did not *cause* members to comply, as if pushing and pulling them in particular directions. In the same way, the formal or informal 'rules' of business settings – such as organizational structure charts, job descriptions, strategy statements, codes of conduct, manuals, guidelines and so on – do not determine what people do at work (Bittner, 1974). The code could not be used to explain or predict the behaviour of organizational members in the way a positivistic science might demand. Rather, the existence of this social order was created by the 'methods of giving and receiving embedded instructions for seeing and describing a social order' (Wieder, 1974, p. 172). The 'rules', 'values' and 'norms' supposedly generating the orderly patterns of behaviour did not exist 'out there'; they had to be continually produced by members using their stock of social knowledge in every situation they faced: they were 'an endogenous concerted achievement' (Maynard & Clayman, 1991, p. 403). It is this sense of social order being an outcome of a *continuous process* of interpretation rather than existing as a set of 'variables' that gives ethnomethodology its affinity to other process theories of organization (see Langley & Tsoukas, 2017).

Conclusion

Ethnomethodology has a special place within management and organization studies because of its distinct position as an alternative paradigm of social science. It is unlike most other approaches to studying the social world and, as such, has a lot to contribute to the study of organizational settings of various kinds. We hope that the reader will take away inspiration from this chapter and consider adopting an ethnomethodological approach in their own research. It might be helpful to consider in the concluding sections of the chapter the different streams of research through which ethnomethodological studies can contribute to our understanding of different forms of organization. We will consider three streams: workplace studies, the study of market transactions and finally a small but important body of work on public inquiries and official sensemaking.

Since the publication of Garfinkel's (1986) edited collection *Ethnomethodological Studies of Work*, ethnomethodologists began to study a range of work settings under the umbrella term 'workplace studies'. These studies have sought to reveal the methods that organizational members use to make coordinated action possible by interacting with each other and artefacts and machines of various kinds. Studies have examined the use of photocopiers (Suchman, 1987; Orr, 1996), the design of a new technology (Button & Sharrock, 1998), air traffic control rooms (Suchman, 1993), London Underground control rooms and train drivers (Heath, Hindmarsh & Luff, 1999; Heath & Luff, 2000) and CCTV operators (Neyland, 2006). This work has also found practical applications, for example in informing the design of human–computer interfaces and information systems (Luff, Hindmarsh & Heath, 2000; Rouncefield & Tolmie, 2011).

Workplace studies have produced a number of insights into how documents, graphs, charts and spreadsheets enable organization that future studies could advance further. Existing work has studied how organizational members use figures in spreadsheets (Gephart, 1988; 2006; Hughes, 2011), order forms (Moore, Whalen & Hankinson Gathman, 2010), formal plans and strategies (Samra-Fredericks, 2010; Neyland & Whittle, 2017; Whittle et al., 2016), the kinds of mundane artefacts used in meetings (Boden, 1994; Hughes et. al., 2010) and paper-based and digital records that are routinely used in workplaces (Watson, 2009; Heath and Luff, 1996; Hartswood et al., 2011). Workplace studies have had much to offer in the study of management processes such as leadership and decision-making. This has included work on leader succession (Gephart, 1978), decision-making in multidisciplinary teams (Housley, 2003), recruitment decisions (Llewellyn, 2010; Llewellyn & Spence, 2009; Bolander & Sandberg, 2013), and senior manager decision-making and leadership interactions (Samra-Fredericks, 2000; 2003; 2004; 2005; Iszatt-White, 2010; 2011; Whittle et al., 2015; Mueller et al., 2013).

A second body of ethnomethodological work has studied market interactions where goods or services are being sold. Studies have examined interactions between salespeople and their customers (Clark & Pinch, 2010; Llewellyn & Hindmarsh, 2013), acts of charitable exchange (Llewellyn, 2011a; 2011b) and auction houses (Heath & Luff, 2010). There is much more still to contribute in this area by management and organization researchers who are interested in how markets are created and enacted. One obvious future research opportunity is in the study of marketing professionals, whose day-to-day work has not been fully explored from an ethnomethodological perspective.

A final body of work where future ethnomethodological studies would have rich insights to contribute is in the study of societal sensemaking. The focus here for management and organization researchers is not on the organization itself but rather how organizations, and the people who manage them, are held to account for organizational actions (in particular disasters, scandals and crises) through accounts produced about them and by them in different social institutions. Two streams of research are potential here: studies of how organizations and their actions are accounted for in media discourse (see e.g. Jalbert, 1999) and how they are accounted for in public enquiries or similar such hearings of official bodies of various kinds (see e.g. Atkinson & Drew, 1979; Pollner, 1987; Gephart, 1993; Lynch & Bogen, 1996; Goodwin, 1997; Whittle, Mueller & Carter, 2016). In doing these studies, ethnomethodology can contribute to management and organization studies in the same way that ethnomethodological studies have contributed to areas such as law, science and medicine (Maynard & Clayman, 1991, p. 408).

End-of-chapter exercises

1. What does the term 're-specify' mean for ethnomethodologists and how does it change the way that research is done by ethnomethodologists?
2. How do mainstream social theory explanations of deviant behaviour, which are based on the assumption that there exists a 'moral code' governing the behaviour of deviant groups, differ from the ethnomethodological approach used in Lawrence Wieder's study?
3. How do ethnomethodologists question the status of 'social facts' (such as norms, values, rules, role structures, etc.) as variables with causal properties that are amenable for use in positivistic social science reasoning about cause and effect?
4. Try out a little experiment to establish how people create a social 'fact' such as a queue. Next time you want to join a queue in a shop, see how far away you can stand behind the person at the back of the queue before the person wanting to join after you asks you 'are you in the queue?' You can try other variations of this exercise, such as facing the opposite direction to everyone else, standing slightly to the side, or appearing to be still shopping. Use this experiment to identify the ethno-methods other people use to construct the social reality of 'a queue'.
5. Next time you have a conversation with someone (ideally a close friend or family member where this will not adversely affect your relationship!), try leaving an unusually long pause when it's your turn to talk. Then, after you have remained silent for a while, ask the person you are talking to how they made sense of the long pause. This will give you some understanding of the documentary method of interpretation they used to generate a meaningful 'pattern' or 'typification' to understand your strange behaviour.
6. Think of an example where you used the documentary method of interpretation to establish a completely different 'pattern' to someone else who was also present when you made sense of an event (for example, a meeting you both attended). How did you create this different sense of social reality, using which 'pattern'? What 'pattern' did they use to create their sense of reality?
7. If you were to design an ethnomethodological study that involved interviews or questionnaire surveys, how would your research design differ from the more conventional social scientific research designs that employ these research methods?

Glossary

Accountable/accountability   In ethnomethodology, accounts produced by members of a social setting are not 'about' the setting but part of the constitution of the setting. Members of the setting work to make their scenes publicly and visibly accountable through the production of accounts that render them 'real'.

Documentary method of interpretation   The documentary method of interpretation is the interpretative activity through which a link is created between an event or 'appearance' and an underlying 'pattern' or assumed meaning structure in a circular fashion, wherein each elaborate the other.

Indexicality   The idea of indexical expressions is extended from its origins within linguistics and in ethnomethodology refers to the notion that the meaning of all utterances and social actions is dependent upon a context that is supplied to make sense of it. Context, from this perspective, is not a fixed set of properties of the social scene but something that is brought into being in the moment-by-moment unfolding of the interaction.

Reflexivity   The term reflexivity used in ethnomethodology does not refer to the forms of self-reflection undertaken by researchers when reflecting on their role in the construction of their data and findings. Rather, reflexivity refers to a property of social action, namely that members of a social setting understand their actions through reference to a context at the same time as that context is being defined through their actions.

Re-specification   Ethnomethodology 're-specifies' conventional sociological analysis by turning the 'social facts' presumed to exist 'out there' into a topic of empirical enquiry. It examines the methods that members use to create the things they take to be social facts and that give them their fact-like status in their moment-by-moment interactions.

Note

1 Many of Garfinkel's most (in)famous studies did in fact involve 'contrived' settings of various kinds. His (in)famous breaching experiments (Garfinkel, 1967, Chapter 2), where he asked his students to deliberately break or 'breach' the normal 'rules' of interaction, for example by asking people to clarify what they really mean or acting like a lodger in your own home, were 'contrived' in the sense of not being naturally occurring. His infamous 'student counselling experiment', where students were told they were speaking to a counsellor who could only answer 'yes' or 'no' to questions they posed (which were in fact randomly generated), was also contrived in this sense of not being naturally occurring. However, they differ from other contrived researcher-designed settings informed by positivism, where conditions are controlled and variables are tested, because their aim was not to test the correlation of variables but rather to surface the kind of common-sense reasoning that is normally so taken for granted and therefore not visible for analysis.

References

Atkinson, J. M., & Drew, P. (1979). *Order in court: The organisation of verbal interaction in judicial settings*. London: Macmillan.

Atkinson, P., & Delamont, S. (2006). Rescuing narrative from qualitative research. *Narrative Inquiry, 16*(1), 164–172.

Bar-Hillel, Y. (1954). Indexical expressions. *Mind, 63*(251), 359–379.

Benson, D., & Hughes, J. A. (1983). *The perspective of ethnomethodology*. London: Longman Publishing Group.

Bittner E. (1974). The concept of organization. In R. Turner (ed.) *Ethnomethodology* (pp. 69–81). Baltimore, MD: Penguin.

Boden, D. (1994). *The business of talk: Organizations in action*. Cambridge: Polity Press.

Bolander, P., & Sandberg, J. (2013). How employee selection decisions are made in practice. *Organisation Studies, 34*(3): 285–311.

Button, G. (ed.) (1991). *Ethnomethodology and the human sciences*. Cambridge: Cambridge University Press.

Button, G., & Sharrock, W. (1998). The organisational accountability of technical work. *Social Studies of Sciences, 28*(1), 73–102.

Cicourel, A. V. (1968). *The social organization of juvenile justice*. New York: John Wiley.

Cicourel, A. V. (1973). *Cognitive sociology: Language and meaning in social interaction*. Harmonsworth: Penguin.

Clark, C., & Pinch, T. (2010). Some major organisational consequences of some 'minor' organised conduct: Evidence from a video analysis of pre-verbal encounters in a showroom retail store. In N. Llewellyn, & J. Hindmarsh (eds) *Organisation, interaction and practice: Studies of ethnomethodology and conversation analysis* (pp. 140–171). Cambridge: Cambridge University Press.

Clegg, S. (1975). *Power, rule and domination: A critical and empirical understanding of power in sociological theory and organizational life*. London: Routledge & Kegan Paul.

Coulon, A. (1995). *Ethnomethodology*. London: Sage.

Dingwall, R. (2000). Language, law, and power: Ethnomethodology, conversation analysis, and the politics of law and society studies. *Law & Social Inquiry, 25*(3), 885–911.

Durkheim, E. (1964 [1895]). *The rules of sociological method*. New York: Free Press.

Durkheim, E. (2008 [1912]). *The elementary forms of religious life*. Oxford: Oxford University Press.

Francis, D., & Hester, S. (2004). *An invitation to ethnomethodology: Language, society and interaction*. London: Sage.

Garfinkel, H. (1967). *Studies in ethnomethodology*. Englewood Cliffs, NJ: Prentice-Hall.

Garfinkel, H. (ed.) (1986). *Ethnomethodological studies of work*. London: Routledge.

Garfinkel, H. (1988). Evidence for locally produced naturally accountable phenomena of order, logic, reason, meaning, method, etc. in and as of the essential haecceity of immortal ordinary society. *Sociological Theory, 6*(1), 103–109.

Garfinkel, H., Lynch, M., & Livingston, E. (1981). The work of a discovering science construed with materials from the optically discovered pulsar. *Philosophy of the Social Sciences, 11*(2), 131–158.

Garfinkel, H., & Rawls, A. (2002). *Ethnomethodology's program: Working out Durkheim's aphorism*. Boulder, CO: Rowman & Littlefield Press.

Garfinkel, H., & Wieder, D. L. (1992). Two incommensurable, asymmetrically alternate technologies of social analysis. In G. Watson, & R. M. Seiler (eds) *Text in context: Contributions to ethnomethodology* (pp. 175–206). London: Sage.

Geertz, C. (1973/2000). *The interpretation of cultures: Selected essays*. New York: Basic Books.

Gephart, R. P. (1978). Status degradation and organizational succession: An ethnomethodological approach. *Administrative Science Quarterly, 23*, 553–581.

Gephart, R. P. (1988). *Ethnostatistics: Qualitative foundations for quantitative research*, Vol. 12. Thousand Oaks, CA: Sage.

Gephart, R. P. (1993). The textual approach: Risk and blame in disaster sensemaking. *Academy of Management Journal, 36*(6), 1465–1514.

Gephart, R. P. (2006). Ethnostatistics and organizational research methodologies: An introduction. *Organizational Research Methods, 9*(4), 417–431.

Giddens, A. (2009). *Sociology*. Cambridge: Polity Press.

Goodwin, C. (1997). The blackness of black: Color categories as situated practice. In L. B. Resnick, R. Säljö, C. Pontecorvo, & B. Burge (eds) *Discourse, tools and reasoning*. NATO ASI Series, Vol. 160. Berlin, Heidelberg: Springer.

Handel, W. H. (1982). *Ethnomethodology: How people make sense*. Englewood Cliffs, NJ: Prentice-Hall.

Hartswood, M., Rouncefield, M., Slack, R., & Carlin, A. P. (2011). Documents. In M. Rouncefield, & P. Tolmie (eds) *Ethnomethodology at work* (pp. 151–171).

Heath, C., & Luff, P. (1996). Documents and professional practice: 'Bad' organisational reasons for 'good' clinical records. In *Proceedings of the 1996 ACM conference on computer supported cooperative work* (pp. 354–363).

Heath, C. & Luff, P. (2000). *Technology in action*. Cambridge: Cambridge University Press.

Heath C, & Luff, P. (2010). Orders of bidding: Organising participation in auctions of fine art and antiques. In N. Llewellyn, & J. Hindmarsh (eds) *Organisation, interaction and practice:*

Studies in ethnomethodology and conversation analysis (pp. 119–139). Cambridge: Cambridge University Press.

Heath, C., Hindmarsh, J., & Luff, P. (1999). Interaction in isolation: The dislocated world of the London Underground train driver. *Sociology, 33*(3), 555–575.

Housley, W. (2003). *Interaction in multidisciplinary teams*. Aldershot: Ashgate.

Hughes, J. (2011). On calculation. In M. Rouncefield, & P. Tolmie (eds) *Ethnomethodology at Work* (pp. 55–72). Farnham: Ashgate.

Hughes, J., Randall, D., Rouncefield, M., & Tolmie, P. (2010). Meetings and the accomplishment of organization. In N. Llewellyn, & J. Hindmarsh (eds) *Organisation, interaction and practice: Studies in ethnomethodology and conversation analysis* (pp. 131–150). Cambridge: Cambridge University Press.

Iszatt-White, M. (2010). Strategic leadership: The effortful accomplishment of valuing practices. *Leadership, 6*(4), 409–424.

Iszatt-White, M. (2011). Methodological crises and contextual solutions: An ethnomethodologically-informed approach to understanding leadership. *Leadership, 7*(2), 121–137.

Jalbert, P. L. (1999). *Media studies: Ethnomethodological approaches*. Lanham, MD: University Press of America.

Jimerson, J. B., & Oware, M. K. (2006). Telling the code of the street: An ethnomethodological ethnography. *Journal of Contemporary Ethnography, 35*(1), 24–50.

Langley, A., & Tsoukas, H. (2017). Introduction: Process thinking, process theorizing and process researching. *The Sage handbook of process organizational studies* (pp. 1–26). London: Sage.

Leiter, K. (1980). *A primer on ethnomethodology*. Oxford: Oxford University Press.

Llewellyn, N. (2010). On the reflexivity between setting and practice: The 'recruitment interview'. In N. Llewellyn, & J. Hindmarsh (eds) *Organisation, interaction and practice: Studies in ethnomethodology and conversation analysis* (pp. 74–95). Cambridge: Cambridge University Press.

Llewellyn, N. (2011a). The gift in interaction: The practice of 'picking up the bill'. *British Journal of Sociology, 62*(4), 718–738.

Llewellyn, N. (2011b). The delicacy of the gift: Passing donations and leaving change. *Discourse & Society, 22*(2), 155–174.

Llewellyn, N. (2014). Garfinkel and ethnomethodology. In Adler, P. S., Du Gay, P., Morgan, G., & Reed, M. I. (eds) *The Oxford handbook of sociology, social theory, and organization studies: Contemporary currents* (pp. 299–317). Oxford: Oxford University Press.

Llewellyn, N., & Hindmarsh, J. (eds) (2010). *Organisation, interaction and practice: Studies in ethnomethodology and conversation analysis*. Cambridge: Cambridge University Press.

Llewellyn, N., & Hindmarsh, J. (2013). The order problem: Inference and interaction in interactive service work. *Human Relations, 66*(11), 1401–1426.

Llewellyn, N., & Spence, L. (2009). Practice as a members' phenomenon. *Organization Studies, 30*(12), 1419–1439.

Luff, P., Hindmarsh, J., & Heath, C. (2000). *Workplace studies: Recovering work practice and informing systems design*. Cambridge: Cambridge University Press.

Lynch, M. (1993). *Scientific practice and ordinary action: Ethnomethodology and social studies of science*. New York: Cambridge University Press.

Lynch, M., & Bogen, D. (1996). *The spectacle of history: Speech, text, and memory at the Iran-Contra hearings*. Durham, NC: Duke University Press.

Lynch, M., Livingston, E., & Garfinkel, H. (1983). Temporal order in laboratory work. In K. Knorr-Cetina, & M. Mulkay (eds) *Science observed: Perspectives on the social study of science* (pp. 205–238). Beverly Hills, CA: Sage.

Maynard, D. W., & Clayman, S. E. (1991). The diversity of ethnomethodology. *Annual Review of Sociology, 17*, 385–418.

Meehan, A. J. (1986). Record-keeping practices in the policing of juveniles. *Urban Life, 15*, 70–102.

Moore, B., Whalen, J., & Hankinson Gathman, E. C. (2010). The work of the work order: Document practice in face-to-face service encounters. In N. Llewellyn, & J. Hindmarsh (eds) *Organisation, interaction and practice: Studies in ethnomethodology and conversation analysis* (pp. 172–197). Cambridge: Cambridge University Press.

Mueller, F., Whittle, A., Gilchrist, A., & Lenney, P. (2013). Politics and strategy practice: An ethnomethodologically-informed discourse analysis perspective. *Business History, 55*(7), 1168–1199.

Neyland, D. (2006). Moving images: The mobility and immobility of 'kids standing still'. *The Sociological Review, 54*(2), 363–381.

Neyland, D., & Whittle, A. (2017). Garfinkel on strategy: Using ethnomethodology to make sense of 'rubbish strategy'. *Critical Perspectives on Accounting, 53*, 31–42.

Orr, J. E. (1996). *Talking about machines: An ethnography of a modern job*. Ithaca, NY: Cornell University Press.

Parsons, T. (1937). *The structure of social action*. New York: Free Press.

Parsons, T. (1951). *The social system*. London: Routledge & Kegan Paul.

Pollner, M. (1987). *Mundane reason: Reality in everyday and sociological discourse*. Cambridge: Cambridge University Press.

Rapley, T. J. (2001). The art(fulness) of open-ended interviewing: Some considerations on analysing interviews. *Qualitative Research, 1*(3), 303–323.

Rawls, A. (2002). Editor's introduction. In H. Garfinkel (ed.) *Ethnomethodology's program: Working out Durkheim's aphorism*. Boulder, CO: Rowman & Littlefield Press.

Rawls, A. W. (2008). Harold Garfinkel, ethnomethodology and workplace studies. *Organization Studies, 26*(5), 701–732.

Rouncefield, M., & Tolmie, P. (eds) (2011). *Ethnomethodological studies of work*. Farnham: Ashgate.

Ryle, G. (1990). The thinking of thoughts: What is 'le penseur' doing? In G. Ryle (ed.) *Collected papers, Volume II: Collected essays 1929–1968*. Bristol: Thoemmes Antiquarian.

Sacks, H. (1975). Everyone has to lie. In B. Blount, & M. Sanches (eds) *Sociocultural dimensions of language use* (pp. 57–80). New York: Academic Press.

Samra-Fredericks, D. (2000). An analysis of the behavioural dynamics of corporate governance – a talk-based ethnographic account of a UK manufacturing board-in-action. *Corporate Governance: An International Review, 8*(4), 311–325.

Samra-Fredericks, D. (2003). Strategizing as lived experience and strategists' everyday efforts to shape strategic direction. *Journal of Management Studies, 40*(1), 141–174.

Samra-Fredericks, D. (2004). Managerial elites making rhetorical/linguistic 'moves' for a moving (emotional) display. *Human Relations, 57*(9), 1103–1143.

Samra-Fredericks, D. (2005). Strategic practice, 'discourse' and the everyday constitution of 'power effects'. *Organization, 12*(6), 803–841.

Samra-Fredericks, D. (2010). Ethnomethodology and the moral accountability of interaction: Navigating the conceptual terrain of 'face' and face-work. *Journal of Pragmatics, 42*(8), 2147–2157.

Schutz, A. (1953). Common-sense and scientific interpretation in human action. *Philosophy and Phenomenological Research, 14*(11), 1–38.

Sharrock, W. (1995). Ethnographic work. *Discourse Analysis Research Group Newsletter, 11*(1), 3–8.

Sharrock, W. (1989). Ethnomethodology. *The British Journal of Sociology, 40*(4), 657–677.

Sharrock, W., & Anderson, R. (1986). *The ethnomethodologists*. London: Tavistock Institute.

Suchman, L. (1987). *Plans and situated actions: The problem of human-machine communication.* Cambridge: Cambridge University Press.

Suchman, L. (1993). Technologies of accountability: Of lizards and aeroplanes. In G. Button (ed.) *Technology in working order: Studies of work, interaction and technology* (pp. 113–126). London: Routledge.

Sudnow, D. (1965). Normal crimes: Sociological features of the penal code in a public defender office. *Social Problems, 12*(3), 255–276.

ten Have, P. (2004). *Understanding qualitative research and ethnomethodology.* London: Sage.

Travers, M., & Manzo, J. F. (2016). *Law in action: Ethnomethodological and conversation analytic approaches to Law.* London: Routledge.

vom Lehn, D. (2016). *Harold Garfinkel: The creation and development of ethnomethodology.* London: Routledge.

Watson, R. (2009). *Analysing practical and professional texts.* Farnham: Ashgate.

Whittle, A., Housley, W., Gilchrist, A., Mueller, F., & Lenney, P. (2015). Category predication work, discursive leadership and strategic sensemaking. *Human Relations, 68*(3), 377–407.

Whittle, A., Mueller, F., & Carter, C. (2016). The 'Big Four' in the spotlight: Accountability and professional legitimacy in the UK audit market. *Journal of Professions and Organization, 3*(2), 119–141.

Whittle, A., Mueller, F., Gilchrist, A., & Lenney, P. (2016). Sensemaking, sense-censoring and strategic inaction: The discursive enactment of power and politics in a multinational corporation. *Organization Studies, 37*(9), 1323–1351.

Wieder, D.L. (1974). *Language and social reality: The case of telling the convict code*, Vol. 10. The Hague: Mouton.

Winiecki, D. (2008). The expert witnesses and courtroom discourse: Applying micro and macro forms of discourse analysis to study process and the 'doings of doings' for individuals and for society. *Discourse & Society, 19*(6), 765–781.

Zimmerman, D. H. (1969). Record-keeping and the intake process in a public welfare agency. In S. Wheeler (ed.) *On record: Files and dossiers in American life* (pp. 319–345). New York: Russell Sage. Selected excerpts reprinted in R. Turner (ed.) (1974) *Ethnomethodology: Selected readings* (pp. 128–143). Harmondsworth: Penguin.

Zimmerman, D. H., & Pollner, M. (1970). The everyday world as phenomenon. In J. D. Douglas (ed.) *Understanding everyday life* (pp. 33–65). London: Routledge.

3   Actor-network theory

Michel Callon, Bruno Latour, John Law

Damian O'Doherty

Chapter objectives

In this chapter we will:

- Provide an answer to the question, why should one study actor-network theory (ANT)?
- Introduce the main tenets of an actor-network approach
- Identify the key writers associated with ANT
- Provide a brief introduction to the intellectual genealogy of ANT in sociology and the social sciences more broadly
- Position ANT within contemporary social theory
- Elicit and induce in the reader a way of thinking compatible with ANT
- Briefly indicate some of the differences between the main protagonists of ANT
- *'De-position'* ANT within emerging approaches influenced by ANT but which also mark the nuances of a post-ANT or 'ANT and after' agenda.

Introduction

Actor-network theory (ANT) has become one of the most popular reference points across the social sciences, drawing in scholars from sociology, anthropology, political theory, philosophy, psychology, geography, international development, international relations and, increasingly, the environmental humanities. It is now becoming one of the most important approaches to management and organization, its influence ranging from the obvious and direct where it is 'applied' or extended (Law, 1994; Bloomfield, 1995; Law & Hassard, 1999; Czarniawska & Hernes, 2005), to approaches where features of ANT are cited as an influence and synthesized (with varying degree of coherence or consistency) with other forms of social theory (Taylor, 1993; Cooren, 2000; Nicolini, 2012).

In the search for origin stories Michel Callon (1945–), Bruno Latour (1947–) and John Law (1946–) are typically identified as the founders of ANT, an attribution they have been reluctant to acknowledge, although at least on one occasion one of the authors confessed the term had been invented sometime between 1978 and 1982 at the Centre de Sociologie de l'Innovation (CSI) of the École Nationale Supérieure des Mines de Paris (Law, 2007).[1] It may have been Michel Callon who first uttered the phrase 'actor-network theory', or 'acteur-réseau' in French, in an attempt to offer a pithy summary of what it was the three of them were doing at the time in terms of prevailing sociological theory. ANT has since been re-labelled in a variety of ways, including 'material-semiotics', 'empirical metaphysics' and 'actant-rhizome ontology', none of which have stuck, and so, each time, the body of work associated with ANT escapes easy definition (Latour, 2005). Hence, we should be cautious in our search for clear lines and single points of originality that allow the narration of a foundation of early principles or axioms giving birth to a progressively expanding body of work that eventually captures the world of higher education and intellectual practice. This would miss the point entirely.

There are now hundreds of introductions to actor-networks, some of them penned by the originators themselves (Latour, 1996; 2005; Law, 2004), as well as many introductory chapters in collections and companions of sociological and social theory designed for a first-time reader (e.g. Restivo, 2003; Harris, 2005; Czarniawska, 2014), all variously sophisticated and attentive to the pitfalls and subtleties that beset the unwary reader of ANT. In this respect it is easier to talk in terms of what makes a well-crafted ANT study rather than to set out a definitive list of principles. In its most basic and distinctive contribution an ANT approach is able to make the assumption that 'the social' does not exist, or to show how what we commonly take to be 'the social' does not exist. (Thatcher was right, as Latour writes, but 'for very different reasons'; Latour, 2005, p. 5.) Rather, what we casually refer to as the social is better thought as the partial and contingent outcome of actors' or actor-networks' ongoing efforts to construct and understand something for which we conveniently use 'the social' as shorthand.[2]

This poses considerable problems to those working in management and organization studies who normally want to use a concept of 'the context', or the bigger picture, in which to place the work of managers and organizations. Management studies typically works with the idea that management is performed by managers – individuals – who variously make policy, negotiate with each other, take decisions, motivate, train and handle their subordinates, etc. To avoid accusations of ignoring the bigger picture, students of business and management tend to bring in a context of social condition-ing that is said to inform and influence what it is managers do in organizations. Hence, there is a social context that partially determines agency, occasionally still a dialectic of macro and micro, structure and agency (see chapters on Archer, Bour-dieu, Giddens and the Frankfurt School, all in this volume), and sometimes a social construction of management (Harding, 2004). All these landmarks and categories familiar to management and organization studies become problematic once we begin to think in terms of ANT.

To get around some of this cluttered furniture of traditional social theory, we can say, by way of introduction, that actors or actor-networks are made up of a dispersal of fine-grained heterogeneous 'socio-technical'[3] materials through which agency emerges as a collective and *relational* phenomenon. One dimension of this is the *symmetry* accorded to the contribution of human and non-human; hence to take a simple example, it is neither the gun nor the man holding the gun that shoots the deer, it is both; or rather it is the properties that emerge out of their relation or *assemblage* that are responsible. Or, perhaps easier to grasp in these preliminaries, it is neither the man nor the cigarette who smokes, but both, in a relation that also give rises to a relational or hybrid actor – the human smoker. As we can easily recog-nize the addictive properties of nicotine we can perhaps find it easier to admit that the human is not always the actor – tobacco or nicotine takes actions in the world and also makes possible certain actions from others. From these very basic insights we can begin to explore a whole series of implications and ramifications that will fill out a wholly different ontology to the one we are used to in social theory.

Of all three authors named in the chapter subtitle, it is Bruno Latour who is widely considered to be the most influential thinker in the social sciences writ large and whose reach extends beyond its confines. Without doubt Latour is a major philosophical figure of the late 20th century, so original and profound is his challenge to modern thought. As a mark of this he received the Legion of Honour in 2012 and the prestigious Holberg prize in 2014 (considered the equivalent of the Nobel for the social sciences) and at the time of writing (2018) his work has attracted over 15 full-length books of introduction, commentary and exegesis, written in many cases by senior established figures in their own right (Blok & Jensen, 2011; Schmidgen, 2014; McGee, 2014; Harman, 2009; de Vries, 2016). This in itself should be sufficient grounds to justify the claim that his work must be taken very seriously and grappled with by anyone who wishes to engage with current conversations in social theory, while the fact that he is also taken seriously by some of the most distinguished European philosophers of the late 20th century must surely establish these credentials beyond doubt. Either explicitly recognized and supported (by people such as Michel Serres, Peter Sloterdijk, Bernard Stiegler and Isobel Stengers), or grudgingly acknowledged – usually by those who have been sufficiently discomfited by the implications of his work to seek to dismiss or distance themselves from it (e.g. Pierre Bourdieu, Jean-Francois Lyotard, Niklas Luhmann) – we can be sure that Latour will be studied and read by increasing numbers of people over the coming decades, and perhaps beyond. This is not to say he is 'difficult' or 'obscure' – in the classic sense to which people normally refer to writers such as Heidegger or Derrida[4] (in which Latour is also steeped of course); in fact he can be as difficult or as simple as you like, and one of the themes that will run through this chapter is what I call his 'profound superficiality'.

In this chapter we first address the question why one might want to explore the work of ANT and, assuming little to no prior knowledge, exemplify some of the most basic and distinctive motifs that through reflection and practice can be developed to help researchers begin to conduct their research in an ANT kind of way. We then move on to introduce and discuss three seminal papers in the history of ANT, namely John Law's 'On the Methods of Long-Distance Control: Vessels, Navigation and the Portuguese Route to India' variously presented in the early 1980s and published in 1986, Michel Callon's 1986 publication 'Some Elements of a Sociology of Translation: Domestication of the Scallops and the Fisherman', and Latour's 1988 essay 'Mixing Humans and Nonhumans Together: the Sociology of a Door-Closer'. The intention here is not to tell you a lot about ANT; we want to help you *think* your way into its way of doing social studies and how this might deepen and support research in management and organization. As we progress it will become increasingly clear that ANT is not a theory, nor something that can be applied in any conventional way. It is instead something more like a method or sensibility (Latour, 2005), one that is constantly evolving and adapting, and one that demands continual conceptual innovation but also rigour that neither reads the empirical off pre-existing theory (ANT or other), nor simply adapts or advances theory in the light of new empirical findings. At a quite profound level, beyond that of an introduction, theory and the empirical is another one of those dualisms that has been dismantled by ANT.

Why study actor-networks?

The question why one might want to adopt or apply ANT is not an idle one, especially if you are reading this as a doctoral student or young researcher who has been told that you must choose an academic theory or body of work in which to position your research question. Those guidebooks that counsel such advice and schematize with boxes and lines in clear linear processual terms showing how one is to build a research project are dangerous and ultimately self-defeating, at least in terms of establishing sustainable research that will contribute to knowledge anything beyond the next academic promotion round (Dunleavy, 2003; Phillips & Pugh, 2010). They might secure a publication or two but they are fundamentally antithetical to the teachings of those associated with ANT – and this is often missed by writers on ANT and especially critics who cannot see anything interesting politically in ANT. So, ANT is not something which one should aim to use, apply or put to work, or even something to which findings or theory can be added. Indeed, before the acronym had really become established, a conference was convened at Keele University[5] in the UK by the main protagonists associated with ANT to debate the problems that were emerging and evident in early appropriations of this newly titled 'school' given apparent licence with the name ANT (Law & Hassard, 1999). In his piece, John Law wrote about the value of working in ways that he called 'After ANT', and Latour (1999) wrote in his characteristic and irrepressible style that there were only four things wrong with ANT – the word actor, the word network, the word theory, and the hyphen![6] As always Latour draws his readers in with a highly entertaining textual performance that appears insouciant and light – easy reading. However, this is his consummate style – and one to be alert for. It forms part of what we called earlier his 'profound superficiality'.

The reason why Callon, Latour and Law developed this acronym was not because they wanted to develop a new social theory or popularize a new approach that would help promote their careers or make them internationally recognized and successful – even if this is what they have become.[7] They did not start from the ambition to design new theory – apart from anything else such ambition would simply create another academic glass bead game. Instead, they were forced to contrive what is almost a *portmanteau* phrase (ANT), which in many ways disfigures customary Western grammatical convention, in order to make sense of their empirical findings that had been accumulating through studies of science and technology. The idea was not to create theory but to find a way of thinking about what is called 'society' in the social sciences when it became clear that something like society could be best described as an *outcome* (or ambition) of scientific endeavour and technological development. Since Durkheim, society has been assumed to be such a large thing, and we use it so casually and usually in inconsistent and contradictory ways. It is assumed to be a container, something stable, a context or something full of stuff. In this alternative ANT way of looking at the world, not only is 'society' something that is a conceptual invention of the modern social sciences, or social theory, in which Durkheim plays a key role; it is also the outcome of efforts to socialize or 'discipline' modern citizens precisely through the very same concepts. Moreover, in an effort to dethrone the pretension of such a grand concept, when we start thinking with ANT we begin to see that society is also only accessible through the study of what at first we might too easily dismiss as small or trivial things. For example, a Bunsen burner, the small contraceptive pill made available in the 1960s, or Louis Pasteur's tiny little laboratory can all be seen to have fundamentally changed the world. What we normally conceive of as that which is solid, powerful and more enduring, 'society', gets chopped back down to size and conceived as a fragile, contingent and emergent thing. With ANT society can be both powerful and almost inexistent, fundamentally derailed or set on a new path and by an apparently incidental thing as a small white pill or things which are only seen inchoately, on the fringes of our carefully disciplined attention, or which have not yet cohered to form a recognizable phenomenon, but immanent, distributed in a myriad of bits and pieces of ideas, texts and devices (Law, 1987).

'Give me a laboratory and I will raise the world' Latour writes, paraphrasing Archimedes' famous 'Give me a lever long enough and a fulcrum on which to place it, and I *shall* move the *world*' (Latour, 1983). Indeed, as Latour (2005) writes in his own introduction to ANT, we might better think of the kind of work done by ANT-designated scholars as ant-like! Crawling through 'society' and its furniture as if one were a busy and obsessive ant reveals a more fine-grained level of detail out of which somehow (partially, and always incoherently) something like society is presumed as an aggregate, a 'lash up' or synthesis. But for the ant, up close and in detail, all they can see is the shifting grains of sand that form a narrow passageway from one point to the next in their itinerary. As we drive in our car along a motorway, for example, we might think of ourselves as being *inside* society, but for the ANT scholar, all they can see, at best, is their participation and agreement in the making of a society of car drivers. Indeed, their own status as road users, or car drivers, requires considerable effort and discipline – especially so for the lowly ant! The road is of course a synthesis of partially stabilized materials, maintained by an army of well-disciplined engineers and repair workers trying to shore up the disintegration of the road at its edges, the potholes, bumps and other cracks and desiderata. Indeed, without signposts and an office for the ordering and a factory for their production, as Latour shows in his study of how the city of Paris is made (Latour & Hermant, 1998), the road would not work – and society, and perhaps not only the society of car drivers, would soon collapse.[8] Moreover, what is typically seen as 'micro' or 'macro' can be seen here to be first inverted (where the big becomes small, and the small big, in which 'the whole is always smaller than its parts'; Venturini, Jensen & Latour, 2015) and then displaced as an opposition, as we need a new language or set of concepts to trace that which comes before and connects macro and micro, or from which macro and micro get invented, extracted and reified.

For an ANT scholar, everything is of interest; there are no shortcuts, or easy summaries, and there are no boundaries behind which we can hold things stable with terms like 'context', for example, which normally serves the purpose of placing boundaries around things in business and management studies. If we want to grasp how actors in management and organization are working on strategy, for example, it is no good conducting the famous PESTEL analysis as part of a SWOT, through which we summarize politics as something which is contextual, i.e. something which we have no capacity to change. The political context of a country is often taken as a given, for example, understood through the popular work of Hofstede (1980). Management textbooks will at best give suggestions as to how one might best operate in different political contexts. HR texts on managing expatriates, for example, represent a popular line of research (see Iles & Zhang, 2013). How we might progress plans to construct a new processing plant in a one-party state with an authoritarian ruler might then be a simple matter of applying a set of rules or a procedure considered best practice for that particular part of the world. For the ANT-like scholar, on the other hand, such broad-brush summaries such as political context, or even something like an organizational policy or process, disappear when you get close to the details. For those predisposed to think like an ant, or those who can accept their status as an ant, we can only follow someone who calls himself/herself a strategist. Or, we might follow documents in which the word 'strategy' appears and observe how these are used by strategists as they pursue strategy (in meetings, for example) and report on and account for its practices in organizational documents.

As we follow the human actor, we will learn how things are currently stacked in, for example, local government planning departments (nothing can be built without local authority planning permission), who has the ear of the chair of such and such a committee, who is on the way up, who on the way down, how local planning rules are perhaps being shaped by central government ambitions and changing ministerial appointments and priorities, what EU grants might be available for certain types of business development, and how one might best influence all this through employer associations and/or other lobby groups and other institutional forms of representation (see Barley, 2010). Before we know where we are, our strategist (and certainly if successful) will soon appear to us as a veritable Machiavelli, in which there is no context other than that which is emergent due to the actions and influence of the business strategists; context is not a given but something that can only be discovered by looking for it, which is what the strategist we are studying here is also doing, with the added sting in the tail that the very way in which we chose to find out about context also changes the very thing we are trying to know or define. Like water, as soon as you reach out and seek to grasp it with your hand, the water recedes, spills out and overflows.

For this ANT-like scholar there is nothing too small or too big that is not potentially relevant to answering any particular question posed in an empirical enquiry. As we can see from these brief illustrations, everything is connected and in often strange and surprising ways. One must be prepared to let the fieldwork be the guide and to follow these connections steered by no *a priori* categories or social theory and no ready-made explanation – such as 'neoliberal capitalism', 'bureaucratization', 'globalization' or any other chapter title from an introduction to the social sciences or social theory. Studying 'culture' in an organization may require that you allow for the possibility that culture is not or not simply a social object but instead a technical or linguistic practice, something that exists as text only. Similarly, the study of what one assumes to be a technical object, a bridge, for example, or the chemical components of the 'thyrotropin releasing factor' (Latour & Woolgar, 1979), might turn out to be a thoroughly social and political phenomenon that would disappear without sufficient political will. Equally, as we have suggested, one may enter fieldwork ostensibly to study business strategy but rapidly find oneself immersed in the world of political wheeling and dealing, having to master the rudiments of Machiavelli's *The Prince* in order to follow your interlocutors. One must even be prepared to acknowledge one's own influence on the object of your research. As your questions become more informed as you read Machiavelli, for example, your interlocutor might respond, 'I never thought of that, yes'. That afternoon, the strategists think about it again during a meeting with his/her CEO, decides to pursue a different approach to seeking agreement to build new premises on a new out-of-town science park. This forms part of what is understood as reflexivity in ANT.

The lack of attention to this reflexivity is fatal for ANT accounts. In a salutary editorial in the prestigious journal *Social Studies of Science*,[9] Mike Lynch wrote that he was becoming a little disgruntled at the number of desk rejects of self-designated ANT papers he had been forced to make during his tenure as senior editor. What he was objecting to was the facile efforts by many to produce research accounts written with the use of ANT as a ready-made and recognizable concept, or concepts developed in previous studies associated with ANT, i.e. delegation, translation, obligatory point of passage, *interessment*, enrolment, immutable mobiles or heterogeneous engineering. Not only does this reduce ANT to a set of principles or axioms that appear to make the collection of empirical data rigorous and methodical, but such efforts typically only *appear* to be an actor-network analysis, in which work is presented in the patina of ANT-like concepts when in actual fact some pretty ordinary kind of social theory is being exercised below the surface. Each of these concepts was derived out of specific fieldwork for very specific purposes and cannot be transplanted wholesale from one field to another. This also puts the proverbial cart before the horse.

Each independent research project will have to discover its own concepts, and indeed construct its own contingent meta-language in which to write up research. ANT is in fact very *minimalist* in terms of concepts, theoretical architectures or methodological rules. Concepts proliferate, but they do not hang around for very long, and each new study has to be prepared to abandon all the conceptual baggage that one acquires in becoming proficient in the main genealogy of texts that define the ANT oeuvre. So, what is important here is the *motivation* or ambition for carrying out an empirical enquiry in the first place. Wanting to know how things actually work in practice is as good a starting point as any, but perhaps more consistent with ANT is to always recall the autobiographic elements that motivate and inspire research and to ask: who are 'we' that make the world around us; where are the possibilities for change; who can have a say on these changes; how can I extend different ways of being-in-the-world that diversify and enrich our shared being-together and how can I connect in as many and different ways with science, politics and technology to learn of the possibilities for living together on a disappearing earth? These are questions that have become increasingly more explicit in the later Latour (2013; 2017). The ambition and scale of such questioning is daunting, but at the same time it provides one way of escaping the parochialism of so many commercially published academic journal articles and reconnects the infinitely expanding detail of specialist scholarship with questions of greater existential import.

Portuguese boats, door closers and scallops

Moving on from introductions and generalizations, we now turn to three of the most important and widely cited texts in the history of ANT and which have perhaps exercised more influence in how one goes about *doing* ANT than any other.[10] It is of course always somewhat arbitrary to select a few exemplary texts as illustrative of an entire field of research, especially one with perhaps the biggest bodies of literature of all the topics dealt with in this book. However, the purpose of so doing is that it will allow us the space to get into the detail and grain of the text and devote some real work to building up an appreciation of what ANT is and how one does it.

The question that animates Law's paper is the 15th- and 16th-century expansion of the Portuguese empire into the East Indies where the Portuguese eventually took control of the spice trade. Even though it might appear on first read to be little more than a secondary reading of an arbitrary episode in the history of boat construction, it is in fact a paper that is right on the cutting edge of contemporary social theory. One is struck on casual acquaintance with this paper by the arcana of technical knowledge about things like hull construction, sails, rigging, planispheric astrolabes, rutters, quadrants and tables of solar declination. We are supposed to be reading sociology, so why do we need to know about the distinction between Hanseatic and Mediterranean forms of shipping and boat design? The point is that the rise and fall of empires might hinge on apparently minor details in the length of the prow of a boat or a degree of increased accuracy in the measurement of the pole star achieved by a breakthrough in glass polishing. Law is partly, if not mainly, interested in how patterns of power and inequality are stabilized and or destabilized historically, as well as the different types of society to which new sources of power give rise. Moreover, the social and the technical are mutually implicated in shaping each other, in which the social *is* technical, and vice versa. Why were the Portuguese able to expand so effectively into new parts of the globe where prevailing winds and tides and other conditions of sailing (piracy, etc.) were so different from those in which they were used to sailing? To answer this, sociology has to invest as much attention to detail to technical and technological factors, and not simply seek to supplement or reverse a history of science and technology, in which technology is privileged as the primary determinant, with a social explanation, i.e. in which new technology is portrayed as the outcome of a social construction as new people, novel ideas and emergent groups arose with new social interests to solve underlying technical impediments that prevented the expansion of empire. We are left to explain what gives rise to the new social interests and, as Law shows, we discover that social interests are in part shaped by what it is possible to conceive and desire based on prevailing scientific and technological conditions of possibility. You might never know you desired a hula hoop, for example, before its arrival on the shelves of the supermarket or in television adverts showing laughing, smiling, nubile bodies swinging their hips to elevate a circular piece of coloured plastic.

The way the story is told by Law is exemplary of ANT. He starts with the basic question,

> How, then, were the Portuguese able to bombard the Samorin of Calicut, to fight and win a naval victory against a powerful combined Gujerati and Egyptian fleet at Diu in 1509 ... and obtain a stranglehold on the vital Indian Ocean spice trade that had previously been monopolised by Muslim sailors.
>
> (Law, 1986, p. 248)

We are then told about the various kings and merchants, as typical in such a tale, but the range of actors permitted extends far beyond that usual cast of characters addressed by conventional history. And so sailors and astronomers appear, navigators and soldiers of fortune, astrolabes and astronomers, etc. Increasingly smaller and smaller items are introduced, each given its potential contribution and agency, right down to the changing position of the alidade[11] abstracted from the carapace once provided by the astrolabe, which takes up its rightful due as a contributor or interlinked component in a vast socio-technical assembly that gives rise to the modern European empire. Everything is laid out on a flat plane of immanence in which nothing is a priori privileged as the explanation for the breakthrough. The story is told in a way that allows the reader to sense the uncertainty and indeterminacy that we all feel in our own historical era (Will war happen? Are we doomed to economic recession? Will England win the World Cup?)[12] but which is often sacrificed for explanatory convenience when dealing with other historical periods. Nor is anything given in terms of context or content, a division which is ultimately debilitating of attempts to explore and explain such matters.

There is no simple context or structure of economy or society in the way Law tells his story. The 'Portuguese problem was to build a new navigational context', which meant that new forms of capital, technical artefacts and new social interests had to be created so that it was possible for new forms of ship design to emerge. There are also no 'social interests' deemed to be struggling to find ways to exercise its will – by inventing new artefacts and technologies, for example, in which to realize its interests. Interests are co-dependent and evolve with the possibilities made available by a prevailing socio-technical 'envelop'. Not only does 'the social' disappear but so too does 'the natural'. Sailing successfully to the Indies also meant that new winds had to be *made* for the Europeans. *The wind is also a sociological phenomenon.* There are material properties we can, of course, attribute to wind, but there is no wind *outside* of social forms of language, designation and signification. There are different winds in different historical time periods. A wind is sometimes a gale, and sometimes a *vent* (in French). If there are 50 different words for snow in Eskimo languages, we might expect a complex lexicon of terms for wind for people whose life depended on telling the difference between a wind that is likely to kill you, and one which might be helpful. Wind is also a phenomenon that is part matter, material, air particles in movement (but even this is a choice of linguistic descriptor, of course) but it is also a *semiotic* phenomenon, by which we mean it cannot exist without meaning and signification systems through which we learn about the wind, what it can do and what it might be able to do.

ANT often refers to such things as material-semiotics, which occasionally draws on the work of Donna Haraway (Law, 2004; 2009) to signal that things are neither matter nor idea, neither object nor subject, but are always in part both whilst also in part escaping this opposition. The natural system is as much a partial and contingent outcome of new socio-technical assemblies as the social system, both of which are only idealized abstractions from this unsteady intermediate world of comings and goings, partial connections and minor technical breakthroughs that resonate across a network of relationally dependent parts. As Law's analysis develops he draws attention to the new and improved methods of sail and rigging that *translate* or *borrow* from the wind (in other words make something of it), '*novel ways of borrowing the power of the wind,* converting it, and using it to exert force upon the sea' (Law, 1986; emphasis in original). We might also say the new type of ship construction (known as the Carreira) *incorporates* (embodies or re-embodies) things such as the wind but also other unique socio-natural features of the Indian Ocean – the lack of regular ports of call and the peculiarly lawless and hostile nature of the place, which itself becomes incorporated and manifest in the design of castles erected on the bow and stern of the boat. The wind and sail are so to speak *folded* together (see also Cooper, 1992) in the movement of the boat as it sails across the sea converting an opposition into a seamless welding of sea–wind–vessel. The design of the boat can be transcribed then as a reflection of wider social and natural conditions of possibility (similar to Bourdieu's 1970 study of the Berber House) but it can also be taken as a force of action itself, something that gives stimulus and shape to a new world emerging around it. Hence, the Carreira makes new worlds possible; it is as much an agent of social change as it is a record or register of what social theory would traditionally call wider social or contextual forces.

A simple door closer can be examined to illustrate many of these features of the social world, which is what Latour does in his essay published under the pseudonym of Jim Johnson in *Social Problems* in 1988. The essay starts by noting how sociology has traditionally avoided dealing with the technicalities of science and engineering and almost appears intimidated by the 'hard sciences'. Conventionally, sociology can do the social context, but leaves qualified engineering experts to explain how material objects and artefacts like a door closer work technically. It is precisely this divide that Latour targets in this paper as he also tries to show how what we think of 'the social' hinges on apparently small and humble unseen artefacts such as the automated door closer. ANT does behove the researcher to try and master technical objects within the language and resources deployed by scientists and engineers but at the same time sociology cannot simply replicate the technical explanation. There are many reasons for this as developed in ANT. How scientists and engineers explain the working of technology is always social in nature, as understanding and explanation are always products of existing social norms and conditions. This has been widely known since the work of Robert Merton in the 1940s (Merton, 1942 is the seminal paper). What begins to emerge as distinctive in this pioneering work of Latour is that there is also a social life of things (see Appadurai, 1986). Beyond this we also have to try and imagine that there is 'society' or rather society at work in a technical artefact: 'technology is society made durable', as Latour (1990) writes elsewhere. As the work of ANT developed, 'society' gets used with increasing caution and is replaced with the concept 'association', which is etymologically related to the same root form *socius* from which our modern term society is derived. However, association better captures the sense of movement and contingency and makes no assumption about what is relevant or what is included in the *socius*. Whereas 'the social' implies some distinctive region that is counterpoised to 'the political', 'the economic' or 'the natural', association cuts across all these divisions (see also Latour, 2005).

The essay on the door closer begins with a startling observation. A handwritten notice has been posted on the door in a corridor at the university of Walla Walla in Washington that reads 'The door closer is on strike, for God's sake, keep the door closed' (Johnson, 1988, p. 298). From this humorous and apparently trivial aside Latour spins a whole world that also rewrites sociology in the process. At first what might strike the reader of this notice is the apparent anthropomorphism – strike action is usually attributed to humans who are deemed to uniquely enjoy things like consciousness, agency and deliberation. In fact, far from an anthropomorphism, as Latour points out, 'strike' is perhaps better thought as deriving from a non-human repertoire (think of the onomatopoeic qualities of a match being struck against the coarse edge of a matchbox), which is then appropriated for something assumed to be exceptional in the human – the capacity to strike.

Can we imagine a world in which an automated door closer decides to take strike action? The challenge to our customary ways of thinking the world is immense, as we witness again in the reactions to contemporary animal and plant studies amongst scientists seeking to defend the canon of scientific rigour and 'objectivity' (Pollan, 2013; Mancuso & Viola, 2015; Myers, 2015). Can a door *think* or *take action*? In many ways, of course it can. The copper rectangular box that compresses air and from which steel arms protrude and fold allows a certain autonomy and independence of action. It is a 'black box' in the conceptual repertoire of ANT, but it is also what is called in this early ANT an example of 'delegation' pursued for the purposes of predictability, regularity and efficiency. A human door closer is harder to control, more expensive, and given current labour practices, more likely to go on strike. How significant is the automatic door closer for sociology? The door closer is, of course, on one level an illustration of how technology works socially and how one best goes about its study.

There is also a literal quality to this study; as Latour explains, imagine what social life would be like when doors would be left open by people each time they passed through the doorway? People are not naturally equipped or disciplined to shut doors automatically and so the cold outside air would blow into buildings, making life very uncomfortable. This could get so bad that even our capacity to socialize would be impaired! The automated door closer is typical of things that get overlooked by sociologists and deemed simply technical and hence off-syllabus for the discipline of sociology. However, the 'boundary work' performed by the door is a marvel of invention and translation and without it social life would be very difficult indeed. The ingenuity of the piston that is gently activated by the movement of the door, borrowing energy from the human hand as it combines with the door to push, storing and slowly releasing this energy to return the door to its closed position, is a marvel of socio-technical agency and collaboration between humans and non-humans. It is therefore worthy of sociological reflection and the development of social theory adequate to its contribution to society. The door performs and participates in social activity. Therefore, we can think of it as partly social as well as technical.[13]

Latour advances a similar approach in papers dedicated to the study of speed bumps or 'sleeping policemen' (Latour, 1994) and hotel keys (Latour, 1993) in which he shows how these artefacts act back, shaping and creating new users and new types of humans, or rather new human-artefactual or socio-technical assemblages. We are always-already technically mediated; indeed 'the human' is borne through technical mediation as careful histories of the anthropos have shown (Stiegler, 1998); in some strands of phylogenetic study even the human body is made or shaped as a tool-using animal. For most conventional sociology 'the human' is treated as something autonomous and independent of such materials and artefacts, in ways that help divide 'the social' and 'the technical'. In these essays on door closers and other seemingly innocuous artefacts, Latour shows how we social humans are extensions and mediators in a complex relational world of technics and practices that by virtue of becoming second nature we take for granted and no longer see (an argument that adapts and develops an approach laid out in Heidegger, 1926). Agency, should we still want to use the traditional language of modern social theory, is therefore better conceived as a form of collective emergence, a relational phenomenon rather than something which can be sourced or found in a coherent, bounded entity.

If Latour extends agency to include things like door openers, Callon goes one step further in his 1984 paper by asking us to consider scallops as actors with important sociological significance through a close study of how three researchers from the *Centre National d'Exploitation des Océans* seek to explore ways of restoring dwindling stocks of St Brieuc Bay scallops that have been, it is believed, overfished but perhaps also partly driven out of the area by changing sea temperatures. Like Latour and Law, Callon writes the story in a way that does not organize and define the empirical world in ways that *historicize*, i.e. reading back with the knowledge we now have to explain things in the past. Instead what becomes known (and how) is part of the story and to allow this to emerge his writing makes efforts to respect the uncertainties and unknowns that would have been experienced by the researchers and other parties mobilized by the problem of dwindling scallops in the St Brieuc Bay.

The events Callon retraces start in 1972 when the three researchers declare an interest in trialling a technique discovered in Japan that cultivates scallops by the use of man-made 'collectors' upon which the scallop larvae have been shown to anchor and on which they are protected from predators. At this point, though, very little is known. Do the fishermen recognize a problem? Is there a group of self-identifying 'fishermen of St Brieuc Bay'? Who speaks for them? Do they want to restore scallops? What are their interests? Nor is there any scientific knowledge of larvae. In fact, the Japanese scallops (*Pecten patinopecten yessoeusis*) are a different species from those of St Brieuc (*Pecten maximus*). Will they behave the same? Can the knowledge of one species be assumed reliable for another species? After ten years, Callon writes, an actor-network was formed through which

> A 'scientific' knowledge was produced and certified; a social group was formed (the fishermen of St. Brieuc Bay) through the privileges that this group was able to institute and preserve; and a community of specialists was organized in order to study the scallops and promote their cultivation.
>
> (Callon, 1986, p. 68)

To give rise to the possibility of such an outcome, however, the three researchers had to become indispensable or place themselves as 'obligatory points of passage' between three different actors who they simultaneously had to define – or *inter-define*: the fishermen, the scientific community and the scallops. This double movement is what is called in ANT *problematization*. The process of interesting these three actors is full of negotiations and representations (called *enrolment*) during which their identities or inter-identities are defined and consolidated. This is called the process of *interessement*. Central to all this is the mobilization of a complex retinue of technological artefacts. To 'interest' the scallops, for example, requires experiments, developments and refinements of various apparatus, including tow-lines, collectors and fine-netted bags. We read that parasites become a problem, the improvements achieved by the use of straw, and how researchers learn about the depths at which larvae like to attach. Everything is in play, mutually, at the same time – knowledge, subjects, objects, nature, the world, etc.

In this paper we can see full actorial dignity being extended to scallops, which has been the cause of some consternation amongst many sociologists and social theorists – though the recent turn to animals and the burgeoning field of plant and animal studies in which this paper is often treated as seminal is testament to its profound originality in sociology. Indeed, it is possible that a new species is being created in the account provided by Callon, in which we learn how a scallop's capacity to sense and act is made possible by an array of socio-technical arrangements. It is in other words actor-network*ing* that is working and through which something like *agency* emerges. During the process both the social and natural world change, and in relation to one another, in which scientists are given equal status in the shaping of the social world, and not just positioned as cultural dopes (Garfinkel, 1967), simple intermediators of prevailing social norms or for a contextual *social construction of scientific facts*. In this paper, Callon is, however, making moves to distinguish and differentiate ANT from the 'strong programme' of social studies of science at Edinburgh which, as we noted earlier, served as a major influence on the development of ANT. Finding a language that does not privilege either the social or natural and which allows for their contingency inspires Callon to pursue the following kinds of formulations for engaging the empirical world: 'Will the masses follow their representatives?' Such a question places scallops and fishermen on the same plane. Will those few scallops that anchored in the study be considered representative or sufficient to prove the success of the experiment? Will the rest of the population of scallops follow these representatives? Similarly, will the fishermen follow their newly elected union officials and representatives?[14]

After ten years, the social context of fishing at St Brieuc is very different; there are new spokespersons (elected), new actors beginning to emerge. The St Brieuc Bay has become different and acts in different ways because of its ongoing use and interventions associated with the experiment, and new forms of power for making one's way politically. This is classic ANT.

Conclusion

Most of us will start out pursuing research projects in management and organization studies assuming we will eventually reach a steady-state of more knowledge or a more secure understanding of the world (cf. Knights & Willmott, 1999). We know little now but we will know so much more when we have cracked our research puzzle through which we aspire to expertise and more complete or deeper forms of knowledge. By contrast ANT brings us back to the surface, or rather displaces the opposition of surface/depth, and in this respect, whilst little known, the writings of Gilles Deleuze are a major influence on ANT, particularly in the work of Latour. As a result there is a constant proliferation of concepts, and nothing stands still. There is no overarching framework, nothing is built, there is no system or Theory in ANT; it achieves in its most accomplished form a radical immanence (Deleuze, 2001).

This chapter has attempted to introduce some of this work whilst paying respect to these minimalist and post-foundational commitments and practices. A more extended introduction would place the work of ANT in a more elaborate genealogy of influence which ranges from the ethnomethodological work of Harold Garfinkel (1967; see chapter in this volume), the structural semiotics of Algirdas Julien Greimas (Greimas & Courtés, 1982), the philosophy of Michel Serres (e.g Serres, 1982; see Serres & Latour, 1995), and the heterodox work of figures on the margins of mainstream modern philosophical and social scientific thought, which includes Alfred North Whitehead, Gabriel Tarde and William James, all of whom are being taken up in the increasingly popular process studies and process theory in management and organization (Hernes & Maitlis, 2010; Langley & Tsoukas, 2016). ANT, however, is radically empirical and exceptionally rigorous. One popular slogan is simply 'to follow the actors' and to use no ready-made concepts or theory in which to try and locate and explain the work of these actors.

In this chapter we have introduced only some of the most basic precepts and concepts of ANT, including the idea that one must try and suspend the customary understanding of 'society' (and indeed nature). In looking closely at three seminal papers in the canon, we have been able to grasp some of the most important formative concepts that show how one can work in the absence of familiar social theory (society, structure, agent, macro/micro, etc.). These include association, problematization, delegation, translation, *interessement*, obligatory points of passage, enrolment, mobilization, incorporation and actants. In a very preliminary way we touched on *reflexivity*, but it is important here to recognize a little more this feature of ANT because it requires us to think of the actor-networks that position and enact the workings of our own texts – including this one! In working with these concepts, all the elements forming the conventional apparatus of sociology are abandoned or rather *reworked*. Reworked because ANT seeks to understand their constitutive and reflexive power of such concepts as they help inform or 'format' (Latour, 2005) our being-in-the-world as social subjects with a certain equipmental sense of society that becomes 'enacted' through the formation of actor-networks. In part, this agnostic treatment of society is a strategic move, in an effort to help render research more sensitive to what Deleuze would call the surface, to track that which is emergent, changing, where society might be imperceptibly beginning to emerge into something new, maybe something that with the vantage point of history might eventually be recognized as a significant period in the evolution of society.

Finally, the full philosophical import and ambitions of ANT have become apparent in some of the more recent work of Callon, Latour and Law. Callon (2017) has recently published his *L'emprise des marchés* which show the results of a methodical deconstruction of the objectification and naturalization of 'the market', a concept which has become so powerful and hegemonic that we can hardly think it might be a complete fabrication. In his turn, Law (2004) has written on 'after methods', distilling the work of ANT scholars to draw out the implications for a mode of study that suggests something beyond the modern social sciences. It is Latour (2013), however, who has perhaps pushed the legacy of ANT the furthest in his most recent work. Here, ANT becomes what he calls one 'mode of existence', of which there are 15 others, including habit, law, technology, fiction, politics, religion and morality. His modes of existence project seeks to come to terms with the end of Europe and the 'modernization' project which is taken up in his increasing attention to political renovation in what some call the 'new climatic regime' addressed in his 'Facing Gaia' project (Latour, 2017). One lesson from this book is that unless we can find new ways of relating to Gaia we might have to learn how to host a 'requiem' for our species (Hamilton, 2015). From scallops to planetary survival the reinvention of social theory through ANT tackles the most profound subjects and upon which we can begin to think about futures again. If you now see the link between scallops and the cosmos, you are doubtless becoming proficient in 'profound superficiality'.

End-of-chapter exercise

Imagine you have been invited to study the management and organization of football (or what might be called soccer in some parts of the world). Your proposal has secured the funding on the basis that no one understands the management of the game beyond popular journalism (i.e. Jonathan Wilson) or the simple 'I did it my way' autobiographies written by celebrity managers such as Alex Ferguson of Manchester United or Pep Guardiola at Barcelona, which you think vests too much significance in 'the great man' version of management.

You have secured access to ethnographically study Manchester United for a season. On the first day you are given a tour of the training grounds. Here you see weight rooms, fitness laboratories equipped with all kinds of monitoring equipment, television rooms and training pitches of various sizes. You meet player agents, dieticians, sports physiotherapists, psychologists and medical experts. There is even a library containing coaching manuals and biographies by famous football managers. The first live game you attend, you are invited to visit Sky TV production studios which record and broadcast the game live from a room full of the most sophisticated audiovisual technologies and monitors that show how the game will be seen on digital, high definition, 3D and interactive platforms.

At dinner after the game you are sitting at a table with a councillor from the city who works in economic regeneration. There is also someone from the Football Association and the guest speaker for the dinner is a representative of FIFA (Fédération Internationale de Football Association). Sitting right next to you is a marketing representative of the Chevrolet car company who are the first team shirt sponsors. She asks you what you are studying. As you look around and reflect on the day, you begin to try and think how football is 'managed'. She sees you struggling and laughs. 'Perhaps it's the little round thing they're all kicking around. Have you read Massumi's essay on football? (Massumi, 2002, pp. 73ff)

Using some of the concepts learned in this chapter, try and think of how you would describe football (or soccer) as an actor-network?

Glossary

Actant   A concept extracted from the structural semiotics of Algirdas Julien Greimas by Callon and Law to acknowledge and help identify agency beyond the customary human agent or collective human agency. Words, things and technologies all have agential properties, particularly as they form part of a collective human and non-human assemblage.

Assemblage   Collection of what might be normally separated out in conventional social science as *social* phenomena, *human* subjects and *technical* materials but which are interrelated, co-dependent and co-emergent. Some trace back to the work of philosopher Gilles Deleuze.

Mediation/Mediators   Nothing is simply an *inter*-mediary, i.e. something passive between structure and agent, or object and subject. If we can see it empirically, or identify an object or artefact, it must enjoy some distinctive contribution co-shaping phenomenon that is normally abstracted and distilled into conventional social scientific artefacts such as 'structure' and 'agency'.

Networks   When used in ANT texts they are best heard in the form net-*works*, i.e. it is the 'net' that works, the 'net' as in the emergent agency brought about through the enrolment of multiple techniques, knowledges, texts, materials and practices. The network in ANT is not the same as a telephone or infrastructural network. It is more like a precautionary methodological warning or principle for empirical research.

Problematization   The ways in which an actor makes himself or herself indispensable to others whilst becoming a link that holds together otherwise disparate actors, materials and knowledge. In this way, they become through their practices and operations an **obligatory point of passage.**

Reflexivity   Many versions of reflexivity play out in ANT texts as they adapt and develop the early Edinburgh School work of Barry Barnes and David Bloor. The most basic property of this multifaceted term in ANT is the awareness that ways of representing or interpreting the world *are also a part of the work we are studying and a part of this world that also makes the world.*

Semiotics   The study and theorization of communication and language in terms of signs and symbols.

Symmetry   Sometimes expressed as generalized or radical symmetry to distinguish the analytical ambitions of ANT from the way this term was introduced and used by early Edinburgh School studies of science. Latour, Callon et al. use the term to explain the importance of giving equal weight to 'the social' and 'technical' and that a common language must be found to their respective contribution to actor-networks.

Translation   The most simple version would suggest this term refers to the work of spokespersons who act to represent and speak for the emerging actor-network. A key term in early ANT, but it began to be used more generally to help orient thinking as to how to better conceive, approach and study technology as something that is inevitably entangled with human collaboration and interaction but whose contribution imparts a difference to agency.

Notes

1   The privileging of these three as the founders of ANT is problematic in many ways, not least of which is the fact that there are many others whose participation and contribution to the practice of ANT in and around the same time is equally important (including Madeleine Akrich, Francois Bastide, Arie Rip, Steve Woolgar), some of whom would balk at the attribution, though their influence as interlocutors in the development of what becomes known as ANT in and through debates with the social studies of science and particularly the Edinburgh School 'strong programme' (Bloor, 1976; Edge & Mulkay, 1976; Barnes, 1977; Barnes & Edge, 1982) was significant.

2   This distinction between practical *construction* and the effort to *understand* becomes increasingly problematic as one's proficiency and experience with ANT develops.

3   We will return to this hybrid term 'socio-technical'. Often confused with that understanding of the socio-technical established through the Tavistock human relations school, from Trist and Bamforth (1951) forward, it is important to understand that to

conduct competent ANT studies requires one to follow the ways 'the social' and 'the technical' are both made and unmade in practice, never reaching a final stabilization or definition. Fundamentally, to posit or to begin these terms assumes a dualism that is conceptually and practically debilitating for empirical study. At best we might say the terms attempt to simplify and make visible complex forces that make and unmake social ties by separating out two aggregate entities – 'the social' and 'the technical'. However, the social is always technical and the technical always social.

4 Correctly read, Latour is doing to the social sciences what Derrida and Foucault or Deleuze in their own ways did to philosophy, and in Foucault's case, history. This is very different from *applying* Foucault or Derrida to social theory, or to the social sciences. Latour undoes the social sciences *from within*, so to speak, and in that respect he is more faithful to the teaching of Derrida et al. than most commentators who self-designate as 'Derridean' or deconstructive, Foucauldian, Deleuzian, or whatever, all of whom show a fundamental error in their appreciation of the authors with whom they seek to align.

5 Strictly this conference occurred at the very point at which ANT was about to go mainstream.

6 The hyphen plays an important part, and we shall leave that as our Hitchcock-like 'Mac-Guffin' to draw the reader through this chapter.

7 Other important papers in the Law and Hassard (1999) collection help illuminate and draw out the ambitions latent and sought after in the original investiture of ANT as a title that summarized the challenge to social theory arising out of studies of science and technology. Mol (1999) talks about 'ontological politics' and Verran (1999) finds way of bringing back questions of morality and moral judgement. How can one best preserve ontological difference, for example, and resist tendencies at universalizing knowledge and truth? These are huge questions, of course, and very engaged and political, but it does show the stakes of entering the world of ANT. A good PhD will not shy clear of these bigger questions, and working through ANT will not provide any ready-made or easy answers.

8 At times it is difficult to tell in a good ANT text whether the examples are literal, figurative, metaphorical or akin to an allegory. Hence, on one reading it appears to be a trivial, and perhaps rather mannered or exaggerated example of – say, as in this example – a simple road. On a second reading, however, it may be that society is being conceived through the thinking evoked by roads and their materials – an allegory, in other words. It seems insignificant and trivial; how can society depend on the regular maintenance of a road? But think about it again. Things would rapidly come to a standstill if we couldn't get to work in the morning because the roads could not be used!

9 One of the most distinguished publications in which scholars working on ANT and related approaches seek to publish their work, though the journal's remit is wider, encompassing a whole series of approaches to the sociology of scientific knowledge (SSK) and the social study of science and technology. A more advanced introduction would have to draw out the subtleties and gradations that distinguish ANT from 'science and technology studies' (STS), within which can be found a number of distinctive groups including an approach called the 'social construction of technology' (SCOT). Within the broad umbrella term STS we might conveniently label three main 'schools of thought', the Edinburgh School that follows the work of early pioneers like David Edge, David Bloor and Barry Barnes; the Bath School focused on the work of Harry Collins, Trevor Pinch and collaborators; and the Paris School, meaning people around Callon, Latour and Law. Part of the ensuing debate, at times quite heated, was collected in Pickering (1992).

10 There are several versions of Law's study of Portuguese methods of long distance control, but the two most widely cited are from *The Sociological Review* in 1984 (later published in Law, 1986), and the version in Bijker, Hughes and Pinch (1987), which has to date attracted some 3,000 references. Latour's infamous paper on the door closer (Johnson, 1988) is perhaps more of a cult, penned under the pseudonym of Jim Johnson for reasons explained in the text, but perhaps because the paper seems so elementary that it would not be taken seriously as a contribution if it had appeared under the name Bruno Latour. However, as an introduction to ANT it is exemplary. The Callon paper has also appeared in a couple of versions, but the one that we are using here is from 1984 and has attracted over 9,000 references.

11 A device or 'pointer' used in surveying and for a period in astronomy for sighting and determining directions so as to measure angles.
12 Christopher Clark's (2013) new history of the First World War is an outstanding effort in an emerging form of historical analysis that seeks to recapture the indeterminacy of events and without relying upon either structure or agency (or any dialectical synthesis) to resolve the question, what was the cause(s) of the First World War?
13 The door is an example of what Latour calls an 'actant', adapting this term from the work of Algirdas Julien Greimas in structuralist semiotics, who is a major influence on the development of ANT (see Greimas and Courtés, 1982). An actant is something that has agency-like qualities but can be human or non-human; a test or even a certain phrase or acronym can 'act', as can something like a business corporation – which can sue and be sued because it has legal personality (see also Akrich & Latour, 1992).
14 An interesting addendum to the empirical enquiry was the fact that the fishermen finally did not observe 'agreements' and one day lost patience and raided the fragile nurseries of maturing scallops to sell on the market, destroying the experiment. Hence, there is always the risk of *dissidence* that breaks the alliances forged in the nascent actor-network as other associations form.

References

Akrich, M., & Latour, B. (1992). A summary of a convenient vocabulary for the semiotics of human and non-human assemblies. In W. Bijker, & J. Law (eds) *Shaping technology-building society: Studies in sociotechnical change* (pp. 259–264). Cambridge, MA: MIT Press.

Appadurai, A. (ed.) (1986). *The social life of things: Commodities in cultural perspective.* Cambridge: Cambridge University Press.

Barley, S. R. (2010). Building an institutional field to corral a government: A case to set an agenda for organization studies. *Organization Studies, 31*(6), 777–805.

Barnes, B. (1977). *Interests and the growth of knowledge.* London: Routledge & Kegan Paul.

Barnes, B., & Edge, D. O. (1982). *Science in context: Readings in the sociology of science.* Cambridge, MA: MIT Press.

Blok, A., & Jensen, T. E. (2011). *Bruno Latour: Hybrid thoughts in a hybrid world.* London: Routledge.

Bloomfield, B. P. (1995). Power, machines and social relations: Delegating to information technology in the National Health Service. *Organization, 2*(3–4), 489-518.

Bloor, D. (1976) *Knowledge and social imagery.* London: Routledge & Kegan Paul.

Bijker, W. E., Hughes, T. P., & Pinch, T. (eds) (1987). *The social construction of technological systems: New directions in the sociology and history of technology.* Cambridge, MA: MIT Press.

Bourdieu, P. (1970). The Berber House or the world reversed. *Information (International Social Science Council), 9*(2), 151–170.

Callon, M. (1986). Some elements of a sociology of translation: Domestication of the scallops and the fishermen of St. Brieuc Bay. In J. Law (ed.) *Power, action and belief: A new sociology of knowledge?* London: Routledge & Kegan Paul.

Callon, M. (2017). *L'emprise des marchés: comprendre leur fonctionnement pour pouvoir les changer.* Paris: La Découverte.

Clark, C. (2013). *The sleepwalkers: How Europe went into war in 1914.* Harmondsworth: Penguin.

Cooper, R. (1992). Formal organization as representation: Remote control, displacement and abbreviation. In M. Reed, & M. Hughes (eds) *Rethinking organization: New directions in organization theory and analysis* (pp. 254–272). London: Sage.

Cooren, F. (2000). *The organizing property of communication.* Amsterdam: John Benjamins.

Czarniawska, B. (2014). Bruno Latour: An accidental organization theorist. In P. S. Adler, P. du Gay, G. Morgan, & M. I. Reed (eds) *The Oxford handbook of sociology, social theory, and organization studies: Contemporary currents* (pp. 87–105). Oxford: Oxford Handbooks.

Czarniawska, B., & T. Hernes (eds) (2005). *Actor-Network Theory and Organizing*. Copenhagen Business School Press.

Deleuze, G. (2001). *Pure immanence: Essays on a life*, A. Boyman (trans.). New York: Zone.

de Vries, G. (2016). *Bruno Latour*. Polity: Cambridge Press.

Dunleavy, P. (2003). *Authoring a PhD: How to plan, draft, write and finish a doctoral thesis or dissertation*. Houndmills: Palgrave

Edge, D., & Mulkay, M. (1976). *Astronomy transformed. The emergence of radio astronomy in Britain*. New York: Wiley.

Garfinkel, H. (1967). *Studies in ethnomethodology*. Englewood Cliffs, NJ: Prentice-Hall.

Greimas, A. J., & Courtés, J. (1982) *Semiotics and language: An analytical dictionary*. Bloomington, IN: Indiana University Press.

Hamilton, C. (2015). *Requiem for a species*. Abingdon, Oxfordshire: Routledge.

Harding, N. (2004). *The social construction of management*. London: Routledge.

Harman, G. (2009). *Prince of networks: Bruno Latour and metaphysics*. Melbourne: re.press.

Harris, J. (2005). The ordering of things: Organization in Bruno Latour. *The Sociological Review*, 53 (1_suppl),163–177.

Hernes, T., & Maitlis, S. (eds) (2010). *Process, sensemaking, and organizing*, Vol. 1. Oxford: Oxford University Press.

Hofstede, G. (1980). *Culture's consequences: International differences in work-related values*. Beverly Hills, CA: Sage.

Iles, P., & Zhang, C. L. (eds) (2013). *International human resource management: A cross-cultural and comparative approach*. London: CIPD.

Johnson, J. (aka Latour, B.) (1988). Mixing humans and nonhumans together: The sociology of a door-closer. *Social Problems*, 35(3), 298–310.

Knights, D., & Willmott, H. (1999). *Management lives: Power and identity in work organizations*. London: Sage.

Langley, A., & Tsoukas, H. (eds) (2016). *The Sage handbook of process organization studies*. London: Sage.

Latour, B. (1983). Give me a laboratory and I will raise the world. *Science Observed*, 141–170.

Latour, B. (1990). Technology is society made durable. *The Sociological Review*, 38 (1_suppl),103–131.

Latour, B. (1993). The Berlin key or how to do words with things. L. Davis (trans.). In P. M. Graves-Brown (ed.) *Matter, materiality and modern culture* (pp. 10–21). London: Routledge.

Latour, B. (1994). On technical mediation. *Common Knowledge*, 3(2), 29–64.

Latour, B. (1996). On actor-network theory: A few clarifications. *Soziale welt*, 369–381.

Latour, B. (1999). On recalling ANT. In J. Law, & J. Hassard (eds) *Actor network theory and after*. Oxford: Blackwell.

Latour, B. (2005). *Reassembling the social: An introduction to actor-network theory (Clarendon Lectures in Management Studies)*. Oxford: Oxford University Press.

Latour, B. (2013). *An inquiry into modes of existence*. Cambridge, MA: Harvard University Press.

Latour, B. (2017). *Facing Gaia*. Cambridge: Polity Press.

Latour, B., & Hermant, E. (1998). *Paris ville invisible*. Paris: LaDécouverte-Les Empêcheurs de penser en rond.

Latour, B., & Woolgar, S. (1979). *Laboratory life: The social construction of facts*. Beverly Hills, CA: Sage.

Law, J. (1984). On the methods of long-distance control: Vessels, navigation and the Portuguese route to India. *The Sociological Review, 32* (1_suppl),234–263.

Law, J. (1986). On the methods of long distance control: Vessels, navigation, and the Portuguese route to India. In J. Law (ed.) *Power, action and belief: A new sociology of knowledge?* (pp. 234–263) Sociological Review Monograph 32, Routledge, Henley.

Law, J. (1987). Technology and heterogeneous engineering: The case of Portuguese expansion. In W. E. Bijker, T. P. Hughes, & J. Trevor (eds) *The social construction of technological systems: New directions in the sociology and history of technology.* Cambridge, MA: MIT Press.

Law, J. (1994). *Organizing modernity.* Oxford: Blackwell.

Law, J. (2004). *After method: Mess in social science research.* London: Routledge.

Law, J. (2007). After ANT: Complexity, naming and topology. In J. Law, & J. Hassard (eds) *Actor network theory and after.* Oxford: Blackwell.

Law, J. (2009). Actor network theory and material semiotics. In B. S. Turner (ed.) *The new Blackwell companion to social theory* (pp. 141–158). London: John Wiley & Sons.

Law, J., Callon, M., & Rip, A. (eds) (1986). *Mapping the dynamics of science and technology: Sociology of science in the real world.* Basingstoke: Macmillan.

Law, J., & Hassard, J. (eds) (1999). *Actor network theory and after.* Oxford: Blackwell.

McGee, K. (2014). *Bruno Latour: The normativity of networks.* London: Routledge.

Mancuso, S., & Viola, A. (2015). *Brilliant green: The surprising history and science of plant intelligence.* Washington, DC: Island Press.

Massumi, B. (2002). *Parables for the virtual: Movement, affect, sensation.* Durham, NC: Duke University Press.

Merton, R. K. (1942). The normative structure of science. In R. K. Merton (ed.) *The sociology of science: Theoretical and empirical investigations.* Chicago, IL: University of Chicago Press.

Mitchell, J. (1969). The concept and use of social networks. In J. Mitchell (ed.) *Social networks in urban situations.* Manchester: Manchester University Press.

Mol, A. (1999). Ontological politics. A word and some questions. In J. Law, & J. Hassard (eds) *Actor network theory and after.* Oxford: Blackwell.

Myers, N. (2015). Conversations on plant sensing. *NatureCulture, 3,* 35–66.

Nicolini, D. (2012). *Practice theory, work, and organization: An introduction.* Oxford: Oxford University Press.

Phillips, E., & Pugh, D. (2010). *How to get a PhD: A handbook for students and their supervisors.* Maidenhead: Open University Press.

Pickering, A. (ed.) (1992). *Science as practice and culture.* Chicago, IL: University of Chicago Press.

Pollan, M. (2013, December 23). The intelligent plant. Retrieved from *The New Yorker.* http://www.newyorker.com/reporting/2013/12/23/131223fa_fact_pollan?currentPage=all.

Restivo, S. (2003). Bruno Latour. In Ritzer, G. (ed.) *The Wiley-Blackwell companion to major social theorists, 1* (pp. 520–540). Oxford: Blackwell.

Schmidgen, H. (2014). *Bruno Latour in pieces: An intellectual biography.* New York: Fordham University Press.

Serres, M. (1982). *The parasite,* L. R. Schehr (trans.). Baltimore, MD: Johns Hopkins University Press.

Serres, M., & Latour, B. (1995). *Conversations on science, culture, and time.* Ann Arbor, MI: University of Michigan Press.

Stiegler, B. (1998). *Technics and time: The fault of epimetheus,* Vol. 1. Stanford, CA: Stanford University Press.

Taylor, J. R. (1993). *Rethinking the theory of organizational communication: How to read an organization.* Norwood, NJ: Ablex.

Trist, E. L., & Bamforth, K. W. (1951). Some social and psychological consequences of the longwall method of coal-getting: An examination of the psychological situation and defences of a work group in relation to the social structure and technological content of the work system. *Human Relations*, 4(1), 3–38.

Venturini, T., Jensen, P., & Latour, B. (2015). Fill in the gap: A new alliance for social and natural sciences. *Journal of Artificial Societies and Social Simulation*, 18(2), 18–29.

Verran (1999). Staying true to the laughter in Nigerian classrooms. In J. Law, & J. Hassard (eds) op cit., pp. 136–155.

4 Anthony Giddens and structuration theory

Ira Chatterjee, Jagat Kunwar and Frank den Hond

Chapter objectives

The relationship between individual action and social structure has been the subject of considerable discussion and debate in social theory. This chapter presents Anthony Giddens' proposal to reconcile the opposition between structure and agency. His *structuration theory* proposes to see structure and agency as mutually constitutive, as a duality: as inseparable as the two sides of a coin (cf. Craib, 1992). It is not just that structure influences human behaviour and that humans are capable of changing the social structures they inhabit; structure enables and constrains action while simultaneously being (re)constituted through action. Such an analysis of the dynamic relationship between individual action and social structure is a topic with important empirical implications. Structuration explains the motivations for actions, the choices – real and perceived – due to structural opportunities and constraints, and the interactions involved.

This chapter discusses:

- Giddens and the development of structuration theory: a prologue to the theory and its genesis
- Core aspects of structuration theory as formulated by Giddens and key developments in the field
- The relationship of structuration theory to other social and organizational theories and some of the major criticisms challenging the theory
- Implications and empirical applications of structuration for research in management and organization studies

Anthony Giddens

Anthony Giddens was born on January 18, 1938 in Edmonton, north London. He was the first member of his family to go to college and, in 1974, obtained his doctorate from the University of Cambridge. He began his working life at the University of Leicester and then worked for some ten years at Cambridge University before he was eventually promoted to a full professorship (Giddens & Pierson, 1998). From 1997 to 2003, he was Director of the London School of Economics. He is currently a Professor Emeritus at the latter institution and a Life Fellow of King's College, Cambridge. Giddens became a member of the House of Lords in June 2004, having received a life peerage as the Baron Giddens of Southgate. Giddens has had a significant impact upon British politics as an advisor to the Blair government. He has received over a dozen honorary doctoral degrees from universities around the globe.

A widely cited and prolific social theorist, Giddens has covered a range of issues in his more than 30 books, 200 articles, essays and reviews. His work spans a variety of disciplines including psychology, linguistics, economics, cultural studies and politics, allowing him to comment on a wide range of issues and to introduce a number of theoretical models that help to explain key aspects of the development of societies at local, national and global levels of analysis. His greatest contribution has arguably been in social theory, through the development of structuration theory.

At the beginning of Giddens' career, Durkheim's *Rules of Sociological Method* was still considered one of the main bases for the examination of society. Having been a commentator on Marx, Weber and Durkheim in his initial writings, in *New Rules of Sociological Method*, originally published in 1976, Giddens turned a critical lens on the founding fathers of sociology and their conceptualizations of power. He believed that the orthodox consensus of the late 1960s and 1970s was being replaced by a variety of emergent perspectives, including critical theory, ethnomethodology, symbolic interactionism, post-structuralism and theories written in the tradition of hermeneutics and ordinary language philosophy. Giddens' critical reinterpretation of the classics is visible in the initial phase of his work.

Indeed, Giddens' academic work can be divided into three stages. In the first stage, he outlined a new role and vision for sociology that found expression in publications such as *Capitalism and Modern Social Theory* (1971) and *New Rules of Sociological Method* (1976). With *New Rules of Sociological Method*, the first stage flows seamlessly into the second. In this stage, he offered an analysis of the interplay of agency and structure with neither holding primacy, culminating in the formulation of structuration theory in works such as *Central Problems in Social Theory* (1979) and *The Constitution of Society* (1984). Books written in the third phase discuss the relationship between the self and society and how people gain a sense of their own identity, for example *The Consequences of Modernity* (1990), *Modernity and Self-Identity* (1991), *The Transformation of Intimacy* (1992), *Beyond Left and Right* (1994) and *The Third Way: the Renewal of Social Democracy* (1998). Structuration theory *per se* forms a relatively small part of his voluminous output but firmly established Giddens' reputation; it is the focus of this chapter.

Key concepts in structuration theory

A central problem in social theory is how to make sense of the opposition, or dualism, of agency and structure. Many people ordinarily experience that their activities are both constrained and enabled by social structures. Considering managerial action, for example, we must allow for agency while recognizing that it is enabled and constrained by, and constitutive of, structures such as organizational designs and institutional embeddedness. It becomes a theoretical problem for social theory, with relevance for organization and management theory, when the analyst postulates that humans have the capacity for sociologically meaningful autonomous action, because they have 'free will'; if so, how can their agency be constrained by structure if not by voluntary choice? Vice versa, if the analyst postulates that structure determines human behaviour, then the question arises, how can there be place for agency? Both can be useful starting assumptions for explaining social phenomena, but they are not easily reconcilable in one theory. The 'paradox of embedded agency', for example, has been extensively discussed as a theoretical problem in the institutional entrepreneurship literature (Battilana, 2006; Greenwood & Suddaby, 2006). Structuration theory is one of several proposals in social theory to address this problem. Other articulations include Bourdieu's and Schatzki's theories of practice (Harvey & Maclean, this volume; Loscher, Spiller & Seidl, this volume), Archer's morphogenesis which is based on Bhaskar's critical realism (Mutch, this volume), and actor-network theory as advanced by Callon, Latour, Law and others (O'Doherty, this volume). In setting out Giddens' proposal, we outline his conceptualizations of duality, agency, structure and time-space, which are constitutive of structuration theory.

Duality

Not only do economists and other adherents of methodological individualism emphasize human intentionality and understanding in the construction of the social world, but phenomenological and interpretive social scientists do as well. Consequently, they believe that to explain social outcomes one needs to study individuals and their interactions. Other social scientists, working from structuralist and functionalist traditions, see unique aspects of the social world that cannot be explained merely by the actions of the sum of individuals present. They give ontological precedence to social structures, entertaining the view that collectives have properties of their own, and that structures determine human behaviour. Both ways of looking – setting aside the many ontological and epistemological differences within each – appeal to common sense and experience, yet they are difficult to reconcile theoretically. What is the place for agency if structure is dominant? What is structure if it cannot always be reduced to the outcome of aggregate human (inter)action?

Rather than finding a synthetic approach to reconciling the opposition between the two perspectives, structuration theory seeks to transcend it. Giddens proposed the concept of the 'duality of structure', in which 'structure is both the medium and the outcome of the reproduction of practices' (Giddens, 1979, p. 5) and structuration the process in which social structures and people's agency interact in mutually constituting ways. Structuration theory does not give primacy to either structure or agency, nor does it presuppose ontological priority of one over the other. As Giddens asserts,

> If interpretative sociologies are founded, as it were, upon an imperialism of subject, functionalism and structuralism propose an imperialism of the social object. One of my principal ambitions in the formulation of structuration theory is to put an end to each of these empire-building endeavours.
>
> (Giddens, 1984, p. 2)

Epistemologically, structuration signifies that human agents deal with a pre-existing, interpreted world, and simultaneously constitute that world through the meanings they assign it (Giddens, 1976). Social structures exist in the very moment they are reproduced by agents while social agents simultaneously constitute themselves as such through structured action. Duality of structure means that both structure and agency are taken into consideration at the same time; structuration refers to giving attention to both past (as structural continuity) and present (as an avenue for innovation and change or, of course, structural reproduction) (Whittington, 2015). Structuration is the instant of the reproduction of agency and structure (Haugaard, 2002).

Agency

One foundational concept of structuration theory is agency: the extent to which social agents are capable of making a difference to everyday social affairs or courses of events, that is: their ability to do otherwise. Giddens ties this ability to the exercise of power. An agent ceases to be an agent when devoid of the ability to act otherwise. 'Agency concerns events of which an individual is the perpetrator, in the sense that the individual could, at any phase in a given sequence of conduct, have acted differently.' (Giddens, 1984, p. 9) This notion of agency is grounded in a set of assumptions about how and why agents can act. Giddens views agents as reflexive and capable beings rather than as the 'cultural dopes' that 'ensue from strong forms of structuralism' (Mutch, 2014, p. 588) or as 'structural dopes of even more stunning mediocrity' (Giddens, 1979, p. 52). Agents then are intentional, reflexive and, to a large extent, rational beings, who behave according to their knowledge or belief regarding their situation and the outcomes of their action (although action may have unintended consequences, sometimes very consequentially so!).

The treatment of agency in structuration theory rests on the premise that agents can have knowledge about what they do and their reasons for it, and about the structural context in which and upon which they act. They can apply this knowledge and exercise reflexivity in the production and reproduction of social practices. Social practices are generalized schemes that agents' employ in their 'doings' and that apply to an indeterminate range of social contexts. Agents use such knowledge to understand the grounds of their everyday life and in the continuation of day-to-day actions (Giddens, 1984).

Giddens supposes that agents' knowledgeability is related to two modes of consciousness: practical and discursive. Discursive consciousness implies the most explicit form of knowledge and is immediately available to the agent. It is, quite simply, the ability to articulate knowledge. The reflexivity of action through which individuals reflect, monitor and modify their action on an ongoing basis is the domain of discursive consciousness (Giddens, 1984). On the other hand, practical consciousness comprises tacit, unarticulated and taken-for-granted knowledge. It facilitates everyday exchanges among social agents; it is mutual knowledge. Albeit unarticulated, social agents have a great deal of knowledge about social life. The process through which they use mutual knowledge to understand the grounds of their everyday life, the continuation of day-to-day actions, is referred to as the rationalization of action.

Giddens also points out the basic relations between ontological security and mutual knowledge and how it leads to the routinized character of social life. Ontological security is the desire of social agents to maintain the cognitively ordered world of self and other. In attempting to maintain a high amount of ontological security, agents engage in routinized behaviour and shy away from radical deviations of the norm (Loyal, 2003). Here, it is necessary to distinguish practical consciousness from common sense, a distinction that Giddens suggests is largely analytical, 'that is to say, common sense is mutual knowledge treated not as knowledge but as fallible belief' (Giddens, 1984, p. 336). Moreover, Giddens contends that the boundary between practical and discursive consciousness is fluid and permeable, and that 'there are only the differences between what can be said and what is characteristically simply done' (Giddens, 1984, p. 7).

Not all action is conscious. Unconscious action can be understood as stemming from repressed desires and cognition or partial refraction of these at practical and/ or discursive modes of consciousness. When an agent takes some action that she cannot necessarily rationalize or articulate, the motivation and memories of that action remain unconscious. According to Giddens (2013, p. 6), 'reasons refer to the grounds of action, [whereas] motives refer to the wants which prompts it'. Although motives cannot always be articulated, reasons can be identified. Reasons may stem from practical consciousness, which can be rationalized and accounted for, and from discursive consciousness, which can always be articulated.

Although Giddens gives primacy to knowledgeability of agents, he argues that they are constrained in spatial dimensions, both laterally and vertically. 'Lateral' refers to different categories of social activities and 'vertical' to the stratified nature of society. That is, agents may be knowledgeable about particular categories of social life, at a particular hierarchical level, but constrained regarding others. Knowledgeability is also bounded, as action may have unanticipated, unintended and uncontrollable outcomes. Still, it is quite evident for Giddens, with his focus on practical consciousness, that the basic domain of social sciences is practices ordered through space and time, and not with either the agent or structure (Whittington, 2015). In many ways, social practice, as an ongoing series of practical activities, acts as a bridge between agency and structure.

Structure

Conventionally, structure refers to anything that has relative endurance and has the effect of bringing order to the given set of 'things'. According to Giddens (2013), the functionalist understanding of structure is the patterning of social relations and phenomena, whereas the structuralist understanding of structure is that of underlying codes or ordered relations beneath the surface level of the society, which must be understood from their surface level manifestations. In any case, these conceptions of structure portray it as external to, independent of and posing constraints on human agency. Structures, thus seen, are primary constituents of social reality; they are ontologically 'real' – as opposed to Levi-Strauss' conceptualization of structure as a model, as a methodological device in the hands of a social scientist (Lizardo, 2010).

Giddens' conceptualization of structure is conventional in subscribing to an ontologically realist position – even if with Giddens, structures are 'virtual', persisting as 'memory traces' – but distinct in its insistence on the *duality* of the structure, highlighting how every act of social production is also an act of social reproduction, and how structure exists during the instant of this constitution. One way to understand the concept of structure, according to Giddens, is by the analogy of language and its relationship with speech. Just as language enables and constrains speech and speech reconstitutes language, so does structure provide the conditions and possibilities for social action.

Giddens amended the definition of structure from patterned social relations to the generative rules and resources underlying patterning. Rules in social life are generalizable procedures, often tacit, which are enacted and reproduced in social practices. They are both constitutive and regulative in nature (Loyal, 2003). Rules not only denote legislations but also less formal routines, habits, procedures and conventions (Whittington, 2015). Rules can be intensive or shallow, tacit or discursive, informal or formalized, and weakly or strongly sanctioned. In this characterization of rules, at one extreme there are rules that are constantly invoked in everyday life, such as the norms or conventions of taking turns in conversations, and at the other extreme, codified laws. A social agent does not need to articulate a rule discursively in order to know it, but she can know the rule tacitly in the form of practical consciousness. Giddens saw more influence on daily life of intensive, tacit, informal and weakly sanctioned rules, indicating that such rules have the potential to affect the very fabric of social life. This belies the commonly held assumption that abstract and codified laws exert greater influence upon the generality of social conduct.

Resources refer to the bases through which power is exercised. Giddens defines power as the transformative capacity of agents to make a difference in the social world. Giddens mentions two types of resources: authoritative and allocative. Authoritative resources grant power over subject–subject relations (people), whereas allocative resources grant power over subject–object relations (material objects). As Giddens mentions, the exercise of power is limited by the inherent desire of agents to invoke routinized patterns of life due to ontological security, by material constraints due to corporeality, and by sanctions and structural constraints which are pre-structured limitations on the possibility for action (Giddens, 1984).

Giddens analytically categorizes structure into structures of domination, signification and legitimation. Whereas rules refer to structures of signification and legitimation, resources refer to structures of domination. Structures of signification deal with the symbols that encode meanings and so shape perceptions, whereas structures of legitimation deal with the meaning of norms that govern social action (Mutch, 2014). Resources as structures of domination refer to power, both authoritative and allocative. Agency is enhanced by control over resources and is exercised through the following or rejection of rules (Whittington, 2015).

Giddens highlighted three different forms of interaction in which agency is performed: communication, power and sanctions. Giddens proposed that the properties of interaction are related to the properties of structure and the modalities of structuration. Structures and interactions are mediated by the modalities of interpretive schemes, facilities and norms. Modalities are the ways through which structural dimensions are expressed in interaction (Whittington, 2015). For example, when communicating (interaction), people draw on interpretive schemes (modality) that are linked to signification (structure). Similarly, the use of power (interaction) involves drawing upon facilities derived from allocative and authoritative resources (modality) that are linked to domination (structure). Finally, the application of sanction (interaction) draws on norms (modality) that are linked to legitimation (structure). Giddens argues that in actual social practices there are various degrees of combination of all three kinds of structure. In fact, Giddens emphasizes reciprocity between all of these properties of structure (Whittington, 2015).

Time-space

A final significant notion related to the theory of structuration is that of time-space. Giddens stated that social interaction occurs across time and space; it is contextual and situated. Further, to understand social interaction, it is important not only to understand the objects and persons present (presencing) but also those absent (absencing). In fact, during social encounters, there is an intersection of interacting agents according to their time-paths at different levels: one at the level of daily experience, one at the level of overall being and in relation to the institutional time (Loyal, 2003). These interactions occur in a definite spatial context, which can be further divided into regions that enclose a time-space providing more specific contexts to social interactions. This has been referred to as regionalization.

In the end, then, more precisely, structure refers to the structuring properties that provide the binding and continuity of time and space in patterned social relations, that is, in social systems (Giddens, 1979). Social systems exist in time-space, manifest themselves empirically and are constituted by social practices. Regular activities bring people together in social systems, which are reproduced over time through continued interaction. Social systems can exist at various levels and may even be somewhat overlapping and contradictory (Whittington, 2015). The participation of agents in different social systems and the inherent contradictions among them are germane to human agency and grant social agents some degree of agency. To study the structuration of a social system is to study the ways in which that system, via the application of general rules and resources, and in the context of unintended outcomes, is produced and reproduced in interaction.

Criticisms of structuration theory

Up until the early 1970s, most of sociology had paid scant attention to the relationship between agency and structure (ethnomethodology perhaps being an exception). Giddens' views on structuration addressed this neglect. Notwithstanding the significant contribution to social theory and the 'intrinsic power and value of structuration' (Stones, 2005, p. 4) evident in the ample empirical applications across disciplines, structuration theory has been the continual target of censure. Critique of the theory can be explained by inherent 'gaps and logical deficiencies' in the theory (Sewell, 1992, p. 5), but if one realizes that from the mid-1970s onward multiple articulations to solve the structure-agency problem where published in a short period of time, some of the intensity of the critique may have resulted from competition for recognition as the 'best' approach.

The criticism meted out to structuration theory can be divided into conceptual critique that targets the fundamental logic of the duality of structure and critique that emphasizes epistemological and methodological deficiencies in the theory. The latter critique can be related to the somewhat wilful sparseness with which Giddens treated structuration theory. The former can be attributed to Giddens' lack of specificity and his penchant for a more abstract rendering of concepts. The concept of duality itself has been severely challenged by, among others, Archer (1982; 1995), Hodgson (2007), Lizardo (2010) and Willmott (2000). Others attacked ambiguity in the notion of power (e.g. Callinicos, 1985) and the concept of time-space (e.g. Urry, 1991), while yet others criticized the overall lack of clarity and comprehensiveness of structuration theory (e.g. Held & Thompson, 1989). Sewell (1992) and Stones (2005) are prominent examples of scholars who sought to salvage structuration theory by proposing ways to overcome its weaknesses and inconsistencies. In this section, we focus, first, on several points of conceptual critique, and then highlight some epistemological and methodological deficiencies.

Conceptual critique – agency

A majority of critics argues that structuration theory is ultimately subjectivist because its notion of duality remains tightly coupled with the voluntarist side of dualism; agency is dominant (Callinicos, 1985; Clegg, 1989). Callinicos (1985), for instance, emphasizes how Giddens' invocation of the agent's capacity to resist – rather than offering historical examinations of the variable conditions of action – privileges agency over structure. For these critics, structuration theory is not a theoretical improvement but a slight neglect of enduring structures over reflexive agency (Mutch, 2014).

Gane (1983) and Bertilsson (1984) argue that the precise meaning of agency, as Giddens uses it, is theoretically ambiguous because in some instances it refers to 'persons' but in other instances to 'dominant sets of practices' that require practical agency. In contrast, Archer (1995) distinguishes the differences between persons, agents and actors in a more nuanced manner (see Mutch, this volume). Giddens' stratified conception of agency has also been criticized on the grounds that it is disembodied from the analysis of social structures and fails to consider the lack of critical intent in the agent's knowledgeability, particularly when actions are undertaken in search of ontological security (Bertilsson, 1984).

The overall gist of the criticisms indicates that Giddens overemphasizes voluntarism. However, in many cases – if not in all – the critique tends to present Giddens as taking an extreme position by quoting him selectively. The argument that Giddens prioritizes agency all the time is somewhat debatable; in our reading, Giddens does not particularly deny the possibility of structural conditions constraining agency. Indeed, Giddens is circumspect in overestimating the ability of agents to act according to their own free will because, although agents always have the 'possibility to do otherwise', this transformative capacity depends on their position in the social world (Giddens, 1984).

Conceptual critique – structure

Just as various critics argued that the concept of agency is flawed, they also argue that there are flaws in the conceptualization of structure. According to Giddens, structure consists of rules and resources, and he categorizes them into interpretative and normative. Some critics (Thompson, 1989; Stones, 2005) find the definition of structure as rules and resources to be imprecise in the sense that Giddens fails to provide a clear and consistent account of rules. Further, what is involved in drawing upon structures remains vague (Stones, 2005).

Critiques point out the difficulty in substituting the conventional concept of social structure with rules and resources (Thompson, 1989; Stones, 2005). Structures are more complex than rules, and resources as rules serve to generate practices only in a very weak sense. The direction of causality and analytical priority of one over the other has also been a contentious issue. Scholars in this vein argue that patterned social relations should have analytical priority over rules and resources to account for the differential capacities of agents and unequal distribution of power, which is so characteristic of social life. Giddens' notion of power, as the transformative capacity of agents, is exercised through the medium of resources which themselves seem to be structurally derived, but without an objective conception of structure this is rendered impossible (Clegg, 1989). Understanding power necessitates assumptions of certain structural conditions based on which the rules of differentiation are themselves derived (Stones, 2005). It is only then possible to categorize institutions and structural pressures acting upon agents that enable specific rules and resources to be drawn.

Giddens suggests that structures, as memory traces, are virtual and exist only at the moment of their instantiation. Ontologically, a structure that resides in a real, material artefact would seem clearly distinct from one that exists only when instantiated in the practices of social agents (Jones & Karsten, 2008; Lizardo, 2010). The notion of action, mediated by various modalities of structure, requires further clarification between virtual and visible social systems (Loyal, 2003). Sewell (1992) proposes that structures as rules and resources are not completely virtual but that 'rules' should instead be conceptualized as virtual schemas whereas 'resources', both authoritative and allocative, do indeed have objective existence. Much of the criticism regarding structure focuses on whether it is appropriate to conceptualize it as generative rules and resources and whether, by doing so, it can sufficiently facilitate the study of social structure and systems as such. The debate also stretches to the extent to which structure manifests materially, given that Giddens emphasizes its virtual nature. The ontological precedence of generative rules and resources or social conditions is also a matter of considerable debate. As will be seen in the next section on duality, the extent to which this sort of conceptualization of structure enables the study of causal relations between agency and structure has led to elaborate criticisms, and modifications in the theory of structuration.

Conceptual critique – duality

Archer (1982) rejects Giddens' concept of duality. According to her, without sufficient differentiation between structural conditions and action, it is very easy to conflate the two, which then results in the loss of analytical value; if structure is inseparable from agency, it cannot be considered as autonomous, emergent, preexistent or causally influential in any sensible way. Thus, the notion of duality disregards the implicit temporality of the process; if structures only exist as memory traces and in the instantiation of practices, the temporality involved in the sequence of relations between structure and agency in the production and reproduction of society is neglected (Stones, 2005). Dismissing the separability and relative temporal autonomy of structure and agency, according to Archer (1982; 1995) and others (Barley & Tolbert, 1997; Thompson 1989; Clegg 1989), precludes any examination of their interplay, causal relationships and relative contribution to enabling and constraining change at any given time. For instance, the theory provides no explanation of how or when agency changes are reflected in structure and at what point agentic forces can be considered significant enough to effect changes in structure (Hodgson, 2007).

Stones (2005) develops the concept of duality in his proposal of 'strong structuration theory' by distinguishing four components in a 'quadripartite nature of structuration'. The four-fold nature of structuration comprises: external structures, internal structures, active agency and outcomes. External structures are conditions of action that the agent faces externally of which the agent may not be necessarily aware. Internal structures are internal to the agent and comprise what and how the agent 'knows' and are further divided into specific knowledge of external structures and general dispositions that are conjunctional. Whereas such specific knowledge relates to the agent's understanding of the external structures and the strategic possibilities to act within it, general dispositions roughly correspond to Bourdieu's (1977) 'habitus' and comprise the agent's schemas, discourses, world views, value commitments, moral and practical principles etc. The third component of the quadripartite nature of structuration, active agency refers to the ways through which an agent either routinely or strategically draws upon internal structures. Outcomes are the effect of an agent's actions on the internal and external structures, which either leads to their reproduction or transformation. In this way, Stones (2005) elaborates on the notion of Giddens' duality with a more nuanced version of structure that makes it more amenable to empirical research.

Epistemological and methodological deficiencies

The second criticism tied to structuration theory, that of a lack of clear methodological procedures, is now 'established wisdom' with Giddens consciously refraining from setting out guidelines for empirical research (den Hond et al., 2012, p. 240). Additionally, the application of structuration theory in empirical studies is hampered by the overall lack of operational definitions of structure and agency, the abstracted level of theorizing, and the very nature of the duality of structure and agency (den Hond et al., 2012; Sewell, 1992; Fuchs, 2001; Whittington, 2015). We attend to a more detailed examination of these criticisms.

At the epistemological level, criticism has been directed at Giddens' rejection to 'wield the methodological scalpel' (Giddens, 1984, p. xxx) and the absence of empirical examples in his work – notwithstanding the few studies Giddens uses to illustrate certain aspects of structuration theory, such as Willis' (1977) *Learning to Labour* (Giddens, 1984; Gregson, 1989). Concerning itself more with answering 'what is' rather than 'how to explain' questions (Lizardo, 2010, p. 658), structuration theory also has neglected to articulate a normative foundation, and is therefore limited as critical theory (Bernstein, 1983). The epistemological difficulty is that 'unless an institution exists prior to action it is difficult to understand how it can affect behaviour' and therefore empirical analysis needs a 'diachronic model of the structuration process' (Barley & Tolbert, 1997, p. 9) to overcome the problem of conflation of action and institution.

Giddens clearly had conceived of structuration theory at the meta-level encompassing a broader range of issues at the ontological level and had been less concerned with the specifics at the methodological and epistemological level. Archer suggests that structuration theory's popularity can be attributed to discontent with the 'old debate' of individualism versus collectivism, but she claims that two competing world views remain relevant given their different ontological conceptions and their distinct implications for practical social theorizing (Archer, 1995, pp. 60–61). However, this explanation for structuration theory's acclaim may be too simplistic and is not borne out by the increasing currency commanded by structuration theory in empirical applications across disciplines. Overall, despite the poor definitional quality of structuration theory, it offers 'much insight into the basic properties and dynamics of human action, interaction, and organization' (Turner, 1986, p. 977) and its 'connection to empirical research is fundamentally important' (Gregson, 1989, p. 236).

Empirical application

Criticisms levied against the various theoretical constructs in structuration theory are belied by the numerous empirical applications in disciplines as varied as accounting, management and organization, political culture, geography, psychology, and technology and information systems (Stones, 2005). The theory's appealing notion of the transformative capacity of human agency finds expression in management and organization studies research that addresses issues of stability, change and process. Unsurprisingly, empirical application is not without its challenges. Firstly, Giddens himself did not explicate how structuration theory could inform empirical research. Instead, he proposed parsimony in applying structuration theory and recommended using the concepts only as 'sensitizing devices', thus consciously limiting 'forays into epistemology' in his own writing (Giddens, 1984, pp. 327, 288). Secondly, empirical operationalization is hampered by the development of key concepts that solely operate at a high level of abstraction (den Hond et al., 2012; Pozzebon & Pinsonneault, 2005; Sewell, 1992; Fuchs, 2001; Whittington, 2015). Responding to this issue, there have been some attempts at making structuration theory operational for empirical research (notably Stones, 2005).

Writing of empirical research, Giddens made an interesting comment when affirming the 'cultural, ethnographic or "anthropological"' element in all social research and the consequent double hermeneutics. The sociological researcher, attentive to agents' complex skills in the 'shifting contexts of time and space' (Giddens, 1984, pp. 284–286), seeks to explain what agents know about how to 'go on' in the daily activities of their social life, by inventing 'second-order' concepts. However, such 'second-order' concepts can also be appropriated in social life by agents as 'first-order' concepts. Translation and interpretation between sociological descriptions and the frames of meaning with which agents understand and orient their conduct is what Giddens referred to as 'double hermeneutics'. Giddens (2013) contended that all social research is characterized by such interplay of two frames of meaning, implicitly arguing how a strict separation of (the language of) social research and (that of) its object – as with Levi-Strauss, see above, and Bourdieu (1990), for example – may not be tenable.

Researchers of management and organization who share structuration theory's primary concern with social groups have adopted, albeit in varying degrees, the theory's concerns with dichotomist thinking (Pozzebon, 2004). In a review of application specific to this discipline, den Hond et al. (2012) found a majority of articles made only a passing reference to Giddens' work, employing it for definitional purposes, as a building block to alternative frameworks, or to emphasize and elaborate on aspects of agency and structure. They found closer engagement with structuration theory in some articles that applied in an in-depth fashion a small number of key concepts from the repertoire of structuration theory. Finally, they found a handful of articles that utilized the theory's three main constructs of duality of structure, agents' knowledgeability, and time-space relations, adopting varying degrees of emphasis on each aspect. Others (Albano, Masino & Maggi, 2010) suggest that even when organizational scholars do not interpret consistently or build fully on structuration theory, they may still realize Giddens' main message: that theory be developed based on an epistemological view that allows the researcher to overcome the objectivist/subjectivist dilemma.

Organization studies and structuration theory

Paradoxically, this lack of clear epistemological and methodological guidelines may have allowed for a wider application of structuration theory in different contexts, accounting for its popularity in shaping a variety of empirical insights. In addition to the particular popularity of structuration theory in information technology and information systems research (reviewed in, for example, Pozzebon, 2004; Pozzebon & Pinsonneault, 2005; Jones & Karsten, 2008), empirical applications can also be seen in institutional research (Barley & Tolbert, 1997), strategy research (Pozzebon, 2004), strategy-as-practice (Whittington, 2015; Seidl & Whittington, 2014), power relations (Courpasson, 2000; Brocklehurst, 2001), and process research methodologies (Sminia, 2009). Complementary to den Hond et al. (2012), who categorized how core concepts of structuration theory were used in empirical studies, we now present examples of empirical work to illustrate how structuration theory has informed some areas in the field of management and organization studies.

Process studies

An especially promising area for management and organization scholars lies in the potential of structuration theory as a process-oriented theory, explaining change in and around organizations (Albano, Masino & Maggi, 2010; den Hond et al., 2012). Drawing simultaneously on the tenets of functionalism and phenomenology, Giddens tries to bridge the gap between deterministic, objective and static notions of structure, on the one hand, and voluntaristic, subjective and dynamic views, on the other, by positing two realms of social order (analogous to grammar and speech) and by focusing attention on points of intersection between the two realms. Since the very term 'structuration' denotes structure as a process that underscores the transformative capacity of human agency in effecting change, concepts such as scripts and routines can present viable process methodology routes (Sewell, 1992). However, capturing recursive relationships implicit in the notion that 'social structures are both constituted by human agency and at the same time are the very medium of this constitution' (Giddens, 1979, p. 121) can be challenging. In this regard, Langley (1999) suggests that temporal bracketing (breaking down into successive periods) can allow for analysis of such 'mutual shaping', although some authors argue that this could distort the 'duality of structure' itself (Jones, 1997; Pozzebon & Pinsonneault, 2005, p. 1361).

Organizational change has been conventionally conceived of as either passive adaptation to exogenous variables or an unpredictable phenomenon resulting from individual strategies and behaviours. Giddens' approach helps in explanation of organizational change by assimilating both the exogenous and individual antecedents in a common framework. Since structuration theory is a meta-theory, it helps in providing a higher level of synthesis of ongoing human activities and enduring social structures (Orlikowski & Robey, 1991). One of the exemplary articles in this regard deals with how organizational structures change over time by applying a Giddensian approach (Ranson, Hinings & Greenwood, 1980; Albano, Masino & Maggi, 2010). Other authors such as Riley (1983) have also adopted structuration theory to study organizational culture and social change (Albano, Masino & Maggi, 2010).

Strategic management

Strategy is considered, at a macro level, an aggregate of actions, transactions, recipes, positions, designs, plans and interpretations. At the same time, strategy can only be empirically grounded in the discrete actions, decisions or routines of a variety of agents at the micro level. Clearly, the link between micro and macro is manifest in a structurationist view of strategy as a matter of ongoing social practices and power relations. The reciprocity between structure and action, so fundamental to structuration theory, has implications for alternative interpretations in the analysis of strategic choice. According to Pozzebon (2004, p. 254), Giddens' theory has more often been adopted as a broad framework (e.g. Coopey, Keegan & Emler, 1998), as a general premise incorporated into existing approaches (e.g. Lowe, 1998; Phillips, Lawrence & Hardy, 2000), or as an integrative theoretical tool (e.g. Child, 1997) than as the primary theoretical foundation in studying strategy and organizational change. She found that structuration has been used substantially to speak to topics such as strategic conversation (Westley, 1990), differentiation between intended and enacted strategy (Sarason, 1995), and strategy making as the ongoing socially structured action of many agents (Rouleau, 2005). From here, structuration has continued to influence strategy formation research (Sminia, 2009). In general, structuration theory has also been applied to analyse managerial work as the 'skilled accomplishment of agents and as an expression of the structural properties of systems of interaction' (Wilmott, 1987, cited in Albano, Masino & Maggi, 2010).

Structuration theory has clear relevance to strategy as practice scholars, with Whittington suggesting that Giddens is a practice theorist since 'for him, understanding people's activity is the central purpose of social analysis' (Whittington, 2015, p. 145). Specifically, Whittington submits that structuration theory has relevance in addressing issues of management control and managerial agency, 'whether and how structures can be used and modified by organizations and their members' (Whittington, 1992, pp. 697–698; den Hond et al., 2012). In addition, this emphasis on people's activity complements the increasing recognition of the role of individuals in the emergent micro-foundations stream of strategy research (Powell, Lovallo & Fox, 2011; Barney & Felin, 2013; den Hond et al., 2012). Structuration theory also complements calls to encourage strategy as practice and institutional theory to work together (Suddaby, Seidl & Lê, 2013; Vaara & Whittington, 2012) since 'to understand activity, we must attend to institutional embeddedness' (Whittington, 2015, p. 145).

Institutional theory

The association between institutional theory and structuration theory is apparent considering both regard institutionalization as a dynamic interactive process. Barley and Tolbert (1997) advance the view that a fusion of the two theories could add to institutional theory since institutionalists have tended to neglect how institutions are reproduced and altered, an area that structuration theory addresses adeptly. Moreover, structuration theory can address problems of institutional determinism (Scott, 2014). Recognizing the lack of empirical direction in structuration theory as to how such study might be operationalized, Barley and Tolbert (1997) provide methodological guidelines for empirical study, but acknowledge that in choosing to focus on the identification and analysis of scripts as an expedient empirical option, they have somewhat relegated the emphasis on cognitive and interpretive frames. For strategy as practice researchers, Wittington (2015) suggests that not only does structuration theory offer the potential to improve understanding of the institutions in which strategy takes place, but indeed the theory demands a 'wide-angled analysis of institutions, as well as the microscopic study of praxis' (p. 146). Poole and Van de Ven (1989), in discussing how to deal with paradox, maintain that structuration theory offers a new conception of the structure–agency paradox, and thereby enables the development of new insights and theory building because it allows researchers to consider action and structure simultaneously.

Power

The relations between human agencies in institutionalized settings are fundamentally related to the dimensions of power. Structural theory emphasizes the transformative capacity of agents and power as defined by social relationships rather than being an attribute of an entity (den Hond et al., 2012). Several researchers have elaborated further on this idea. For instance, Leflaive (1996), building on structuration theory, proposed that instead of viewing power as a property of agents or originating due to unequal control of information, it should be seen as a collective organizational capacity. He argues that the process of surveillance is at the same time constituted and constitutive of organizations and agents have the capacity to both resist and change these processes. Based upon Giddens' conceptualization of power, Brocklehurst argues that working at home changes organizational relationships, including issues of control, because of the transformative capacity (i.e. power) of the employees to change the material and social world (Brocklehurst, 2001, p. 447). Courpasson (2000) uses structuration theory broadly to argue that organizations are governed both via centralized and entrepreneurial governance forms through structures of domination and as structures of legitimacy. It is quite clear that structuration theory has relevance to the issues of use of power in managerial control and agency and in setting up or modifying structures of domination (Whittington, 1992; den Hond et al., 2012).

Organizational routines

With the focus of practical consciousness and routinized nature of social life, structuration theory is quite compatible with the study of organizational routines, especially the relationship between structure and recurrent social practices. For instance, Giddens (1991) mentions that when structuration theory is used as an analytical tool, the researcher should focus on the analysis of 'recurrent social practices', assuming that structures exist in practice. Indeed, structuration theory has been applied in the study of organizational routines to show them as a source of both stability and change. Organizational routines, for instance, have been referred to as 'generative systems' (Feldman, 2000). There are both ostensive and performative aspects to organizational routine following. In many cases, organizational routines are not just taken for granted but are performed by skilful agents. Indeed, for 'recurrent social practices' to be considered routine, agents should display some amount of knowledgeability of these practices (den Hond et al., 2012). When an agent reflexively selects from a menu of choices from the repertoire available, this has inherent possibilities for organizational change. Any kind of patterned activity in a situational context can be a source of both stability and change, as knowledgeable agents innovate on the available repertoire offered by routines.

Organizational intelligence and learning

Structuration theory can provide a more comprehensive view of organization intelligence including cognitive, behavioural and affective processes (Akgun, Byrne & Keskin, 2007). Organizational intelligence has been referred to as the organization's capacity to collect, process and interpret information to support decision-making and is also closely related to the organizational communication process (Feldman & March 1981). Scholars have investigated organizational learning (Berends, Boersma & Weggeman 2003), communication (Yates & Orlikowski, 1992), knowledge (Orlikowski, 2002) and discourse (Heracleous & Hendry, 2000). In this area, the first application of structuration theory is seen in the domain of information processing and technology, with it being subsequently applied to knowledge and learning in organizations. The application of structuration theory in the former (e.g. Yates & Orlikowski, 1992; DeSanctis & Poole, 1994) can be considered more substantial than the latter. Exceptions to this are the application of structuration theory in organizational learning by Hargadon and Fanelli (2002) and to organizational knowledge by Berends, Boersma and Weggeman (2003). There are some direct applications of structuration theory in the area of organizational intelligence (Akgun, Byrne and Keskin, 2007). Yates and Orlikowski (1992) illustrate how a structurational perspective can provide insight to the emergence of communication genres through the interaction of individual communicative actions and the institutionalized practices. This view suggests that discourse is composed of a duality of communicative actions (utterances) and deep structures (such as root metaphors, central themes or fundamental assumptions), interacting through the modality of agents' interpretive schemes (Heracleous & Barrett, 2001; Heracleous & Hendry, 2000).

Conclusion

Undoubtedly, structuration theory is not only relevant but also poses challenges to organization theory due to the lack of a detailed methodology and the usage of obscure and complex terms, possibly compounded by difficulties posed by Giddens' favoured ethnographic approach and time-consuming data collection (Whittington, 2015). Critics see structuration theory as a 'second-order theory ... conceptualizing the general constituents of human society' (Gregson, 1989, p. 245), or as a metatheory (Weaver & Gioia, 1994). Giddens expressed unhappiness about how his concepts were employed in empirical research, arguing that structuration theory's concepts should be applied 'in a spare and critical fashion', and as sensitizing devices rather than *in toto* (Giddens, 1991, p. 213; Giddens, 1984). However, as Stones (2005) points out, Giddens' focus on ontology rather than on specifics does not preclude structuration theory from contributing to situated analyses. Indeed, the abstract level concepts in structuration theory may have inadvertently permitted a flexible approach to data, thus offering insights to a wider research field (Heracleous, 2013).

Thus, notwithstanding the limitations of structuration theory, and contrary to Gregson's (1989) assessment in consigning structuration theory to inconsequentiality due to its inability to inform empirical research, structuration theory has seen widespread practical application in management and organizational studies and holds promise for future research. Indeed, in his proposal for a stronger theory of structuration, Stones (2005, p. 8) suggests that structuration theory contains within it even greater 'untapped potential at the empirical, substantive level'. A point echoed in Pozzebon and Pinsonneault's (2005, p. 1354) assertion that organization theorists' application of structuration theory in empirical studies remains at a nascent stage with the potential to provide a powerful alternative to other 'dichotomous systems of logic'.

End-of-chapter exercises

1. What is the difference between dualism and duality?
2. (Regarding the duality of structure) What is the sociological meaning of a formal rule (law) that nobody observes any longer, or that has passed into oblivion? Of a norm or custom that has become obsolete?
3. How does knowledgeability relate to agency?
4. What are, in your view, the major criticisms of Giddens' outline of structuration? Why do you consider them important?
5. What is, in your opinion, the relevance and purchase of social theory for research? Should social theory be directly applicable in research? Or should it be considered as meta-theory, unfalsifiable by virtue of being meta-theory, but supportive of and a source of inspiration for research by explicating a point of view on society and social change?

Glossary

Agency The ability of people ('agents') to act upon the world; their capacity to make a difference.

Allocative resources Resources that grant control over subject–object relations (material objects).

Authoritative resources Resources that grant control over subject–subject relations (people).

Domination Structure resulting from or associated with control over allocative and authoritative resources that can stretch from relations regarded as authority where legitimacy is bestowed, to relations lacking legitimacy, tyranny.

Double hermeneutics The two-way, interpretive and dialectical relationship between social scientific knowledge and human practices (hermeneutics itself referring to interpretation or meaning making).

Dualism Mutual exclusiveness of opposing concepts, such as agency *versus* structure, subject *versus* object, voluntarism *versus* determinism, and individual *versus* society.

Duality Inseparability and mutual constitution of opposing concepts, such as agency/structure, subject/object, voluntarism/determinism and individual/society.

Interaction The agent's activity within the social system, space and time; forms of interaction in which agency is performed include communication, the exercise of power and sanction.

Knowledgeability Closely related to reflexivity, the capacity/ability of people to 'know' their place and condition in the social world (unconscious knowledge, practical knowledge and discursive knowledge).

Legitimation Structure resulting from, or associated with, the norms that govern social action.

Modalities The ways through which structural dimensions are expressed in action.

Power The transformative capacity of agents to make a difference in the social world.

Reflexivity Closely related to knowledgeability, the capacity/ability of people to 'reflect' on their place and condition in the social world.

Resources The bases or vehicles through which power is exercised; distinction between allocative and authoritative resources.

Rules Generalizable procedures, often tacit, which are enacted and reproduced in social practices; once deeply sedimented in time-space, they have become institutions.

Signification Structure resulting from, or associated with, the symbols that encode meanings and so shape perceptions.

Strong structuration A reinforced version of structuration theory put forth by Stones (2005); it encompasses 'ontology-in-situ' and involves both hermeneutics and structural analysis, with a view to overcoming the more abstract visualization of structure and agency in Giddens theory.

Structuration The process in which social structures and people's agency interact in mutually constituting ways; the very instant of the reproduction of agency and structure.

Structure The relatively stable and enduring elements in social life: Giddens distinguishes domination, signification and legitimation as different structures.

Time-space Shorthand for the temporal and spatial extension of structures; their influence at a distance.

Unintended consequences Just what they are: the unforeseen, unexpected, sometimes desired, but unintended outcomes of action.

Weak structuration Giddens' formulation of structuration theory, and in opposition to Stones' (2005) reformulation of the theory labelled strong structuration.

Acknowledgment

Parts of this chapter build on our previous work, as published in den Hond et al. (2012).

References

Akgun, A. E., Byrne, J., & Keskin, H. (2007). Organizational intelligence: A structuration view. *Journal of Organizational Change Management, 20*(3), 272–289.

Albano, R., Masino, G., & Maggi, B. (2010). *The relevance of Giddens' structuration theory for organizational research.* TAO Digital Library.

Archer, M. S. (1982). Morphogenesis versus structuration: On combining structure and action. *British Journal of Sociology, 33*(4), 455–483.

Archer, M. S. (1995). *Realist social theory: The morphogenetic approach.* Cambridge: Cambridge University Press.

Barley, S. R., & Tolbert, P. S. (1997). Institutionalization and structuration: Studying the links between action and institution. *Organization Studies, 18*(1), 93–117.

Barney, J., & Felin, T. (2013). What are microfoundations? *Academy of Management Perspectives, 27*(2), 138–155.

Battilana, J. (2006). Agency and institutions: The enabling role of individuals' social position. *Organization, 13*(5), 653–676.

Berends, H., Boersma, K., & Weggeman, M. (2003). The structuration of organizational learning. *Human Relations, 56*(9), 1035–1056.

Bernstein, R. (1983). *Beyond objectivism and relativism: Science, hermeneutics, and praxis.* Philadelphia, PA: University of Pennsylvania Press.

Bertilsson, M. (1984). The theory of structuration: Prospects and problems. *Acta Sociologica, 27*(4), 339–353.

Bourdieu, P. (1977). *Outline of a theory of practice.* Cambridge: Cambridge University Press.

Bourdieu, P. (1990). The scholastic point of view. *Cultural Anthropology, 5*(4), 380–391.

Brocklehurst, M. (2001). Power, identity and new technology homework: Implications for new forms of organizing. *Organization Studies, 22*(3), 445–466.

Callinicos, A. (1985). Anthony Giddens: A contemporary critique. *Theory and Society, 14*(2), 133–166.

Child, J. (1997). Strategic choice in the analysis of action, structure, organisations and environment. *Organization Studies, 18*(1), 43–76.

Clegg, S. R. (1989). *Frameworks of power.* London: Sage.

Coopey, J., Keegan, O., & Emler, N. (1998). Managers' innovations and the structuration of organizations. *Journal of Management Studies, 35*(3), 263–284.

Courpasson, D. (2000). Managerial strategies of domination. Power in soft bureaucracies. *Organization Studies, 21*(1), 141–161.

Craib, I. (1992). *Anthony Giddens.* London: Routledge.

den Hond, F., Boersma, F. K., Heres, L., Kroes, E. H., & van Oirschot, E. (2012). Giddens à la Carte? Appraising empirical applications of structuration theory in management and organization studies. *Journal of Political Power, 5*(2), 239–264.

DeSanctis, G., & Poole, M. S. (1994). Capturing the complexity in advanced technology use: Adaptive structuration theory. *Organization Science, 5*(2), 121–147.

Feldman, M. S. (2000). Organizational routines as a source of continuous change. *Organization Science, 11*(6), 611–629.

Feldman, M. S., & March, J. G. (1981). Information in organizations as signal and symbol. *Administrative Science Quarterly, 26*(2), 171–186.

Fuchs, S., (2001). Beyond agency. *Sociological Theory, 19*(1), 24–40.

Gane, M. (1983). Anthony Giddens and the crisis of social theory. *Economy and Society, 12*(3), 368–398.

Giddens, A. (1976). *New rules of sociological method: A positive critique of interpretative sociologies.* London: Hutchinson.

Giddens, A. (1979). *Central problems in social theory.* London: Macmillan.

Giddens, A. (1984). *The constitution of society: Outline of the theory of structuration.* Cambridge: Polity.

Giddens, A. (1991). Structuration theory: Past, present and future. In C. G. A. Bryant, & D. Jary (eds) *Giddens' theory of structuration: A critical appreciation* (pp. 201–221). London: Routledge.

Giddens, A., & Pierson, C. (1998). *Conversations with Anthony Giddens: Making sense of modernity.* Berkeley, CA: Stanford University Press.

Greenwood, R., & Suddaby, R. (2006). Institutional entrepreneurship in mature fields: The big five accounting firms. *Academy of Management Journal, 49*(1), 27–48.

Gregson, N. (1989). On the (ir)relevance of structuration theory to empirical research. In D. Held, & J. B. Thompson (eds) *Social theory of modern societies: Anthony Giddens and his critics* (pp. 235–248). Cambridge: Cambridge University Press.

Hargadon, A. B., & Fanelli, A. (2002). Action and possibility: Reconciling dual perspectives of knowledge in organizations. *Organization Science, 13*(3), 290–302.

Haugaard, M. (2002). *Power: A reader.* Manchester: Manchester University Press.

Held, D., & Thompson, J. B. (eds.) (1989). *Social theory of modern societies: Anthony Giddens and his critics.* Cambridge: Cambridge University Press.

Heracleous, L. (2013). The employment of structuration theory in organizational discourse. *Management Communication Quarterly, 27*(4), 599–606.

Heracleous, L., & Barrett, M. (2001). Organizational change as discourse: Communicative actions and deep structures in the context of information technology implementation. *Academy of Management Journal, 44*(4), 755–778.

Heracleous, L., & Hendry, J. (2000). Discourse and the study of organization: Toward a structurational perspective. *Human Relations, 53*(10), 1251–1286.

Hodgson, G. M. (2007). Institutions and individuals: Interaction and evolution. *Organization Studies, 28*(1), 95–116.

Jones, M. (1997). Structuration and IS. In W. L. Currie, & R. D. Galliers (eds) *Re-thinking management information systems.* Oxford: Oxford University Press.

Jones, M. R., & Karsten, H. (2008). Giddens's structuration theory and information systems research. *MIS Quarterly, 32*(1), 127–157.

Langley, A. (1999). Strategies for theorizing from process data. *Academy of Management Review, 24*(4), 691–710.

Leflaive, X. (1996). Organizations as structures of domination. *Organization Studies, 17*(1), 23–47.

Lizardo, O. (2010). Beyond the antinomies of structure: Levi-Strauss, Giddens, Bourdieu, and Sewell. *Theory and Society, 39*(6), 651–688.

Lowe, S. (1998). Culture and network institutions in Hong Kong: A hierarchy of perspectives. A response to Wilkinson: 'Culture, institutions and business in East Asia'. *Organization Studies, 19*(2), 321–343.

Loyal, S. (2003). *The sociology of Anthony Giddens.* London: Pluto Press.

Mutch, A. (2014). Anthony Giddens and structuration theory. In P. S. Adler, P. du Gay, G. Morgan, & M. Reed (eds) *The Oxford handbook of sociology, social theory, and organization studies: Contemporary currents* (pp. 587–604). Oxford: Oxford University Press.

Orlikowski, W. J. (2002). Knowing in practice: Enacting a collective capability in distributed organizing. *Organization Science, 13*(3), 249–273.

Orlikowski, W. J., & Robey, D. (1991). Information technology and the structuring of organizations. *Information Systems Research, 2*(2), 143–169.

Phillips, N., Lawrence, T. B., & Hardy, C. (2000). Inter-organizational collaboration and the dynamics of institutional fields. *Journal of Management Studies, 37*(1), 22–43.

Poole, M. S., & Van de Ven, A. H. (1989). Using paradox to build management and organization theories. *Academy of Management Review, 14*(4), 562–578.

Powell, T. C., Lovallo, D., & Fox, C. R. (2011). Behavioral strategy. *Strategic Management Journal*, 32(13), 1369–1386.

Pozzebon, M. (2004). The influence of a structurationist view on strategic management research. *Journal of Management Studies*, 41(2), 247–272.

Pozzebon, M., & Pinsonneault, A. (2005). Challenges in conducting empirical work using structuration theory: Learning from IT research. *Organization Studies*, 26(9), 1353–1376.

Ranson, S., Hinings, C. R., & Greenwood, R. (1980). Structuring of organizational structures. *Administrative Science Quarterly*, 25(1), 1–17.

Riley, P. (1983). A structurationist account of political culture. *Administrative Science Quarterly*, 28(3), 414–437.

Rouleau, L. (2005). Micro-practices of strategic sensemaking and sensegiving: How middle managers interpret and sell change every day. *Journal of Management Studies*, 42(7), 1413–1441.

Sarason, Y. (1995). A model of organizational transformation: The incorporation of organizational identity into a structuration theory framework. *Academy of Management Paper Proceedings*, 47–51.

Scott, W. R. (2014). *Institutions and organizations. Ideas, interests and identities*, 4th edn. Thousand Oaks, CA: Sage.

Seidl, D., & Whittington, R. (2014). Enlarging the strategy-as-practice research agenda: Towards taller and flatter ontologies. *Organization Studies*, 35(10), 1407–1421.

Sewell, W. H. (1992). A theory of structure: Duality, agency and transformation. *American Journal of Sociology*, 98(1), 1–29.

Sminia, H. (2009). Process research in strategy formation: Theory, methodology and relevance. *International Journal of Management Reviews*, 11(1), 97–125.

Stones, R. (2005). *Structuration theory*. New York: Palgrave Macmillan.

Suddaby, R., Seidl, D., & Lê, J. K. (2013). Strategy-as-practice meets neo-institutional theory. *Strategic Organization*, 11(3), 329–344.

Thompson, J. B. (1989). The theory of structuration. In D. Held, & J. B. Thompson (eds) *Social theory of modern societies: Anthony Giddens and his critics* (pp. 56–76). Cambridge: Cambridge University Press.

Turner, J. (1986). The theory of structuration. *American Journal of Sociology*, 91(4), 969–977.

Urry, J. (1991). Time and space in Giddens' social theory. In C. G. A. Bryant, & D. Jary (eds) *Giddens' theory of structuration. A critical appreciation* (pp. 160–175). London: Routledge.

Vaara, E., & Whittington, R. (2012). Strategy-as-practice: Taking social practices seriously. *Academy of Management Annals*, 6, 285–336.

Weaver, G. R., & Gioia, D. A. (1994). Paradigms lost – incommensurability vs structurationist inquiry. *Organization Studies*, 15(4), 565–590.

Westley, F. R. (1990). Middle managers and strategy: Microdynamics of inclusion. *Strategic Management Journal*, 11(5), 337–351.

Whittington, R. (1992). Putting Giddens into action: Social systems and managerial agency. *Journal of Management Studies*, 29(6), 693–712.

Whittington, R. (2015). Giddens, structuration theory and strategy as practice. In D. Golsorkhi, L. Rouleau, D. Seidl, & E. Vaara (eds) *Cambridge handbook of strategy as practice*, 2nd edn (pp. 145–164). Cambridge: Cambridge University Press.

Willmott, R. (2000). The place of culture in organization theory: Introducing the morphogenetic approach. *Organization*, 7(1), 95–128.

Yates, J., & Orlikowski, W. J. (1992). Genres of organizational communication: A structurational approach to studying communication and media. *Academy of Management Review*, 17(2), 299–326.

5 Morphogenesis and reflexivity

Margaret Archer, critical realism and organizational analysis

Alistair Mutch

Chapter objectives

This chapter explores the potential of ideas drawn from the tradition of critical realism, particularly the work of Margaret Archer, to aid in the task of organizational analysis.

The chapter discusses:

- The broad trajectory of Archer's work and the key influences on its development
- Some key features of critical realism, notably the concepts of stratification and emergence
- The morphogenetic approach to the relationship between structure and agency
- The formulation of agential reflexivity as based on internal conversations about valued projects, giving rise to distinctive modes of reflexivity
- Some concerns and absences in Archer's work
- The potential for an engagement with aspects of institutional logics

Introduction

Margaret Archer is a leading social theorist working in the critical realist tradition. This chapter focuses on her morphogenetic framework, as a tool for organizational analysis, and her conceptualization of reflexivity, as a rich source of ideas for exploring organizational life. Before considering these two main areas, I supply a brief outline of her voluminous output and of some key ideas in critical realism. I conclude by addressing some gaps in her work, before suggesting the potential of an engagement with her ideas in the context of work on institutional logics.

Career and key concerns

Archer began her academic work as a sociologist of education. Her first major published work was the 1979 book *Social Origins of Educational Systems*. She sought to examine the nature of change in educational systems, which she carried out through a comparative analysis of four countries over a 200-year period. Her selection of Russia, France, Denmark and England was shaped by the desire to explore variability in both educational practice and cultural and social structure. She demonstrated that the structures that had emerged historically, structures of either centralized or decentralized governance, shaped the fate of educational reforms. The concern to stress the importance of the context in which educational reform efforts operated was at the root of her rejection of what she termed 'process without system', something which she found in particular in the espousal of practice theory by Pierre Bourdieu (Archer, 1983). At this early stage, themes that would be elaborated in her later work made their appearance.

Her first major work of social theory appeared with the publication of *Culture and Agency* in 1988 (later revised to align with her elaboration of a morphogenetic framework – Archer, 1996). Drawing in particular on Karl Popper's 'three worlds' conceptualization of knowledge, she argued for the relatively autonomous status of culture in the analysis of social action. For Popper, world one was the world of natural types, with world two being our response to those types (Popper, 1979). Out of this relationship emerged world three, the domain of theories of the world, theories that, once emergent, took on objective status as items, as it were, in the world's library. Once emergent, argued Archer, such cultural items entered into logical relations with other items in the cultural universe, relations that could be ones of contradiction or complementarity. Such relations could exist regardless of whether they were picked up by social actors or whether conflict existed at the level of social interaction. Archer was concerned in particular to challenge what she saw as the enduring myth of cultural integration, a myth which saw 'culture' as a homogeneous and unitary whole. By contrast, she emphasized the possibility of contradiction at the level of both the social and the cultural system. Her elaborate schema was revisited after the publication of her next and most widely cited work, *Realist Social Theory* (Archer, 1995).

Three sources were important for the development of her ideas. The first was the distinction between system and social integration developed by the British sociologist David Lockwood. The second was the work of American sociologist Walter Buckley on the nature of systems. Finally, and perhaps most significant for the future direction of her work, was her engagement with the philosophy of critical realism as developed by Oxford philosopher Roy Bhaskar. We will discuss critical realism in a little detail following this brief outline of Archer's work. However, it is important to note that, while her engagement with critical realism provided Archer with conceptual resources to develop her perspectives, those perspectives were already substantially present in her work on educational systems. *Realist Social Theory* is the site of her development of the morphogenetic framework, a crystallization of the relationship between agency and structure that will be discussed in much more detail later. It is important, however, to note that her first two books of social theory can be seen as a restatement and clarification of classical approaches designed to frame a much more important concern, for her, with the nature of agential reflexivity.

In *Realist Social Theory*, Archer outlined a threefold distinction between persons, agents and actors that she elaborated on in her subsequent work. In *Being Human*, she sought to argue for the primacy of practice in the formation of persons (Archer, 2000). Before developing social identity, she argued, persons in their ontogenetic development established the capacity to distinguish between 'me' and 'not-me', that is, to develop a sense of self. Concepts of self, shaped in particular by linguistic conventions, followed. Persons, argued Archer, had to engage with three domains of reality: the natural, the practical and the social. In each they had to develop distinctive capacities for going on in contexts not of their own selection. The key to doing so, suggested Archer, was the development of reflexive capacities, something that we will explore in much more detail later. The starting point for consideration of the distinctive modes of reflexivity was an engagement with ideas about the internal conversations that Archer, building on the work of the American pragmatists, argued were central to the practice of reflexivity. Previous work had been largely conceptual but *Structure, Agency and the Internal Conversation* saw the beginning of Archer's empirical work, drawing as it did on a series of in-depth interviews (Archer, 2003). Based on these interviews she suggested a number of modes of reflexivity, modes to be explored in subsequent work. In *Making Our Way through the World: Human Reflexivity and Social Mobility*, empirical investigations combined life histories with the development of an instrument named 'ICONI' which was designed to surface modes of reflexivity (Archer, 2007). Continuing with extended interviews of university students, Archer argued in *The Reflexive Imperative in Late Modernity* for a situational logic of opportunity created by extended competition between contending structural and cultural logics that might foster the growth of what she termed 'meta reflexivity' (Archer, 2012). The adequacy of such arguments will be revisited later. Archer's work continued with an engagement with the relational sociology of the Italian sociologist PierPaulo Donati (Donati & Archer, 2015). Archer's conclusion to one of her sections of their joint-authored book sums up some of her concerns and the importance of ideas drawn from critical realism in shaping her conclusions:

> As the world changes and with it the generative mechanism underlying socialization-as-internalization (involving the transmission of consensual messages; the existence of clear and durable role expectations; and the pervasiveness of normative consistency), so too must the conceptualization of the process of socialization within social theory. The latter needs to move from a concept of a passive process to an active one; from assuming an unreflexive acceptance by the young to acknowledging their highly reflexive selectivity; and from stereotyped assumptions about relations and relationality between 'socializers' and 'socializants' to incorporating their variations and varying contributions to different outcomes.
>
> (Donati & Archer, 2015, p. 154).

It is that use of the term 'generative mechanism' that points us towards the contribution of critical realism, so meriting our next brief excursion into some key themes from that body of work. The conclusion also reminds us that Archer's agenda is always to place agents and their actions in the context of the changing contexts in which they find themselves, in order to understand better the actions open to them which might in turn change that world. Her later work, together with that of her collaborators, is concerned with the elaboration of a social ontology adequate to the analysis of the contemporary world.

Critical realism: stratification and emergence

Starting with the undoubted achievements of science as manifest in not only successful experiments but also in technological artefacts, Roy Bhaskar (1979) posed the question, 'what must the world be like for scientific practice to be possible?' From this starting position he suggested the potential of a revived realism, one which posited the existence of a world independent of our conceptions of it but only partially and imperfectly observable through our theoretical conceptions. This is a realism not to be confused with the naïve realism of common-sense experience or the satisfaction with superficial correlations of scientific realism. Rather, it is a realism which proposes an ontology of depth which leads to three distinctive commitments, summarized as ontological boldness, epistemological relativism and judgemental rationality (for accessible summaries of, and introductions to, critical realism and Bhaskar's early work, see Collier, 1994; Sayer, 2000; 2010; Danermark et al., 2002; Edwards, O'Mahoney & Vincent, 2014). The boldness of ontology is in the claim to a mind-independent reality that is conceived of as stratified. The real is not that which can be sensed but rather the mechanisms that produce the sensations that can be experienced. At the level of the observable is the empirical; however, what can be observed may be misleading. Beyond these surface appearances is the domain of the actual, which is the playing out of the consequences of the real, the mechanisms that set the actual in motion. It is the search for these mechanisms, argues Bhaskar, which animates the scientific enterprise. Thus it is necessary to place ontology, the nature of the world, at the forefront of our investigations. The world is not limited to our conceptions of it, because these can be fallible when put to the test of the world. To confuse epistemology with ontology, argues Bhaskar, is to commit the 'epistemic fallacy', to conflate reality with our imperfect understanding of it. From this it follows that the way we understand particular aspects of the world depends on our understanding of its nature. Our methods of inquiry, that is, need to be configured to address the particular nature of that aspect of the world that we are interested in; hence the adherence to epistemological relativism. That is, our methods of inquiry are relative to the phenomena we are seeking to understand. Finally, this tradition argues that there are ways of adjudicating between different knowledge claims, that some ways of understanding the world are more adequate than others. In part, this colours the attaching of the term 'critical' to realism, although this has a number of meanings. In one sense, it seeks to firmly demark this understanding of realism from other, cruder, appellations. However, it also indicates a certain emancipatory intent, whereby better understanding of the world is a necessary, if not sufficient, part of seeking to change that world to promote human flourishing (for debates about this claim from within the tradition, see Frauley & Pearce, 2007).

The stratification of reality into the empirical, the actual and the real is accompanied by another sense of stratification, one coupled with the notion of emergence. Emergence refers to the way that phenomena emerge from mechanisms which operate at one level of existence but, once emergent, cannot be reduced back to those mechanisms. Thus, at the level of physical phenomena, the discipline of physics has pointed to the complex interaction of particles governed by the mechanisms of quantum physics (Norris, 2000). Their interactions produce outcomes which then provide the basis for chemical interactions, interactions that in turn form the grounds for biological processes and sensate beings. Emergent from such biological underpinnings is the psychological. In other words, properties of one level of existence might emerge from an underlying level, albeit that they cannot be reduced back to that level. Once combined at the new level of existence, the properties form part of a system proper to that level. The social world that emerges from the relationships between embodied beings produces effects, which, once emergent, cannot be reduced to the individual properties of persons. We have noted that, for Archer, once ideas have emerged from human interaction, they are lodged in the cultural library of the human species. History is thus central to the social theory that flows from critical realism, as we will see in the next section, which outlines the central idea of the morphogenesis of society.

The morphogenetic cycle

From her early work, one of Archer's enduring concerns has been to explore the relationship between agency and structure. This relationship has been a continuing puzzle for social theory – how to explain, to paraphrase Marx, that 'people make history, but not in circumstances of their choosing'. In *Realist Social Theory*, Archer examines, and rejects, some common approaches before formulating her morphogenetic framework as a means of tackling the issues. She expresses existing approaches as consisting of a series of 'conflations': the 'downwards conflation' of structuralism, the 'upward conflation' of forms of methodological individualism and the 'central conflationism' that she associates with the work of Anthony Giddens and Pierre Bourdieu. She rejects all these forms of conflationism, arguing for the need to maintain a relational approach that pays due attention to history and emergence.

A common tradition in social theory is that associated with forms of structuralism, in which social action is, as it were, 'read off' the particular structure chosen for explanatory priority. The classic case is the crude form of Marxism, in which social action is determined by the state of development of the means of production. The objection, for Archer, is that this treats people as cultural dopes, the puppets of forces beyond their control. It is not just Marxism that provides such 'downward conflation', in which, once we know the parameters of the structure involved, we have no need to examine social action further, for it is predetermined. Forms of economic determinism fall under this umbrella, as do formulations that give explanatory preference to language or genetics. In reaction to such perspectives, argues Archer, some theorists have chosen to stress the action of social actors, who produce society as an epiphenomenon of social interaction. Here she is thinking in particular of currents such as symbolic interactionism. In this tradition, society is produced and reproduced through the interactions of knowledgeable actors; knowledgeable, that is, in terms of 'how to go on' in social situations through knowing tacit rules. The problem here is that the sensitive analyses of situated action provided by writers such as Erving Goffman lack, in the words of Richard Sennett, a grasp of how the contexts that frame action provide strong guides to action. As he argues,

> Each of the 'scenes' in his purview is a fixed situation. How the scene came into being, how those who play roles in it change the scene by their acts, or, indeed, how each scene may appear or disappear because of larger historical forces at work in the society – to these questions Goffman is indifferent.
>
> (Sennett, 2002, p. 35)

It was as a response to the perceived inadequacies of these two approaches that both Giddens and Bourdieu sought to formulate approaches that overcame the dichotomies they found. Giddens is a social theorist who has explored aspects of the nature of late modernity, being associated, in particular, with the formulation of the 'Third Way' in politics which was influential in British politics in the late 1990s (Giddens, 1990; 1991). Influenced both by the British Marxist historian E. P. Thompson, whose work stressed the processual nature of class as a form of becoming rather than as a static reflection of economic positions and the symbolic interactionism of writers such as Goffmann, Giddens outlined his 'structuration theory' (Giddens, 1984). This suggested that structures, conceptualized as rules and resources, had virtual status, existing as memory traces instantiated in action. Structuration theory has had considerable impact in organization studies. It forms, for example, the core of Richard Scott's (2008) influential expression of new institutionalist theory. It has shaped the development of the thread of strategy research known as 'strategy in practice'. Richard Whittington, for example, has argued 'Structuration theory has real purchase where circumstances are plural and fluid, where firms enjoy oligopolistic powers of discretion or where middle managers or others are confident and knowledgeable enough to exploit their powers' (Whittington, 2010, p. 124).

However, other writers have pointed to problems with the notion of structure that Giddens works with. Wanda Orlikowski has enthusiastically taken up structuration theory in the domain of information systems. Her earlier position (Orlikowski, 1992) was that structures were in some sense embodied in technologies but the contradiction between this and Giddens' conception of structures was squarely faced. 'Seeing structures as embodied in artifacts,' argues Orlikowski (2000, p. 406), 'thus ascribes a material existence to structures which Giddens explicitly denies'. The consequence of this move was that Orlikowski's formulations were now firmly in the camp of agency. 'Technology structures' were now nothing to do with either the material properties of artefacts or with wider structures (whether of organization or society) but they were now about 'technology-in-use'. These were 'virtual, emerging from people's repeated and situated interaction with particular technologies' (Orlikowski 2000, p. 407). By this move structures had shrunk in scope from organizations to those rules and resources governing local practices. There was a nod to wider structures but these shrank into the background as they are 'bracketed' (Orlikowski, 2000, p. 410). The problem is that such bracketing renders them all but invisible in practice. This shift then puts the focus on radically tailorable tools and the transformational nature of agency. As she concluded, citing Giddens, 'a practice lens thus allows us to deepen the focus on human agency and recognize "the essentially transformational character of all human action, even in its most utterly routinized forms"' (Orlikowski, 2000, p. 425). Other writers also noted this tendency to underplay the enduring nature of structures (Callinicos, 1985). The historian William Sewell argued that 'it is ... hard to see how such material resources can be considered as "virtual", since material things by definition exist in space and time' (Sewell, 2005, p. 133). Archer went further, arguing that Giddens' formulation of the mutual constitution of structure and action 'precludes examination of their interplay, of the effects of one upon the other and of any statement about their relative contribution to stability and change at any given time' (Archer, 1995, p. 14). Giddens' failure to hold structure and agency apart in order to explore their relationships was, she argued, a form of central conflationism which, rather than providing an answer to the enduring puzzle of such relationships, collapsed it into practice.

Such, also, was her response to the work of the French social theorist Pierre Bourdieu. Building on early ethnographic work with the Kabyle people of Algeria, he devised a tripartite framework of field, capital and habitus, a framework applied to subjects such as education and, most famously, the sociology of taste (Bourdieu & Passeron, 1977; Bourdieu, 1984). His focus was on the nature of practice, practice that took place in fields. Fields were collections of objective relations in which distinctive forms of capital appropriate to success in the field were accumulated. Success in the field was produced in practice by the habitus, structured dispositions to act, which produced appropriate performances. Expressed in typically elliptical form, Bourdieu explains,

> The conditionings associated with a particular class of conditions of existence produce *habitus*, systems of durable, transposable dispositions, structured structures predisposed to function as structuring structures, that is, as principles which generate and organize practices and representations that can be objectively adapted to their outcomes without presupposing a conscious aiming at ends or an express mastery of the operations necessary in order to attain them. Objectively 'regulated' and 'regular' without being in any way the product of obedience to rules, they can be collectively orchestrated without being the product of the organizing action of a conductor.
>
> (Bourdieu, 1990, p. 53)

These formulations were seen as a way of escaping from the determinism of structuralism without collapsing into an unrestrained individualism in which rational actors took optimal decisions. Habitus was thus a key term and one that we will consider more when we explore Archer's work on reflexivity. It is one term that has entered organizational theory, although the importance of another term, the notion of the field in new institutionalism, owes much to Bourdieu's influence. Although in *Realist Social Theory* Archer's main interlocutor is Giddens, we have already noted that in her work on educational systems that Archer found that Bourdieu's focus on practice caused him to develop ideas that did not acknowledge their origins in a particular context, in his case the strong centralizing state traditions in France (Archer, 1983).

Against what she saw as the central conflationism of both Giddens and Bourdieu, Archer formulated her 'morphogenetic framework' (Figure 5.1). The term morphogenesis derives from Greek terms for change and agency:

> The 'morph' element is an acknowledgment that society has no pre-set form or preferred state; the 'genetic' part is a recognition that it takes its shape from, and is formed by, agents, originating from the intended and unintended consequences of their activities.
>
> (Archer, 1995, p. 5)

It is contrasted to 'morphostatis', which is a recognition that actions in the social world often (indeed, perhaps usually) reproduce and confirm existing social arrangements. The focus on the relationship between structure and agency means that this is seen as a dynamic approach in which history needs to be fully considered. Archer provides a summary:

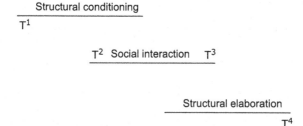

Figure 5.1 The morphogenetic cycle

Source: Adapted from Archer (1995, p. 82). Reproduced with permission of Cambridge University Press

Every morphogenetic cycle distinguishes three broad analytical phases consisting of (a) a given structure (a complex set of relations between parts), which conditions but does not determine (b), social interaction. Here, (b) also arises in part from action orientations unconditioned by social organization but emanating from current agents, and in turn leads to (c), structural elaboration or modification – that is, to a change in the relations between parts where morphogenesis rather than morphostasis ensued.

(Archer, 1995, p. 91)

Structure here also includes, in the fuller scheme, a relationship to culture. As we have noted, Archer draws on ideas of emergence from critical realism to posit the status of ideas, once emergent from human activity, as entities with causal powers in their own right, notably in relations of contradiction with other sets of ideas. As with structural components, such as organizations, which once emergent from human activity cannot be reduced to the activities of current actors (although dependent on those activities), ideas form part of the situational logics which shape and condition activity. They do so not in any deterministic way but by shaping the universe of possibilities which agents face. This is stronger than a simple matter of choice, for these situational logics make powerful suggestions about appropriate courses of action. This is particularly the case when these options seem so obvious as to be 'natural', to have concealed the social conditions of their own production. However, while in many cases actors will choose to act in ways consistent with the avenues suggested by structural and cultural logics, this is in no way predetermined. If they are prepared to pay the opportunity costs, then they can choose to take alternative courses, opening the possibilities for change.

What this formulation suggests is the importance of history, with the injunction from Archer being the need to construct what she terms 'analytical histories of emergence'. These she suggests

Can never ever be grand precisely because the imperative to narrate derives from recognizing the intervention of contingency and the need to examine its effects on the exercise or suspension of the generative powers in question – since outcomes will vary accordingly but unpredictably. On the other hand, analytical narratives are obviously distinct from any version of historical narration tout court, for although social realists in general have no difficulty in accepting the strong likelihood of uniqueness at the level of events, the endorsement of real but unobservable generative mechanisms directs analysis towards the interplay between the real, the actual and the empirical to explain precise outcomes.

(Archer, 1995, p. 343)

It is interesting to note that this formulation is one that organizational theorists often work with, even when they purport to draw on other sources. Stephen Barley and Pamela Tolbert (1997, p. 99) suggested a rapprochement between institutional theory and structuration theory in an article that expressly discounted an Archerian approach. Citing her critique, amongst others, they note

Because Giddens argues that institutions exist only insofar as they are instantiated in everyday activity, critics have charged that he 'conflates' structure with action [...]. Conflation concerns the problem of reducing structure to action (or vice versa) and the difficulty of documenting the existence of an institution apart from activity. Unless institutions and actions are analytically as well as phenomenologically distinct, it is difficult to understand how one can be said to affect the other.

However, despite this they persist with structuration theory to argue for the need to examine repeated cycles of interaction between institution and action. Here, they note that Giddens' 'models are only implicitly temporal, since he usually treats duration as a background assumption rather than a focus of attention' (Barley & Tolbert, 1997, p. 100). As their argument develops, it seems to owe much more to the formulation of structures as enduring elements that Archer presents. They also support the need for historical work to explore the formation and development of such enduring structures. There is a strong sense here that Archer has crystallized the working 'common sense' of many organizational researchers, even if her influence is not explicitly acknowledged. We will return to the further contributions of the morphogenetic framework later. It is the aspect of Archer's work which has perhaps been most adopted as a guide to practical research. As she argues

Analytical dualism can be used by any researcher to gain theoretical purchase on much smaller problems where the major difficulty of seeing the wood from the trees becomes much more tractable if they can be sorted out into the components of temporal cycles of morphogenesis – however short the time-span involved may be.

(Archer, 1996, p. 228)

However, her formulation of the morphogenetic framework can be seen as simply clearing the ground for her major project, that of examining the nature and impact of agential reflexivity, and it is to this that we turn next.

Agential reflexivity

In *Realist Social Theory*, Archer (1995) broached her distinction between persons, agents and actors. She did so in part to resist the claims of those, especially economists, who saw individuals as rational actors. She argued strongly against *homo economicus*, arguing for persons as strong evaluators of personal projects formed on the basis of cherished values (Archer & Tritter, 2000). In formulating a notion of persons as unique she also wanted to resist the claims of those who saw persons as simply the products of discourse, especially the anti-humanism associated with figures such as Michel Foucault. Against their reduction, as she saw it, of persons to artefacts of linguistic constructions, she argued for the distinction between the sense of self and concepts of the self. Drawing on work on childhood development, Archer (2000) argued for the temporal primacy of embodied inter-actions with the natural world, first in the separation from the mother and then in encountering the resistance of physical objects. This focus on ontogeny was strongly developed in *Being Human*, the work prefiguring her focus on reflexivity (Archer, 2000). However, the formulation was to allow for the influence of pre-social factors in the shaping of the person, not at all ignoring the impact of the social. That influence came through the involuntary positioning of persons as agents. Agents are seen as a collective category, in which life chances are shaped in similar ways for persons who find themselves born into particular contexts. Such locations shape the acquisition of distinctive capacities, capacities that enable persons to act in particular roles. Actors thus come to act in particular circumstances governed by the positions available in specific structural configurations. These are the roles or, in Bhaskar's (1979) words, 'position-practices', which face actors as the objective conditions of action but which they can modify dependent on the capacities they vary in relation to these objective conditions. Much depends, therefore, on how actors perceive and respond to the 'situational logics' which combinations of culture and structure provide them with.

The form of evaluation is the internal conversation, in which persons engage in debate on their concerns (Archer, 2003). This notion is developed from the American pragmatist tradition, in particular the work of Charles Pierce, George Herbert Mead and William James. In their exploration of agency, Mustapha Emirbayer and Ann Mische (1998, p. 974) also suggest that such conversations are central to the exercise of agency: 'we ground this capacity for human agency', they write, 'in the structures and processes of the human self, conceived of as an internal conversation possessing analytic autonomy vis-a-vis transpersonal interactions'. However, this conversation, Archer argues, takes very different forms and so leads to different forms of reflexivity. In turn, these different modes of reflexivity suggest why some come into collision with structures and seek to change them.

Following her elaboration of the notion of the internal conversation, Archer argued that there were relatively few examples of its operation in practice. Holding it amenable to investigation through qualitative investigation, she conducted a series of 20 in-depth interviews. Quite clearly this was an exploratory study with the limitations being clearly discussed in Archer's extended treatment of the selection and conduct of interviews. However, the process enabled her to suggest four categories of reflexivity, although one category is marked more by the relative absence of reflexivity (Archer, 2003). These forms of reflexivity are shaped by the interplay between 'context' (that is, the social situation) and 'concerns' (that is, the personal concerns of agents). This is, then, a sociological conception of reflexivity, albeit one underpinned by the cognitive affordances possessed by embodied agents. For some (the majority in her exploratory study) the internal conversation needs to be completed in the context of others. Concerns, that is, have to be verbalized and shared with others in order for resolution to be obtained. This group are the 'conversational reflexives' and their engagement with the world is characterized by measures to maintain continuity of context. In this they will tend to avoid contact with structures or work 'with the grain', in sharp contrast to the 'autonomous reflexives'. The autonomous reflexive completes their own internal conversation in relative (and these terms are all relative) isolation from the concerns of others. This has the potential to bring them into conflict with and seek to change the structures that surround them. This feature is shared to some extent by the third category, that of the 'meta reflexive'. The meta reflexive uses the internal conversation not only to monitor personal projects but also to reflect upon the process of reflection itself. This does not necessarily lead to broader change, however, so much as to the dissatisfaction of the person with the nature of the world and their efforts in it. The final category is that of the 'fractured reflexive', the person who, for some reason, never acquires the ability to conduct a satisfactory internal conversation. These are society's victims, never able to achieve their personal projects and remaining in the position of what Archer would term 'primary agents', that is, with their life chances determined to a significant degree by their involuntary positioning.

Her interlocutors in formulating her modes of reflexivity once again feature Giddens and Bourdieu in prominent positions. For Giddens, reflexivity is the examination and reconstitution of social practices in the light of incoming information, something that he argues is central to modernity. 'What is characteristic of modernity', he argues in *The Consequences of Modernity*, 'is not just an embracing of the new for its own sake, but the presumption of wholesale reflexivity – which of course includes reflection upon the nature of reflection itself' (Giddens, 1990, p. 38). For Archer, this is to make reflexivity the property of structures rather than of persons. The consequence is to smooth over differences in reflexive modalities. Her main concern, however, is to argue against what she sees as the deterministic elements of Bourdieu's notion of habitus. The focus in his work on the connection between the habitus and particular social contexts, plus his argument that the habitus is a durable disposition, one which can be transferred between fields of action, are, for Archer, inimical to considerations of reflexivity. She has engaged in an extended critique of habitus, arguing that it envisages subjects 'so enmeshed in the strands of their own coherent culture as to be unable to question their own thinking and incapable of acquiring the requisite distance for being reflexive about their own doings' (Archer, 2010, p. 130). What she further suggests is that the situational logics of early 21st-century societies will tend to foster the growth of, respectively, autonomous and meta reflexives. The autonomous reflexive is characterized by an internal conversation, which is 'the lone exercise of a mental activity, which its practitioners recognize as being an internal dialogue with themselves and one which they do not need and do not want to be supplemented by external exchanges with other people' (Archer, 2003, p. 210).

This makes such reflexives society's strategists because they are swift to take decisions, decisions that they do not develop in conversation with others. They pursue their own projects in a way likely to bring them into conflict with existing structures, structures that they either seek to use or to change in pursuit of their wider projects. There are three further consequences, argues Archer. These are that autonomous reflexives are much more likely to exhibit a pattern of contextual discontinuity in their lives, uprooting themselves in pursuit of their projects; they are likely to solve potential clashes by prioritizing work, and they are independent people whose concerns tend to make them 'loners'. In considering what contributes to this constellation, Archer suggests that early contextual discontinuity might be important. That is, autonomous reflexives may not have formed at an early stage the rich ties to a particular community that characterize communicative reflexives. Her 'conversational reflexives', with a rich and dense set of ties into networks that they need in order to help themselves make sense of the world, place their prime stress on maintaining such contextual stability. They are likely, therefore, to seek to avoid conflict with anything that threatens this stability. If they are aware of the broader structures of society, they are likely to seek to minimize their contact with them, and to operate with the known and the given. By contrast, the autonomous reflexive has no need of such rich ties. They are more likely to strike out on their own in the pursuit of personal projects. In pursuing such projects, they are likely to be aware of the constraints and enablements that existing structures afford, and to seek to work with and change these to suit their own requirements. This does not mean that they will be successful in their endeavours: 'to call "autonomous reflexives" strategists no more implies that they possess great strategic virtuosity than does the fact that someone is called a military strategist' (Archer, 2003, p. 253). However, it does mean that they are more likely to be aware of the broader features of the environment in which they operate and seek to manipulate such features so as potentially to afford them success in their projects. As such, they may thrive in the conditions of the multinational business organization, with its emphasis on analysis and calculability.

Archer also suggests that developments in technology are fostering a situational logic of opportunity, as a wide set of competing structural and cultural alternatives are presented. She suggests that the growth of the third sector, in a situational logic that 'depends on free-giving, flexible involvement, and crowd-sourcing' is providing enhanced opportunities for the exercise of meta reflexivity (Donati & Archer, 2015, p. 325). She suggests that we are seeing an era of increased morphogenesis. She has provided a richly suggestive set of ideas with which to think, although there are some areas of her work that prompt questions. It is to these that we turn now, before considering one area of organizational analysis that offers a fruitful way forward to engage with her ideas.

Concerns and potential

There are some areas that Archer does not cover. Drawing attention to these is not a matter of criticism; no thinker, especially one as productive and innovative as Archer, can cover all the aspects of social life. Thus, she has relatively little to say about gender. In part, this is because she is concerned with dealing with common features of humanity, ones which operate, as far as typical humans are concerned, equally – as does another thinker on the nature of personhood in the critical realist tradition, Christian Smith (2010). One suspects that she would hold to the distinction between sex as a biological feature of human animals and gender as the socially constructed behaviours and expectations projected onto those differences that is developed in a critical realist argument by Caroline New (2005). This reminds us that there is an intellectual division of labour that applies just as well to those in the broad intellectual tradition of critical realism, where writers such as New and Lena Gunnarson (2014) have advanced arguments about gender.

Another area where Archer lacks discussion is on materiality. It is arguable that her observations about digital technology – 'This has not been seriously examined in the social sciences, because it tends to be assumed that those with contemporary competitive advantages in the market will be able to prolong them by simply annexing digital advances – as, indeed, they try to do' – are a little naïve (Donati & Archer, 2015, p. 326). They neglect work that has been carried out in the information systems domain that suggests, among other things, that information technologies can make existing structural arrangements more durable by inscribing their features into software that, once created, is resistant to change and provides the taken-for-granted context for social action (Mutch, 2010a).

Another area, and one that can also be linked to developments in information systems, is the character of organizations. Like other social theorists, such as Giddens, Archer is providing an account at a high level of generality, which covers large sweeps of time and trends at the level of societies. That is what we should expect from a social theorist and it is up to organizational scholars to explore the implications for organizations and, if necessary, to turn those implications back on social theory in order to refine it. One such area is the relationship of autonomous reflexivity to the modern corporation. The widespread deployment of data-intensive systems, reflected in the spread of 'big data' and analytics, is likely to create the conditions for the wider spread of autonomous forms of reflexivity (Mutch, 2010b). This is not just because they permeate a culture of data analysis and 'rational' decision-making which tends to favour the strategic and planning aspects so important to autonomous reflexivity, but also because they challenge the traditional boundaries supporting the contextual continuity which supports the communicative reflexive. Developments in analytical techniques pioneered in large corporations can in turn be applied in ever-wider areas of social life, especially through the deployment of practices such as performance league tables. Such developments may be thought to call into question the rather optimistic picture that Archer paints of the spread of meta reflexivity and so the questioning of existing arrangements. These are, of course, matters for empirical investigation and Archer provides us with excellent tools for carrying out such investigations.

It is possible to be a little more critical of some of her formulations, especially the persistent focus on the outcomes of particular modes of reflexivity with relatively little attention being paid to how such modes are formed. It is surprising in somebody whose formation was in the sociology of education to find so little attention being paid to the role of secondary education. Indeed, in her study of university students that constitutes the body of her examination of *The Reflexive Imperative in Late Modernity*, she jumps straight from the family to university, pausing only to reflect, rather late in the day, that the modes of reflexivity that she observed had been formed before her subjects got to university, something which would justify 'paying more detailed attention to the quality of family relations and those at school and college' (Archer, 2012, p. 326). Her work, just like that of Bourdieu on the habitus, tends to pay much more attention to describing the nature of reflexivity and its relation to situational logics than to its formation. As another sociologist of education wrote of Bourdieu's habitus,

Habitus is described in terms of what it gives rise to, and brings, or does not bring about. It is described in terms of the external underlying analogies it regulates. But it is not described with reference to the particular ordering principles or strategies, which give rise to the formation of a particular habitus. The formation of the internal structure of the particular habitus, the mode of its specific acquisition, which gives it its specificity, is not described. How it comes to be is not part of the description, only what it does. There is no description of its particular formation.

(Bernstein, 1996, p. 136)

That observation from Basil Bernstein was in the context of his ambition to write what he termed 'grammars' for the acquisition of particular forms of habitus. Archer rather dismisses such attempts to explore the impact of different forms of schooling on the formation of modes of reflexivity but this seems to be a missing dimension to her work. It seems in part to be because she sees 'the traditional loci of socialization, the home and the school, are better viewed as introduction bureaux rather than as induction agencies' (Archer, 2012, p. 106). More widely, her focus on reflexivity might be seen in the eyes of some as part of her commitment to a Catholic theology of the soul (Pilgrim, 2017, p. 480). (Archer is a leading member of the Pontifical College of Social Science and has written, with other critical realists, on the relationship of religious belief to social inquiry; Archer, Collier & Porpora, 2004.) It can be argued that

Archer's laudable desire to stress and preserve individual agency seems to have had the impact of tending to stress agency at the expense of the subtle and indirect ways that structure can mediate agency without there being any direct encounter.

(Mutch, 2004, p. 442)

Having raised these concerns about some potential omissions and challenges, I wish to end on a more positive note in considering how Archer's ideas might be brought into fruitful engagement with some aspects of the body of work under the broad heading of 'institutional theory'. The so-called 'new institutionalism' – to distinguish it from the 'old institutionalism of Philip Selznick (1996) – has become one of the prime streams of inquiry in organizational studies, especially those conducted in North America. There are a number of concerns that can be raised about this body of work. It has tended to operate with a diffuse notion of what an institution is, one that focuses on change as a matter of agential choice. However, within this broad body of work is a stream with intriguing parallels with ideas drawn from critical realism. This is the work on 'institutional logics' pioneered by Roger Friedland and Robert Alford in a foundational essay in 1991 and further developed by Friedland (2009; 2014). Friedland, a sociologist of religion, not an organization theorist, argues that institutional logics should be seen as a combination of substance and practices. The substance is not something that can be apprehended (so a real mechanism in the terms of critical realism) other than through the practices it sets in motion and which obtain their value from belief in the substance. The substance can be love, justice, honour, loyalty or a variety of other abstract terms depending on the institutional order to which the logic pertains. This is an approach which, just as Archer, sees actors as motivated by values which they believe in and which, often, exceed instrumental reasons for action. Conceiving of society as a set of relatively autonomous institutional orders, each with its own internal logic and comprising both material practices and symbolic constructions, seems like a good way of formulating the social ontology which has been Archer's enduring project. Rick Delbridge and Tim Edwards (2013) have used Archer's ideas about reflexivity in order to provide some conceptual clarity to institutional theory in their exploration of 'inhabited institutions'. This seems like a promising line of inquiry and a way of connecting Archer's sometimes abstract-seeming arguments to the messy world of organizational life.

Conclusion

The discussion here can only be a summary of a rich body of ideas that has been developed in not only a series of groundbreaking books but also in numerous edited collections. It is important to remember that, across all of this work, there is a concern with social ontology, with the situated nature of social actions in contexts that have been entered into in involuntary fashion. Just as the ideas from critical realism that Archer works with have had to be contextualized to the study of the social world in her work, so too must organization scholars engage with her ideas to help them explain organizational life. While the effort required to assimilate a large body of ideas is substantial, it is a worthwhile investment.

End-of-chapter exercises

1. Take an aspect of organizational life with which you are familiar. How helpful do you find the morphogenetic approach in seeking to understand it?
2. Do you consider that the availability of data and tools for their analysis in organizations is likely to foster autonomous reflexivity?
3. What broader factors might shape the development of modes of reflexivity in a context with which you are familiar – schooling, family or other sources of cultural norms?
4. Do you think that third-sector organizations are likely to lead to the growth of meta reflexivity, or are they likely to be colonized by practices drawn from multinational businesses?

Glossary

Agential reflexivity   The capacity of agents to evaluate their personal projects. Based on her assertion that agents enter into internal conversations in order to reflect on their personal projects, Archer argues that four modes of reflexivity can be entered into. *Conversational reflexives* need others to complete their internal conversations, whereas *autonomous reflexives* carry out their assessments independently. *Meta reflexives* reflect on the process of reflection itself, whereas *fractured reflexives* are unable to conduct a satisfactory conversation. These modes are found in different combinations, but one tends to be dominant.

Critical realism   A philosophical tradition which argues that there is a world independent of our knowledge of it, one that can only be apprehended by our theories of it. The real is taken to be the mechanisms that produce events, events which lie behind the sensations that we experience – thus, reality is stratified into the real, the actual and the empirical.

Institutionalism (new)   Formulated in the United States, institutions' taken-for-granted practices that are seen to be legitimate. The emphasis is placed on the adoption and maintenance of practices for reasons other than 'objective' rationality.

Institutionalism (old)   Associated with the work of Philip Selznick, this approach stresses the process whereby practices and organizations come to be invested with value and so institutionalized.

Institutional logics   Argues that institutions such as religion possess a logic of their own which can condition organizational action and enter into relations of either contradiction or complementarity with other institutional logics. Much of the work in this tradition has been concerned with contending logics at the level of the field, a structured set of relationships between organizations pursuing similar ends. There has been focus on the ways in which economic logics have invaded and colonized activities previously characterized by different logics.

Morphogenesis   A framework associated with the work of Margaret Archer, expressing the way in which change in social structure is the result of agential action. Also associated with *morphostasis*, which is where agential action results in the reproduction of existing arrangements.

References

Archer, M. (1979). *Social origins of educational systems*. London: Sage.

Archer, M. (1983). Process without system. *Archives Europeenes de Sociologie*, 24(4), 196–221.

Archer, M. (1995). *Realist social theory: The morphogenetic approach*. Cambridge: Cambridge University Press.

Archer, M. (1996). *Culture and agency: The place of culture in social theory*. Cambridge: Cambridge University Press.

Archer, M. (2000). *Being human: The problem of agency*. Cambridge: Cambridge University Press.

Archer, M. (2003). *Structure, agency & the internal conversation*. Cambridge: Cambridge University Press.

Archer, M. (2007). *Making our way through the world: Human reflexivity & social mobility*. Cambridge: Cambridge University Press.

Archer, M. (2010) Can reflexivity & habitus work in tandem? In M. Archer (ed.) *Conversations about reflexivity* (pp. 123–143). Abingdon: Routledge.

Archer, M. (2012). *The reflexive imperative in late modernity*. Cambridge: Cambridge University Press.

Archer, M., Collier, A., & Porpora, D. (2004). *Transcendence: critical realism & God*. London: Routledge.

Archer, M., & Tritter, J. (2000). *Rational choice theory: Resisting colonization*. London: Routledge.

Barley, S., & Tolbert, P. (1997). Institutionalization & structuration: Studying the links between action & institution. *Organization Studies*, 18(1), 93–117.

Bernstein, B. (1996). *Pedagogy, symbolic control and identity*. London: Taylor & Francis.

Bhaskar, R. (1979). *The possibility of naturalism*. Hemel Hempstead: Harvester.

Bourdieu, P. (1984). *Distinction: A social critique of the judgement of taste.* London: Routledge.

Bourdieu, P. (1990). *The logic of practice.* Cambridge: Polity.

Bourdieu, P., & Passeron, J.-C., (1977). *Reproduction in education, society & culture.* London: Sage.

Callinicos, A. (1985). A Giddens, a contemporary critique. *Theory & Society, 14,* 133–166.

Collier, A. (1994). *Critical realism: An introduction to the philosophy of Roy Bhaskar.* London: Verso.

Danermark, B., Ekstrom, M., Jakobsen, L., & Karlsson, J. (2002). *Explaining society: Critical realism in the social sciences.* London: Routledge.

Delbridge, R., & Edwards, T. (2013) Inhabiting institutions: Critical realist refinements to understanding institutional complexity and change. *Organization Studies, 34*(7), 927–947.

Donati, P., & Archer, M. (2015). *The relational subject.* Cambridge: Cambridge University Press.

Edwards, P., O'Mahoney, J., & Vincent, S. (2014). *Studying organizations using critical realism: A practical guide.* Oxford: Oxford University Press.

Emirbayer, M., & Mische, A. (1998). What is agency? *American Journal of Sociology, 103*(4), 962–1023.

Frauley, J., & Pearce, F. (2007). *Critical realism and the social sciences: Heterodox elaborations.* Toronto: University of Toronto.

Friedland, R. (2009). Institution, practice & ontology: Towards a religious sociology. *Research in the Sociology of Organizations, 27,* 45–83.

Friedland, R. (2014). Divine institution: Max Weber's value spheres and institutional theory. *Research in the Sociology of Organizations, 41,* 217–258.

Friedland, R., & Alford, R. (1991). Bringing society back in: Symbols, practices, & institutional contradictions. In W. Powell, & P. DiMaggio (eds) *The new institutionalism in organizational analysis* (pp. 232–266). Chicago, IL: University of Chicago Press.

Giddens, A. (1984). *The constitution of society: Outline of the theory of structuration.* Cambridge: Polity.

Giddens, A. (1990). *The consequences of modernity.* Cambridge: Polity.

Giddens, A. (1991). *Modernity and self-identity: Self and society in the late modern age.* Cambridge: Polity.

Gunnarson, L. (2014). *The contradictions of love: Towards a feminist-realist ontology of sociosexuality.* London: Routledge.

Mutch, A. (2004). Constraints on the internal conversation: Margaret Archer and the structural shaping of thought. *Journal for the Theory of Social Behaviour, 34*(4), 429–445.

Mutch, A. (2010a). Technology, organization & structure: A morphogentic approach. *Organization Science, 21*(2), 507–520.

Mutch, A. (2010b). Organizational use of information and communication technology & its impact on reflexivity. In M. Archer (ed.) *Conversations about reflexivity* (pp. 243–258). London: Routledge.

New, C. (2005). Sex and gender: A critical realist approach. *New Formations, 56,* 54–70.

Norris, C. (2000). *Quantum theory and the flight from realism: Philosophical responses to quantum mechanics.* London: Routledge.

Orlikowski, W. (1992). The duality of technology: Rethinking the concept of technology in organizations. *Organization Science, 3*(3), 398–427.

Orlikowski, W. (2000). Using technology and constituting structures: A practice lens for studying technology in organizations. *Organization Science, 11*(4), 404–428.

Pilgrim, D. (2017). Critical realism, psychology and the legacies of psychoanalysis. *Journal of Critical Realism, 16*(5), 468–482.

Popper, K. (1979). *Objective knowledge: An evolutionary approach.* Oxford: Clarendon Press.

Sayer, A. (2000). *Realism and social science*. London: Sage.

Sayer, A. (2010). *Method in social science: A realist approach*. London: Routledge.

Scott, W. (2008). *Institutions and organizations: Ideas and interests*. London: Sage.

Selznick, P. (1996). Institutionalism 'old' & 'new'. *Administrative Science Quarterly*, *41*, 270–277.

Sennett, R. (2002). *The fall of public man*. London: Penguin.

Sewell, W. (2005). *Logics of history: Social theory and social transformation*. Chicago, IL: University of Chicago Press.

Smith, C. (2010). *What is a person? Rethinking humanity, social life, and the moral good from the person up*. Chicago, IL: University of Chicago Press.

Whittington, R. (2010). Giddens, structuration theory and strategy as practice. In D. Golsorkhi, L. Rouleau, D. Seidl, & E. Vaara (eds) *Cambridge handbook of strategy as practice* (pp. 109–126). Cambridge: Cambridge University Press.

6 Pierre Bourdieu and elites
Making the hidden visible[1]

Mairi Maclean and Charles Harvey

> There exists a correspondence between social structures and mental structures, between the objective divisions of the social world – especially the division into dominant and dominated in the different fields – and the principles of vision and division that agents apply to them.
>
> (Pierre Bourdieu, 1996a, p. 1)

Chapter objectives

This chapter applies the work of the French social theorist Pierre Bourdieu to the study of elites, power and domination, highlighting his ability to reveal and make manifest the hidden mechanisms of social stratification that often remain invisible in organizational and social life.

The chapter discusses how:

- Bourdieu's sociological imagination helps to identify the enduring processes of class domination and cultural reproduction in big business
- Cultivating reflexive practice might influence life chances
- Some elites may turn to charitable giving and philanthropy for legitimizing purposes
- Material goods provide the 'props' and accoutrements for elites that conceal the arbitrary nature of elite power and make it appear as if preordained
- A new neoliberal discourse creates a social space within which wealthy elites can position their selves, necessitating the continued exploration of their activities in the global field of power

Introduction

One of Bourdieu's greatest skills and gifts to organizational researchers is his ability to reveal and make manifest the hidden mechanisms of social stratification that often remain invisible in organizational and social life. This chapter draws on a body of research, conceptual and empirical, on Bourdieu and elites conducted by the authors over 20 years, particularly in the context of France and the UK but also more broadly. In what follows, we explore Bourdieu's contribution to the study of elites, which has emerged as an important theme in organization studies in recent years (Reed, 2012). We do so with regard to four research domains: class domination and cultural reproduction in big business; the importance of reflexivity for social mobility; the transactional nature and legitimizing function of entrepreneurial philanthropy; and the discerning processes of taste formation, including transmission, legitimization and embedding. Prior to this, we consider Bourdieu's oeuvre in relation to his background and personal experience.

The writings of Bourdieu are marked by a tendency to perceive binary oppositions in all aspects and strata of social life, which are conceived of as populated by dominant or subordinated agents. Oppositions such as noble/common, inheritors/parvenus and Parisian/provincial, operate as underlying cognitive structures. The initial act of cognition, however, is essentially recognition of an order that exists also in the mind (Bourdieu, 1986a, p. 172), an order whose being there is projected on to the world perceived, sometimes as a form of *mis*-recognition. Nobility exists, for example, for and by those nobles or commoners who perceive and recognize it, due to their situatedness in a world organized according to such structuring principles (Bourdieu, 1999).

For Bourdieu, all symbolic systems – whether cultural or linguistic – are sources of domination, helping to fix and preserve social hierarchies. Bourdieu, much as Foucault, considers power to be exercised from innumerable points, being inherent in other types of relationship, such as economic processes. According to this view, power comes not only from above but is also supported from below, so that power depends on those who bear its effects, on rulers and ruled in equal measure (Bourdieu, 1996a; 1999; Foucault, 1978). The ultimate source of power in society derives from the possession of four types of capital – economic, cultural, social and symbolic (Bourdieu, 1986b; Harvey & Maclean, 2008). The power that these afford, however, is not stable and static; capital formation is an ongoing, dynamic process, subject to accumulation or attrition. As in a game of cards, the hand which players are dealt must still be played, with greater or lesser skill. Agents' positioning in social space is contingent upon their 'overall volume and relative composition of capital' (Anheier, Gerhards & Romo, 1995, p. 892). Material and symbolic power are intertwined, making it difficult for social agents, as practical strategists, to transcend their situational understanding of the world intellectually, rooted as it is in 'habitus', a structured and structuring principle given and reproduced in daily interaction and the means whereby life chances are 'internalized and converted into a disposition' (Bourdieu, 1986a, p. 70; Hartmann, 2000; Mutch, 2003). The relationally embedded nature of power, however, causes it to be misunderstood or 'misrecognized' by those held in its sway. This applies especially to symbolic power, as Bourdieu (1991, pp. 163–164) explains:

> Without turning power into a 'circle whose centre is everywhere and nowhere', which could be to dissolve it in yet another way, we have to be able to discover it in places where it is least visible, where it is most completely misrecognized – and thus, in fact, recognized. For symbolic power is that invisible power which can be exercised only with the complicity of those who do not want to know that they are subject to it or even that they themselves exercise it.

Bourdieu's personal history and subjective experience

Bourdieu arguably is well qualified to speak for both dominant and dominated categories, having experienced the 'habitus' or 'lifeworld' of both in his career, as a 'sociologist whose origins are in what is called the people and who has reached what is called the elite' (Bourdieu, 1990a, p. 178). From provincial, lower-middle-class social origins, he ascended to the apex of the academic pyramid (Maclean, Harvey & Press, 2006). Born in 1930 in the Béarn region of southwestern France, the son of a farmer-turned-postman, Bourdieu proved to be an industrious, able pupil, eventually entering the prestigious Ecole Normale Supérieure (ENS) in Paris. This, the most academic of the Parisian *grandes écoles*, had a policy of opening its doors to a small number of academically gifted recruits (including Georges Pompidou, who overcame his peasant origins to become president of France). The ENS has served over the years as a breeding ground for French intellectuals, featuring, as former students, Althusser, Bergson, Deleuze, Derrida, Durkheim, Foucault, Lévi-Strauss and Sartre. Here, however, lacking the social and cultural capital of his peers, Bourdieu was made to feel an outsider. Set apart by his provincial origins, denied the 'unselfconscious belonging of those born to wealth, cultural pedigree and elite accents', he saw himself as a frustrated 'oblate' (Swartz, 1997, p. 18). The experience of alienation instilled in him a desire for revenge against the institutions to which he owed his success, angered by the gulf between their professed ideals and perceived ingrained prejudice against the lower classes (Bourdieu, 1996a). He criticized their role as institutions of social reproduction (Bourdieu, 1970; 1979); indeed, it was as a 'crisis of reproduction' that he viewed the events of May 1968 (Bourdieu, 1984). He objected to the university mandarins who determined the curriculum and engaged in little empirical research while acting as gatekeepers to aspiring academics by controlling access to the higher echelons of academe (Swartz, 1997).

After graduation in 1951, Bourdieu taught in a *lycée* outside Paris, and in 1955, he was sent to do military service in Algeria. Here, finding that the agrarian society of Kabylia had much in common with the peasant community of Béarn, he commenced social scientific research as a self-taught ethnographer, an experience which later influenced his thinking on issues of social domination (Bourdieu, 1962; 1979). Opposed to the French war in Algeria, he left and took up sociology, which at the time enjoyed little prestige and academic recognition in French universities. However, this also presented Bourdieu with the freedom to elaborate his own theories and research methods. He established his own academic *avant-garde*, creating a school, a Centre for European Sociology and, in 1975, a journal to promote his own brand of sociology, the *Actes de la Recherche en Sciences Sociales*, theoretical yet empirically researched. In 1981, his academic achievements were crowned by his election to the Chair of Sociology at the Collège de France, joining the ranks of Raymond Aron and Claude Lévi-Strauss. In the 1990s, having established his position at the pinnacle of French intellectual life, his international renown spread, facilitated by the translation into English of a growing number of his major works, and by regular visits to the United States, Japan and other European countries. He was extraordinarily prolific during his career, publishing over 30 books and 350 articles by the time of his death at the age of 71 in January 2002. His body is interred in the prestigious Père Lachaise Cemetery in northeast Paris, alongside writers Marcel Proust and Oscar Wilde, singers Edith Piaf and Jim Morrison, composers Bizet and Chopin, and artists Delacroix and Modigliani – a prodigious achievement for the provincial boy from Béarn. Only the Panthéon confers greater honour.

Bourdieu's dual status as a provincial outsider excluded from the Parisian social elite, an outsider–insider, imbues his writing with an anti-institutional *esprit de critique* (Calhoun & Wacquant, 2002). The Collège de France is a highly prestigious institution but is arguably marginal rather than mainstream. Bourdieu's status as outsider within the academic community was underscored by the fact that he lacked a *doctorat d'Etat*, the fundamental qualification for a university chair, which meant that his career lacked one essential element of state-conferred legitimacy and personal distinction: he could not, for example, preside over a committee for the *soutenance* (*viva voce*) of a doctoral thesis. Such an absence of an exemplary manifestation of symbolic capital must have stung Bourdieu, for whom the state is the key instigator of symbolic violence in society, partly because of its power to *name*, to confer upon an individual or group, 'its social titles of recognition (academic or occupational in particular)' (Bourdieu, 1999, p. 337). Symbolic violence refers to an unseen means of domination that is exercised symbolically rather than physically, whereby individuals may be treated as inferior or restricted in their personal aspirations. In short, Bourdieu's personal history and subjective experience were crucial to his interpretation of the social processes that order and govern society (Bourdieu & Wacquant, 1992).

Power, elites and domination

The battle to 'unmask' power and domination demands examining afresh the role of social class. The role of social origin in determining which individuals come to occupy 'strategic command posts' in society is neglected (Mills, 1956, p. 4; Zald & Lounsbury, 2010), arguably obscured by emphases on gender and ethnicity (Bennett et al., 2009). This has enabled the influence of social class to persist largely unseen, shielded from scrutiny in part by a pervasive belief that class is somehow *passé* and obsolete, no longer relevant and hence immaterial (Boltanski & Chiapello, 2007). Mike Savage and his collaborators have done much to promote the study of social class in recent years in a British context, identifying new classes, including the precariat at the bottom of the scale (Savage et al., 2015). However, there is a need also to consider the ongoing role of social class in the acquisition and maintenance of power at the highest levels (Maclean, Harvey & Kling, 2015; 2017). Rising inequalities have attracted renewed interest in scholarly and policy circles in recent years, especially since the publication of Piketty's (2014) landmark study on the topic, but if one is to grapple with inequalities it is important to engage with the rich and powerful in society. Given the disproportionate exercise of power by a small number of elite players, who function as 'hyper agents' or 'playmakers' in society (Maclean, Harvey & Kling, 2014; Schervish, 2003), there is a corresponding need to investigate further the 'contemporary dynamics of elite production', the processes and structures that lead to enduring inequalities in society (Clegg, Courpasson & Philips, 2006, p. 357). This entails a re-examination of the social struggles which inform stratification: uncovering the contests for control in fields and the capacities and strategies of agents to optimize their positioning in social space; illuminating settlements and processes of change within what Bourdieu (1996a) termed the 'field of power'. This 'space of power positions' (Bourdieu, 1990a, p. 127) is the integrative social domain that transcends individual fields and organizations, serving as a metafield of contestation for dominant agents – individuals holding a controlling position within an organizational field – from different walks of life.

Bourdieu (1986a, p. 476) observes in *Distinction* that:

> Every real inquiry into the divisions of the social world has to analyse the interests associated with membership and non-membership... the laying down of boundaries between the classes [being] inspired by the strategic aim of 'counting in' or 'being counted in'.

The problem is that the boundaries of inclusion or exclusion are themselves unseen (Ibarra & Barbulescu, 2010); social reality being composed of 'an ensemble of invisible relations, those very relations which constitute a space of positions' (Bourdieu, 1989, p. 16). For Bourdieu (ibid., 23), 'the power to make visible and explicit social divisions that are implicit, is political power par excellence'. The means to impose such divisions becomes objectified as academic qualifications and credentials, for example. In this way, the institutions of consecration play a critical part in funnelling or filtering opportunities for access. Unlike Foucault, who speaks of polymorphous techniques of power, Bourdieu's reflexive sociology is grounded in social reality, geared to actual social spheres – of elite schools and the state, academia, art, cultural taste and distinction (Bourdieu, 1984; 1986a; 1996a; 1996b). Hence, his world is not only relational; it is also material (Bourdieu, 1998). The objectification of the principles of domination occurs indirectly through the 'intermediary of mechanisms', being mediated by material things (Bourdieu, 2011, p. 137; Le Wita, 1994). The effect of this process of objectification of class-based difference in qualifications, memberships, symbolic and material goods is to obscure the arbitrary nature of their power while simultaneously institutionalizing the principles that inform stratification. In this way, elite reproduction is accomplished by agents in conjunction with specific rules, frameworks and material artefacts that are teleologically charged (Bourdieu, 1990b); dependent on the 'constitutive entanglement of the social and the material' that serves to sanction and endorse differences that are socially relevant (Orlikowski, 2007, p. 1435).

Bourdieu's 'master concepts' of capital (economic, cultural, social and symbolic resources), field (social spaces of objective relations between positions) and habitus (internalized dispositions) have attracted much attention in organizational research (Swartz, 2008). His conceptual arsenal – including field theory, capital theory, habitus, reflexivity, class dispositions, doxa, homologies and the field of power – provide a set of constructs and ideas that shed light on elite structures, power and reproduction, illuminating what is really going on beneath ostensible appearances. Important in the context of elites is his notion of 'doxa', a set of core discourses which specifies the main principles of a field, and which require submission despite their essentially arbitrary nature. Also fundamental is 'illusio', the belief that the game is worth the candle, or as Bourdieu (1998, pp. 76–77) puts it: 'the fact of being caught up in and by the game, of believing that ... playing is worth the effort ... and that the stakes created in and through the fact of playing are worth pursuing'. Within this theoretical armoury, however, his concept of the field of power is arguably underutilized, despite its considerable conceptual and empirical potential. What he does with these constructs and ideas is to elucidate elite structures, power and reproduction, to help bring the unseen processes and mechanisms that determine (growing) inequalities under the spotlight. We now take four examples of how he achieves this in practice, drawing in turn on the enduring processes of class domination and cultural reproduction in big business; the importance of reflexivity for social mobility; the legitimizing function of entrepreneurial philanthropy; and the discerning processes of taste formation.

The enduring processes of class domination

Figure 6.1 displays our conceptualization of the field of power, explicating and developing Bourdieu's (1993; 1996a; 2011) ideas. It depicts institutional life as divided vertically into fields, each defined by the activities conducted within a given social space, delineated by the prevailing rules of competition, practices and dispositions (Hilgers & Mangez, 2015). As individual agents undergo career progression, they may gradually ascend the hierarchy within their selected field; eventually penetrating the field elite should they continue to progress. Progression to the level of field elite affords the potential of accessing the field of power, which a minority of candidates enter while the majority do not. Here, coalitions between elites drawn from different lifeworlds form, reform and reconfigure in response to new challenges and different interests. Bourdieu's (1996a) writing on the field of power refers specifically to the business elite closely intersected with those who serve the state, who form the 'state nobility' (Dudouet & Joly, 2010; Hartmann, 2011). While 'all positions of arrival are not equally probable for all starting points' (Bourdieu, 1986a, p. 110), the expertise of individual agents in playing the hand they are dealt is critical, helping to determine the outcome of struggles in the field of power – struggles that do not represent a smooth process. Bourdieu elaborates this point in *The Field of Cultural Production* (1993, pp. 145–160), where he populates a fictional field of power with an array of heirs and upstarts drawn from the cast of Flaubert's (1869/1972) novel, *L'Education Sentimentale*. The trump

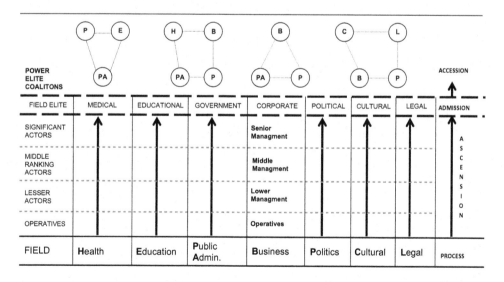

Figure 6.1 Elite actors in the field of power

cards the wealthy characters hold are the inherited assets and assimilated attributes of their habitus – 'elegance, ease of manner, beauty and so forth' (Bourdieu, 1993, p. 150) which define the possibilities intrinsic to the field. However, to prosper the characters must still play the game skilfully.

Figure 6.1 highlights the extraordinary concentration of power in the hand of a small number of dominant elites in the corporate economy in both France and Britain (Maclean, Harvey & Chia, 2010). Those with the highest levels of economic, social, cultural and symbolic capital are found to be especially active within the field of power. Power, as mentioned, is relational, and those most energetic in the field of power tend to bridge different lifeworlds, networking both inside and outside the corporate world. Doing so enhances their power base and allows them to form coalitions to pursue changes in public opinion, laws and regulations. Lindsay (2008, p. 62) calls this a form of 'convening power', which he identifies as one of the most compelling resources at the disposal of elites. A recent illustration of this in the UK is the pressure exerted by some members of the elite in favour of so-called 'light touch' regulation in financial services, whose devastating consequences were exposed when the financial crisis struck in 2007–2008.

One question that arises is, in the field of power why is power so concentrated? Why do so few agents enter and remain active in the field of power, the 'dominant dominants'? One of Bourdieu's (1989, p. 18; 1990a, p. 131) most important insights is his recognition that 'the structuring structures, the cognitive structures, are themselves socially structured, because they have a social genesis'. Our analysis again highlights the importance of social class, confirming the advantages enjoyed by those from the upper echelons, and highlighting the specific advantage they gain in bridging different lifeworlds beyond the corporate sphere. 'Dominant dominants' are, by definition, 'boundary spanners' (Geletkanycz & Hambrick 1997). In Bourdieu's terms, they are 'multipositional', participating in public, private and charitable organizations in cultural, educational, governmental and sporting networks and arenas, engaging with several lifeworlds beyond the corporate world (Boltanski, 1973).

Where a high-status background is lacking, 'educational socialization' can help compensate, but not entirely (Reay, Crozier & Clayton, 2009, p. 1105). While it is undoubtedly beneficial, it is usually in itself insufficient to afford passage to the field of power, since 'the school does not create *ex nihilo* [but] ... relies on the family and educational transmission rests on familial transmission' (Wacquant, 1993, p. 31). This is important, since the occupants of command posts hold positions of power over capital, the exercise of corporate power being heavily implicated in the exercise of economic power. For lower-class aspirants, class serves as a limiting force, inducing a 'capping effect', so that they often achieve second-tier positions, failing to emerge as 'hyper-agents' in their own right. France is described as a meritocracy, but as Hartmann (2000, p. 243) points out, the espoused societal logic of meritocracy is not the overriding logic when 'the important thing is to know without ever having learnt'. Agents from the uppermost classes, on the contrary, benefit from the reassuring mutual resemblance or in-group bias that makes them attractive to their peers. They recognize one another, seek each other out, and co-opt one another onto the various boards on which they serve (Kling, Harvey & Maclean, 2017; Stern & Westphal, 2010), such that dominant elites choose the schools, the clubs, the boards that have already chosen them (Bourdieu, 2007, p. 5). This may not be apparent to the outside observer, however, to whom inner subdivisions of the corporate class may be imperceptible and hence go unnoticed (Flemmen, 2012).

Reflexive practice and social mobility

How, then, might corporate actors from lower-class backgrounds make it to the top, as a small minority of them undeniably do? One answer proposed by Bourdieu and Wacquant (1992) entails learning to think in a novel way. The conscious adoption of reflexive practices may help to overcome the limitations of familial class habitus, such that 'the more [agents] become aware of the social within them by reflexively mastering their categories of thought and action, the less likely they are to be actuated by the externality which inhabits them' (Bourdieu & Wacquant, 1992, p. 49; Maclean, Harvey & Chia, 2012).

Bourdieu argues that it is only by means of a reflexive stance that agents can objectively make sense of the social world. For Bourdieu (2004, p. 4), reflexivity has the power to direct an 'ironic gaze on the social world, a gaze which unveils, unmasks, brings to light what is hidden'. Defined as the self-critical contemplation of 'unthought categories of thought that delimit the thinkable and predetermine the thought', his concept of reflexivity is closely related to his notion of habitus, a system of internalized dispositions that is socially constituted and acquired through experience (Bourdieu, 1990a, p. 178). Habitus is not a static system but may be interpreted as a 'grammar of dispositions' (Vaara and Faÿ, 2011, p. 35), which is dynamic and open to re-education, inducing a sense of the potential opportunities for repositioning available to an individual agent in what Bourdieu (2007, p. 4) terms the 'space of possibles'. At key points of disjuncture, dislocation may foster distanciation, reappraisal and the development of fresh understanding. Bourdieu experienced such a disjuncture in elite education when 'being a stranger and a misfit gave [him] a definite distance from the illusions of those professors to whom the "regal vision" of the social world goes without noticing because it is the vision of their class of origin' (Bourdieu & Wacquant, 1992, p. 45).

Our analysis suggests a connection between reflexive practice and the potential for career progression, particularly in the case of non-privileged elites. This may be because the greater distance covered in traversing social space facilitates perspective-taking, enhancing multi-positionality. Lacking capital in the 'economy of exchange' (Vaara & Faÿ, 2011, p. 28), the need of those from non-privileged backgrounds to remake themselves through their own reconstructive efforts is arguably greater. An uncomfortable awareness of social position can trigger nascent strategies for self-advancement, which may evolve into fine-tuned reflexive practices. In contrast, established elites may be less likely to develop well-honed reflexive practices because, like Bourdieu's professors, their 'regal vision' of their social world is perfectly attuned to their class of origin. Interestingly, new entrants to the corporate elite may be more inclined to take on the mantle of the establishment than seek to change it, thereby playing an active part in ensuring and reinforcing cultural reproduction. Corporate elites are special cases of self-serving communities, where the barriers to entry are social, as members serve also as gatekeepers. Hence, it improves the chances of the non-privileged of admission into prized elite circles if they adopt the manners, bearing and dispositions of established elite members.

Bourdieu's conception of the mediating duality of reflexivity and habitus is modelled in Figure 6.2. This figure locates individual agents as engaged within fields that exist in a state of flux due to internal dynamics and contingencies. Field dynamics impinge on actors, who in turn engage strategically in pursuit of personal goals. Such

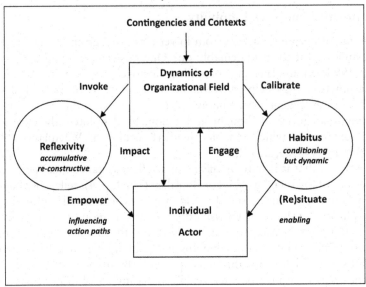

Figure 6.2 Mediating role of reflexivity and habitus

engagements between actor and field are mediated through the operation of habitus and reflexivity (Bourdieu, 1993). Habitus, functioning dispositionally, serves as a personal guidance system that helps actors situate themselves within their social milieu. Reflexivity, operating intellectually, enables actors to think critically and for-mulate appropriate tactics in response to everyday challenges. Figure 6.2 shows that there are two aspects to reflexivity in the context of social mobility and career pro-gression, these being accumulative and reconstructive. The accumulation of different forms of capital is critical. At the same time, reconstructive reflexivity in response to perspective-taking induces repositioning and recalibration.

The legitimizing function of philanthropy

In conducting research on elites from a Bourdieusian perspective in a context of rising inequalities (Piketty, 2014), one overriding question presents itself which refuses to be suppressed: what do they do with all the money? This question became more insistent as the financial crisis deepened. As Rego, Cunha and Clegg (2012) point out, virtue is exacted of today's elites, whom society expects to engage in business ethically (Piff et al., 2012). Bourdieu's writing casts new light on the practice of philanthropic giving by elites by showing that philanthropy brings accumulative rewards in cultural, social and symbolic capital, which in turn may generate further economic capital (Harvey et al., 2011). This highlights the hidden benefits agents may derive from nominally non-economic endeavours, which nevertheless boost their overall capital stock (Swartz, 2008). Philanthropic giving emerges as the prod-uct of specific representational strategies, the most profitable of which must appear disinterested, 'on the hither side of all calculation and in the illusion of the most "authentic" sincerity', to succeed (Bourdieu, 1977, p. 214). Viewed in this light, agents may be seen to have an interest in disinterestedness. This marks a departure from the notion of philanthropy as 'pure gift', born of altruism (Acs & Phillips, 2002; Boulding, 1962; Radley & Kennedy, 1995), to the notion of philanthropic giving as something altogether much more *interested* (Maclean, Harvey & Kling, 2015).

The example of Andrew Carnegie provides a useful illustration of Bourdieu's notion that there is profit to be found in ostensible disinterestedness (Maclean, Harvey & Clegg, 2016). Carnegie (1835–1919) was a Scottish bobbin boy who migrated to the United States, and in due course emerged as a steel magnate (Carnegie, 1920/2006a). His reputation had been severely damaged by his habit of exploiting customers, friends and foes alike, and most dramatically by the 1892 Homestead strike, when he locked out workers and called in the army. His promise to share out most of his fortune during his lifetime, however, singles him out as a pioneer who reframed expectations for other super-rich business leaders to emulate. In writing *The Gospel of Wealth*, he enabled the relationship between wealthy individuals and their wider communities to be redrawn, strengthening the legitimacy of the former by means of a compact to give back to the latter (Carnegie, 1889–1906/2006b; Harvey et al., 2011). He altered the meaning of wealth as something that it was permissible to enjoy on condition that it was redistributed during the lifetime of the holder. Bill Gates and Warren Buffet, as entrepreneurial philanthropists, have followed his example by taking on his maxim that 'he who dies rich dies disgraced'; in this sense they are 'Carnegie's children' (Bishop & Green, 2008). Philanthropy proved to be a trump card in Carnegie's campaign to accumulate symbolic capital. In terms of symbolic association, the scale of his giving set him apart and gave him access to elite actors denied to others. The philanthropic activities of the wealthy enhance their leverage in society in a way that gives them 'special power', which may not always be employed for social good (Piff et al., 2012). As Schervish (2005, p. 267) puts it,

> The wealthy are well aware of their special power and … most take special steps to be careful about its effects. But such concern provides no guarantee that the effects will be salutary. Hyperagency presents a formidable temptation to manipulation.

Figure 6.3 makes explicit the relationship between philanthropic engagement and capital accumulation, revealing the various forms of capital as inherently interconnected. Through philanthropy, Carnegie increased his stocks of social and symbolic capital and access to prized networks. This enhanced his ability to achieve personal objectives through the exercise of an increasingly extensive policymaking role in society (Ball, 2008; Villadsen, 2007). In other words, philanthropy facilitates what Bourdieu (1987) calls 'world-making', which we might conceive of as the 'embedded ways in which agents relate to and shape systems of meaning and mobilize collective action to change social arrangements' (Creed, Scully & Austin, 2002). This illustrates in turn the 'competitive advantage of social orientation' identified by Dees and Anderson (2006, p. 56), underlying the self-interest which imbues philanthropic engagement (Maclean, Harvey & Gordon, 2013).

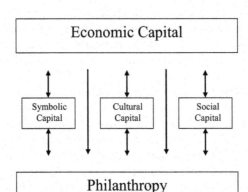

Figure 6.3 A capital theoretic model of entrepreneurial philanthropy

Processes of taste formation

In making the hidden visible, Bourdieu's aim is to reveal the social as central to the most subjective experience (Swartz, 2008). His world, as mentioned, is material as well as relational, and within this taste is critical. Taste is presented not as neutral but rather as a form of social orientation: 'Taste classifies, and it classifies the classifier' (Bourdieu, 1986a, p. 6). Tastes, the manifest cultural preferences of individuals, groups and social classes, he argues, cannot be understood independent of class and social hierarchies. There is, he notes, a 'correspondence between goods and groups', as social structures are internalized and embodied as mental structures (Bourdieu, 1986a, p. 467). Considered thus, taste stems not from internally generated aesthetic preferences but from the conditioning effects of habitus and the availability (or otherwise) of economic and cultural capital, with each class fraction having its own habitus and correlative set of cultural practices. Bourdieu concludes that relative distance from necessity is the primary determinant of habitus and the formation of tastes and preferences, inducing the 'taste of necessity or the taste of luxury' (Bourdieu, 1986a, p. 175).

Culture and taste are thus central to Bourdieu's understanding of habitus, domination and the exercise of power by elites, engendering 'a "sense of one's place" which leads one to exclude oneself from the goods, places and so forth from which one is excluded' (ibid., p. 471). Habitus works by adjusting expectations to lifeworlds as well as life chances. Being 'bourgeois' means mastering a whole system of objects and artefacts in addition to words and gestures, which together comprise a defined culture (Le Wita, 1994). In this way, *being* becomes equated with *being perceived* (ibid., p. 483), and with the consumption of goods, which function as 'props' and accoutrements to a specific lifestyle, concealing the arbitrary nature of elite power and making it seem preordained. Hence, cultural practices and artefacts denote underlying status distinctions, serving as subtle yet powerful forms of social distinction, such that good taste emerges as a means of exercising power in its own right (Turner & Edmunds, 2002, p. 221).

Bourdieu articulates processes of taste formation that otherwise remain nebulous, difficult to circumscribe and pin down. In Figure 6.4, we present a process model of taste formation that builds on Bourdieu's analysis as presented in *Distinction* (1986a, pp.

PROCESS	CULTURAL HOMOLOGIES		
	Field of Production	⇔	*Field of Consumption*
Objectification	Translation of abstract ideas into cultural artefacts	⇔	Formation of cultural dispositions through homologous movements in society
Legitimization	Production, marketing and endorsement of a new genre of cultural products	⇔	Establishment through symbolic appropriation of a leading edge community of taste
Transmission	Range of products extended to include lesser emblems of distinction	⇔	Community of taste extended across different sections of society
Institutionalization	Original models exploited in the production of sentimentally evocative goods	⇔	Community of taste renewed across generations through cultural reproduction

Figure 6.4 Cultural homologies and the four processes of taste formation

226–256) and *The Rules of Art* (1996b, pp. 141–173). Each of the four processes delineated in Figure 6.4 involves a series of interactions between the field of production and consumption, referred to by Bourdieu as functional and structural homologies. *Objectification* defines the translation of ideas into artefacts – new products attuned to the *Zeitgeist* of the times. *Legitimization* stems from acceptance on the part of the cultural elite that a new class of goods meets and satisfies prevalent standards of good taste. *Transmission* entails the gradual expansion of a community of taste while preserving status distinctions between consumers. This is realized, we suggest, through the production of 'lesser emblems of distinction' (Harvey, Press & Maclean, 2011), 'copies of copies' in Deleuze's (1972, p. 7) terms, purchased by consumers lacking the economic capital to acquire more original, bespoke, distinctive items. In this way, for example, the catwalk is linked to the high street, as sought-after items are reproduced and trickle down in a more accessible format, as lesser emblems of distinction. In the fourth process, *institutionalization*, the cultural elite elevates selected products to classic status, the embodiment of good taste, while consumers cherish them as part of a cultural heritage. It is through the ongoing dialogue between the cultural elite and consumers that tastes become embedded.

Conclusion

Bourdieu offers us, through his conceptual arsenal, ways of making visible and bringing out into the open that which would otherwise remain hidden from view. In this regard, he is an exemplar of the French philosophical-sociological tradition. Especially pertinent to this making visible is the study of elites and the ways in which they are changing (or not changing) their strategies and tactics in an increasingly globalized and unequal world. The 21st century has seen a progressive rise in inequality (Piketty, 2014; Stiglitz, 2012). In times defined as those of austerity, states no longer choose to meet growing welfare needs, facilitating the emergence of a neo-liberal 'common sense' which deems the private sphere more effective than the public in serving the common interest (Davis & Walsh, 2017). This new discourse also creates a social space into which wealthy agents can move and take up position (Ball, 2008; Villadsen, 2007). Engaging with rich and powerful elites may not always be popular in social science research, partly because of academic dispositions (Brewer, 2013), and partly because of the difficulties of gaining access (Pettigrew, 1992). However, there is growing recognition that it is timely now, as the crisis of inequality deepens, to take up the challenge of engaging directly with wealth, power and privilege without losing criticality.

Bourdieu's theoretical arsenal is far from exhausted in its exploration by students of management and organizations, enabling new avenues of enquiry to be opened up. We need it most of all to continue our explorations of the activities of elites in the global field of power as – unseen and largely unobserved – they tighten their grip or stranglehold on global wealth and resources.

End-of-chapter exercises

1. Why do so few agents enter and remain active in the field of power?
2. In what way might reflexive practice help to compensate for a lower-class background in career progression?

3. Given the strong interest in philanthropic giving, why is society currently experiencing growing inequalities?
4. Drawing on Bourdieu's capital theory, how might philanthropic giving be seen as a strategy of interest available to elites, rather than purely disinterested?
5. How did philanthropic giving enhance Carnegie's ability to realize personal goals, and how does this illustrate Bourdieu's theory of capital accumulation?
6. In what way does taste stem from the conditioning effects of habitus and the availability (or otherwise) of economic and cultural capital, as opposed to being independently generated by individual preferences? Do you agree with Bourdieu's assessment?
7. How might Bourdieu's concept of the field of power help us to understand growing inequalities?

Glossary

Capital   A generalized resource, which may be monetary or non-monetary in form, tangible or intangible, and represents a power over a given field. Its four main types are economic, cultural, social and symbolic capital.

Doxa   A collection of essential discourses and values that together establish the principles of a given field, misrecognized as true despite being fundamentally arbitrary.

Field   Individual competitive arena that constitutes a recognized area of organizational or social life, marked by an ongoing struggle for capital.

Field of power   The integrative social domain, transcending individual fields and organizations, that represents a metafield of contestation for dominant agents.

Habitus   An internalized disposition which emerges and is developed in response to the objective conditions that individuals encounter in their development, and which serves as a structured and structuring principle given and reproduced in daily interaction.

Homologies   Similarities between fields that lead dominant actors to share similar dispositions across domains.

Illusio   Recognition of and investment in the game and its stakes.

Misrecognition   Recognition of a taken-for-granted order that exists also in the mind and appears like second nature.

Reflexivity   A systematic, self-critical practice that challenges unthought categories of thought that restrict the thinkable and preset the thought.

Symbolic violence   An invisible mode of domination that is exercised symbolically rather than physically, whereby individuals may be treated as inferior or constrained in their personal aspirations.

Note

1 This article partly draws on a keynote address entitled 'Making the hidden visible: Applying Bourdieu's ideas in elites research', given by Mairi Maclean at the London School of Economics symposium on 'Changing Elites in Europe', hosted by the LSE and the Norwegian Research Council, November 26–27, 2015, London, UK. She shared the keynote address with Jérôme Bourdieu, Pierre Bourdieu's son.

References

Acs, Z. J., & Phillips, R. J. (2002). Entrepreneurship and philanthropy in American capitalism. *Small Business Economics, 19*, 189–294.

Anheier, H. K., Gerhards, J., & Romo, F. P. (1995). Forms of capital and social structure in cultural fields: Examining Bourdieu's topography. *American Journal of Sociology, 100*(4), 859–903.

Ball, S. J. (2008). New philanthropy, new networks and new governance in education. *Political Studies, 56*(4), 747–765.

Bennett, T., Savage, M., Silva, E., Warde, A., Gayo-Cil, M., & Wright, D. (2009). *Culture, class, distinction.* London: Routledge.

Bishop, M., & Green, M. (2008). *Philanthropcapitalism: How giving can save the world.* London: Black.

Boltanski, L. (1973). L'espace positionnel: Multiplicité des positions institutionnelles et habitus de classe. *Revue Française de Sociologie, 14*(1), 3–26.

Boltanski, L., & Chiapello, E. (2007). *The New Spirit of Capitalism.* London: Verso.

Boulding, K. (1962). Notes on a theory of philanthropy. In F. G. Dickinson (ed.) *Philanthropy and public policy* (pp. 57–72). Boston, MA: NBER.

Bourdieu, P. (1962). *The Algerians.* Boston, MA: Beacon Press.

Bourdieu, P. (1970). *La Reproduction: Eléments pour une théorie du système d'enseignement.* Paris: Minuit.

Bourdieu, P. (1977). *Outline of a theory of practice.* Cambridge: Cambridge University Press.

Bourdieu, P. (1979). *The inheritors: French students and their relation to culture.* Chicago, IL: University of Chicago Press.

Bourdieu, P. (1984). *Homo academicus.* Paris: Minuit.

Bourdieu, P. (1986a). *Distinction: A social critique of the judgement of taste.* London: Routledge.

Bourdieu, P. (1986b). The forms of capital. In J. G. Richardson (ed.) *Handbook of theory and research for the sociology of education* (pp. 241–258). New York: Greenwood.

Bourdieu, P. (1987). *Choses dites.* Paris: Minuit.

Bourdieu, P. (1989). Social space and symbolic power. *Sociological Theory, 7*(1), 14–25.

Bourdieu, P. (1990a). *In other words: Essays towards a reflexive sociology.* Stanford, CA: Stanford University Press.

Bourdieu, P. (1990b). *The logic of practice.* Cambridge: Polity Press.

Bourdieu, P. (1991). *Language and symbolic power.* Cambridge: Polity Press.

Bourdieu, P. (1993). *The field of cultural production.* Cambridge: Polity Press.

Bourdieu, P. (1996a). *The state nobility: Elite schools in the field of power.* Cambridge: Polity Press.

Bourdieu, P. (1996b). *The rules of art: Genesis and structure of the literary field.* Cambridge: Polity Press.

Bourdieu, P. (1998). *Practical reason.* Stanford, CA: Stanford University Press.

Bourdieu, P. (1999). Scattered remarks. *European Journal of Social Theory, 2*(3), 334–340.

Bourdieu, P. (2004). *Science of science and reflexivity.* Cambridge: Polity Press.

Bourdieu, P. (2007). *Sketch for a self-analysis.* Cambridge: Polity Press.

Bourdieu, P. (2011). Champ du pouvoir et division du travail de domination. *Actes de la Recherche en sciences sociales, 190*(5), 126–193.

Bourdieu, P., & Wacquant, L. (1992). *An invitation to reflexive sociology.* Cambridge: Polity Press.

Brewer, J.D. (2013). *The public value of the social sciences.* London: Bloomsbury.

Calhoun, C., & Wacquant, L. (2002). Social science with a conscience: Remembering Pierre Bourdieu (1930–2002). *Thesis Eleven, 70*, 1–14.

Carnegie, A. (1920/2006a). *The autobiography of Andrew Carnegie.* New York: Signet Classics.

Carnegie, A. (1889–1906/2006b). The gospel of wealth essays and other writings. In D. Nasaw (ed.) *Andrew Carnegie* (pp. 1–109). New York: Penguin.

Clegg, S. R., Courpasson, D., & Philips, N. (2006). *Power and organizations*. London: Sage.

Creed, W. E. D., Scully, M. A., & Austin, J. R. (2002). Clothes make the person? The tailoring of legitimating accounts and the social construction of identity. *Organization Science, 13*(5), 475–496.

Davis, A., & Walsh, C. (2017). Distinguishing financialization from neoliberalism. *Theory, Culture and Society, 34*(5–6), 27–51.

Dees, J. G., & Anderson, B. B. (2006). Framing a theory of social entrepreneurship: Building on two schools of practice and thought. In R. Mosher-Williams (ed.) *Research on Social Entrepreneurship: Understanding and contributing to an emerging field* (pp. 39–66). Indianapolis, IN: ARNOVA.

Deleuze, G. (1972). *Différence et repetition*, 2nd edn. Paris: Presses Universitaires de France.

Dudouet, F-X., & Joly, H. (2010). Les dirigeants français du CAC 40: Entre élitisme scolaire et passage par l'Etat. *Sociologies Pratiques, 21*(2): 35–46.

Flaubert, G. (1869/1972). *L'Education sentimentale*. Paris: Librairie Générale Française.

Flemmen, M. (2012). The structure of the upper class: A social space approach. *Sociology, 46*(6), 1039–1058.

Foucault, M. (1978). *The history of sexuality: Volume I, introduction*. Harmondsworth: Penguin.

Geletkanycz, M., & Hambrick, D. C. (1997). The external ties of top executives: Implications for strategic choice and performance. *Administrative Science Quarterly, 42*(4), 654–681.

Hartmann, M. (2000). Class-specific habitus and the social reproduction of the business elite in Germany and France. *Sociological Review, 42*, 241–261.

Hartmann, M. (2011). Internationalisation et spécificités nationales des élites économiques. *Actes de la Recherche en Sciences Sociales, 190*(5), 10–23.

Harvey, C., & Maclean, M. (2008). Capital theory and the dynamics of elite business networks in Britain and France. *The Sociological Review, 56*(S1), 105–120.

Harvey, C., Maclean, M., Gordon, J. & Shaw, E. (2011). Andrew Carnegie and the foundations of contemporary entrepreneurial philanthropy. *Business History, 53*(3), 424–448.

Harvey, C., Press, J., & Maclean, M. (2011). William Morris, cultural leadership and the dynamics of taste. *Business History Review, 85*(2), 245–271.

Hilgers, M., & Mangez, E. (eds) (2015). *Bourdieu's theory of social fields: Concepts and applications*. Abingdon: Routledge.

Ibarra, H., & Barbulescu, R. (2010). Identity as narrative: Prevalence, effectiveness and consequences of narrative identity work in macro work role transitions. *Academy of Management Review, 35*(1), 135–154.

Kling, G., Harvey, C., & Maclean, M. (2017). Establishing causal order in longitudinal studies combining binary and continuous dependent variables. *Organizational Research Methods, 20*(4), 770–799.

Le Wita, B. (1994). *French bourgeois culture*. Cambridge: Cambridge University Press.

Lindsay, D. M. (2008). Evangelicals in the power elite: Elite cohesion advancing a movement. *American Sociological Review, 73*(1), 60–82.

Maclean, M., Harvey, C., & Chia, R. (2010). Dominant corporate agents and the power elite in France and Britain. *Organization Studies, 31*(3), 327–348.

Maclean, M., Harvey, C., & Chia, R. (2012). Reflexive practice and the making of elite business careers. *Management Learning, 43*(4), 385–404.

Maclean, M., Harvey, C., & Clegg, S. R. (2016). Conceptualizing historical organization studies. *Academy of Management Review, 41*(4), 609–632.

Maclean, M., Harvey, C., & Gordon, J. (2013). Social innovation, social entrepreneurship and the practice of contemporary entrepreneurial philanthropy. *International Small Business Journal, 31*(7), 747–763.

Maclean, M., Harvey, C., Gordon, J., & Shaw, E. (2015). Identity, storytelling and the philanthropic journey. *Human Relations, 68*(10), 1623–1652.

Maclean, M., Harvey, C., & Kling, G. (2014). Pathways to power: Class, hyper-agency and the French corporate elite. *Organization Studies, 35*(6), 825–855.

Maclean, M., Harvey, C., & Kling, G. (2015). Business elites and the field of power in France. *Research in the Sociology of Organizations, 43*, 189–219.

Maclean, M., Harvey, C., & Kling, G. (2017). Elite business networks and the field of power: A matter of class? *Theory, Culture and Society, 34*(5–6), 127–151.

Maclean, M., Harvey, C., & Press, J. (2006). *Business elites and corporate governance in France and the UK.* Basingstoke: Palgrave Macmillan.

Mills, C. W. (1956). *The power elite.* Oxford: Oxford University Press.

Mutch, A. (2003). Communities of practice and habitus: A critique. *Organization Studies, 24*(3), 383–401.

Orlikowski, W. J. (2007). Sociomaterial practices: Exploring technology at work. *Organization Studies, 28*(9), 1435–1448.

Pettigrew, A. (1992). On studying managerial elites. *Strategic Management Journal, 13*(S2), 163–182.

Piff, P. K., Stancato, D. M., Côté, S., Mendoza-Denton, R., & Keltner, D. (2012). Higher social class predicts increased unethical behavior. *PNAS, 109*, 4086–4091.

Piketty, T. (2014). *Capital in the twenty-first century.* Cambridge, MA: Belknap.

Radley, A., & Kennedy, M. (1995). Charitable giving by individuals: A study of attitudes and practice. *Human Relations, 48*(6), 685–709.

Reay, D., Crozier, G., & Clayton, J. (2009). 'Strangers in paradise'? Working-class students in elite universities. *Sociology, 43*(6), 1103–1121.

Reed, M. I. (2012). Masters of the universe: Power and elites in organization studies. *Organization Studies, 33*(2), 203–221.

Rego, A., Cunha, M. P., & Clegg, S. R. (2012). *The virtues of leadership: Contemporary challenges for global managers.* Oxford: Oxford University Press.

Savage, M., Cunningham, N., Devine, F., Friedman, S., Laurison, D., McKenzie, L., Miles, A., Snee, H., & Wakeling, P. (2015). *Social class in the 21st century.* Harmondsworth: Penguin.

Schervish, P. G. (2003). *Hyperagency and high tech donors.* Boston, MA: Social Welfare Research Institute.

Schervish, P.G. (2005). Afterword. In P. G. Schervish, P. E. Coutsoukis, & E. Lewis (eds) *Gospels of wealth: How the rich portray their lives* (pp. 39–66). London: Praeger.

Stern, I., & Westphal, J. D. (2010). Stealthy footsteps to the boardroom: Executives' backgrounds, sophisticated interpersonal influence behavior, and board appointments. *Administrative Science Quarterly, 55*(2), 278–319.

Stiglitz, J. E. (2012). *The price of inequality.* New York: W.W. Norton.

Swartz, D. (1997). *Culture and power: The sociology of Pierre Bourdieu.* Chicago, IL: University of Chicago Press.

Swartz, D. L. (2008). Bringing Bourdieu's master concepts into organizational analysis. *Theory and Society, 37*(1), 45–52.

Turner, B. S., & Edmunds, J. (2002). The distaste of taste: Bourdieu, cultural capital and the Australian postwar elite. *Journal of Consumer Culture, 2*(2), 219–240.

Vaara, E., & Faÿ, E. (2011). How can a Bourdieusian perspective aid analysis of MBA education? *Academy of Management Learning & Education, 10*(1), 27–39.

Villadsen, K. (2007). The emergence of 'neo-philanthropy': A new discursive space in welfare policy. *Acta Sociologica, 50*(3), 309–323.

Wacquant, L. J. D. (1993). From ruling class to field of power: An interview with Pierre Bourdieu on *La noblesse d'État. Theory, Culture & Society, 10*(3), 19–44.

Zald, M. N., & Lounsbury, M. (2010). The wizards of Oz: Towards an institutional approach to elites, expertise and command posts. *Organization Studies, 31*(7), 963–996.

7 Theodore Schatzki's practice theory and its implications for organization studies

Georg Loscher, Violetta Splitter and David Seidl

Chapter objectives

Our objective for this chapter is to introduce the practice theory developed by Theodore R. Schatzki and to illustrate its potential for studying organizations by discussing the:

- Central concepts of Schatzki's theoretical approach
- Implications of these central concepts for studying organizations
- Application of Schatzki's theory in empirical research
- Advantages and limitations of Schatzki's theory for studying organizations

Introduction

Theodore Schatzki counts as one of the main promoters of the 'practice turn' in contemporary social theory (Schatzki, Knorr Cetina, & Savigny, 2001). The practice turn is based on earlier work by such social theorists as Giddens (1984), Bourdieu (1977), Foucault (1977), Garfinkel (1967) and Wittgenstein (1953) and demarcates a stream of diverse theories sharing a common aspect: they consider practices as the constitutive element of social life (Seidl & Whittington, 2014). Based on a critique of Bourdieu and Giddens – the two most prominent practice theorists (Schatzki, 1996) – Schatzki also developed his own version of practice theory, known as 'site ontology' (Schatzki, 2002). It offers a general theoretical apparatus for examining the relationship between human activity and the social. It is based on the premise that there is just one level of social reality (i.e. there is no distinction between micro and macro levels) and that all human activity and all social phenomena are situated within intertwined practices.

Although Schatzki is a general social theorist, he frequently uses organizations as examples to illustrate his theoretical concepts (Schatzki, 2002), which may be one of the reasons why his work has become extremely popular in organization and management studies. Researchers have applied the site ontology in such fields as strategy (e.g. Hydle, 2015) and accounting (e.g. Ahrens & Chapman, 2007; Jørgensen & Messner, 2010), as well as in the study of specific organizational phenomena such as individual and collective knowledge (Nicolini, 2011), management learning (Zundel, 2012), the theory–practice relation (Zundel & Kokkalis, 2010), institutional complexity (e.g. Smets et al., 2015), and financial markets (e.g. Jarzabkowski, Bednarek & Spee, 2015). As we argue in this chapter, Schatzki's theory is particularly compelling for three reasons. It allows researchers to address the micro foundations of organizational phenomena, it allows analysing the embeddedness of organizations in their wider social context, and it can advance our understanding of the temporal and spatial dimension of organizations.

This chapter is organized as follows. After a brief overview of Schatzki's life and work, we introduce the central concepts of Schatzki's site ontology. We then discuss the implications of his theory for the study of organizations and illustrate how his theory can be applied empirically. We conclude with a short summary of our main points and the main advantages and limitations of Schatzki's theory to the study of organizations.

General life and work of Theodore Schatzki

Theodore Schatzki was born in Boston in 1956. He began his academic career studying mathematics at Harvard University, before switching to philosophy at the University of California Berkeley and the University of Oxford. After having been appointed Professor of Geography and Philosophy at the University of Kentucky, Schatzki published his first key book on practice theory, entitled *Social Practices: A Wittgensteinian Approach to Human Activity and the Social* (1996). In this seminal book he presented a Wittgensteinian version of practice theory based on a critique of the practice theories of Giddens and Bourdieu. In his second book, *The Site of the Social: A Philosophical Account of the Constitution of Social Life and Change* (2002), Schatzki revisited earlier ideas presented in his first book and connected them to the constitution and transformation of social life more generally. He developed them into a highly distinctive practice approach, which he referred to as 'site ontology'. This theory was subsequently refined in a number of publications, which focused on such specific aspects of the social domain as materiality, discourse, space, learning, change, and large social phenomena (see Table 7.1 for an overview of Schatzki's main publications). Despite Schatzki's extensive oeuvre, which he developed over the past 20 years, his work is still ongoing; some concepts have changed, some have been specified, and new concepts are still emerging. This ongoing development may be the reason why some people consider his work bulky and at times confusing (e.g. Nama & Lowe, 2014). Against this background, we seek in this chapter to offer an overview of Schatzki's approach and discuss its potential for studying organizations.

Central concepts of Schatzki's site ontology

Similar to all theories of social practice, Schatzki's site ontology is based on the presumption that all social phenomena are rooted in practices (Schatzki, 1996). Yet, in contrast to other practice theorists, such as Bourdieu and Giddens, Schatzki assumes that there is only one single level of social reality: the level of social practices (Seidl & Whittington, 2014). This means that Schatzki's practice theory is based on a 'flat ontology', which does away with the common idea that there are different levels of reality: micro and macro levels, for example (Schatzki, 2011). In this sense, he defines large social phenomena – which other practice theorists would describe as macro phenomena – as a web of intermingled practices (Schatzki, 2011). In the following, we explain this particular aspect of Schatzki's theory in greater detail, introducing the main concepts upon which this theory is based.

Practices

At the heart of Schatzki's approach is the concept of practice, which he defines as 'a temporally evolving, open-ended set of doings and sayings linked by practical understandings, rules, teleoaffective structure, and general understandings' (Schatzki, 2002, p. 87). In what follows, we elaborate on the various elements of this definition.

The fundamental elements of a practice are formed by doings and sayings, both of which are also called *activities*. *Doings* are, or are ultimately grounded in, voluntary bodily movements, hence in the human body. This active body bears three sorts of expressive relationship to how things stand and are going for a person; that is, to the mental and action dimensions of that person's existence (Schatzki, 1996):

1. Manifestation: the bodily manifestation of states of the mind, which means that the body expresses sensations, emotions and states of consciousness
2. Signification: the bodily signification of cognitive conditions, which means that the body signifies desires, beliefs, hopes and expectations
3. Instrument: the instrument to perform actions; it is through bodily actions that other actions are performed in particular situations

These three relationships apply also to *sayings*, which Schatzki (1996; 2017) conceptualizes as speech acts or a particular form of bodily doings.

Schatzki (2002) conceptualizes doings and sayings as 'open-ended' as there is typically a wide range of different ways in which to respond to the particular situation one is confronted with: doings and sayings are altered, disputed and changed in reaction to particular situations. However, the range of doings and sayings that are appropriate in reaction to a specific situation is restricted by the ways in which doings and sayings are tied to a particular practice. Schatzki (2002) outlines four organizing principles through which doings and sayings are tied to a particular practice:

1. Doings and sayings are tied to or embedded in a practice through the practice's *teleoaffective structure*. The first part of the term, 'telos', denotes that all practices entail 'a set of ends that participants should or may pursue' (Schatzki, 2002, p. 80) and the second part of the term, 'affective', denotes an emotional component encompassing the appropriate emotions. The teleoaffective structure of an accounting practice is 'efficiency' (Loscher, 2016), for example, which means that the doings and sayings embedded in this practice are aimed at efficiency. The central end of efficiency ensures profitability by focusing on the cost-utility ratio of activities (i.e. doings and sayings), thereby prioritizing certain activities over others. Although efficiency *per se* is not very emotional, one could argue that it contains an emotional attachment towards the goal of profitability.
2. Doings and sayings are also embedded in a practice through *practical understanding*. Practical understanding denotes the abilities of actors to react appropriately to specific situations. A practical understanding contains the bodily

know-how and implicit knowledge to conduct, recognize and react to other activities. Experienced accountants have a practical understanding of the ratios in balance sheets, for example, and can therefore react appropriately to anomalies in the balance sheet.

3. Doings and sayings are also embedded in a practice through *general understanding* – a reflexive understanding of the overall practice in terms of its values and aesthetics, including a cultural and societal sense of appropriateness and rightness. Professional accounting practice, for example, includes a general understanding of such aspects as values, aesthetics and manners of the accounting practice, including a certain degree of conservatism.

4. *Rules* can also embed doings and sayings in a practice. Rules refer to explicit prescriptions, procedures and principles of proceeding. The practice of accounting, for example, includes rules about explicating certain doings and sayings, such as the prescribed steps to verify a balance sheet or to book 'debit to credit'.

The teleoaffective structure as well as the general and practical understandings constitute the normative 'background' of the doings and sayings. Together with the rules they form the four 'organizing principles' of a practice that give doings and sayings their meaning.

Material arrangements

A material arrangement (or short: arrangement) is a specific constellation of material entities that gives meaning to the doings and sayings of a practice, while simultaneously providing meaning to the individual entities of the constellation (e.g. a table and a chair in a kitchen vs. in a classroom). Schatzki (2002) differentiates between four types of entities: 1) human beings as carriers of practices; 2) artefacts as objects formed by human activity; 3) organisms (animals, plants and other creatures); and 4) non-living elements of nature (e.g. mountains, rivers). Based on this differentiation, Schatzki (2013) highlights several ways in which the entities of material arrangements and (the activities of) practices are related:

1. Activities within a practice change material arrangements: an accountant writes on a piece of paper, or a carpenter transforms wood into furniture using tools.
2. Activities within a practice react to events within an arrangement: a chair breaks in a classroom, and a person fetches a new chair; a saleswoman arrives at the office and a manager stops her to greet her.
3. An entity of a material arrangement is causally related to an activity within a practice: a client enters the room and the auditor greets her; an alarm bell rings, and the firefighters rush to their vehicle.
4. Material arrangements prefigure a particular practice: an auditor follows the steps of a checklist to verify the existence of an asset or the assembly line in a plant prefigures the activities of workers to produce a car.
5. The performance of particular practices depends on specific material arrangements: the use of auditing software depends on the existence of hardware and software; online chatting depends on the existence of technical equipment (e.g. hardware, software protocols)

6. Practices and material arrangements co-disseminate: writing an e-mail requires the dissemination of the internet so someone can receive it or respond to it; the dissemination of the practice of process management co-evolved with the dissemination of enterprise resource-planning software.
7. The performance of a specific practice changes the meaning of material arrangements: an auditor is casually reviewing a balance sheet in the office kitchen instead of using the kitchen for taking a break.

Schatzki (2002; 2012) highlights the notion that practices and arrangements are always linked in one or several of these ways, forming an inseparable amalgam, which he refers to as practice-arrangement bundles.

Practice-arrangement bundles and sites

Schatzki (1996; 2002) argues that practices and material arrangements necessarily hang together, forming 'practice-arrangement bundles'; yet the respective relations, which we described above, can differ in density. While some practices and material arrangements are strongly entangled with or dependent on each other – as when a particular accounting software can only be used to perform a particular accounting practice, other practices and material arrangements are more open and fluid, allowing for different combinations of material arrangements and practices – as when a city square is open to such practices as going to work, attending meetings, playing, etc.

Practice-arrangement bundles tend to change over time. The respective changes might result from changes in the practice or the material arrangement (Schatzki, 2002). These changes in turn are often triggered by external events (Schatzki, 2006). While in most cases actors can proceed unhampered, as the events may not require a change of the practice or arrangement, in other cases, parts of the practice or material arrangements must be altered in order to continue. For Schatzki (2013), these small alterations of a practice can lead to an evolution of practice-arrangement bundles over time. Prominent among the ways bundles can evolve are the following four possibilities (Schatzki, 2013):

1. The introduction of new material arrangements can extend an existing practice. For example, the introduction of video conferencing technology has affected meeting practices.
2. Practices can bifurcate and develop differently. For example, the practices in two plants within a corporation, which originated from their mother firm, might develop differently over time, as they are adapted to the local situation (e.g. human resource management practices are adapted to the different national laws of the respective plants, work practices are adapted to the different cultural peculiarities of the respective plants, etc.), which give rise to new bundles within these different plants.
3. Practice-arrangement bundles evolve through hybridization. Hybridization means that two practice-arrangement bundles are merged (e.g. two firms merge and the different accounting practices of the two firms get merged as well).
4. Practice-arrengement bundles can change because an entity (human, artefact, organism, things) 'flees' from the practice-arrangement. This can have two

effects: the practice-arrangement bundle from which the entity has fled has to adapt, and the fleeing entity integrates into another practice-arrangement bundle. For example, an employee might leave his employer and start with another company.

According to Schatzki (2013), the different ways through which practice-arrangement bundles evolve have one thing in common: new practical understandings must emerge in order to consolidate the change. This emergence of new practical understandings takes time, because the participants of a practice react differently, because the elements of practices are interdependent and therefore resilient to change, and because material arrangements tend to persist. Therefore, various versions of practices (within practice-arrangement bundles) can co-exist, leading to experimentations and uncertainty on behalf of the actors who participate in a practice (Schatzki, 2013).

Practice-arrangement bundles generally form the 'frame' or context in which activities are performed and in which entities and activities gain their meaning; Schatzki (2002) refers to such frames as 'sites' of activity. Thus the elements of practice-arrangement bundles constitute the site, and, through their specific constellation, provide entities and activities their particular meaning. For Schatzki, sites also form a field of 'action intelligibility' in which it makes sense to participants to perform certain actions in a given situation (Schatzki, 2002; 2011). The sites in which actors conduct their doings and sayings also characterize the situations in which they are located. As actors become participants of practice-arrangement bundles, they learn which actions and goals are appropriate, expected and allowed. That means they develop what Schatzki refers to as *practical intelligibility*, which enables them to discern the appropriate action and proceed for the ends they pursue and according to events that confront them.

Large phenomena

As Schatzki's theory focuses on sites and the activities that happen within these sites, it may seem that his site ontology was restricted to the analysis of small and local phenomena. Beyond the observable, situated action within a single site, however, Schatzki's theory is suited to examine larger social phenomena like organizations, states or markets. Schatzki (2002; 2016a) argues that large phenomena can be conceptualized as webs of interconnected practice-arrangement bundles. Phenomena that would be considered 'macro' (e.g. state or market) in a traditional sense are, from Schatzki's theoretical perspective, conceptualized as dense relationships of practice-arrangement bundles that have a wider spatial and temporal extension (Schatzki, 2016a). This extension implies that large phenomena, such as a multinational corporation, expand to a large geographical space, and, similar to a state, are long-lasting. Furthermore, to analyse large phenomena, one needs to study the specific connections of the practice-arrangement bundles that constitute these phenomena. Specifically, practice-arrangement bundles can be related to each other in three ways (Schatzki, 2016a):

1. A practice-arrangement bundle can connect to the practice of another practice-arrangement bundle. The practice-arrangement bundle of going shopping in

a grocery shop, for example, is connected to the practice of chatting with a neighbour within the bundle of forming a friendly community.

2. A practice-arrangement bundle can be interdependent with another practice-arrangement bundle. Schatzki (2016a) speaks of interdependence between practice-arrangement bundles if the bundles draw on the same elements of a practice (its activities, or organizing principles) or the same material arrangements. The practice-arrangement bundle of having a meeting and of having a farewell party may be interdependent because they both draw on the same office space – the same material arrangement.

3. A practice-arrangement bundle can be related to the material arrangement of another practice-arrangement bundle through causal relations (e.g. the ringing of the alarm by the security guard leads the firemen to debark on a firefighting mission), through physical proximity (e.g. the physical proximity of the accounting office and marketing office links the practice arrangement-bundles of accounting and marketing), or through physical structures (e.g. a telephone cable linking the accounting and marketing offices and the related practice-arrangement bundles of sales coordination).

Webs of practice-arrangement bundles can generally range in size from small to extremely large webs. Accordingly, we can distinguish large phenomena of different scales. Large multinational organizations comprise a larger net of practice-arrangement bundles than small local organizations do, for example.

Time-space

Schatzki (2009) emphasizes that practice-arrangement bundles define distinctive temporal and spatial dimensions for the activities taking place within them. In contrast to objective time (such as clock time) and objective space (such as geographic location), temporality and spatiality are relative to the particular practice-arrangement bundle. They are defined by the particular teleology of the practice (which is part of the teleoaffective structure) – that is, the aims and focus of the practice.

As Schatzki (2009) explains, spatiality differs from objective space, such as a length and geographical location, in that it describes 'the world around (an actor) in its pertinence to and involvement in human activity' (Schatzki, 2009, p. 36). Yet, even though spatiality is relative to the activity in which it is involved, it is always anchored in objective space by artefacts and objects. A fence in objective space, for example, may limit the spatial expansion of the practice of playing football in a garden. Spatiality is formed by the *places* where specific activities happen (e.g. shops in which selling activities occur) and *paths* connect different places (e.g. roads between the shops). Arrays of places and paths between them form larger *settings* for activities.

Analogous to the spatial dimension, Schatzki (2009) distinguishes between objective time, such as clock time, and temporality as the temporal horizon of activities. Accordingly, temporality is conceptualized as past, present and future of activities: the past shapes activities, in that they start from a particular state of affairs; the future shapes activities, as they are performed for a particular future end; the present is the moment in which the situated acting occurs and in which future and past come together in the activity. For example, in their present strategic actions, managers may be motivated by past situations (e.g. bad performance) while aiming at particular future states (e.g. career progression). Thus, temporality describes the teleological dimensions of acting, rather than a sequence of events and activities (Schatzki, 2009). Acting becomes teleological by aiming at a future state of affairs (a goal) informed by the particular practice-arrangement bundles.

While Schatzki (2011) presents temporality and spatiality as two analytically distinguishable dimensions, he stresses that they are intimately connected in the activities. In order to describe this connectedness, Schatzki (2011) coined the term *time-space* and, accordingly, speaks of the 'time-space of human activity'. Furthermore, he introduced the term 'interwoven time-spaces' to refer to the interconnectedness of the time-spaces of different people's activities.

Overview of the different elements of the site ontology

In Figure 7.1, we bring together graphically the various concepts of Schatzki's site ontology and offer an overview of their relationship. On the left of the figure we have an exemplary practice-arrangement bundle. On the upper half of it we find the material arrangement consisting of human beings, artefacts, things and organisms. On the lower half we find the practice with its organizing principles of teleoaffective structures, rules, general and practical understandings, and at the bottom the embedded activities (doings and sayings) in reaction to concrete events. The teleological aspect of the teleoaffective structure shapes the time-space within which the activities of the practice-arrangement bundle take place. All elements of the practice-arrangement bundle are intermeshed, shaping the practical intelligibility of

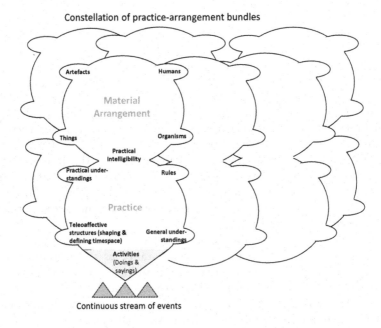

Figure 7.1 An overview of the central elements of Schatzki's site ontology

actors, which determines actors' interpretation of the situation and their activities in reaction to it. As indicated by the other shapes around the focal practice-arrangement bundle, a practice-arrangement bundle is typically linked to other practice-arrangement bundles forming larger constellations of practice-arrangement bundles as the overall site for activities.

Implications for studying organizations

Schatzki's site ontology offers a rich theoretical corpus for analysing organizational phenomena (see Table 7.2 for an overview of existing studies in organization and management drawing on Schatzki's site ontology.) We now highlight three implications of this approach for the study of organizations: the micro-foundations of organizational phenomena, the embeddedness of organizations in wider social context, and the temporal and spatial dimensions of organizing.

Micro-foundations of organizational phenomena

One of the fundamental tenets of Schatzki's practice theory is the focus on the micro activities through which organizational phenomena emerge. In this way, it fits well with the increasing interest of organization scholars in the micro-foundations of organizations (Felin, Foss & Ployhart, 2015), even though Schatzki would disagree with the predominant assumption of methodological individualism of that stream of work. There are two aspects of Schatzki's site ontology of relevance to an understanding of the micro-foundations of organizations: situatedness of activities and materiality of organizational practices.

The first aspect concerns the *situatedness of activities* within particular practice-arrangement bundles. The practice-arrangement bundles in which activities are embedded provide actors with an orientation as to the appropriate activities in a given situation, which Schatzki refers to as 'practical intelligibility'. There are five studies that have focused on Schatzki's account of activities as situated within practice-arrangement bundles, two of which focus on actors' practical understandings and the skilful performance of practices. Lindberg and Rantatalo (2015) examine the competence of professional staff in police departments and hospitals by conceptualizing competence as the capacity to act appropriately in professional practice. The authors show that acting appropriately requires sufficient bodily capabilities, such as a police officer's ability to carry 30 kg of gear and a physician's ability to remain calm and to exhibit positive emotions. Thus the appropriate behaviours of police officers and physicians include appropriate bodily actions, indicating that they possess the practical understanding to carry out their professional practices. Another study by Smets et al. (2015) examines the situated activities of the traders of reinsurance at Lloyd's of London. They describe how some activities of these practices, such as dressing up, dressing down or moving between spaces, were expressed through particular bodily movements, such as rolling up their sleeves, shining their shoes before leaving the office or syncronizing their walking pace with colleagues. The study shows that the timing and pace of these embodied activities were tightly coupled to switching among practices: traders dressing up (e.g. wearing a tie, buttoning down their sleeves) when leaving their office for Lloyd's of London (Smets et al., 2015). A second set of three studies focuses particularly on Schatzki's concept of practical intelligibility within practice-arrangement bundles. Ahrens and Chapman (2007) and Nama and Lowe (2014) show practical intelligibility in terms of the situated functionality of management accounting numbers; in both studies, accounting numbers were used as a means for attaining different goals depending on the setting (e.g. as a planning instrument to attain profitability, or as a means to legitimize a performance review). Specifically, Nama and Lowe (2014) highlight how the practical intelligibility within private equity firms determines how accounting is intermeshed with other practices and how other practices in the firm prefigure the situated functionality of accounting (Nama & Lowe, 2014). In sum, these sets of studies point to the important role of analysing activities and their meaning within their specific setting. Moreover, all these studies take the immersion of practitioners in their practices and arrangements as the starting point for understanding such organizational phenomena as competencies, conflicting goals, and interactions. Simultaneously, these studies focus on the bodily expressions and performances of practices and actors' know-how to act appropriately, enabling them to analyse how practitioners perceive and react to the 'mini-contingencies' (Ahrens & Chapman, 2007) of a situation based on the repertoire of available practices.

The second aspect of Schatzki's site ontology of relevance to an understanding of the micro-foundations of organizations concerns the *materiality* of practices. Schatzki emphasizes that practices and material arrangements constitute each other, and that physical structures – such as telephone cables – connect sites. There are several studies that have drawn on Schatzki's site ontology to examine the role of materiality in organizational activities. In their study of management accounting in a restaurant chain, Ahrens and Chapman (2007) show that several practices centred on the menu and its design as particular material artefacts. It was the central artefact for practices of strategic choice and to ensure profitability. Similarly, Jørgensen and Messner (2010), in their study of a manufacturing firm, highlight the critical role of materiality in the practices of product development, by showing how the misuse of one of its products by one customer opened up a range of new practices related to the use of that product. Hydle (2015), in turn, shows how material arrangements are interwoven with the practices of strategizing in a global professional service firm, describing the way in which a technology was used to structure the coordination of strategy practices and connect the different locations of the global firm. Together, these studies reveal how Schatzki's theory allows an analysis of the role of materiality for particular organizational practices. Future studies could go beyond that, however, by applying the theory to a study of the co-constitution of arrangements and practices within organization. Specifically, researchers could examine the implications of how organizations are created by connecting sites through material arrangements.

Embeddedness of organizations in the wider social context

Schatzki's site ontology can also advance our understanding of the embeddedness of organizations in their wider social context. As elaborated here, Schatzki (2005) treats organizations as constellations of practice-arrangement bundles (e.g. constellations of accounting bundles, marketing bundles and production bundles) that are themselves connected to wider constellations of practice-arrangement bundles of the respective industry (e.g. mechatronics, consulting) and other regional practice-arrangement bundles (e.g. suppliers, state). Such a conceptualization implies an understanding of organizations as a knot within wider constellations of practice-arrangement bundles. This conceptualization has two key implications for studying organizations: first, organizations cannot be treated as entities in themselves, but must be seen as constellations of individual practices and arrangements forming a heterogeneous network linking to other practices and arrangements around it. Accordingly, when studying practices and arrangements of an organization, the researcher needs to consider the links of those practices and arrangements that constitute these constellations. Second, the particular conceptualization of organizations also unfolds the very notion of 'context' by highlighting the fact that the context itself comprises practice-arrangement bundles. Hence, rather than treating the wider social context as an amorphous entity, the researcher needs to spell out the relevant practices and arrangements of which the context is composed (Seidl & Whittington, 2016).

Two empirical studies have focused on the embeddedness of organizations in wider constellations of practice-arrangement bundles. The first one is Lodhia's (2015) case study, which examines the introduction of integrated financial, environmental and social reporting in an Australian bank. Lodhia traced the bank's connections to global practices of cooperative banking, banking regulation in Australia, and environmental, financial and social reporting practices. She shows how the emergence of integrated reporting practices in the Australian bank was connected to the wider economic, social and environmental aspects of cooperative banking. In a second study, Jarzabkowski, Bednarek and Spee (2015) examine the practice of reinsurance, analysing global reinsurance practice as a result of the activities of interconnected actors. The authors show how the actors developed a dense network of interconnected activities (e.g. valuation of risks by consensus pricing and collective risk bearing), going beyond the domain of the individual reinsurance firms.

In summary, Schatzki's site ontology allows researchers to study organizations as phenomena that are open and intertwined with their environment. Its potential lies in directing attention to the nestedness of organizational practices and arrangements in wider constellations of activities and arrangements. Based on an understanding of organizations as an interconnected compound of practice-arrangement bundles, Schatzki's theory points to the importance of analysing interfaces between different practice-arrangement bundles (e.g. accounting and organizing) within an organization and beyond organizational boundaries (e.g. industry or professional associations). His theory also stresses the importance of understanding the interplay of the empirical context (e.g. the industry) and the functional practices (e.g. human resources management), and the ways in which these factors interact in the emergence, persistence and dissolution of practices in organizations. A Schatzkian approach therefore allows researchers to trace the interconnected activities within industries or value networks and, generally, to describe the entwinement of phenomena that are traditionally conceptualized as separate.

Temporal and spatial dimensions of organizing

Schatzki's site ontology can also advance our understanding of the temporal and spatial dimensions of organizing, which have received increasing attention from organization scholars (Langley et al., 2013; Weinfurtner & Seidl, forthcoming). It allows researchers to gain a deeper understanding of the ways in which organizations structure temporality and spatiality. Schatzki's basic argument is that temporality and spatiality in social life are interwoven with practice-arrangement bundles and that they are characterized by the ends for which practices are performed.

Hydle (2015) provides a good example of an empirical study drawing on Schatzki's site ontology to explore temporal and spatial dimensions of organizing. She examines spatio-temporal patterns of strategy work in a transnational professional service firm and found that the time-space of this work differed across contexts. Some time-spaces were strongly structured according to actors' previously decided strategy practices and others were open to emerging strategy practices. Hydle (2015) thereby demonstrated how different temporal-spatial patterns of strategy work enabled distributed agency in a global professional service firm. Schatzki's notions of temporality and spatiality has been used in other research as well. Jarzabkowski et al.'s (2015) study, for example, offers insights into the market cycles of the reinsurance industry and examines the way in which renewal dates of contracts coordinate actions within the industry. Furthermore, they demonstrate how the market as a whole was shaped by the particularities of different places in which market activities were carried out and the events confronted in different places such as earthquakes or floods. In the study by Smets et al. (2015), temporal aspects of structuring the day (office work, change of location to Lloyd's of London, meetings) were shown to be closely related to particular places.

In summary, integrating the temporal and spatial dimension in studies of organizational phenomena based on Schatzki's theory offers a better way of conceptualizing the experience of organizational phenomena by practitioners.

Applying Schatzki's theory through methodologies empirically

After having highlighted the potential of Schatzki's approach for advancing organization research, we offer some general suggestions as to how to apply the site ontology in empirical work. In particular, we comment on suitable empirical methods and some more specific guidelines on how to organize such an empirical project.

Ethnography and interviews as key methods

According to Schatzki (2012), ethnography is the main method for uncovering practices and their relationships to the social. Researchers must engage extensively with the field in order to uncover the activities and the material arrangements bound to a practice. The basic step to uncover the activities and arrangements bound to a practice is to reconstruct the abstract elements of the practice itself. To do so, researchers need, on the one hand, to develop a deep understanding of the practice, and on the other hand, to abstract analytically from the concrete activities to uncover the organizing principles of the practice (Schatzki, 2012). Ethnography is the method best suited to develop such a deep understanding.

In addition to ethnographic methods, Schatzki (2012) suggests that researchers conduct interviews in order to analyse practices and the bundles in which they are embedded. In contrast to ethnographic methods, which allow scholars to examine practices in real-life settings, interviews allow researchers to examine the intentions, as related to the teleoaffective structure involved in enacting particular practices.

Even if practitioners aren't typically fully aware of their intentions, interviews can still help reveal how participants reflect the goals of their activities, the reasons behind them, and links to other practices (Schatzki, 2012). In this sense, interviews allow scholars to analyse the 'normativity' of a practice, as interviewees' use of language to describe their practices indicates how the practices should be enacted and what they are supposed to achieve (Schatzki, 2017). Regarding the sayings of actors, however, Schatzki (2012) remains cautious: although sayings accompanying an activity of a practice can be considered accurately descriptive of practices, the decontextualized sayings within an interview – abstracted from the concrete experience of individual practices – tend to reflect particular 'discourses' rather than providing accurate descriptions of practice. Those interview sayings reflect ideology, politics and desired status, rather than provide 'accurate' descriptions of the concrete activities.

To supplement these qualitative methods, Schatzki (2012) proposes statistical methods to grasp large social phenomena. Quantitative methods allow researchers to obtain an overview and to compare measurable aspects of larger phenomena (Schatzki, 2012). Qualitative methods to apply Schatzki's practice theory have not yet been combined with quantitative methods, however – at least not in organization and management studies.

Some guidelines for applying the site ontology empirically

Though Schatzki has pointed to the empirical methods that could be used in applying his site ontology (Schatzki, 2012), few studies have actually done so. Drawing on these few existing examples, we develop in the following subsections some tentative guidelines for the empirical application of the site ontology with regard to micro-foundations, organizational embeddedness, and temporal and spatial dimensions.

Micro-foundations. When studying the micro-foundations of organizations, researchers need to analyse the relationships among individual practices, among arrangements, and among practice-arrangement bundles to uncover the situatedness of organizational phenomena as well as the role materiality. This requires researchers to immerse themselves in the world of the practitioners. An exemplary study in this regard is that of Ahrens and Chapman (2007), who engaged with their empirical research object over an extensive period, gathering data on the day-to-day activities of individuals (e.g. interviewees talking them through their practices of accounting by using documents), to observe different settings (central and peripheral places in the organization) and formal and informal interactions of practitioners (e.g. meetings, office work, coffee breaks, gossip), and to learn the practice (e.g. passing through trainings for practitioners). As their study shows, the data should be 'rich' in the sense of integrating different groups (e.g. managers, workers), their perspectives and activities and artefacts (e.g. outputs of activities, process maps of activities) to triangulate observations and interviews. Such data allowed them to trace relationships among practices, arrangements, their elements and the way actors engage with them.

Embeddedness of organizations in wider social context. When studying the embeddedness of organizations in their wider social context, researchers need to examine the relationships of organizational practices, arrangements and practice-arrangement bundles. An illustrative example is Jarzabkowski et al.'s (2015) study, in which the researchers conducted ethnographic observations to capture the embeddedness of reinsurance companies in their market. In order to trace connections among practices, the researchers followed different human and non-human actors to different sites at different times, which allowed them to capture the connections, links and relationships among practice-arrangement bundles. In this way, the authors were able to examine the nestedness of organizational phenomena in wider practices and the relationality of the respective activities.

Temporal and spatial dimensions. Studies of temporal and spatial dimensions of organizations can relate to single practice arrangements or to larger networks of practice-arrangement bundles. In the case of *single practice arrangements*, researchers could use similar methods to gather data, as described with regard to the micro-foundations. In applying these methods, the aim is to uncover how time and space are practised and how this relates to the teleology of the respective practice. Schatzki (2011) illustrates this point by showing how the practice of horse breeding influences space in the Kentucky farmland (e.g. archetypal horse farms). An example from organization studies regarding time, albeit not explicitly based on Schatzki, is the study by Kaplan and Orlikowski (2013) in which the authors conducted an ethnography within an organization to capture how mangers constructed past, present and future in their practices of developing strategy. In contrast to such focused data collection, researchers studying the spatial and temporal dimensions of *larger networks of practice-arrangement bundles* must collect data across different locations and times. To do so, researchers may choose team-based multisite ethnographies (Jarzabkowski, Bednarek & Cabantous, 2014). In contrast to traditional ethnographies, such ethnographies involve a team of researchers who conduct ethnographies at different research sites simultaneously. Jarzabkowski et al.'s (2015) study of reinsurance market is a good example of that as well. The authors examined the spatio-temporal dimensions of the reinsurance market using ethnographic observations of three market cycles over three years at various locations. Beyond such ethnographic methods, researchers may also draw on archival data and interviews to explore changes of temporal and spatial experiences over time. For example, Quattrone (2004), even though not explicitly drawing on Schatzki, showed how the time-space of accounting practices changed over the decades as a result of the introduction of new technologies and ideologies.

Conclusion

Our chapter offers an introduction to Schatzkian practice theory, providing an overview of its main concepts and their relations. We have argued that his practice theory has the potential to advance our understanding of the micro-foundations of organizational phenomena, the embeddedness of organizations in their wider social context, and the spatial and temporal dimension of organizing. We also illustrated how Schatzki's theory can be applied empirically. In conclusion, we now want to reflect briefly on the general strengths and weaknesses of the site ontology as an approach to studying organizations.

One of the main strengths of Schatzki's site ontology is that it offers a set of theoretical concepts applicable to all areas of social life, including organizational life. It provides an extremely powerful, new perspective for understanding organizational practices (Schatzki, 2005; 2006). As the studies of Ahrens and Chapman (2007), Jørgensen and Messner (2010), Nicolini (2011), Nama and Lowe (2014), Hydle (2015), Jarzabkowski et al. (2015), and Lindberg and Rantatalo (2015) have shown, drawing on Schatzki's site ontology can result in novel insights into various organizational phenomena. The fact that Schatzki's theory can also easily be combined with established organization and management theories is a further strength, differentiating the site ontology from many other grand theories, such as Luhmann's system theory, which cannot be easily combined with other theories and whose concepts cannot be used eclectically. There are three possibilities for combining Schatzki's site ontology with other established theories: first, researchers can draw on some individual concepts of his theory in order to grasp issues or aspects within an established theory (e.g. Smets et al., 2015); second, one can use Schatzki's concepts to reframe concepts within other established theories (e.g. Loscher, 2016); third, one can also combine the site ontology as a basic and general account of social life with theories that focus on a particular aspect of social life – as long as the latter theory is compatible with the basic tenets of the site ontology. For example, Schatzki (forthcoming) suggests that we might complement interactionism, which focuses on interactions as one particular aspect of social life, with his site ontology in order to provide a more comprehensive account of social life.

Alongside its great strengths, Schatzki's site ontology has three limitations. His theoretical apparatus is relatively complex, as his conceptual vocabulary is extremely rich, a situation that can be challenging for scholars unfamiliar with his work. This complexity constantly increases as Schatzki continues to develop and refine his theory by adding new terminology and concepts. A further challenge is that the empirical application of the site ontology is still in its infancy, meaning that not all of his concepts have yet to be used in empirical studies and the different concepts may not be easily distinguished empirically (Nama & Lowe, 2014). Finally, in contrast to other practice theories such as Bourdieu's praxeology, Schatzki's site ontology does not explain social phenomena, but offers merely 'sensitizing concepts' for describing them (Nicolini, 2012). Schatzki himself emphasizes that his philosophical approach has to be complemented by social science, which develops explanatory theories (Schatzki, 2002).

The reception of Schatzki's theory in management and organization studies is still in its infancy and is still ongoing. His site ontology, however, enables researchers to reconceptualize every aspect of organizational life, offering them new insights and contributions for organization and management research. With this chapter, we hope to contribute to the ongoing absorption of Schatzki's work in management and organization studies.

End-of-chapter exercises

1. Traditionally, boundaries play an essential role for organizations. How can boundaries be reinterpreted in light of the concept of 'the web of practice-arrangement bundles'?
2. How does the site ontology contribute to micro-fundations of organizations?

3. Why is the site ontology useful for studying large phenomena such as markets, organizations, etc.?
4. How can multinational corporations be conceptualized as a 'compound of practice-arrangement bundles'?
5. How does the site ontology change traditional theoretical concepts of organizations?
6. Describe the practice-arrangement bundles of an organizational function (like finance, marketing, strategy or human resource management) and its interconnectedness to wider practice-arrangement bundles.
7. Why is ethnography an appropriate method for studying practices?

Glossary

Activities   Doings and sayings of human actors.
Arrangement   Interrelated material entities.
Doings   Bodily performances signifying, manifesting and constituting actions and states of mind.
Flat ontology   An ontology in which reality is seen as consisting only of one level.
General understanding   Shared senses of things, including values, aesthetics, morals and the cultural appropriateness of activities.
Paths   Connections between places.
Places   Locations to perform particular activities.
Practical intelligibility   The sense of what to do, given a situation and an end.
Practical understanding   The bodily ability to perform activities within practices and the sense for appropriate reactions in a practice.
Practice   An open-ended temporal and spatial manifold of sayings and doings, organized by teleoaffective structures, general understandings, practice understandings and rules.
Practice-arrangement bundles   The connection of practices and arrangements.
Rules   Explicit prescriptions on the way to proceed.
Sayings   Specific bodily performances for linguistic expressions.
Setting   Configuration of places and paths.
Spatiality   The world around an actor in its pertinence to and involvement in activity, in contrast to objective space (e.g. geographic space).
Site   A specific form of context constituting and being constituted by its elements (practice-arrangement bundles).
Teleoaffective structure   A normative structure composed of prioritized goals, end projects and appropriate emotions.
Temporality   Temporal horizon of activities, in contrast to objective time (e.g. clock time).
Time-space   The connectedness of temporality and spatiality.

Acknowledgements

We thank Theodore Schatzki for his comments on earlier drafts of this chapter.

Appendix

Table 7.1 Overview of Schatzki's main work

Books

Year	Title	Content
1996	*Social Practices: A Wittgensteinian Approach to Human Activity and the Social*	Introduction to a theory of social practices based on Wittgenstein's work and focusing on the way practices constitute the social
2002	*The Site of the Social: A Philosophical Account of the Constitution of Social Life and Change*	Development of a site ontology and the way social practices constitute the social
2011	*The Timespace of Human Activity: On Performance, Society, and History as Indeterminate Teleological Events*	Introducing the concept of activity timespaces to conceptualize human activity as teleological

Edited books

Year	Title	Content
2001	*The Practice Turn in Contemporary Theory (with Karin Knorr Cetina and Eike von Savigny)*	Various chapters by leading theorists constituting fundamental texts for the practice turn
2017	*The Nexus of Practices: Connections, Constellations, Practitioners (with Alison Hui and Elizabeth Shove)*	Various chapters specifying concepts of practice theory

Selected examples of articles and contributions in edited books

Year	Title	Content
2005	The sites of organizations	Conceptualization of organization as a compound of practice-arrangement bundles and a justification of Schatzki's ontology
2006	On organizations as they happen	The role of events, past, present and future for organizations
2012	A primer on practices	An introduction to practice theory, constituting elements and the way to research practices
2013	The edge of change: On the emergence, persistence and dissolution of practices	An introduction to the way practices emerge, evolve and persist
2016	Keeping track of large phenomena	Discussion on the way phenomena like markets and states can be conceptualized by practice theory
	Practice theory as a flat ontology	Introducing the meaning of an ontology, focusing on only one level of reality
	Crisis and adjustments in ongoing life	Discussion of the way crises and adjustments are part of social life and that activity always has the potential to end in a novel form of acting
2017	Sayings, texts and discursive phenomena	Discussing the importance of sayings and discursive phenomena from a practice theoretical point of view
	Practices and learning	Discussion of learning from a Wittgensteinian point of view and how being part of a practice is a form of learning
	Practices and people	Discussion of the relationship and dependence of people and practices

Table 7.2 Overview of exemplary empirical studies drawing on Schatzki's site ontology in management and organization studies

Author	Title	Content	Method	Empirical setting
Ahrens & Chapman (2007)	Management accounting as practice	'Situated functionality' of accounting numbers	Interviews, archival records, direct observations	Restaurant chain
Hydle (2015)	Temporal and spatial dimensions of strategising	Timespaces in an organization and their role for strategizing	Interviews, group interviews, documents, observation	Transnational professional service firm (engineering consultancy)
Jarzabkowski, Bednarek & Spee (2015)	*Making a Market for Acts of God: The Practice of Risk Trading in the Global Reinsurance Industry*	Sites and practices constituting a market	Work observations, additional field interactions (e.g. social events), interviews	Reinsurance industry
Jørgensen & Messner (2010)	Accounting & strategising: A case study from new product development	The relationship of accounting and strategizing in decisions during new product development	Interviews, archival material, participant observation	R&D intensive company
Lindberg & Rantatalo (2015)	Competence in professional practice: A practice theory analysis of police and doctors	Teleoaffective structures and general understandings of competent practitioners	Interviews	Police work and medical work
Lodhia (2015)	Exploring the transition to integrated reporting through a practice lens: An Australian customer owned bank perspective	Development and evolution of reporting, drawing on social, environmental and financial practices	Interviews and documents	Banking
Loscher (2016)	*The Management of Public Accounting Firms: Between Trustee and Commercial Logic*	The way commercial and professional practices are combined	Interviews, participant observation and documents	German public accounting
Nama & Lowe (2014)	The 'situated functionality' of accounting in private equity practices: A social 'site' analysis	Analysis of the role of accounting figures in the context of various other practices	Interviews, field interactions (e.g. public talks)	Private equity
Nicolini (2011)	Practice as the site of knowing: Insights from the field of telemedicine	The way knowing is bound to practices and sites rather than to an individual	Interviews, ethnographic observations, documents, tools and pictures	Medical work
Smets, Jarzabkowski, Burke & Spee (2015)	Reinsurance trading in Lloyd's of London: Balancing conflicting-yet-complementary logics in practice	Practitioners as competent to balance conflicting yet complementary logics	Ethnographic observations, interviews and documentary data	Reinsurance trading at Lloyd's of London

References

Ahrens, T., & Chapman, C. S. (2007). Management accounting as practice. *Accounting, Organizations and Society, 32*(1), 1–27.

Bourdieu, P. (1977). *Outline of a theory of practice*. Cambridge: Cambridge University Press.

Felin, T., Foss, N. J., & Ployhart, R. E. (2015). The microfoundations movement in strategy and organization theory. *Academy of Management Annals, 9*(1), 575–632.

Foucault, M. (1977). *Discipline and punish: The birth of the prison*. New York: Vintage Books.

Garfinkel, H. (1967) *Studies in ethnomethodology*. Englewood Cliffs, NJ: Prentice-Hall.

Giddens. A. (1984). *The constitution of society: Outline of the theory of structuration*. Cambridge: Polity Press.

Hydle, K. M. (2015). Temporal and spatial dimensions of strategizing. *Organization Studies, 36*(5), 643–663.

Jarzabkowski, P., Bednarek, R., & Cabantous, L. (2014). Conducting global team-based ethnography: Methodological challenges and practical methods. *Human Relations, 66*(1), 3–33.

Jarzabkowski, P., Bednarek, R., & Spee, P. (2015). *Making a market for acts of god: The practice of risk trading in the global reinsurance industry*. Oxford: Oxford University Press.

Jørgensen, B., & Messner, M. (2010). Accounting and strategising: A case study from new product development. *Accounting, Organizations and Society, 35*(2), 184–204.

Kaplan, S., & Orlikowski, W. J. (2013). Temporal work in strategy making. *Organization Science, 24*(4), 965–995.

Langley, A. N. N., Smallman, C., Tsoukas, H., & Van de Ven, A. H. (2013). Process studies of change in organization and management: Unveiling temporality, activity, and flow. *The Academy of Management Journal, 56*(1), 1–13.

Lindberg, O., & Rantatalo, O. (2015). Competence in professional practice: A practice theory analysis of police and doctors. *Human Relations, 68*(4), 561–582.

Lodhia, S. (2015). Exploring the transition to integrated reporting through a practice lens: An Australian customer owned bank perspective. *Journal of Business Ethics, 129*(3), 585–598.

Loscher, G. (2016). *Die Steuerung von Wirtschaftsprüfungsgesellschaften: Zwischen managementorientierter und berufsständischer Logik. Zukunftsfähige Unternehmensführung in Forschung und Praxis*. Wiesbaden: Springer Gabler.

Nama, Y., & Lowe, A. (2014). The 'situated functionality' of accounting in private equity practices: A social 'site' analysis. *Management Accounting Research, 25*(4), 284–303.

Nicolini, D. (2011). Practice as the site of knowing: Insights from the field of telemedicine. *Organization Science, 22*, 602–620.

Nicolini, D. (2012). *Practice theory, work and organization. An introduction*. Oxford: Oxford University Press.

Quattrone, P. (2004). Accounting for God: Accounting and accountability practices in the Society of Jesus (Italy, XVI–XVII centuries). *Accounting, Organizations and Society, 29*(7), 647–683.

Schatzki, T. R. (1996). *Social practices: A Wittgensteinian approach to human activity and the social*. Cambridge: Cambridge University Press.

Schatzki, T. R. (2002). *The site of the social: A philosophical account of the constitution of social life and change*. University Park: The Pennsylvania State University Press.

Schatzki, T. R. (2005). The sites of organizations. *Organization Studies, 26*, 465–484.

Schatzki, T. R. (2006). On organizations as they happen. *Organization Studies, 27*, 1863–1873.

Schatzki, T. R. (2009). Timespace and the organization of social life. In E. Shove, F. Trentman, & R. Wilk (eds) Cultures of consumption series. *Time, consumption and everyday life. Practice materiality and culture* (pp. 35–49). Oxford: Berg.

Schatzki, T. R. (2011). *The timespace of human activity: On performance, society and history as indeterminate teleological events*. Plymouth: Lexington Books.

Schatzki, T. R. (2012). A primer on practices. In J. Higgs, R. Barnett, S. Billett, M. Hutchings, & F. Trede (eds) *Practice, education, work and society: Practice-based education: Perspectives and strategies* (pp. 13–26). Rotterdam and Boston: Sense Publishers.

Schatzki, T. R. (2013). The edge of change: On the emergence, persistence, and dissolution of practices. In E. Shove, & N. Spurling (eds) *Sustainable practices: Social theory and climate change* (pp. 31–46). London: Routledge.

Schatzki, T. R. (2016a). Keeping track of large phenomena. *Geographische Zeitschrift, 104*(1), 4–24.

Schatzki, T. R. (2016b). Practice theory as flat ontology. In G. Spaargaren, D. Weenink, & M. Lamers (eds) *Practice theory and research: Exploring the dynamics of social life* (pp. 28–42). Abingdon, Oxford and New York: Routledge.

Schatzki, T. R. (2017). Sayings, texts and discursive formations. In A. Hui, T. R. Schatzki, & E. Shove (eds) *The nexus of practices: Connections, constellations, practitioners* (pp. 126–140). Abingdon, Oxford, New York: Routledge.

Schatzki, T. R. (forthcoming). On practice theory or, what's practices got to do [got to do] with it? In. P. Grootenboer, & C. Edwards-Groves (eds) *Education in an era of schooling: Critical perspectives of educational practice and action research. A Festschrift for Stephen Kemmis*. Singapore: Springer.

Schatzki, T. R., Knorr Cetina, K., & Savigny, E. v. (eds) (2001). *The practice turn in contemporary theory*. London: Routledge.

Seidl, D., & Whittington, R. (2014). Enlarging the strategy-as-practice research agenda: Towards taller and flatter ontologies. *Organization Studies, 35*(10), 1407–1421.

Smets, M., Jarzabkowski, P., Burke, G. T., & Spee, P. (2015). Reinsurance trading in Lloyd's of London: Balancing conflicting-yet-complementary logics in practice. *Academy of Management Journal, 58*, 932–970.

Weinfurtner, T., & Seidl, D. (forthcoming). Toward a spatial perspective: An integrative review of research on organizational space. *Scandinavian Journal of Management*.

Wittgenstein, L. (1953). *Philosophical investigations*. Oxford: Blackwell.

Zundel, M. (2012). Walking to learn: Rethinking reflection for management learning. *Management Learning, 44*(2), 109–126.

Zundel, M., & Kokkalis, P. (2010). Theorizing as engaged practice. *Organization Studies, 31* (9&10), 1209–1227.

8 Mary Douglas and institutions

Dean Pierides and Graham Sewell

Chapter objectives

We present a way of ordering Mary Douglas's thinking that demonstrates its continued relevance for institutional approaches to understanding organization. We extend the ways in which Douglas's writing on institutions has been used for this purpose by considering how her notions of Grid-and-Group allowed her to develop critiques of rational agency and methodological individualism.

The chapter discusses:

- The limited manner in which the new institutionalists have so far made use of Douglas's ideas and what is lost by persisting with this restricted reading
- How the insistence that there is one rationality against which all others can be measured prevents institutional analysis from understanding its own cultural biases
- How Douglas's Grid-and-Group heuristic device avoids a retreat to methodological individualism and what is gained from using it
- How Barnard's organization theory is closer to Douglas's understanding of a way of life than it is to any of the new institutionalists, whether in economics or sociology
- One way to work through select texts from Douglas's writing and proposes how to relate these texts to concepts and problems in organizational institutionalism

Introduction

In current institutional theory an institution is defined as a system of rules. Since the rules may arise spontaneously in response to a variety of problems, and perform many functions without any single overall objective, 'institution' is to be distinguished from 'organization' when that refers to a purposive arrangement for achieving a specific goal.

(Douglas, 2013a, p. 36)

If one were asked to summarize in a single sentence the central concern in all of Mary Douglas's scholarship it would be difficult to improve on the following: '[T]he relation between forms of association and the forms of moral judgment that ratify the former' (Douglas, as cited in Fardon, 1987, p. 4). The simplicity of this core argument belies the richness of Douglas's oeuvre. Strongly influenced by the idea that classifications are social conventions (Durkheim & Mauss, 1963 [1903]), Douglas (1986a) develops her own powerful theory of classification, one that has been picked up by scores of organizational scholars who study institutions. However, most of these scholars have only ever used her ideas superficially and largely in the absence of the broader theoretical edifice in which these emerge (for a discussion of this shortcoming, see Logue, Clegg & Gray, 2016). In light of this, the purpose of this chapter is to expand the scope of how Douglas's ideas might be used by organizational scholars interested in institutions.

Margaret Mary Tew was born on March 25, 1921 in San Remo and died on May 16, 2007 in London. She was raised by her mother's parents after being sent to Devon at the age of five while her parents were stationed in Burma with the British civil service. Though it was common for children of civil servants in the Far East to be sent home at such a young age, this did affect Douglas in a variety of ways, about which she would write throughout her life. Living with her grandparents she developed what she calls a 'feeling for hierarchy',[1] after experiencing the 'hierarchical home' (Douglas, 2013b, p. 299). When her mother died in 1933, she and her sister were taken back into her father's care and they were transferred to the Sacred Heart Convent in Roehampton. In this schooling system, her 'feeling' for hierarchy was further intensified and the difference between life at home and life in the convent provided a stark contrast; implicit rules in the former, and explicit rules in the latter.

At Oxford University, she chose to study philosophy, politics and economics, and, following her graduation in 1942, she was mobilized into the Colonial Office as part of the war effort. Whilst on post, she met various anthropologists and through reading their work became increasingly interested in anthropology. She returned to Oxford in 1946 to study the subject at the same time E. E. Evans-Pritchard had been appointed as Chair of Social Anthropology. In our chapter, we describe how Evans-Pritchard's ideas would allow her to theorize the feeling for hierarchy she had developed intuitively in her earlier life. In 1949, as part of her doctoral study, Douglas went to the Belgian Congo to do fieldwork among the Lele of the Kasai. She moved to University College London (UCL) in 1951, married James Douglas and in 1953 completed her doctorate. At UCL, where Daryll Forde was head of department, she first published work that was based on her African fieldwork, later extending her ideas into new areas, now publishing about food and consumption theory.

Douglas remained at UCL until 1977, after which she moved to the United States. There she was Research Scholar and later Director of Research on Culture at the Russell Sage Foundation in New York. This facilitated her collaboration with political scientist Aaron Wildavsky on the topic of risk perceptions and environmentalism before she moved again for a joint appointment across Humanities and Religious Studies at Northwestern University in 1981. At Northwestern, she returned to some of her earlier interests in religion and theology, whilst continuing to develop her ideas about hierarchy in new and interesting directions. She was a visiting professor at Yale and Princeton. Douglas left Northwestern in 1985 but continued to publish. She was awarded Commander of the Most Excellent Order of the British Empire in December 2006 shortly before her death.

We do not aim to provide a précis that readers would use in place of Douglas's original texts. Instead, we start with a discussion about how her ideas have been taken up by organizational scholars who study institutions, much in the same manner as a newcomer to the study of business and organizations might encounter her work. Next we discuss what is lost by not reading her work directly. We use this format so that we can provide a guide for how to approach Douglas's ideas directly and so that we can point to secondary literature that might be relevant for studying institutions. Our aim in doing this is to build on Douglas's legacy in the broadest way possible so that we can make room for new organizational research on institutions that will be inspired by her important contributions to the social sciences. By the same token we will avoid providing the customary list of 'suggestions for future research' because we want to reinforce the message that Douglas's books should be consulted directly by anyone seeking inspiration. If, as Douglas argues, organizational actions are understood to be related to the correspondence of forms of association and forms of moral judgement, then we hope our reader can see how Douglas provides us with a rich theory and method for better understanding the ethical tension between how organizations are and how they ought to be.

Why the new institutionalism has tried to do the thinking for us

Why would someone studying the world of business and organizations be interested in institutions? If modern organizations emerge because magic, myths and superstition are increasingly replaced by processes of intellectualization and rationalization,[2] then understanding how the rise and fall of different institutions has influenced the development of the modern world would help us better understand why organizations are the way they are. By extension, it could also help us understand why organizations are not different from how they are now or it could even help us work out how they might be different. We could simply say that understanding the institutionalized organization of life can help us make a difference (e.g. March & Olsen, 1984). Trying to understand these processes of rationalization better, Meyer and Rowan (1977) concluded that the formal organizational structures that sustain the coordination and control of activities of organizations arise in highly institutionalized contexts, as is evident in their incorporation of prevailing practices and procedures. This, in turn, increases the legitimacy and long-term survival of organizations, even if adopting these practices and procedures goes against the short-term efficacy of doing something else. They proposed that these rationalized myths arise in an institutional context alongside complex networks of social organization and exchange, which subsequently also support and sustain the diffusion of these myths. Since the publication of Meyer and Rowan's (1977) landmark article, there has been an ever-increasing interest amongst organizational scholars to understand the role of institutions in the world of business and organizations.

In their introduction to the influential edited volume *The New Institutionalism in Organizational Analysis*, DiMaggio and Powell (1991) sought amongst other things to differentiate this new institutionalism of organization theory and sociology from the new institutionalism of economics and public choice. They draw on two main arguments from Douglas's book titled *How Institutions Think* (1986a).[3] First, they build on her critique that the behavioural conventions of rational actors, on which economists and public choice theorists rely, are on their own too unstable and unsustainable to be the starting point and foundation for an institution. Her critique poses a series of questions that would be difficult for rational choice theorists to adequately answer. What prevents individuals from repeatedly misbehaving in a haphazard manner? What prevents an individual from altering a convention on a whim? And what prevents individuals from free riding? Douglas proposes that it is the relationship between behavioural conventions and cognitive conventions that can provide continuity and order and that under certain conditions, an institution can emerge from this relationship.

Second, in *How Institutions Think*, Douglas provides a theory which explains what the conditions for the emergence of an institution actually are, and, why understanding them is a necessary component for analysing the origins and continuity of any institution. Since individual people in Douglas's theorization do not determine the fit between conventions and the order of the universe, new institutionalists can follow her lead and exclude from their definition of institutions 'any purely instrumental or provisional practical arrangement that is recognized as such' (Douglas, 1986a, p. 46). Drawing on the ideas of both Émile Durkheim and Ludwik Fleck,[4] Douglas encourages us to think of an institution as a 'legitimized social grouping', its legitimacy derived from its 'fit with the nature of the universe' (Douglas, 1986a, p. 46). This analogy, between behavioural and cognitive conventions, on the one hand, and the natural order of the cosmos for a given group of people, on the other hand, is what Douglas means when she refers to a 'naturalizing analogy' (see 1986a, pp. 48, 50, 52).

Institutional theorists after the publication of DiMaggio and Powell's edited volume have demonstrated a strong preference for using only Douglas's (1986a) *How Institutions Think*, usually in a perfunctory manner, failing to explore the full implications of what it means for an analogy to become naturalized in the manner she theorizes. This is unfortunate, since, as we argue in this chapter, there is more to Douglas's thought in that particular book, and much more than that particular book on its own would reveal. One notable exception is a recent paper by Logue, Clegg and Gray (2016) that focuses on what Douglas's core arguments can contribute to the theorizing of institutional logics. Next, we briefly introduce what institutional logics are, we summarize the advances that Logue et al. (2016) make using Douglas's ideas and then we consider the broader contributions of *How Institutions Think* in order to identify just how much more we could glean from this book alone.

Scholarship on institutional logics predominantly takes as its starting point the chapter by Friedland & Alford (1991) titled 'Bringing society back in: Symbols, practices, and institutional contradictions' published in the DiMaggio & Powell edited book that we mentioned above. In that chapter, Friedland & Alford (1991) argued that institutional logics are the symbolic and material patterns that organize the institutionalized social world and that these logics constitute 'society as a potentially contradictory interinstitutional system' (Friedland & Alford, 1991, p. 240), an idea that was later developed to provide a meta-theory of society which aims to explain 'actors' choices for sensemaking, the vocabulary they use to motivate action, and their sense of self and identity' (Thornton, Ocasio, & Lounsbury, 2012, p. 2).[5] Like DiMaggio and Powell (1991), Friedland and Alford draw on Douglas's critique of rational choice theory and her insistence on the importance of cognition but they also criticize Douglas for under-theorizing the incompatibility of different institutions, attributing this lacuna to her concern with establishing 'the basis of social solidarity in shared categories of knowledge' (Friedland & Alford, 1991, p. 262, fn. 22). Boxing Douglas in the consensus category, within a consensus versus conflict dualism is, perhaps, too hasty.

As Mary Douglas's biographer, Richard Fardon (1999, pp. 210–211), tells us, *How Institutions Think* is only one side of the coin. Her essay on *Cultural Bias*

(Douglas, 1978; 1982b, pp. 183–254) is the other. In fact, if we start with yet another of her essays titled 'Passive voice theories in religious sociology' (Douglas, 1982b, pp. 1–15) and couple this with *Cultural Bias*, what we start to see is that accountability is foundational for social solidarity and it provides the mechanism by which voluntary, intended agency is granted by everyone, collectively, to every individual. This mutually agreed form for individual responsibility is the flip side of the attribution of blame.

Logue et al. (2016, p. 1602) remind us that the original conception of institutional logics that was developed by Friedland and Alford was centrally concerned 'with how analogies ground new practices and narratives achieving naturalness' but that 'this insight has faded from more recent institutional work'. Although some organizational scholars have used analogies to study institutions (e.g. Cornelissen, Holt & Zundel, 2011; Etzion & Ferraro, 2010), their accounts have been much narrower in their scope than Logue et al. (2016) suggest they could be if we follow Douglas instead. Where organizational scholars have so far treated analogies only based on representations-in-use (e.g. text, images), Douglas (1986a, p. 45) would urge us to consider analogies as foundational for institutions, 'in reason and in nature'. In short, where organizational scholars have thus far merely treated analogies as discursive formations that accompany institutions, we think that organizational scholars could go further and study them as cosmologies on which all institutional life is founded. Importantly, this expansion of representation beyond the bounds of the narrow psychologism of individual cognition is an invitation to explore how membership of social entities – in this instance, organizations – involves a consideration of actions that are not simply the enactment of schemas or logics. In short, Douglas is advocating a European social anthropology of institutions drawing on Durkheim and Mauss rather than a US cultural anthropology of institutions drawing on Boas and Benedict. While the former would take its object of study as the social collective itself, the latter has a tendency to reduce the social to an epiphenomenon of rules of behaviour as they apply to individuals.

The intellectual antecedents of a social anthropology of institutions

The intellectual backdrop to what was happening in British anthropology before World War II can be conveniently caricatured as a struggle between Malinowski's functionalism at the London School of Economics (LSE) and an emerging structuralism at Oxford (see Goody, 1995, pp. 68–76; Kuper, 1983, pp. 6–93). Douglas went up to Oxford in 1939 to study as a member of the Society for Home Students (later St Anne's College), which allowed her to attend lectures and tutorials across the university, including those given by Alfred Radcliffe-Brown who had been appointed to the foundational chair in social anthropology two years earlier.

The attempt to establish a true 'science of the social' at Oxford was self-consciously a rejection of the individualism of Malinowski's *Argonauts of the Western Pacific* (1922). Here Malinowski aimed to show that the Trobriand Islanders had customs and laws that were entirely rational in so far as they met an individual's need to make sense of their world. Describing it as a 'classic of descriptive ethnography' (Evans-Pritchard, 1951, p. 93), Malinowski's student Evans-Pritchard was nonetheless critical of this effort because it treats 'only a part of social life for particular and limited problems of investigation, taking the rest into consideration only in so far as it is relevant to these problems' (1951, p. 96); a kind of functional analysis that he similarly identifies in Margaret Mead's *Coming of Age in Samoa* (1929).

Between 1926 and 1938, Evans-Pritchard was doing fieldwork amongst the Azande in Sudan and the Nuer in Kenya. Unlike prior anthropologists, such as Malinowski, who studied much smaller, island populations in Oceania, Evans-Pritchard and his contemporaries who were studying African societies were confronted with the vast governmental systems of tribes and nations which colonial authorities were having trouble disciplining. The lack of centralized political institutions amongst the Nuer, for example, is one of the reasons that Evans-Pritchard was led to abandon the Malinowskian mode of generalizing from single societies and toward Radcliffe-Brown's comparative approach. Evans-Pritchard and Fortes (see Goody, 1995, pp. 58–67), however, also departed from Radcliffe-Brown's position by emphasizing

> The lineage as part of the system of political relationships, rather than as a mode of organizing personal relationships ... [so that the] term 'social structure' came to connote the structure of relationships between groups and, in Fortes's work, offices, rather than between persons.
>
> (Kuper, 1983, p. 86)

Radcliffe-Brown and Evans-Pritchard also disagreed about whether anthropology was to be considered a science or part of the humanities.

The 'new paradigm', as Kuper (1983, p. 84) has referred to it, thus ushered structuralism into British anthropology, creating a rift between those who followed Malinowski at the LSE and those who followed the Oxford tradition established by Radcliffe-Brown and developed further by Evans-Pritchard and Meyer Fortes. Of course, it is worth noting that in spite of their differences what both Malinowski and Radcliffe-Brown were doing was constituted as the science of society, a commitment which many succeeding generations of cultural anthropologists would drop, thereby returning anthropology to the humanities. The new paradigm marked a shift from function to meaning. Structural analysis meant 'the integration of abstractions from social life' (Evans-Pritchard, 1951, p. 96). It was a shift from 'the concrete, institution-based functionalism of Malinowski ... [to] a sociological, structuralist position' (Kuper, 1983, p. 97). This new British structuralism was later to be developed by Edmund Leach and Rodney Needham, and even later by Mary Douglas (Kuper, 1983, p. 169).

Like Durkheim, Evans-Pritchard aimed to show that societies otherwise considered primitive are not irrational and plagued by superstition. Instead, the people in these societies follow a logic that makes sense *to them*, that is rational *to them*. If an anthropologist could understand their witchcraft, they could explain misfortune rather than treat people's belief about it as irrational. In adopting a sociological position, anthropologists following Radcliffe-Brown took social facts, in Durkheim's sense, to be central to understanding this system (Stocking, 1984; 1995). Social life is analogous to organic life in so far as the function of a social institution is the correspondence between that institution and the conditions of the existence of the social. Institutions are situated within a social structure that is made up of individuals who are finitely connected into an integrated whole (see Evans-Pritchard, 1951, p. 54; Radcliffe-Brown, 1935, p. 394).

Where Evans-Pritchard (1965, p. 111) parted ways with Durkheim is in believing that anthropology 'deals with relations, not with origins and essences' as Durkheim did. We now turn to Douglas's (1980) book on Evans-Pritchard to show how she takes all of these different sociological elements in a direction that is particularly useful for investigating institutions. Evans-Pritchard was, of course, hugely influential in Douglas's thinking, a personal friend of hers and an intellectual compass of sorts. Her book on Evans-Pritchard was written after both of the two influential books in which she synthesizes her ideas, *Purity and Danger* (1966) and *Natural Symbols* (1970), and must therefore be read as a retrospective account (Fardon, 1999, p. 33). According to Fardon (1999, p. 26), 'at different stages in the development of her own thought Mary Douglas was able to turn back to Evans-Pritchard to experience again the recognition that he had been there before her in important respects'. Although her 'interpretation of what was of value in Evans-Pritchard work ... is one with which few will agree' (Schneider, 1981, p. 721) and for some even 'turns out to resemble Mary Douglas' herself (Beidelman, 1980), we would suggest that Douglas's work can be approached from a different point of view.

Interestingly, the second chapter of her book on Evans-Pritchard focuses on 'human mental faculties' and can be seen as a restorative account of British and French psychology for the purposes of the sociology of knowledge. The former had failed 'to develop a sociological dimension to their experimental thinking' and the latter had failed to 'benefit from the British methodological advances' (Douglas, 1980, p. 28). Evans-Pritchard, she argues, shows us a way forward. What differentiates Evans-Pritchard from any other scholar focusing on 'the power to suspend attention ... was his confidence that the selective principles were to be found in social institutions' (1980, p. 27). This was precisely the argument made by Durkheim and Mauss, and Douglas tells us that Evans-Pritchard's life can therefore be presented as a tribute to them.[6] The focus on mental faculties might seem ridiculous were it not for this point which directs us to the relationship between cognition and institutions which Douglas herself would later come to tackle.

If philosopher Immanuel Kant was right that the mind could organize immediate experience, how can any knowledge system be explained without defaulting to a transcendental divinity or collapsing all explanation into the individual?[7] Durkheim resolves the tension between classical empiricism and Kantian *apriorism* by rendering epistemology sociological. This was Durkheim's great insight. His ingenious solution is summarized in the conclusion of a book Durkheim wrote with his nephew Marcel Mauss which aimed to demonstrate that primitive classifications are essentially no different from modern classifications: 'they are systems of hierarchized notions' and they 'have a purely speculative purpose' (Durkheim & Mauss, 1963 [1903], p. 81). Taking *How Institutions Think* as our starting point, we can start to see that Douglas picks up on Durkheim's effort to understand pre-modern classification and she extends this to the modern world. What needs to be understood in any specific analysis is how a classificatory enterprise is matched with social requirements, ultimately producing the foundations of a sociological epistemology (Douglas, 1986a, pp. 62–63).

Almost an entire century later, the problem that Evans-Pritchard poses about human mental faculties still haunts us. Psychologists, economists and rational theorists of all flavours still insist in various ways that there is one rationality against which all others can be measured. Ultimately, however, both institutions and organizations are epiphenomena of ongoing human habits and experience (cf. Dewey, 1922). But according to Kant's formulation, experience is structured by a priori categories and intuition that comprise the necessary and universal basis for all knowledge. The link then must be that attention is controlled by principles that are derived from interests, which can only be constituted in society, not the individual mind.[8] By attention, Evans-Pritchard probably meant something similar to what organizational institutionalists mean (e.g. Thornton & Ocasio, 2008, pp. 113–114), since he was in conversation with neurologists and psychologists such as Frederick Bartlett, Henry Head and Charles Sherrington. However, the mechanism Evans-Pritchard was proposing undermines the one the new institutionalists would inherit from psychology because it locates interests in society rather than the individual mind. Accordingly, the 'contrast between primitives and ourselves is much exaggerated by pretending that we think scientifically all the time ... [and to] prevent that error the proper method is to compare like with like, our everyday thought with their everyday thought' (Douglas, 1980, p. 31).[9]

What can be gleaned from Douglas's interpretation of Evans-Pritchard's ethnographic work that is helpful for understanding institutions? Douglas tells us that Evans-Pritchard was interested in how the things that the Azande and the Nuer do in moments of misfortune can be used to study accountability. Since misfortune must be explained somehow, people resort to systems that require them to either blame or accept responsibility. The movement from consciousness to action is thoroughly institutionalized and accordingly requires the invocation of existences and powers that differ from one system to another. Methodologically, the researcher traces this accountability as it surfaces. When institutions are guarded an 'awesome cosmos' is established and 'the initial convention is buried' (Douglas, 1999, p. xv). As Douglas says about Durkheim's model, delusion is necessary and this entire setup creates the delusion that institutions confer certainty. The analyst who idly goes along with this implicit assumption fails to understand the process by which institutions are created and maintained.

Grid-and-Group

'It is easy to be scathing about whether communities divide into hierarchical groups, egalitarian groups, individualist groups: They do not, and no one ever said they do' (Douglas, 1999, p. 225).

In *Purity and Danger* (1966), Douglas built on the critique of 'primitive mentality' we have outlined above (Evans-Pritchard, 1934) and famously showed the universality of cognitive blocks on matter that is 'out of place'. She showed that rituals of cleanliness in contemporary households are underwritten by classification in much the same way as rituals related to defilement in societies described as primitive. In other words, from the point of view of studying social controls on institutionalized classification, there is no difference between primitive and contemporary societies. All institutions and organizations impose a classificatory order but the specific classifications in each do vary. What was missing was a parsimonious tool with which comparisons can be made. This new problem enters Douglas's repertoire in conversation with the work of sociologist of education Basil Bernstein.

Douglas took inspiration from a paper delivered by Bernstein at the London Institute of Education, titled 'Ritual in education'. Bernstein's argument was that speech acts were not psychologically determined but rather that forms of speech are subjected to controls on social position and social individualization. He had developed a model for understanding cultural transmission that struck a chord for Douglas because it lent credence to the argument that one did not need to go and study remote peoples to learn about what it means to be human. It also promised to introduce a potential dynamism to her earlier model. Thus, after meeting Bernstein, Douglas proceeded to apply his ideas about 'speech, thought and social structure to the study of religion' (Douglas, 2001, p. 113), updating her earlier work on purification. Starting with *Natural Symbols* (1970), which was a product, at least in part, of many discussions with Bernstein, she began to revise one of the central theses of *Purity and Danger*. Bernstein urged her to consider those people who can go on with few concerns about matter that is out of place; where do they belong? This is when she started to differentiate classification systems.

In this work we start to see that values, the division of labour and social organization are differently upheld depending on the culture that produced them as classification systems. Throughout different editions of the book, features of this 'grid-group' typology, as she would eventually call it, draw inspiration from different aspects of Bernstein's work. What ties them together, however, is the work of Durkheim, especially his book on suicide (Durkheim, 1951). The common influence can be summarized as follows: 'different forms of suicide are the products of different degrees of group regulation (or constraint) and group bonding (or affection)' (Richards, 2008, p. 406). As its name suggests, the grid-group schematic has two dimensions for grounding ideation in social life. Fardon summarizes how these appeared in the first edition of *Natural Symbols*:

> The first of these, 'group' – the experience of a bounded social unit – ... is prerequisite to the classic instance of the Durkheimian hypothesis in which society is expressed through ritual ... [G]roup is independent of the second variable, which Douglas calls 'grid'... On this first definition, grid consists of 'rules which relate one person to others on an ego-centred basis' (Douglas, 1970, p. viii, as cited) ... Group evokes boundary, an enclosing circle; grid may either picture the individual as a nodal point from which relations radiate, or else place the individual within a 'cross-hatching' of rules, distinctions and regulations. The thought of individuals grounded in these social dimensions is channelled into the 'grooves' worn by the thoughts of previous residents of the same institutional space. The formal characteristics of both the 'thought-style' and the institutional space within which it arises are similar.
>
> (Fardon, 1999, p. 111)

This sets up three conditions: *group and grid*, so that boundaries and internal order are well established; *group not grid*, so that boundaries are rigid but there is internal disarray; and *grid not group*, so that ego-centred networks prevail. In the second edition of the book, Douglas extends this. Justification for a system of knowledge is given by a cosmology, which elaborates principles and the associated conduct that follows.[10] The group dimension had to be enlarged to accommodate for the kinds of demands that Bernstein saw were being placed on students: '[t]he difference between strong boundary maintenance and weak boundary maintenance in education is analogous to the difference between ritual and anti-ritual in types of religion' (Douglas, 1996a, p. ix). This extends the central thesis of *Purity and*

Danger in new and interesting ways, as Douglas explains in one of her many acknowledgements to Bernstein:[11]

> In that study I emphasized the communication function of all boundings of experience, without facing the empirical fact that some societies persist very well without strongly bounded cognitive categories and some tolerate anomaly more easily than others. *Natural Symbols* is an attempt to answer questions raised by myself from the programme of the earlier book.
>
> (Douglas, 1996a, p. ix)

These changes maintain parsimony in the schema while introducing many new explanatory dimensions to it, including not least the capacity to place societies in more than one quadrant and a dynamism that accounts for different lengths of time. In sum, as we tend toward a system of shared classifications (upon the vertical axis), it becomes increasingly possible to exercise control through classification. As we tend toward the origin and toward private classification, the associated control also changes (either through brute force or strong personal relationships). The ego with respect to others (the horizontal axis) varies according to whether control is being exercised against others (left) or by others (right). In other words, control is not the same concept in all locations of the schema.

In this diagram (see Figure 8.1), Douglas is clear that she is reducing, rearranging and adding to Bernstein's model but that ultimately she is returning to the intentions behind it. It is a model for 'deriving cosmology from control systems, or rather showing how cosmology is a part of the social bond, according to [three] principles' (1996a, p. 57): (1) the entire cosmos and the place of humans

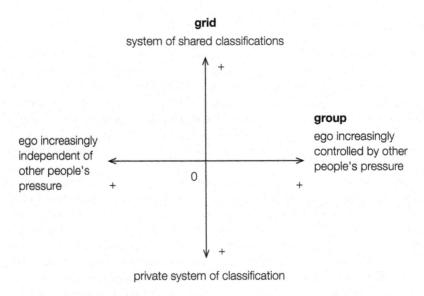

Figure 8.1 Grid-and-group diagram

Source: Adapted from Douglas (1996a, p. 60)

in it has to match up with the control system imposing it; (2) the medium of control (speech codes and rituals) interacts with the control system; and (3) the coding of the medium matches up with the control system. The first of these principles, as Douglas notes, is attempting to address what Weber refers to as legitimation. When she combines this with the second and third principles, to produce the concepts of Grid-and-Group, we have descriptive tools for addressing 'the way that social pressures reach an individual and structure his consciousness' (Douglas, 1996a, p. 86).

The Bernstein–Douglas diagrams had wide-ranging influence in many different circles, not least of which, amongst a group of scholars who sought to develop this line of work explicitly (Douglas, 1982a). What does the Grid-and-Group typology do? According to Fardon (1987, p. 5), it operationalizes:

> The correlations which should exist between types of social interactions and the moral and cognitive universes in which they took place. To each social environment there should be a corresponding world of ideas. 'Cultural bias' would tally with social experience, and social experience could be represented in terms of the qualities of relationships and the boundedness of social networks.

For us the importance of Grid-and-Group is not that it should be deployed blindly as a tool to classify human behaviour; rather it is a compelling illustration of the explanatory importance Douglas attaches to our membership of a particular social collective when considering how we try to rationalize our behaviour with respect to others deemed to be inside or outside that social collective. In a sense, this is Douglas's own attempt to deal with the familiar structure/agency dualism, but in a way that makes space for a treatment of institutions that avoids a retreat to methodological individualism.

Beyond methodological individualism and the myth of the rational actor

Melvin A. Eggers, the Chancellor of Syracuse University, wrote the foreword of *How Institutions Think*[12] and in it he notes that the book is the product of five lectures which Mary Douglas gave as part of the Abrams lecture series at Syracuse.[13] The head of the lecture series planning committee was Guthrie S. Birkhead, Professor of Public Administration and Political Science and Dean of the Maxwell School of Citizenship and Public Affairs. The other members of the committee were the Vice Chancellor, the Dean of the School of Management, a Syracuse law professor, the Chairman of the University's Board of Trustees and the President of the Exxon Education Foundation. That Douglas would be chosen by this committee is telling of not only who respected Douglas's contributions to academic knowledge but also those whom Douglas was willing to engage with through her ideas.

The lecture series was funded by the Exxon Education Foundation in memory of Frank W. Abrams who was Chairman of the Board of the Standard Oil Company of New Jersey. Abrams is worth mentioning in this context because of his commitment to responsible and professional management, which he believed could be achieved when 'individual objectives ... are identified with the common good' (Abrams, 1951, p. 34). According to Swanson (2008, p. 235), Abrams's call – for

executives to accept their responsibilities to society by adopting a professional attitude toward a wide variety of stakeholders – has been credited with influencing the
development of stakeholder theory and the role of executive leaders in corporate
social responsibility. Abrams's commitment to civic duty echoes a form of responsible management that one of his contemporaries, Chester Barnard, tried to develop
throughout his career. Barnard made some of the most important contributions to
our understanding of management and organizations to date (Perrow, 1986), but
his work has largely fallen out of favour. Douglas saw similarities in this part of
Barnard's work with her own interests but identified major shortcomings in the
way that one of Barnard's central concerns had been interpreted by subsequent generations of economists and management scholars. She took them on and tried to
vindicate Barnard.

In the spring of 1988, economist Oliver E. Williamson, who just over two decades
later would become the recipient of the Sveriges Riksbank Prize in Economic Sciences
in Memory of Alfred Nobel, held a visiting post as Professor of Economics and
Transamerica Professor of Business Administration at the University of California,
Berkeley. As is often customary with such appointments, he was asked to convene an
interdisciplinary seminar, the theme of which became Chester Barnard's classic book
The Functions of the Executive (1938). The contributions to this seminar were eventually published as a book entitled *Organization Theory: From Chester Barnard to
the Present and Beyond* (1990; expanded edition published in 1995). Alongside
contributors more easily identifiable as management scholars, such as James
March, Dick Scott, Glenn Carroll and Jeff Pfeffer, Mary Douglas has a chapter
entitled 'Converging on autonomy: Anthropology and institutional economics'. It
is the 1995 version we refer to, although it was also reproduced under the title
'Autonomy and opportunism' in her book, *Risk and Blame: Essays in Cultural
Theory* (1992).

Douglas's focus on Barnard is, at first blush, rather unpromising, for what
could such a venerable commentator possibly offer for today's organizational
researcher? According to Douglas, however, what Barnard was trying to achieve –
an adequate theory of the interaction of individuals with the organization they
work in – had largely eluded us for decades. Still, Barnard did offer
a rudimentary theory that links the purposes of members of organizations with
the purposes of their organizations. The problem for Douglas is that readers of
Barnard's work had relied on an economistic view of human agency that has
achieved its most developed status in the transactions costs approach of Oliver
Williamson.[14] As such, how *homo economicus* maintains his autonomy in an
organization for them is a matter of rational choice, i.e. establishing equilibrium
between the utility of self-interested behaviour and the pursuit of collective goals.
Doing so bespeaks a methodological individualism founded on an 18th-century
notion of autonomy that is still evident in economics and social theory alike
where people rationally choose their ideas, unlike primitives who are bound by
the stultifying effects of culture. Such interpretation went against the grain of
Douglas's critiques of rational agency and methodological individualism, which
we introduced above. It also betrays Barnard's original attack on *homo economicus* and his attempt to develop organization theory that is closer to Douglas's
understanding of a way of life than it is to any of the new institutionalists (cf. du
Gay, 2015), whether in economics or sociology.[15]

Douglas contends that this attempt to relate the structure of individual goals to the organization is founded on impossibility. This starting point gets in the way of any attempt to relate the structure of individual goals to the goals of an organized social environment, such as an organization. It is a sleight of hand because it is based on something that cannot be known: the genuine desires of the actor. Nevertheless, maintaining the conceit that economic actors behave according to some internal rational calculus of cost has undeniably been very successful, at least in a performative sense. Thus, unacceptably high costs for a particular choice will make a rational being change his or her mind about the ordering of their goals vis-à-vis those of the organization without the need to consider any social influences. In other words, it treats individuals' objectives as independent of those of other people or the organization. Indeed, the only environmental factors that need be considered are expressed through the price setting of the market; preferences arise mysteriously from within the individual (Wildavsky, 1987). In terms of classifying organization, the implications are stark in that we end up with Williamson's binary choice of either hierarchy or market. Douglas, however, proposes a way of classifying organizations using an anthropological approach that relies on seeing them as systems of shared meaning that afford their members more or less autonomy while simultaneously defining what that autonomy consists in.

This is where Grid-and-Group analysis comes into its own. Drawing on the work of her one-time student, Gerald Mars, Douglas shows that different organizational arrangements are associated with alternative economies of reward and esteem. Although economists since Adam Smith have acknowledged that the esteem in which others hold us is part of the calculus of cost, this has been limited to economizing around transactions and in this sense Williamson is simply following a venerable tradition. In contrast, Mars shows a parallel economy of personal utility can exist, based on four characteristic shared understandings of the interaction of opportunistic behaviour and mutual esteem. Importantly these play out across the dimensions of Grid-and-Group to capture the social environment that affects the relations between an organization's members by mapping onto easily apprehensible notions of structure and boundary. While Group represents where the boundary between insiders and outsiders lies, Grid is a measure of the extent to which those on the inside have to interact with those on the outside insulated from those on the inside.

An exemplary illustration of the Grid-and-Group typology in *Natural Symbols* (1973a) is David Bloor's (1978) analysis of how the discipline of mathematics responds to cultural differences (see also: Barnes, 1983). Bloor looks at the organization of mathematics departments in 19th-century Germany and shows that there is a correspondence between their institutional form, on the one hand, and the curriculum and their chosen research topics, on the other hand. Drawing on Lakatos's (1963) study of the way in which German mathematical departments dealt with subsequent challenges to Euler's formulae concerning complex polyhedra, Bloor shows how a group of people bound together by a set of common intellectual principles deal with challenges to their world view. Much in the same way Douglas looked at rituals of cleanliness or defilement, Bloor is able to show that organization corresponds to classification schemes.

The key insight that Bloor takes from Douglas to establish this line of institutional reasoning is that members of social groups understand the world through the categories they derive from their shared intellectual and material resources. This is where institutions crash into the messy world of human experience and here the key question arises: what happens when members of the group encounter an anomaly (or what Lakatos called a 'Monster') that does not neatly fall into one of the existing categories they use on a day-to-day basis? For Lakatos this was a polyhedron that did not accord with Euler's formulae, which meant that the formulae themselves needed revision or the monster had to be redefined. But what passes for a monster in 19th-century geometry also goes for today's organizations. For example, how do we classify forms of organization that are neither captured by the rigidities of formal bureaucracy nor by the anarchy of the unfettered market? This is a challenge for organization studies and other disciplines that are so wedded to this simple binary choice. Small and isolated groups of scholars who do not have the intellectual and material resources nor the autonomy associated with the great European and North American universities (i.e. low Grid/high Group) would have good reason to fear these monsters as abominations and avoid the challenges they pose to their comfortably simple view of the world (an act of 'Monster Barring', as Bloor puts it). In contrast, larger and better resourced groups of scholars – well-credentialed members of the intellectual mainstream if you like – are much better placed to accommodate monsters simply by creating new sub-disciplines with suitably revised theoretical and empirical instruments. This is, nevertheless, still a conservative strategy of high Grid/high Group that attempts to control disruption to its intellectual world view by containing the monster, rather than by embracing it (according to Bloor an act of 'Monster Adjustment' or, perhaps more graphically, a practice of sweeping the problem under the carpet, as Douglas describes it). This is because the autonomy of Monster Adjusters is constrained by their membership of the very community that is the source of most of their privileges. The scholars who are most receptive to the challenges posed by an anomaly, however, are those who have both the material and intellectual resources and the autonomy (i.e., low Grid/low Group) to indulge in what Bloor calls 'Monster Embracing' activity. In this case the presence of an anomaly is not a threat to be ignored or closed down but is an opportunity for individuals to advance their career and enhance their status vis-à-vis other organizational scholars by proposing a new category of organization. Of course, if sufficient numbers come to accept this new formulation, it becomes the new orthodoxy and effectively the institution has changed.

Categories are developed to address organizational problems, problems that are the product of usually implicit institutional processes. Norms then emerge from organization. If we follow Bloor's analysis of various forms of organizing which uses Douglas's Grid-and-Group typology together with Douglas's consideration of ritual, we can significantly expand the institutional analysis of categories from merely looking at vocabularies (Loewenstein, Ocasio & Jones, 2012), or temporally protracted rituals (Tracey & Creed, 2017) and myths (Sewell, 2018), to capture the full anthropological richness of organizational experience. An institutional analysis of this sort would thus yield a noticeably enriched understanding of organizations and undoubtedly displace the overly determined individual extant institutional analysis inherits from the weakest assumptions of psychology and economics.

Conclusion: how institutions really think

> Nearly the whole effort of British social anthropology ... was developed under the assumption that organization results from the process of adapting categories of thought. When I write that common categories are the basis of the social bond, reviewing anthropologists castigate me for stating the obvious.
>
> (Douglas, 1995, p. 104)

The preface that Douglas wrote for *How Institutions Think* provides a good a place to finish for our purposes. Here she is upfront about her attack on ideas of human cognition that lack sociological awareness and on the weaknesses of institutional analysis in economics. Indeed, as she pointedly says, 'Not just any busload or haphazard crowd of people deserves the name of society' (Douglas, 1986a, p. 9). This much is consistent with the lessons that organizational institutionalists take from the book. But she then explains that the lectures from which the book is drawn repeat ideas she had already developed in her earlier work but in the book these are restated with the aim of shedding new light on them, clarifying them, making them more persuasive and refining their delivery. Douglas goes even further and suggests that there is an important link between *How Institutions Think* and her previous writing to date that responds to her critics. This link is repeated at various points throughout her work, reminding us that all her different books make incremental modifications to the others. In the table below we attempt (with an obvious sense of irony) to classify her advice and the advice of her critics and commentators to produce a rough guide on how to approach the relationship between different books (for elaborated versions of many of the same points, see: Fardon, 1987; 1999; Mamadouh, 1999). This is neither a complete bibliography of Douglas's work, nor a definitive guide; it is just one way to work through select texts and relate them to concepts and problems in organizational institutionalism (see Table 8.1). We present this as a thematic rather than strictly chronological approach to Douglas's writings; something that is particularly important, as she was apt to draw heavily on previous work in complex ways. We look forward to seeing institutional analyses of organization that are centrally inspired by Douglas's important ideas and hope that our discussion assists in achieving this objective.

End-of-chapter exercises

1. Think about the ways in which individuals are classified in and by organizations. How did these forms of classification come about? How does it affect the people who are classified in this way? Must we accept such classification or can we resist them?
2. Carefully consider Douglas's concepts of Grid-and-Group and think about how they might be used by you to understand your position in a social group and your relationship to others inside and outside the group.
3. If institutions are social constructions, then, conceivably, there could be an infinite number of different ones, yet so few alternatives seem to present

themselves at any one time. Why do you think this is case? How can Douglas help us to answer this question?

4. What alternatives are there to thinking of individuals as examples of *homo economicus* (i.e. the utility maximizing, self-interested, rational actor)?

Glossary

Durkheim (1858–1917)   A prominent and influential French sociologist who sought to explain how and why societies were able to maintain their integrity in a modern world in which traditional sources maintaining coherence and stability such as magic and religion no longer held sway.

Institution   Organizational studies refers to institutions as complex social forms that reproduce themselves. An organization is thus itself an institution but an organization's members live across many others such as family, religions, the legal system, governments, etc. For institutionalism to be a meaningful contribution to our understanding of organizations, however, it must be able to explain how they emerge, endure, change and are ultimately replaced. In this sense, institutional analysis focuses on how individuals create but are also constrained by things like organizational structures (e.g. bureaucratic hierarchy), systems of rules, and taken-for-granted ways of behaving.

Methodological individualism   The claim that social phenomena are best explained by showing how they result from the actions of individuals. In turn, those actions are best explained by developing an understanding of the specific intentional states that motivate the individual actors. As a form of atomism it is most closely associated with the work of Max Weber but it has become the dominant epistemological approach in many social science disciplines today, especially economics and social psychology. It stands in opposition to Emile Durkheim's notion of methodological holism where social phenomena cannot easily be explained by reducing them to the actions of individuals.

Naturalization   A form of legitimization where a group tries to justify its preferred social arrangements by claiming they are a natural state of affairs. This may be strengthened by claiming additional support from ostensibly scientific evidence. For example, evolutionary psychology legitimates prevailing social arrangements by claiming they are part of our inherited human nature.

Rational actor   The idea of rational actor can be traced back to the origins of Western philosophy in ancient Greece, but it is now most closely associated with a post-Enlightenment notion of humans who assess the costs and benefits of their action before making a decision. A variant of this in the limited circumstances of economic exchange is the rational, utility maximizing, self-interested actor sometimes known as *homo economicus*.

Social anthropology   An approach to the study of societies and cultures that focuses on the composition of social institutions and their interrelationships.

Appendix

Table 8.1 A thematic presentation of Mary Douglas's major works as they relate to the study of institutions

Title (reference)	A description of the contribution	Our reflection of the contribution	Implications for institutionalism
How Institutions Think (Douglas, 1986a)	Establishes presuppositions and foundations. Points an accusing finger at professional blind spots and rooted resistance. A post hoc introduction or prolegomenon to *Risk Acceptability*. *How Institutions Think* is only one side of the coin. Her essay on *Cultural Bias* (Douglas, 1978; 1982b, pp. 183–254) is the other	Develops a theoretical and logical anchoring that presents a coherent argument about the social control of cognition (for background and context, see Douglas, 2013b). Start with her essay entitled *Passive Voice Theories in Religious Sociology* (Douglas, 1982b, pp. 1–15) and couple this with *Cultural Bias*. Accountability is foundational for social solidarity and it provides the mechanism by which voluntary, intended agency is granted by everyone, collectively, to every individual. This mutually agreed form for individual responsibility is the flip side of the attribution of blame	An institutional theory that can interpret the multiple interactions that individuals have with the organization in which they work that relies on the actual experiences of humans instead of the now-common abstractions that are too often made about individuals (for an important critique of these abstractions, which has still not adequately been answered but would be if our propositions are developed, see Willmott, 2011)
Implicit Meanings (Douglas, 1975)	An introduction to Douglas's thinking in three parts	Boundaries can be used forensically because they reveal how order is created	The capacity to compare institutions across cultures without resorting to ethnocentric assumptions about individuals (a problem that was articulated by Meyer, 2008)
Edward Evans-Pritchard (Douglas, 1980) *Thought Styles* (Douglas, 1996b)	The allocation of responsibility for misfortune Why different people reason differently in everyday life		A 'forensic' method for tracing how accountability is allocated by institutional thinking (on method and for a discussion about using risk, see Douglas, 1990)

(Continued)

Table 8.1 (Cont.)

Title (reference)	A description of the contribution	Our reflection of the contribution	Implications for institutionalism
Purity and Danger (Douglas, 1966)	An attempt to generalize from Africa to our own condition	Classification in different societies as this relates to social conventions	Case studies for: (1) understanding Douglas's early formulation of the dynamics between classification and order; and (2) how detailed descriptions of social organization can be achieved
Rules and Meanings (Douglas, 1973b)	A reader that reinforces the argument of *Purity and Danger*		
The Lele of the Kasai (Douglas, 1963)	A collection of ethnographic writings from her fieldwork on the Lele that provides an analysis of their organizational form		
Natural Symbols (Douglas, 1970)	Introduces Grid-and-Group to describe the relationship between social classification and membership	Operationalizes the earlier theory of how social order and the behavioural/cognitive conventions cohere to make a world	A primer for understanding how Grid-and-Group can be used as a heuristic device for analysing different kinds of cultural bias that would be compared when doing institutional analysis. A wide range of secondary sources can be read alongside this (e.g. Law, 1986; Thompson, Grendstad, & Selle, 1999; Wuthnow et al., 1984)
Cultural Bias (Douglas, 1978)	Summary and refinement of Grid-and-Group		
Essays in the Sociology of Perception (Douglas, 1982a)	A collection of essays that apply Douglas's model to a wide range of topics		
The World of Goods (Douglas & Isherwood, 1996)	Extends the argument to consumption		
Risk Acceptability According to the Social Sciences (Douglas, 1986b)	Extends the argument to judgements about risk. Risk acceptability is an introduction to *Risk and Culture* (see also: Douglas, 2013a)	Shows how the anthropological analysis of public beliefs can be extended to our own case	
Risk and Culture (Douglas & Wildavsky, 1982)			
Risk and Blame (Douglas, 1992)			
Missing Persons (Douglas & Ney, 1998)	Her theory of personhood and agency (see important discussion by Munro, 1997)	Against the critique of reductionism and an oversocialized individual (cf. Wrong, 1962)	The criticism of the passive voice could easily be extended and applied to organizational institutionalism and all its variants
In the Active Voice (Douglas, 1982b)	A collection of older essays that impress the necessity of not treating humans as passive and impersonal objects		

Notes

1 Douglas (2013b, pp. 15–36) describes this 'feeling for hierarchy' in a lecture she gives when she receives the Marianist award on October 9, 2001 to honour her as 'a Roman Catholic whose work has made a major contribution to the intellectual life'. It is important to note that one of Douglas's overall interests is in cultural bias, so rather than adopting a pro-hierarchical or anti-hierarchical attitude herself, she wants to understand what kind of culture leads to such attitudes.

2 Max Weber borrows the term (*Entzauberung*) from Friedrich Schiller to refer to the 'disenchantment' of the world, in a process of transformation from traditional to complex societies. He makes the analysis of this process one of the core problems he pursues throughout his work.

3 DiMaggio's own ideas about cultural entrepreneurship owe much to Mary Douglas's early thinking about classification and framing (especially Douglas, 1966, and the influence of Bernstein after this), as developed in her 'Mass Media and Mythology' seminar at the NYU Institute for the Humanities (see acknowledgments in DiMaggio, 1982, p. 49; also fn. 3, p. 35).

4 Four important thinkers who set the way for *How Institutions Think* are named in the preface: anthropologists E. E. Evans-Pritchard and Claude Lévi-Strauss, and sociologists Émile Durkheim and Robert Merton. Douglas dedicates the book to Merton. These are all figures who are now often too hastily dismissed with the label 'functionalists', a flippant charge which should not get the accuser off the hook from having to adequately engage with any of their primary texts (cf. Cummings et al., 2017; Hinings, Greenwood & Meyer, 2018; Thornton, 2009).

5 Thornton, Ocasio & Lounsbury (2012) who wrote the first textbook on institutional logics, titling it *The Institutional Logics Perspective*, essentially ignored both the importance of Douglas's thought for Friedland & Alford's (1991) conception of institutional logics, and as Logue et al. (2016) argue, they and others ignored the importance of naturalizing analogies for founding institutions. The literature on institutional logics has developed significantly since then and it has become highly differentiated; however, the use of Douglas's work in this literature, which is what concerns us here, remains superficial.

6 And similarly as a tribute to Lévy-Bruhl and Halbwachs for sociologizing the mind.

7 In this note, Douglas (1986a, pp. x–xi) gives us a personal insight into how she reconciles two incompatible problems: 'My husband deserves a special tribute. When two problems seem insoluble, our long experience of domestic life has suggested an oblique approach. Instead of a head-on attack on each separate issue, one set of problems can be made to confront the other. This strategy, which produces new definitions of what has to be solved, gives the framework of this book.'

8 If Evans-Pritchard's work was to be held together as a sociological theory of knowledge, then Douglas maintains that there are three essays published in the *Bulletin of the Faculty of Arts* at the Egyptian University on the subjects of magic (Evans-Pritchard, 1933), comparison (Evans-Pritchard, 1934) and rationality (Evans-Pritchard, 1936) which exemplify this.

9 The symmetry which Evans-Pritchard sought to promote between logic (reason and rationality), pre-logic (Lévy-Bruhl) and non-logic (Pareto) seemingly foreshadows the later problems of the sociology of scientific knowledge; local realities are to be anchored in local systems of accountability (Douglas, 1980, p. 35). Scientific culture is just as mystical as any other culture.

10 This move is analogous to the one Bernstein makes when he turns his attention from restricted and elaborate speech codes to curriculum and the transmission of culture (e.g. Bernstein, 1996).

11 Douglas says that this second edition of *Natural Symbols* 'shows up more obviously as the other side of [Bernstein's] thesis' (Douglas, 1996a, p. ix). What she means is that the relationship between ritual and restricted code in her work – that weak boundaries are associated with ritualism – is the reverse of what it is in Bernstein's. In this edition, grid also changes so that it is 'the scope and coherent articulation of a system of classification' (Douglas, 1996a, p. 59) whilst maintaining Durkheim's thesis that systems of classification are products of social relations.

12 Eggers was an economist who received his PhD from Yale in 1950.
13 A very similar foreword appears in other books that were published from this series (e.g. Calabresi, 1985; Coleman, 1982; Dahl, 1985; Hoffmann, 1981). Douglas also writes in her preface that some of the chapters were previously tested in other venues, including importantly a conference in memory of Nelson Goodman, the Hollingshead Lecture at Yale University, the American Sociological Association meeting and the ethics seminar series organized by the late Russell Hardin (editor of the journal *Ethics* at the time) at the University of Chicago.
14 Careful readers of Douglas and Barnard will know that Douglas is using Barnard here as a linchpin to critique the institutional economists and not Barnard himself. This has the unfortunate effect of appearing as though she is overly critical of Barnard when in fact we believe that it is his interpreters whom she sees as the real problem.
15 This passage in Douglas (2005, p. 95) reveals a certain kind of ethos that is not unlike what du Gay (2015) refers to as a classical stance in organization theory: 'I see [hierarchy] as a spontaneously created and maintained inclusive system, organizing its internal tensions by balance and symmetry, and rich in resources for peace and reconciliation. I miss it when it is not there, and grieve when it falls into any of its besetting traps.'

References

Abrams, F. W. (1951). Management's responsibilities in a complex world. *Harvard Business Review*, 29(3), 29–34.

Barnard, C. I. (1938). *The functions of the executive*. Cambridge, MA: Harvard University Press.

Barnes, S. B. (1983). Social life as bootstrapped induction. *Sociology*, 17(4), 524–545.

Beidelman, T. O. (1980). The ethnographer as translator. Evans-Pritchard by Douglas, Mary (author). *The Times Literary Supplement*, December 12(4054), 1420.

Bernstein, B. (1996). *Pedagogy, symbolic control, and identity: Theory, research, critique*. London: Taylor & Francis.

Bloor, D. (1978). Polyhedra and the abominations of Leviticus. *The British Journal for the History of Science*, 11(3), 245–272.

Calabresi, G. (1985). *Ideals, beliefs, attitudes, and the law: Private law perspectives on a public law problem*. Syracuse, NY: Syracuse University Press.

Coleman, J. S. (1982). *The asymmetric society*. Syracuse, NY: Syracuse University Press.

Cornelissen, J. P., Holt, R., & Zundel, M. (2011). The role of analogy and metaphor in the framing and legitimization of strategic change. *Organization Studies*, 32(12), 1701–1716.

Cummings, S., Bridgman, T., Hassard, J., & Rowlinson, M. (2017). *A new history of management*. Cambridge: Cambridge University Press.

Dahl, R. A. (1985). *Controlling nuclear weapons: Democracy versus guardianship*. Syracuse, NY: Syracuse University Press.

Dewey, J. (1922). *Human nature and conduct. An introduction to social psychology*. London: George Allen & Unwin.

DiMaggio, P. (1982). Cultural entrepreneurship in nineteenth-century Boston: The creation of an organizational base for high culture in America. *Media Culture Society*, 4(1), 33–50.

DiMaggio, P., & Powell, W. W. (1991). Introduction. In W. W. Powell, & P. DiMaggio (eds) *The new institutionalism in organizational analysis* (pp. 1–38). Chicago, IL: University of Chicago Press.

Douglas, M. (1963). *The Lele of the Kasai*. London: Oxford University Press.

Douglas, M. (1966). *Purity and danger: An analysis of concepts of pollution and taboo*. London: Routledge & Kegan Paul.

Douglas, M. (1970). *Natural symbols: Explorations in cosmology*. London: Barrie and Rockliff, Cresset Press.

Douglas, M. (1973a). *Natural symbols: Explorations in cosmology*, 2nd edn. London: Barrie and Jenkins.

Douglas, M. (1973b). *Rules and meanings: The anthropology of everyday knowledge: Selected readings*. Harmondsworth: Penguin.

Douglas, M. (1975). *Implicit meanings: Essays in anthropology*. London: Routledge & Kegan Paul.

Douglas, M. (1978). *Cultural bias*. London: Royal Anthropological Institute.

Douglas, M. (1980). *Edward Evans-Pritchard*. New York: Viking Press.

Douglas, M. (1982a). *Essays in the sociology of perception*. London: Routledge & Kegan Paul, published in co-operation with the Russell Sage Foundation.

Douglas, M. (1982b). *In the active voice*. London: Routledge & Kegan Paul.

Douglas, M. (1986a). *How institutions think*. London: Routledge & Kegan Paul.

Douglas, M. (1986b). *Risk acceptability according to the social sciences*. London: Routledge & Kegan Paul.

Douglas, M. (1990). Risk as a forensic resource. *Daedalus, 119*(4), 1–16.

Douglas, M. (1992). *Risk and blame: Essays in cultural theory*. London: Routledge.

Douglas, M. (1995). Converging on autonomy: Anthropology and institutional economics. In O. E. Williamson (ed.) *Organization theory: From Chester Barnard to the present and beyond* (pp. 98–115), expanded edn. New York: Oxford University Press.

Douglas, M. (1996a). *Natural symbols: Explorations in cosmology*. London: Routledge.

Douglas, M. (1996b). *Thought styles: Critical essays on good taste*. London: Sage.

Douglas, M. (1999). *Implicit meanings: Selected essays in anthropology*, 2nd edn. London: Routledge.

Douglas, M. (2001). Basil Bernstein. In B. Bernstein, & S. Power (eds) *A tribute to Basil Bernstein, 1924–2000* (pp. 109–113). London: Institute of Education.

Douglas, M. (2005). A feeling for hierarchy. In J. Heft (ed.) *Believing scholars: Ten Catholic intellectuals* (pp. 94–120). New York: Fordham University Press.

Douglas, M. (2013a). *Culture and crises: Understanding risk and resolution*, Vol. 2. London: Sage.

Douglas, M. (2013b). *A very personal method: Anthropological writings drawn from life*, Vol. 1. London: Sage.

Douglas, M., & Isherwood, B. C. (1996). *The world of goods: Towards an anthropology of consumption*, rev. edn. New York: Routledge.

Douglas, M., & Ney, S. (1998). *Missing persons: A critique of the social sciences*. Berkeley, CA: University of California Press.

Douglas, M., & Wildavsky, A. (1982). *Risk and culture: An essay on the selection of technical and environmental dangers*. Berkeley. CA: University of California Press.

du Gay, P. (2015). Organization (theory) as a way of life. *Journal of Cultural Economy, 8*(4), 399–417.

Durkheim, É. (1951). *Suicide: A study in sociology*. Glencoe, IL: Free Press.

Durkheim, É., & Mauss, M. (1963 [1903]). *Primitive classification*. Chicago, IL: University of Chicago Press.

Etzion, D., & Ferraro, F. (2010). The role of analogy in the institutionalization of sustainability reporting. *Organization Science, 21*(5), 1092–1107.

Evans-Pritchard, E. E. (1933). The intellectualist (English) interpretation of magic. *Bulletin of the Faculty of Arts, I*, 282–311.

Evans-Pritchard, E. E. (1934). Lévy-Bruhl's theory of primitive mentality. *Bulletin of the Faculty of Arts, II*, 1–36.

Evans-Pritchard, E. E. (1936). Science and sentiment: An exposition and criticism of the writings of Pareto. *Bulletin of the Faculty of Arts, II*, 163–192.

Evans-Pritchard, E. E. (1951). *Social anthropology*. London: Cohen & West.

Evans-Pritchard, E. E. (1965). *Theories of primitive religion*. Oxford: Clarendon Press.

Fardon, R. (1987). The faithful disciple: On Mary Douglas and Durkheim. *Anthropology Today*, 3(5), 4–6.

Fardon, R. (1999). *Mary Douglas: An intellectual biography*. London: Routledge.

Friedland, R., & Alford, R. R. (1991). Bringing society back in: Symbols, practices, and institutional contradictions. In W. W. Powell, & P. DiMaggio (eds) *The new institutionalism in organizational analysis* (pp. 232–263). Chicago, IL: University of Chicago Press.

Goody, J. (1995). *The expansive moment: The rise of social anthropology in Britain and Africa, 1918–1970*. Cambridge: Cambridge University Press.

Hinings, C. R., Greenwood, R., & Meyer, R. (2018). Dusty books? The liability of oldness. *Academy of Management Review*, 43(2), 333–343.

Hoffmann, S. (1981). *Duties beyond borders: On the limits and possibilities of ethical international politics*, 1st edn. Syracuse, NY: Syracuse University Press.

Kuper, A. (1983). *Anthropology and anthropologists: The modern British school*, rev. edn. London: Routledge & Kegan Paul.

Lakatos, I. (1963). *Proofs and refutations*. London: Nelson.

Law, J. (1986). *Power, action, and belief: A new sociology of knowledge?* London: Routledge & Kegan Paul.

Loewenstein, J., Ocasio, W., & Jones, C. (2012). Vocabularies and vocabulary structure: A new approach linking categories, practices, and institutions. *The Academy of Management Annals*, 1–46.

Logue, D. M., Clegg, S., & Gray, J. (2016). Social organization, classificatory analogies and institutional logics: Institutional theory revisits Mary Douglas. *Human Relations*, 69(7), 1587–1609.

Malinowski, B. (1922). *Argonauts of the Western Pacific: An account of native enterprise and adventure in the archipelagoes of Melanesian New Guinea*. London and New York: Routledge and Kegan Paul.

Mamadouh, V. (1999). Grid-group cultural theory: An introduction. *GeoJournal*, 47(3), 395–409.

March, J. G., & Olsen, J. P. (1984). The new institutionalism: Organizational factors in political life. *The American Political Science Review*, 78(3), 734–749.

Mead, M. (1929). *Coming of age in Samoa: A psychological study of primitive youth for Western civilisation*. London: Jonathan Cape.

Meyer, J. W. (2008). Reflections on institutional theories of organizations. In R. Greenwood, C. Oliver, R. Suddaby, & K. Sahlin (eds) *The Sage handbook of organizational institutionalism* (pp. 790–811). Los Angeles, CA: Sage.

Meyer, J. W., & Rowan, B. (1977). Institutionalized organizations: Formal structure as myth and ceremony. *The American Journal of Sociology*, 83(2), 340–363.

Munro, R. (1997). The consumption view of self: Extension, exchange and identity. *The Sociological Review*, 44 (1_suppl), 248–273.

Perrow, C. (1986). *Complex organizations: A critical essay*, 3rd edn. New York: Random House.

Radcliffe-Brown, A. R. (1935). On the concept of function in social science. *American Anthropologist*, 37(3), 394–402.

Richards, P. (2008). Mary Tew Douglas (1921–2007). *American Anthropologist, 110*(3), 404–407.

Schneider, D. M. (1981). Review: Edward Evans-Pritchard by Mary Douglas. *American Anthropologist*, 83(3), 719–721.

Sewell, G. (2018). Myths that work: Toward a mythology of organizations and organizing. In Ø. Ihlen, & R. L. Heath (eds) *The handbook of organizational rhetoric and communication* (pp. 155–168). Hoboken, NJ: Wiley-Blackwell.

Stocking, G. W. (1984). Dr. Durkheim and Mr. Brown: Comparative sociology at Cambridge in 1910. In G. W. Stocking (ed.) *Functionalism historicized: Essays on British social anthropology* (pp. 106–130). Madison, WI: University of Wisconsin Press.

Stocking, G. W. (1995). *After Tylor: British social anthropology, 1888–1951*. Madison, WI: University of Wisconsin Press.

Swanson, D. L. (2008). Top managers as drivers for corporate social responsibility. In A. Crane (ed.) *The Oxford handbook of corporate social responsibility* (pp. 227–248). Oxford: Oxford University Press.

Thompson, M., Grendstad, G., & Selle, P. (1999). *Cultural theory as political science*. London: Routledge.

Thornton, P. H. (2009). The value of the classics. In P. S. Adler (ed.) *The Oxford handbook of sociology and organization studies: Classical foundations* (pp. 20–36). Oxford: Oxford University Press.

Thornton, P. H., & Ocasio, W. (2008). Institutional logics. In R. Greenwood, C. Oliver, K. Sahlin, & R. Suddaby (eds) *The Sage handbook of organizational institutionalism* (pp. 99–129). Los Angeles, CA: Sage.

Thornton, P. H., Ocasio, W., & Lounsbury, M. (2012). *The institutional logics perspective: A new approach to culture, structure and process*. Oxford: Oxford University Press.

Tracey, P., & Creed, W. E. D. (2017). Beyond managerial dillemas: The study of institutional paradoxes in organization theory. In P. Jarzabkowski, W. K. Smith, A. Langley, & M. W. Lewis (eds) *The Oxford handbook of organizational paradox* (pp. 162–177), 1st edn. Oxford: Oxford University Press.

Wildavsky, A. (1987). Choosing preferences by constructing institutions: A cultural theory of preference formation. *The American Political Science Review*, 81(1), 4–21.

Williamson, O. E. (1990). *Organization theory: From Chester Barnard to the present and beyond: Spring seminar: Papers*. New York: Oxford University Press.

Williamson, O. E. (1995). *Organization theory: From Chester Barnard to the present and beyond*, expanded edn. New York: Oxford University Press.

Willmott, H. (2011). 'Institutional work' for what? Problems and prospects of institutional theory. *Journal of Management Inquiry*, 20(1), 67–72.

Wrong, D. H. (1962). The over-socialized conception of Man in modern sociology. *Psychoanalysis and the Psychoanalytic Review*, 49(2), 53–69.

Wuthnow, R., Hunter, J. D., Bergesen, A., & Kurzweil, E. (1984). *Cultural analysis: The work of Peter L. Berger, Mary Douglas, Michel Foucault, and Jürgen Habermas*. Boston: Routledge & Kegan Paul.

9 Norbert Elias and organizational analysis

Towards process-figurational theory

Robert van Krieken

Chapter objectives

This chapter examines the process-figurational theoretical perspective of Norbert Elias in order to outline how it can enhance organization theory more broadly. The chapter examines:

- The mid-life crisis characterizing the most pervasive approach in organization studies, neo-institutionalism, highlighting how the never-ending concern with the supposed 'agency/structure' problem is itself a problem
- The main elements of Elias's broader conceptual approach, focusing on his distinctive theoretical vocabulary of process, relation, figuration, habitus, power balance, unplanned order and his rejection of dualisms such as agency/structure and individual/society
- The two areas of his work with most direct relevance for organization studies, his study of court society and of the process of civilization, including accompanying concepts such as decivilization and informalization
- A selection of key works by organization theorists drawing on process-figurational theory.
- Some preliminary suggestions as to the future directions that might be taken with process-figurational theory in organization studies.

Introduction

Sociological theory has been characterized at least since the middle of the 20th century by an ongoing concern with dualisms: individual/society, micro/macro and agency/structure, which have been a source of never-ending and indeed irresolvable debate. Michael Reed has observed that it is a genuine puzzle why agency/structure is such a dominant theme in organization theory. 'Why', he asks, 'do we keep returning to it like an old pimple or sore that we can't resist picking? Why not let it alone when we know only too well that further probing will only make matters worse?' (2005, p. 2) Why indeed, since it is anchored in another equally false dualism, that of individual/ society (Collins, 1992). However, his answer is simply to search for more effective ways to pick at that sore (Reed, 1997; 2005).

The siren call of agency/structure dualism drives many of the problems in organization theory, in the form, for example, of the reification of institutions (Suddaby, 2010) and entanglement within an opposition between institutional isomorphism and entrepreneurship (Clegg, 2010). The current situation in (neo-)institutional theory, as Alvesson and Spicer observe, is that of a mid-life crisis, caught up in vague and tautological understandings of the core concept, 'institution', resulting in 'a body of research which seems to produce much more heat than light' (2018, p. 5). The theoretical move most commonly pursued to move organization theory beyond a static and reified conception of organizations has been a turn to writers such as Foucault, actor-network theorists such as Callon, Law (in Callon & Law, 1997) and Latour (1993), philosophers such as Wittgenstein, Heidegger, Serres, Derrida, and Deleuze and Guattari, or ethnomethodologists such as Harold Garfinkel (Chia, 1995; 2005; see also Weick, 1969; 1995; 2012), often broadly captured under the headers of post-structuralism and postmodernism.

An effective alternative or complement to the postmodern and actor-network turn is available, however; Norbert Elias's approach to sociology provides a rich body of conceptual tools and means of orientation for organization theory that help transcend these tired and ultimately pointless disputes in organization studies and generate significant new insights and conceptual innovations in the study of organizational stability and change.[1] His analysis of 'court society' is usefully read alongside Weber's account of the rationalization process and bureaucracy; his account of the process of civilization has various linkages with both Weber and Foucault on the historical development of a disciplined psychic apparatus (van Krieken, 1990); his theory of figurations is in many ways stronger than the concept of 'network' in actor-network theory as well as Bourdieu's (1985) concept of 'field'; he was emphasizing the importance of the concept of 'habitus' long before Bourdieu took it up, while his theory of power is a useful alternative to that of Foucault or Latour. As Tim Newton and Dennis Smith have argued, Elias weaves together a number of otherwise disparate theoretical concerns in organization studies – power, subjectivity, networks, processes of change, subjectivity and the self, strategy and leadership, emotions and violence (Newton & Smith, 2002, p. viii) in a single conceptual framework.

If, as Stewart Clegg and Ad van Iterson have argued, organization studies can now usefully be reinvigorated through a 'creative re-reading of the sociological classics' (2013, p. 623), Elias's particularly imaginative mobilization of development of sociological and psychological thought from Marx, Weber, Simmel, William James and Freud onwards is one of the better ways of engaging in such a re-reading, constituting a valuable 'source of inspiration for organizational studies' (van Iterson, 2009).

Although Elias was content initially to present his approach as organized around the concept of 'figuration' he grew to dislike the term 'figurational sociology' and ended up preferring 'process sociology'. Both terms are equally important, which is why I am using the admittedly clumsy term 'process-figurational' theory to come as close as possible to a convenient label.[2]

Elias's conceptual framework

Elias would not have referred to himself as 'radical' but this is actually true of his approach to sociology generally and his contribution to organization studies in particular. In agreeing with Benjamin Lee Whorf's (1956) analysis of the constraints placed on thought processes by the structure of European languages, Elias was concerned with developing a distinctive form of *perception* of the social world. He believed that many of the problems and obstacles in contemporary social science were built into the very categories and concepts around which thought about society and human behaviour was organized, with his work constituting an argument for a new sociological vocabulary and conceptual framework that he argued would be closer to the reality of human social life. A number of concepts are important here, including: figuration, process, habitus, civilization, relation, power balance and power-ratio, interweaving, interdependence, unplanned order and established/ outsiders. These terms are not only useful in themselves but also as radical alternatives to the standard concepts used in most social theory: society, system, role, action, structure, interaction, individual, society, organization and institution. For all of these concepts, Elias either argued for alternatives or for different understandings of them.

Processual and relational theory

One of Elias's core concerns, which he shared with the philosopher Ernest Cassirer (1953 [1910]), Georg Simmel (1971), the Frankfurt School theorists (Adorno, Horkheimer, Marcuse) and others influenced by Marxist social thought, was the necessity to avoid seeing social life in terms of states, objects or things. Influenced by Cassirer's emphasis on relational thinking and most likely by Georgy Lukács' (1971) arguments concerning the *reification* ('turning into a thing or object') of what are in fact dynamic social relationships, he shared the concern to avoid freezing relations and processes into impenetrable objects, indeed, often into subjects capable of thought and action.

Elias's efforts consisted, in the first place, of a double movement: first, towards an insistence on the *processual* character of social life; second, towards an emphasis on social life as *relational*. Instead of thinking about social life in terms of static 'states' or phenomena, such as capitalism, rationality, bureaucracy, organization, modernity or postmodernity, Elias always aimed to identify their processual character. He thought in terms of rationalization, modernization, bureaucratization, civilization, etc. Individuals, families, communities and organizations were thus to be regarded as *dynamic*, in a state of flux and change, as processes. Indeed, suggested Elias, although it is not how we are used to thinking about ourselves, 'it would be more appropriate to say that a person is constantly in movement; he not only goes through a process, he *is* a process' (2012 [1978], pp.113–114). Clearly the same point applies to organizations, which should also be regarded as ongoing processes rather than stable entities only occasionally subjected to change.

Elias spoke of the 'change impetus (*Wandlungsimpetus*) of every human society', and regarded 'the immanent impetus towards change as an integral moment of every social structure and their temporary stability as the expression of an impediment to social change (2009 [1997], p. 27). Often it is difficult to come up with the appropriate concept; 'capitalism' is difficult to render in this way, and while 'bureaucratization' works (Jacoby, 1973) well enough, it is not immediately obvious how one could turn 'organization' into a process – Weick's (1969) 'organizing' moves in that direction. Haridimos Tsoukas and Robert Chia (2002) make a similar point about organizational change being the pervasive norm and stability the exception. Elias also emphasized the existence of a *plurality* of processes, all of which interweave with each other, with no causal primacy being given to any one of them. Transformations in social relationships and organizational life are thus intertwined with a variety of other process of change: economic, political, psychological, geographical and so on.

A closely connected element of Elias's critique of thinking in terms of stable objects was his argument for the necessity 'to give up thinking in terms of single, isolated substances and to start thinking in terms of relationships and functions' (2010 [1939], p. 23). A 'person' or 'individual' is thus not a self-contained entity or unit, they do not exist 'in themselves', they only exist as elements of sets of relations with other individuals. The same applies to families, communities, organizations, nations, economic systems – in fact to any aspect of the world, human or natural, for the concept arose from Einstein's physics. The primary object of sociological study and the very stuff of historical change was thus the relations between people, the ties binding them to each other. In distancing himself from the accepted conception of 'structure', Elias argued that '"circumstances" which change are not something which comes upon people from "outside": they are the relationships between people themselves' (2012 [1939], p. 444; see also Bourdieu, 1990, p. 192; Emirbayer, 1997).

Unplanned order

While Elias agreed that sociology is fundamentally concerned with a 'problem of order', he directed his attention to a very particular construction of that problem, namely, the apparent *independence* of social order and social structure from intentional human action. Elias formulated the problem in this way:

> Again and again ... people stand before the outcome of their own actions like the sorcerer's apprentice before the spirits he has conjured up and which, once at large, are no longer in his power. They look with astonishment at the convolutions and formations of the historical flow that they themselves constitute but are unable to control.
>
> (Elias, 2010 [1939], p. 61)

The most acute question for Elias was the apparent *lack* of relationship between social order and human intentions, the seemingly *alien* character of the social world to the individuals making it up.

He saw 'society' not as some entity existing separately from its individual members but as consisting of the structured interweaving of the activity of interdependent human agents, all pursuing their own interests and goals, producing distinct social forms signified by terms such as 'Christianity', 'feudalism', 'patriarchy', 'capitalism', or whatever culture and nation we happen to be part of, which cannot be said to have been planned or intended by any individual or group. This means that, for Elias, it makes no sense at all to speak of organizations or institutions as 'actors' that perceive, think and do things – they are the outcome of the ever-changing interweaving of the actions of myriad human individuals.

The constraints surrounding human agency are best understood not as those of a reified social 'structure' or institutions but rather as the crystalized and sedimented outcomes of the interweaving of multiple lines of action, all colliding with each other in ways that cannot be predicted beforehand. Social order is precisely the 'order of interweaving human impulses and strivings' (2012 [1939], p. 404) A favourite example in discussions of the unintended consequences of human action is that of the queue outside the baker – people came there to buy a croissant, not to form a queue, yet that is the result of the intersection of their actions, as Boudon (1982, p. 2) notes, making the same point that Elias is making about social institutions and structures more broadly.

One of the primary foci of sociological analysis for Elias is the *relationships* between intentional, goal-directed human activities and the unplanned or unconscious process of interweaving with other such activities, past and present, and their consequences. As he put it:

> It is simple enough: plans and actions, the emotional and rational impulses of individual people, constantly interweave in a friendly or hostile way. This continuous interweaving of people's separate plans and actions, can give rise to changes and patterns that no individual person has planned or created. From this interdependence of people arises an order *sui generis*, an order more compelling and stronger than the will and reason of the individual people composing it.
>
> (2012 [1939], p. 404)

It is a line of argument that is also connected to his emphasis on long-term processes, since the analysis of the interrelationships between intentional action and unplanned social processes had to be undertaken over periods of time for, as Johan Goudsblom put it, 'yesterday's unintended social consequences are today's unintended social conditions of 'intentional human actions' (1977, p. 149).

Interdependence – figurations – habitus – power

For Elias, the structure and dynamics of social life could only be understood if human beings were conceptualized as *interdependent* rather than autonomous, comprising what he called *figurations* rather than social systems or structures, characterized by socially and historically specific forms of *habitus*, or personality-structure, always bound up with relations of *power*. He emphasized seeing human beings in the plural rather than the singular, as part of collectivities, of groups and networks, stressing that their very identity as unique individuals only existed within and through those networks or figurations.

Rather than seeing individuals as ever having any autonomous, pre-social existence, Elias emphasized human beings' interdependence with each other, the fact that one can only become an individual human being within a web of social relationships and within a network of interdependencies with one's family, school, church, community, ethnic group, class, gender, work organization and so on. The essential 'relatedness' of human beings, said Elias, began with being born as a helpless infant, over which we have no control: 'Underlying all intended interactions of human beings is their unintended interdependence' (2009 [1969], p. 179).

He developed this point in part through his critique of what he called the *homo clausus*, or 'closed person' image of humans. Elias argued for a replacement of this *homo clausus* conception with its emphasis on autonomy, freedom and independent agency with:

The image of man as an 'open personality' [*homines aperti*] who possesses a greater or lesser degree of relative (but never absolute and total) autonomy vis-a-vis other people and who is, in fact, fundamentally oriented toward and dependent on other people throughout his life. The network of interdependencies among human beings is what binds them together. Such interdependencies are the nexus of what is here called the figuration, a structure of mutually oriented and dependent people.

(2012 [1968], p. 525)

Elias said that he introduced the concept of 'figuration' in the 1960s because it 'puts the problem of human interdependencies into the very heart of sociological theory' (2012 [1978], p 129), and he hoped it would 'eliminate the antithesis ... immanent today in the use of the words "individual" and "society"' (2012 [1968], p. 526).

For Elias, organizations need to be understood as figurations of interdependent individuals and groups can be small or large, all bound together by shorter or longer, simpler or more complex chains of interdependence, only properly understood as existing over time, in a constant process of dynamic flux and greater or lesser transformation (see Figure 9.1). Figurations themselves also form larger figurations (Couldry & Hepp, 2017, p. 73) and 'nesting' within each other (Kuipers, 2018, pp. 427–428). Just as human individuals only exist in relations of interdependence and power *within* organizations, the same is true of organizations themselves, which are also constitutively bound up in relations of interdependence and power with other organizations and figurations.[3]

The dynamics of figurations also depend on the formation of a shared social *habitus* or personality make-up that constitutes the collective basis of individual human conduct. Elias called the concept of 'national character' 'a habitus problem *par excellence*' (2010 [1987], p. 164), which he argued needed to be seen as being continually transformed along with the nation-states within which individuals lived. He also referred to it as 'second nature' or 'an automatic, blindly functioning apparatus of self-control' (2012 [1939], pp. 136, 406). The organization of psychological make-up into a *habitus* was also a continuous *process* which began at birth and continued throughout a person's life,

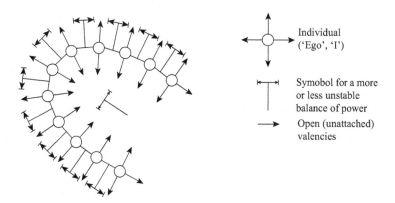

Figure 9.1 Figurations of interdependent individuals – 'family', 'group', 'state', 'society', etc.
Source: Elias (2012 [1978], p. 9)

For although the self-steering of a person, malleable during early childhood, solidifies and hardens as he or she grows up, it never ceases entirely to be affected by his or her changing relations with others throughout his or her life.

(2012 [1939], p. 415)

What Elias found most important about human figurations was the way in which they were constituted as *power* relations, so that he develops his point about relations in most detail with reference to 'the relational character of power' (2012 [1978], p. 70). For Elias it was crucial that the concept of power be 'transformed from a concept of substance to a concept of relationship'. More precisely:

At the core of changing figurations – indeed the very hub of the figuration process – is a fluctuating, tensile equilibrium, a balance of power moving to and fro, inclining first to one side and then to the other. This kind of fluctuating balance of power is a structural characteristic of the flow of every figuration.

(2012 [1978], p. 126)

If we see power in relational terms, it also becomes possible to recognize that questions of power are quite distinct from questions of 'freedom' and 'domination', and that power 'is not an amulet possessed by one person and not another; it is a structural characteristic of human relationships – of *all* human relationships' (2012 [1978], p. 70)

Elias understood power in terms of *power-ratios* or 'constantly shifting balances of tensions' (2006 [1969], p. 157) and regarded these concepts as the best successors to debates about freedom and determinism. He said that the recognition that all human beings possess some degree of freedom or autonomy 'is sometimes romantically idealized as proving the metaphysical freedom of man' (2006 [1969], p. 157), its popularity arising primarily from its emotional appeal. However, he argued that it was important to go beyond thinking in terms of a fictional antithesis between 'freedom' and 'determinism' – fictional because of human beings' essential interdependence – and move to thinking in terms of power balances that are at least bi-polar and frequently multi-polar (2012 [1978], p. 69).

Elias stressed the *reciprocal* workings of power, so that within the network of relations binding the more and less powerful to each other, apparently less powerful groups also exercise a 'boomerang effect' back on those with greater power chances (2006 [1969], p. 283). This was, he felt, a problem with concepts such as 'rule' or 'authority', since they 'usually make visible only the pressures exerted from above to below, but not those from below to above' (2006 [1969], pp. 283–284). He referred to the well-known Hegelian example of the master–slave relationship and also to the relation between parents and children: parents clearly have greater power chances than their children, but because children fulfil particular functions and needs for their parents, they also have power over their parents, such as calling them to their aid by crying and requiring them to reorganize their lives (2012 [1978], p. 69; 2008 [1980]).[4]

One of the key examples of the breadth and subtlety of power relations was for Elias that between established and outsider groups in larger or smaller communities and social groups, based on his study of a suburb of Leicester, named 'Winston Parva', *The Established and the Outsiders*, researched together with John Scotson in the 1950s and 1960s (Elias & Scotson, 2008 [1965]). The power relation they observed was between the residents who had lived there for several generations and the more recent arrivals, based not on differences in income and wealth but on differences in the forms and degree of organization and communal cohesion across the two groups. The very fact that the established had known each other for a long time, developed shared norms, language and orientations created a particular power balance between them and the outsiders, who were more fragmented and individualized, less able to counter the mechanisms of exclusion and stigmatization mobilized by the established group. 'Exclusion and stigmatisation of the outsiders by the established group', wrote Elias and Scotson, 'were two powerful weapons used by the latter to maintain their identity, to assert their superiority, keeping the others firmly in their place' (Elias & Scotson, 2008 [1965], p. 4)

Court society and the process of civilization

The Court Society was Elias's first major sociological work, completed in 1933 as his *Habilitationsschrift* under Karl Mannheim. It was the foundation upon which Elias's *On the Civilizing Process* was built and for organizational theorists it is probably one of the better places to start reading Elias, since it is precisely about a particular mode of organizing social relations of power. There are three aspects of Elias's account of court society that are of particular significance for organizational theory:

* His argument for identifying royal and aristocratic courts as key social organizational units that played a vital role in the emergence of modern bureaucratic society
* The differentiation of the concept of 'rationality' into two forms: a 'courtly rationality' that both preceded instrumental-legal rationality and continues as an undercurrent to it
* The identification, in the dynamics of social relations in court society, of particular mechanisms of power, competition, distinction and social differentiation, which continue to operate in contemporary social and organizational life

Elias extends our understanding of the development of modern societies by highlighting the ways in which the aristocracy and its organizational setting, court society, should be understood as far more than an outmoded form of ostentatious consumption, not just a feudal relic destined for the historical scrap heap. Court society, Elias argued, was a historically significant form of social organization, with a dual relationship to the bourgeois society that followed it.

On the one hand, bourgeois morality and forms of life – the distinction between public and private life, the organization of life around criteria of instrumental, economic rationality and the placement of a dedication to work at the centre of human existence – were developed precisely in *opposition* to those of the courts. On the other hand, Elias saw that many features of the forms of social relations in court society also continued into the post-Enlightenment world, so that an understanding of court society also illuminates many aspects of contemporary social relations which are less visible to us precisely because we, as good citizens of the Enlightenment, believe we have left the world of *Dangerous Liaisons* and the *Ancien Régime* in the past. 'By studying the structure of court society and seeking to understand one of the last great non-bourgeois figurations of the West', argued Elias, 'we indirectly gain increased understanding of our own professional and commercial, urban-industrial society' (2006 [1969], p. 44).

The social process of 'courtization' which underpinned the transformation of feudal society subjected first knights and warriors and ever-expanding circles of the population to an increasing demand that expressions of violence be regulated, that emotions and impulses be subjected to ever-increasing self-reflection and surveillance, and placed ever more firmly in the service of the long-term requirements of complex networks of social interaction imposing increasingly ambivalent expectations. In court society we see the beginnings of a form of mutual and self-observation that Elias referred to as a 'psychological' form of perception, which is now analysed in terms of reflexive self-awareness.

Elias's analysis of court society reveals more than simply the pre-history of bourgeois society; it also reveals a deeper layer of social relations that continues to the present day. The organization of power relations around the representation of social prestige still plays an important role in contemporary societies, despite the lack of fit with our self-image as instrumentally rational moderns. Much of the dynamics of court society can still be seen today in the day-to-day workings of any organization, with success in contemporary social life maybe more dependent on adept display, performance and representation than we are usually willing to admit. As Elias put it:

> Despite their formal organizational framework based on written contracts and documents, which was developed only in rudimentary form in the state of Louis XIV, in many organizations of our time, even industrial and commercial ones, there are rivalries for status, fluctuations in the balance between groups, exploitation of internal rivalries by superiors, and other phenomena that have emerged in the study of court society. But as the main regulation of human relationships in large organizations is formalized in a highly impersonal manner, such phenomena usually have a more or less unofficial and informal character today. In court society we therefore find quite openly and on a large scale many phenomena that exist below the surface of highly bureaucratized organizations.
>
> (2006 [1969], p. 152)

The roots of informal organizational structures and organizational culture can, therefore, be seen to have originated in the dynamics of court society, continuing an older form of rationality beneath the surface of the instrumental-legal rationality which modern organizations are supposed to revolve around.

Reinhard Bendix, for example, pointed to the parallels between the transformation of fighting knights into restrained courtiers and the shift from an approach to authority in the workplace framed in muscular terms of dominance and obedience to one framed in terms of the considered, self-reflexive management of human relations. Referring to Elias's account of the 'courtization of warriors', he argued that the model managerial *habitus* had come to take the following form:

> The calm eyes which never stray from the other's gaze, the easy control in which laughter is natural but never forced, the attentive and receptive manner,

the well-rounded, good-fellowship, the ability to elicit participation and to accomplish change without upsetting relationships, may be so many devices for personal advancement when the man is on his way up.

(Bendix, 1974 [1956], p. 335)

As Tim Newton and Dennis Smith argue, *The Court Society* is an important case study in the 'crystallization' of other fluid networks, how the distinctive dynamics of court society, organized around language, etiquette and ceremony, drove the production of a particular kind of organizational subjectivity, that of the courtier. Elias's insights have the potential, they suggest, to inform the analysis of corporate takeovers, large-scale meta-organizations such as the European Union or the World Trade Organization (Newton & Smith, 2002, p. ix); really, the analysis is useful for grasping the varieties of 'rationality' in any organization.

The process of civilization

The concept of 'the process of civilization' aims at understanding those social and political conditions, practices and strategies that have produced changing conceptions and experiences of civilization. Elias shows that what is experienced as 'civilization' is founded on a psychic structure or *habitus* which had changed over time, and that it can only be understood in connection with changes in broader social relationships. For Elias, civilization refers not to a state or a condition but to a process of civil-*ization*. The aim is then an understanding of those social and political forms, practices, strategies and figurations that have produced changing conceptions and experiences of civility.

The state-formation process in Europe was accompanied, necessarily, by an increasing monopolization of the means of violence and a pressure towards other means of exercising power in social relations. Rather than the use of violence, social 'success' became more and more dependent on 'continuous reflection, foresight, and calculation, self-control, precise and articulate regulation of one's own affects, knowledge of the whole terrain, human and non-human, in which one acted' (2012 [1939], p. 439). Elias argued that this 'rationalization' of human conduct, its placement at the service of long-term goals and the increasing internalization of social constraint were closely tied to the process of state formation and development of monopolies of physical force. The 'requirement' placed on each individual is not a direct one but one mediated by one's own reflection on the consequences of differing patterns of behaviour.

Although Elias and his followers use the concept most precisely and in the greatest depth, it is important to note that it also usefully captures a cluster of developments examined by a variety of other social theorists who have observed and analysed the emergence of a specifically modern disciplined character, mode of conduct or *habitus* along similar lines. Both Weber and Foucault, for example, agree that one can trace a developmental trend towards increasing self-discipline, a regularization and routinization of the psyche, so that one's inner 'economy of the soul' coordinates with the outer economy of an increasingly bureaucratized, rationalized and individualized social world. Their work converges on the notion that there has been 'societalization of the self', a transition in European history from a social order based on external constraint to one increasingly dependent on the internalization of constraint (van Krieken, 1990).

The restraint imposed by such differentiated, complex networks of social relations became increasingly internalized and less dependent on its maintenance by external social institutions, underpinning the development of what Freud (1961 [1923]) recognized as the super-ego. These transformations are to be understood in the context of developments in the structuring of social relations, including the development of a money economy and urbanization, but for Elias the two most important ones were: (1) the process of state formation with its monopolization of the means of violence; and (2) the gradual differentiation of society, the increasing range, diversity and interdependence of competing social positions and functions composing European societies.

The increasing monopolization of the means of violence associated with state formation created a pressure towards other means of exercising power in competitive social relations, so that social success and distinction is increasingly dependent on 'continuous reflection, foresight, and calculation, self-control, precise and articulate regulation of one's own affects, knowledge of the whole terrain, human and non-human, in which one acted' (Elias, 2012 [1939], p. 439). The increasing density of European societies, produced by a combination of population growth and urbanization, and the increasing circles of people with whom any single individual would be interdependent, no matter how fleetingly, also facilitated the 'rationalization' of human conduct, its placement at the service of long-term goals and the increasing internalization of social constraint, eventually making the highly regulated mode of conduct characteristic of 'organization man' (Whyte, 1956) effectively 'second nature'.

Important driving forces behind the civilizing process are *competition* and the opportunities for advantage offered by being *distinctive* in the realm of manners and morals. Continuing competition between various social groups has generated both the willingness to submit to the demands of etiquette and the increasing subjection of people's bodies, emotions and desires to stringent controls and ever more demanding forms of self-discipline. Competition has also driven the spread of the civilizing process, first to the higher bourgeois strata, in their attempts to enter court society, and then, in turn, to the strata below them.

There are two additional important developments in the understanding of the process of civilization that are important to highlight here. The first concerns the emergence of more detailed explorations of the extent to which it can be regarded as unilinear, the ways in which it can reverse its direction under particular circumstances and how it can also be accompanied simultaneously by processes of *decivilization* (Mennell, 1990; Fletcher, 1997). There is also increasing examination of the issue of contradictions and conflicts within civilizing processes and the question of 'civilized barbarism' (van Krieken, 1999), whether the infliction of violence should be seen simply as having been 'reduced', or as changed in form, such as from physical to symbolic violence.

The second relates to the evolution of the shaping of habitus in the process of civilization in the course of the 20th century, accelerating from the 1950s onwards, towards more reflexive, flexible and informal modes of self-regulation, from the constraint and repression of emotions to their careful and modulated management, a development which Elias and Dunning (2008 [1986], p. 77) referred to, in relation to leisure activities, as 'controlled decontrolling', and which Elias scholar Cas Wouters has termed 'informalization' (1977; 1986; 2004; 2007). Wouters highlights how increasing democratization and reduction of social and cultural differentials between distinct social groups, the move away from rigid, hierarchical organizational structures and formulaic management styles towards flatter and more egalitarian institutional forms, was accompanied by intensified social competition, requiring a broader range of more flexible modes of self-regulation, a transition Wouters describes as 'from conscience to consciousness' (2004, p. 208). He also captures the shift with the term 'third nature': if Elias had analysed the development of 'second nature', understood as an apparatus of social control functioning relatively automatically and blindly, that automaticity gradually became less socially effective, with the shifting character of increasingly democratized social relations requiring the formation of a 'third nature', based on 'a more reflexive and flexible self-regulation' (Wouters, 2004, p. 210).

Elias and organization studies

Although discussions of Elias and organization theory are often prefaced with the observation that his work has had limited impact, in fact there is now quite a rich body of process-figurational literature covering a wide variety of topics. The topics covered have included the relationships between Elias's theoretical orientation and that of Foucault in relation to organizational subjectivity (van Krieken, 1990; 1996; Kieser, 1998), the comparison of Weber and Elias in relation to organizations (Breuer, 1994), transformations of the National Health Service (NHS) and the medical profession (Dopson & Waddington, 1996; Dopson, 1997; 2001; 2005), the longer-term history of organizational forms, emotional management and management discourses (Mastenbroek, 1993; 1996; 2000; 2002a; 2002b; 2005), the Lillehammer Winter Olympics and the Sydney Summer Olympics (Lesjo, 2000; Frawley, 2015), shame and humiliation in organizations (Smith, 2001; 2002), the film industry (Blair, 2003), Elias's concept of 'survival units' (Kaspersen & Gabriel, 2008), a critique of governmentality approaches in relation to urban regeneration (Lever, 2011), talent management (Lever & Swailes, 2017), medical unionism in Belgium (Gourdin & Meul, 2013), gossip in organizations (Soeters & van Iterson, 2002), corporate governance (Stokvis, 2002), Elias's and Wouters' concept of informalization (van Iterson, Mastenbroek & Soeters, 2001), the wine market in China (Maguire, 2017), firms' online communities (van Iterson & Richter, 2017), corporate responsibility and unintended outcomes (Vertigans, 2017), organizational learning and complex responsive processes (Stacey, 2003; 2012) and violence in organizational life (Costas & Grey, 2018).

In what follows, the focus, albeit brief, will be on the following five bodies of work to clarify exactly what process-figurational theory contributes to organization studies: (1) Tim Newton's theoretical arguments about how Elias's work can be mobilized in relation to organizations; (2) Wilbert van Vree's analysis of how meetings shape the dynamics of organizational life; (3) Paddy Dolan and John Connelly's critique of institutional theory; and (4) Stewart Clegg and Ad van Iterson's (2013) use of Elias to analyse increasingly fluid and liquid organizational forms.

Tim Newton – power and subjectivity

One of the first organization theorists to examine how Elias's work could be drawn upon was Tim Newton, who from around 1998 has drawn attention to the importance of the relationship between interdependency, power and subjectivity in organizations, partly in the context of a critique of Foucauldian approaches to power and subjectivity. Over the course of his engagement with the question of Elias and organizations, Newton has argued for a number of points of contact with questions such as organizational strategy, emotions and violence, and discursive change, making the following points.

First, Elias's analysis of the broader social forces driving the historical formation of subjectivity within asymmetrical relations of power and interdependence is crucial for any linkage of the study of organizations and behaviour within organizations to their changing social contexts, with his relational theory of power deserving as much, if not more, attention in organization studies as Foucault's account of the relationship between power and freedom in his theory of governmentality. Elias thus helps to place shifts in organizational life in the context of broader lines of social transformation – the process of civilization, changes in *habitus*, and the shifts from external to internal compulsion, with our relationship to time a key dimension of the longer-term shift from external to internalized restraint. Newton suggests that it is important to place any discussion of corporate culture in the context of a changing balance between collectivism and individualism (1999, p. 432) and he sees *The Court Society* as a highly instructive case study of how emotions and subjectivity constitute the heart of the exercise of power in organizational settings.

Second, there are strong parallels and connections between Elias's critique of the *homo clausus* conception of human beings as well as his concepts of interdependence and figurations, and the understanding of networks in the work of actor-network theorists such as Callon and Latour. Michel Callon, for example, notes how the arguments of Elias, Granovetter and actor-network theory all share a critique of the 'person closed in on himself – *homo clausus*, to use Elias' expression' (Callon, 1999, p. 185), with John Law commenting that 'the explanatory attitude of [actor network] writers is not so different from that of Norbert Elias' (Law, 1994, p. 113). As Newton argues,

> There is a close correspondence between the Eliasian emphasis upon interdependency networks/chains and *Homines aperti*, and that observed in actor network theory. Both question the sovereignty and independence of the individual actor, since the actions of any actor are seen continually to condition, and be conditioned by, the wider networks in which they operate.
>
> (1999, p. 428)

However, Elias's particular concept of figurations of interdependent actors, in *The Court Society* and in his game models, adds sensitivity to the dimension of asymmetrical power relations, alerting us to 'the likelihood that actor networks will be characterised by social hierarchies'(1999, p. 429).

Third, his critique of the *homo clausus* conception of human beings, his emphasis on the interdependence of human action and his stress on the frequent disjunction between planned action and its outcomes are enormously important for the understanding of how and why organizational change take place and how we should approach the concept of 'strategy'. As he puts it, 'strategic change is always likely to be a fraught process because strategic "outcomes" often represent the interweaving of action and argument between numerous "players", such as competitors, clients, suppliers, different professional groupings, government agencies' (2001, p. 482), rather than being the rational result of strategic action driven by decisive actions of especially insightful and effective managers and CEOs. This does not mean, however, that the relationship between strategies and plans is entirely opaque, merely that is it complex; thus, his analysis of different types of game configurations (2012 [1978]) aims to provide a range of models for how the analysis of strategic action can be undertaken.

Wilbert van Vree – the meetingization of society

Wilbert van Vree's (1999; 2002; 2011) work on meetings in organizational life is another especially important contribution to process-figurational theory in organization studies. He points out that studying meetings is a strategic means of grasping the inner dynamics of organizations. The everyday activity in all forms of organizations is dominated, observes van Vree, with, if not actively taking part in meetings, preparing for them or processing their results (van Vree, 2011, p. 242). Meetings are an essential aspect of lengthening chains of interdependence, constituting the means by which interdependent interweaving actions are realized and negotiated (van Vree, 2011, p. 245). Looking at the long-term history of meeting behaviour, he draws attention to gradually changing standards of behaviour expected of meeting participants, especially the restraint of violence and outbursts of emotion. When one sees opposing politicians in a legislative assembly break out in physical assaults on each other, these cases are especially notable because they are exceptions to the rule of the enormous number and variety of meetings that take place around the world in an entirely pacified way – usually to the point of tedium.

Van Vree highlights a particular historical shift, from 'parliamentary' to 'professionalized' meeting styles. The parliamentary style, which dominated meeting styles from 1750 to 1950, is highly rule-governed, with rules and formal codes designed to restrain highly oppositional adversaries within a workable framework of regulated debate, decision-making and action, orientated to the principles of democratic politics, with clear voting procedures and decision-making rules. An important part of the courtization of warriors, then, was also their 'parliamentarization' (van Vree & Bos, 1989), where courtiers had to extend their regulation of their emotions in the interests of peaceful negotiation of all the issues underpinning the exercise of governmental power and authority, such as taxation, military service, education, healthcare, social welfare, police, the regulation of property rights and so on. It was this parliamentary meeting style that then served as the template for a wide variety of other types of meetings through society, of civil associations and business firms.

Looking at manuals for associations and meetings, rules of order and meeting textbooks (such as Zelko, 1969 [1957]), van Vree observes that these meeting manuals show that meeting manners have shifted significantly over the last 50–60 years. Rather than deliberative assemblies, they are

> More differentiated, especially professional and business meetings; from formal rules to informal codes; from debating to discussing; from majority decisions to consensus; from the attitude of parties, administration and opposition to the

behaviour of individual meeting participants; and from a chairman's function to the duties of ordinary meeting participants.

(2011, p. 255)

Organizations now require a different kind of habitus and a different, more professionalized and business-like meeting style, orientated towards efficiency and effectiveness rather than due process and democratic decision-making. As van Vree puts it, 'compared with parliamentary-like meetings, company-like meetings demand more knowledge and abilities, more team spirit, more mutually anticipated self-control and flexibility' (2011, p. 258). Referring to Elias's and Cas Wouters' (1986; 1999) theory of informalization and the development of a 'third nature', he highlights how it is no longer just a matter of internalizing social rules but also of developing a highly strategic, flexible understanding of how the rules are to be mobilized, perhaps in fact broken or adjusted, in particular circumstances and local conditions. As networks of interdependence become larger and broader and power differentials decrease, the role of meetings in social coordination becomes increasingly significant, 'an ever increasing precise, more equal and more embracing regulation of impulses and short-lived affects' (2011, p. 259), exactly what Elias analysed as the long-term process of civilization.

Meetings are 'the frontline of civilization' and the obligation to attend meetings 'has become the fate of civilized people' (2011, p. 250), because 'the development of meeting behaviour is a process in which people constrain each other towards control of their mutual relations and thus also of themselves, by orientation to ever-longer, more permanent, and more differentiated chains of action' (2011, p. 245). Indeed, given the globalization of organizational structures, van Vree also refers to meetings as 'the trailblazers of contemporary, continental and global, integration processes' (2011, p. 257). He draws the obvious parallel with court society, observing that:

> Courtiers gathered in set places and at set times to perform specific acts according to exact rules. They bitterly complained about these useless rituals, but went through them again and again. The court etiquette endured as a 'ghostly perpetuum mobile' (Elias, 2006 [1969], p. 95) because of the current power relationships between the most important social groupings. The slightest modification of a ritual might have been interpreted by a group or faction as an attempt to upset the shaky social power balance. In the same way contemporary organization men seem to be socially fated to meet and to meet again with the same colleagues at set places and set times to perform similar acts every time.
>
> (van Vree, 2011, p. 253)

We saw earlier how Bendix noted, with the spread of meeting activities in business firms, the emergence of an upper class of 'moderate' managers, 'even-tempered when others rage, brave when others fear, calm when others are excited, self-controlled when others indulge' (Bendix, 1974 [1956], p. 332). Today it is those individuals who are most skilled in this management of emotional style who are most successful in organizational life. Being a successful manager, then, means being 'good at running meetings', having a high tolerance for their tedium and repetition and being skilled at managing the emotional dynamics of a smaller or larger group of members of the organization. Van Vree, agreeing with Bendix, notes the historical emergence of an 'upper class' of professional chairmen (and increasingly chairwomen) functioning at the top of a wide variety of organizations, part and parcel of the phenomenon of interlocking directorships and the 'revolving door' between management positions in government, the public sector and private corporations.

John Connolly and Paddy Dolan – beyond agency/structure

In a number of articles since around 2010, John Connolly and Paddy Dolan have significantly developed a process-figurational approach in organization studies, with a particular focus on two Irish case studies: the development of the Gaelic Athletic Association (GAA) from the late 19th century to the present, and the changing approach to advertising and marketing amongst the management of the Guinness brewery between the 1880s and the 1960s (Connolly, 2016; 2017; Connolly & Dolan 2011; 2012a; 2012b; 2016; 2017; Dolan & Connolly, 2017). There is not the space here to discuss their close analysis of organizational change in these two settings, but it is possible to identify the key conceptual points that they make. First, they draw attention to the continued heavy reliance in institutional theory on dualisms such as structure/agency, individual/society and micro/macro, dualisms which essentially misperceive social reality, failing to grasp the multi-polarity and multi-directionality of power relations, the long-term historical processes within which organizational change is always embedded. In relation to Arthur Guinness and the company's approach to advertising, for example, they argued that changes within the organization need to be understood in relation to shifts in class relations in England, a 'changing power ratio between bourgeoisie and those above (the aristocracy and gentry) and those below (lower class groups)', which 'shaped, propelled and constrained opportunities for innovation across a myriad of social spheres' (Dolan & Connolly, 2017, p. 142). In relation to the professionalization of the GAA, they argue that the changes which took place can only be properly understood in relation to Elias's conception of a broader process of civilization, in the sense of lengthening chains of interdependencies underpinning increased requirements for foresight and management of one's emotional life.

Second, while Bourdieu's concept of 'field' has frequently been turned to in order to resolve the problems besetting the structure/agency dualism, they point out that 'fields' are relatively constrained and closely defined social spaces – art, education, sport – and the concept is less suited than figuration to capture the overlapping of fields, as well as the social spaces between fields (Dolan & Connolly, 2017, p. 143). They illustrate the difference between Elias's emphasis on long-term processes and the ways in which institutional and organizational change is usually explained by contrasting Rao, Monin and Durand's (2003) account of the shift towards nouvelle cuisine in France from the 1970s onwards – focusing on how the nouvelle cuisine movement was driven by the anti-authoritarian ethos of the May 1968 student movement – with the way Elias would have approached the same question, by suggesting the geological metaphor of change resulting from an earthquake (in this case, May 1968), to change resulting from the much slower and more gradual movement of tectonic plates – in this case, gradually shifting power balances between different social, professional and consumer groups (Dolan & Connolly, 2017, p. 145). While

Dolan and Connolly do not mention this, a striking absence in Rao et al.'s account is the diner, and their explanation is framed almost entirely in the 'great man' terms of the culinary concepts, norms and orientations of activist chefs, a *homo clausus* type of explanation which ignores the broader figurations – linking them with diners, food and alcohol producers, hotels, cafés, food journalists – and the changing competitive logic of these various intersecting figurations – as a Bourdieusian would say, 'fields'.

Stewart Clegg and Ad van Iterson – liquid organizations

For Stewart Clegg and Ad van Iterson (2013), agreeing with Tim Newton, Elias's analysis of the place of habitus and subjectivity within power relations has significant implications for organization theory, both over the long term and with respect to the arguments concerning 'informalization' in the civilizing process. They are especially concerned with an understanding of how self-regulation has been transformed within the long-term shift from 'iron cage' organizations such as monasteries, armies, factories and Weberian bureaucracies to the de-differentiated, de-specialized, decentralized, organic and networked organization characteristic of 'liquid modernity' (Clegg, 1990; Clegg & Baumeler, 2010; Clegg & Cunha, this volume). They examine aspects of Elias's arguments in relation to the question of the salience of proximity versus distance in relations of interdependence, as well as reflecting on the tightness of the connection between lengthening chains of interdependence and the forms taken by self-regulation. For Elias, longer and more complex interdependence chains lead to greater self-regulation, but Clegg and van Iterson point out that it is possible that this depends on proximity and visibility. To the extent that interdependence and its supposed constraints remain invisible, it may be that the effect is the reverse, lessening self-regulation. They refer here to Mouzelis (1995) and Newton's (2001) critical accounts, arguing that it appears that 'not all interdependence leads to a conversion in self-regulation and subjectivity. The hypothesized relation has to be tested everywhere, in various time periods, to assess whether a connection exists, and, if so, to assess its exact nature and form' (Clegg & van Iterson, 2013, p. 629; see also Breuer, 1991, p. 407, who makes the same point).

On the one hand, then, they agree that non-hierarchical relationships do require higher levels of informalized self-regulation – Wouters (2011) would use the term 'third nature' – to function effectively (van Iterson, 2009, pp. 337–338; see also van Iterson, Mastenbroek & Soeters, 2001). In loosening organizational structures and making them more flexible and fluid, there is an effective transfer of the regulatory mechanisms from the organizational structure to the level of self-regulation – exactly what Elias was referring to in the shift from external to self-restraint. 'Postmodern organizations thus represent increasingly lengthy and complex webs of interdependency that require people to take each other into greater consideration', and de-specialized workers have to be as proficient as 'network players' as were the courtiers at Versailles, needing to juggle 'anxious, disciplined behavior and relaxed, informal behaviour' (Clegg & van Iterson, 2013, p. 629).

On the other hand, the opposite effect can also be discerned, given how abstract and purely functional the organizational constraints have become. 'Why be concerned,' ask Clegg and van Iterson rhetorically, 'with people whom you only see once a week or month? ... with people with whom collaboration will end in the very near future? ... with people who hardly understand what you can do or what you actually do?' (Clegg & van Iterson, 2013, p. 630). The potential for increased rather than decreased violence of various sorts – bullying, abuse, anger – is then as much a part of liquefied organizational relationships as increased self-regulation, and it remains an open question exactly how the two possibilities are balanced out. They conclude by indicating an important line of future research in organization studies, drawing on process-figurational theory: the possibility of working to 'unravel the dynamics between the two faces of civilizing processes' (Clegg & van Iterson, 2013, p. 631).

Future directions

My aim in this chapter has been to provide some useful reflections on the various ways in which Elias's process-figurational theory might be equally if not more effective in overcoming the main theoretical problems in organization theory. Elias provides a conceptual toolbox well suited to overcoming stubborn theoretical difficulties, dissolving, indeed rendering meaningless, the supposed agency/structure problem. The absence of discussions of power is already an important problem in organization theory, as Stewart Clegg has been arguing for some time now, but in addition to turning to theorists such as Foucault and Latour, Elias's theory of power is also a valuable theoretical resource. His work helps address the question of how organizations have been transformed from rational, mechanistic forms to networked forms (Clegg, 1990), their anchorage in surrounding social dynamics and relations, and above all, the constantly increasing interdependence of human action. His ideas constitute a powerful critique of much management thinking as 'magico-mythical' (Stacey, 2007) and constitute theoretical foundations that make it possible to see a range of different things about organizational life and change, as well as seeing things we are used to, more clearly, that otherwise become caught up in tired and irresolvable conceptual disputes.

It should also be said that the relationship between Elias and organization theory is most productive when it is critical and two-way, when a clearer focus on the organizational dimensions of social life might enhance Elias's analyses, perhaps nudge them in new directions. It is true that Elias often placed the institutional form taken by social relations and processes very much in the background of his account and his emphasis on the unintentional, unplanned nature of social order often underplayed the ways in which intentions are in fact realized (van Krieken, 1990). It is not, then, simply a matter of looking at organizations in terms of process-figurational theory but also of reading Elias through an organizational studies lens.

There are a variety of possible directions into which organizational research drawing on Elias might travel, including:

- How Elias's account of the structure and dynamics of court society can be used to analyse contemporary organizational forms, the performative dynamics of organizational culture

- How the concept of figurations can be used as an alternative to the agency/structure dualism to analyse what writers like Karl Weick (2012) term the 'impermanence' of organizations
- How Elias's concept of unplanned order as the interweaving of intentional action by figurations of interdependent individuals and groups can be used to analyse the emergence of new organizational forms such as Google, Facebook and Uber
- How Dolan and Connolly's close analysis of the Gaelic Athletic Association and the Guinness brewery can be drawn upon to develop similar analyses of other organizations, using process-figurational theory
- The broader implications of Wilbert van Vree's account of the 'meetingization' of society, how decision-making processes in different organizations revolve around the formation of particular kinds of habitus and psychological disposition. (Judith Brett [2002], for example, drawing on van Vree, highlights how the disjunction between the parliamentary and professional styles of meeting affect how the realm of politics is perceived and how it might play a role in the declining legitimacy of political parties and governments.)
- How Elias's theory of power-in-figurations can provide alternative explanations to those dependent on theorists such as Foucault
- How changing forms of the organization of work can be analysed with an emphasis on long-term processes, figurational relations and the changing formation of habitus. Elias's conceptual approach would generate a range of new insights into, for example, the emergence and spread of 'McDonaldization' (Ritzer, 2013) and the 'deformalization' of organizations in the 'Uberfication' (Fleming, 2017, p. 34) of forms of work
- The ways in which the expression of various forms of violence and emotions more broadly are both continually reshaped in organizations and also continue to play an important role, the dialectic of civilizing and decivilizing processes and informalization
- The impact of social media on organizational dynamics, power relations and the formation of subjectivity both within organizations and linking with broader social relations
- The ways in which the connections between process-figurational and actor-network theories – so far only lightly observed – can be developed into a more robust dialogue with empirical applications
- How networked, postmodern organizations balance the opposing tendencies that they generate. Clegg and van Iterson, for example, note that 'how the tension between discipline and expression in postmodern organizations will affect organizational members' disposition is an intriguing issue for further study' (Clegg & van Iterson, 2013, p. 631)
- In terms of methodology and possible research projects, Clegg and van Iterson point to the possibility of following Elias's own method and examining etiquette manuals and their equivalents over time, management texts, as well as surveys and interviews, and ethnographies. One could add to those empirical sources studies of 'how to succeed' books, TED talks, the organizational rules and norms built into popular culture (*Mad Men*, police dramas, films, etc.) the discursive performance and impact of public figures such as Jordan Peterson, Donald Trump, as well as the narratives around celebrity CEOs – the likes of Richard Branson, Elon Musk, etc.

The potential of Elias's process-figurational theory for organizational analysis is really only in its early stages but this chapter has sketched the basic contours of how Elias's sociology can contribute to both theoretical development and empirical research in organization studies.

End-of-chapter exercises

1. Critically examine Elias's argument that most, if not all, social and organizational change is the unplanned outcome of the interweaving of intentional individual actions. Is this true, for example, of the emergence of Facebook and Google, or the 'Uberfication' of work organization?
2. Why use the concept 'figuration', instead of network, or structure and agency?
3. Explain the central features of social interaction in court society and how court society relates to what you know about the changing structure and dynamics of organizations today?
4. How does Elias explain the power dynamics of the relationships between established members of any community and outsiders or newcomers, and to what extent can those power dynamics be seen as a model for conflict within organizations?
5. Take any topic in organization studies and explain how the combination of a 'processual' and a 'relational' approach might provide a distinctive way of analysing that topic.
6. Using that same example, outline the ways in which seeing that topic as part of a long historical process would facilitate a particular kind of analytical perspective.
7. To what extent and in what ways is it true to say that organizations are caught in ever-lengthening chains of interdependence; for example, in processes of globalization, which require ever more subtle and nuanced management of emotions and dispositions in organizational life?
8. What difference does it make to the analysis of power and subjectivity in organizations to think in terms of *homines aperti* (open persons) as opposed to the *homo clausus* (closed person)?

Glossary

Court society The social form characterizing aristocratic and royal courts from the 15th to the 18th centuries, constituting the negative reference point for bureaucratic organizational forms from the 18th century onwards. It was organized around a distinctive 'court rationality' which both preceded bureaucratic, instrumental-legal rationality, but also accompanies it today as an undercurrent, with its particular mechanisms of power, competition, distinction and social differentiation continuing to operate in contemporary social and organizational life.

Figuration Derived from the concept 'configuration' in Gestalt psychology, the term is used to refer to the form taken by human social life at a number of different levels. Used as an alternative to concepts such as 'network', it encompasses the following points: that humans can only be understood in their relations of interdependence, shaped by the figurations they are part of; that figurations are constantly undergoing processes of change, and that they have their own dynamic driven by the interweaving of intentional human action; and that they are characterized by constantly shifting power balances.

Habitus   Internalized social constraint, sometimes translated as 'personality structure', a psychological and emotional orientation and set of dispositions experienced as 'second nature', in the sense of feeling as self-evident as if it was simply 'human nature'.

Homo clausus/homines aperti   Closed person/open persons. Referring to the need always to think of human individuals in their *relations of interdependence* with others (*homines aperti*), rather than as autonomous and separate from 'society' (*homo clausus*).

Informalization   Term used occasionally by Elias but in greater depth by Cas Wouters, to refer to emergence of less rigid and standardized modes of self-regulation. Elias had analysed the development of 'second nature' – an apparatus of social control functioning relatively automatically and blindly – and informalization refers to the ways in which that automaticity gradually became less socially effective, with the shifting character of increasingly democratized social relations requiring the formation of a 'third nature', based on more reflexive and flexible forms of self-regulation.

Power   Understood as a *relation*, not a thing, object or resource, characterizing *all* social life and all figurations, constituting a *reciprocal*, not a one-way, relationship between individuals or groups, often multi-polar rather than only bi-polar.

Process and relation   Two core concepts constituting Elias's rejection of 'reification', arguing for thinking of human social life in terms of long-term historical processes, and with an emphasis on relations between individuals and groups as opposed to thinking in terms of their apparently separate, autonomous characteristics.

Process of civilization   The long-term shift in the balance between external, social constraint and internalized psychological constraint towards the latter, driven by constantly lengthening chains of interdependence requiring increasingly complex, nuanced and balanced forms of self-regulation.

Reification   Turning dynamic, ever-changing social relationships into a static thing or object.

Unplanned order   An alternative to 'social structure' or 'society', the outcome of the interweaving of the intentional actions of interdependent individuals and groups, generating changes and patterns usually unintended by any of those individuals or groups. The term is also useful to capture the form and dynamics of organizations.

Notes

1   There are now a number of useful general introductions and overviews of Elias's sociology, including Fletcher (1997), van Krieken (1998), Mennell (1999), Dunning and Hughes (2013), and Loyal and Quilley (2004).

2   The term should probably be 'relational-processual-figurational', but that's even more unwieldy.

3   For a useful discussion of the strengths of the concept 'figuration' in comparison with 'network' or 'assemblage', see Couldry & Hepp (2017, pp. 61–73). As they put it: 'Missing from both concepts (network and assemblage) is an attention to the complexity of our

changing interrelations and interactions through communications, and specifically mediated communications. The strength of "network" is the attention to the structural features of actor constellations, whereas the strength of "assemblage" is its attention to the fine detail of practice and its entanglement with material technologies. But neither concept discusses comprehensively how complexity is built up in and through processes of meaning-construction and resource-distribution' (p. 62).

4   See also Simmel (1896; 1971 [1908], pp. 97–98).

References

Note on works by Elias: In addition to *On the Process of Civilization*, first published in German in 1939, Elias published extensively from the 1950s onwards, and there have been multiple versions, with differing translations, of some of his works. *On the Process of Civilization*, in particular, was published again in German in 1969, in English as separate volumes, at different times, in 1978 and 1982, as a combined volume in 1994 and then revised in 2000. Here reference is always to the version in *The Collected Works of Norbert Elias*, volumes 1–18, published by UCD Press. I have also ordered the Elias references according to their date of original publication, rather than the date of publication in the collected works.

Alvesson, M., & Spicer, A. (2018). Neo-institutional theory and organization studies: A mid-life crisis? *Organization Studies*. https://doi.org/10.1177%2F0170840618772610.

Bendix, R. (1974 [1956]). *Work and authority in industry*. Berkeley, CA: University of California Press.

Blair, H. (2003). Winning and losing in flexible labour markets: The formation and operation of networks of interdependence in the UK film industry. *Sociology, 37*(4), 677–694.

Boudon, R. (1982). *The unintended consequences of social action*. London: Macmillan.

Bourdieu, P. (1985). The genesis of the concepts of habitus and of field. *Sociocriticism, 2*(2), 11–24.

Bourdieu, P. (1990). *In other words*. Cambridge: Polity.

Brett, J. (2002). Parliament, meetings and civil society. *Papers on Parliament, 38*, 43–60.

Breuer, S. (1991). The denouements of civilization: Elias and modernity. *International Social Science Journal, 128*, 405–416.

Breuer, S. (1994). Society of individuals, society of organizations: A comparison of Norbert Elias and Max Weber. *History of the Human Sciences, 7*(4), 41–60.

Callon, M. (1999). Actor network theory – the market test. In J. Law, & J. Hassard (eds) *Actor network theory and after* (pp. 181–195). Oxford: Blackwell.

Callon, M., & Law, J. (1997). After the individual in society: Lessons on collectivity from science, technology and society. *Canadian Journal of Sociology, 22*(2), 165–182.

Cassirer, E. (1953 [1910]). *Substance and function and Einstein's theory of relativity*. New York: Dover.

Chia, R. (1995). From modern to postmodern organizational analysis. *Organization Studies, 16*(4), 579–604.

Chia, R. (2005). Organization theory as a postmodern science. In C. Knudsen, & and H. Tsoukas (eds) *The Oxford handbook of organization theory* (pp. 113–140). Oxford: Oxford University Press.

Clegg, S. (1990). *Modern organizations*. London: Sage.

Clegg, S. (2010). The state, power, and agency: Missing in action in institutional theory? *Journal of Management Inquiry, 19*(1), 4–13.

Clegg, S., & Baumeler, C. (2010). Essai: From iron cages to liquid modernity in organization analysis. *Organization Studies, 31*(12), 1713–1733.

Clegg, S. R., & van Iterson, A. (2013). The effects of liquefying place, time, and organizational boundaries on employee behaviour: Lessons of classical sociology. *M@n@gement*, *16*(5), 621–635.

Collins, R. (1992). The romanticism of agency/structure versus the analysis of micro/macro. *Current Sociology*, *40*(1), 77–97.

Connolly, J. (2016). Elias and habitus: Explaining bureaucratisation processes in the Gaelic Athletic Association. *Culture & Organization*, *22*(5), 452–475.

Connolly, J. (2017). Figurational dynamics and the function of advertising at Arthur Guinness & Sons Ltd, 1876–1960. In J. Connolly, & P. Dolan (ed.) *The social organisation of marketing* (pp. 61–91). Cham: Palgrave Macmillan.

Connolly, J., & Dolan, P. (2011). Organizational centralization as figurational dynamics: Movements and counter-movements in the Gaelic Athletic Association. *Management & Organizational History*, *6*(1), 37–58.

Connolly, J., & Dolan, P. (2012a). Re-theorizing the 'structure–agency' relationship: Figurational theory, organizational change and the Gaelic Athletic Association. *Organization*, *20*(4), 491–511.

Connolly, J., & Dolan, P. (2012b). Sport, media and the Gaelic Athletic Association: The quest for the 'youth' of Ireland. *Media, Culture & Society*, *34*(4), 407–423.

Connolly, J., & Dolan, P. (2016). Social class tensions, habitus and the advertising of Guinness. *Sociological Review*, 1–18.

Connolly, J., & Dolan, P. (2017). Figurational theory, marketing and markets: Moving from description and technological empiricism to empirical–theoretical explanations. In J. Connolly, & P. Dolan (ed.) *The social organisation of marketing* (pp. 205–221). Cham: Palgrave Macmillan.

Costas, J., & Grey, C. (2018). Violence and organization studies. *Organization Studies*, June 12. https://doi.org/10.1177%2F0170840618782282.

Couldry, N., & Hepp, A. (2017). *The mediated construction of reality*. Cambridge: Polity.

Dolan, P., & Connolly, J. (2017). Beyond logic and norms: A figurational critique of institutional theory in organisation studies. *Cambio. Rivista sulle trasformazioni sociali*, *7*(14), 139–149.

Dopson, S. (1997). *Managing ambiguity and change*. Basingstoke: Macmillan.

Dopson, S. (2001). Applying an Eliasian approach to organizational analysis. *Organization*, *8*(3), 515–535.

Dopson, S. (2005). The diffusion of medical innovations: Can figurational sociology contribute? *Organization Studies*, *26*(8), 1125–1144.

Dopson, S., & Waddington, I. (1996). Managing social change: A process-sociological approach to understanding organisational change within the National Health Service. *Sociology of Health & Illness*, *18*(4), 525–550.

Dunning, E., & Hughes, J. (2013). *Norbert Elias and modern sociology*. London: Bloomsbury.

Elias, N. (2010 [1939]). The society of individuals. In R. van Krieken (ed.) *The society of individuals. The collected works of Norbert Elias, Vol. 10* (pp. 7–62). Dublin: UCD Press.

Elias, N. (2012 [1939]). *On the process of civilisation. The collected works of Norbert Elias, Vol. 3*, S. Mennell, E. Dunning, J. Goudsblom, & R. Kilminster (eds). Dublin: UCD Press.

Elias, N. (2012 [1968]). Postscript. In S. Mennell, E. Dunning, J. Goudsblom, & R. Kilminster (eds) *On the process of civilisation: Sociogenetic and psychogenetic investigations. The collected works of Norbert Elias, Vol. 3* (pp. 493–527). Dublin: UCD Press.

Elias, N. (2006 [1969]). *The court society. The collected works of Norbert Elias, Vol. 2*, S. Mennell (ed.). Dublin: UCD Press.

Elias, N. (2009 [1969]). Sociology and psychiatry. In S. Mennell, & E. Dunning (eds) *Essays III: On sociology and the humanities. The collected works of Norbert Elias, Vol. 16* (pp. 159–179). Dublin: UCD Press.

Elias, N. (2012 [1978]). *What is sociology? The Collected Works of Norbert Elias, Vol. 5*, A. Bogner, K. Liston, & S. Mennell (eds). Dublin: UCD Press.

Elias, N. (2008 [1980]). The civilizing of parents. In R. Kilminster, & S. Mennell (eds) *Essays II: The collected works of Norbert Elias, Vol. 15* (pp. 14–40). Dublin: UCD Press.

Elias, N. (2010 [1987]). Changes in the we–I balance. In R. van Krieken (ed.) *The society of individuals. The collected works of Norbert Elias, Vol. 10* (pp. 137–212). Dublin: UCD Press.

Elias, N. (2009 [1997]). Towards a theory of social processes. In S. Mennell, & E. Dunning (eds) *Essays III: On sociology and the humanities. The collected works of Norbert Elias, Vol. 16* (pp. 9–39). Dublin: UCD Press.

Elias, N., & Dunning, E. (2008 [1986]). *Quest for excitement. The collected works of Norbert Elias, Vol. 7*, E. Dunning (ed.). Dublin: UCD Press.

Elias, N., & Scotson, J. L. (2008 [1965]). *The established and the outsiders. The collected works of Norbert Elias, Vol. 4*, C. Wouters (ed.). Dublin: UCD Press.

Emirbayer, M. (1997). Manifesto for a relational sociology. *American Journal of Sociology*, 103(2), 281–317.

Fleming, P. (2017). *The death of homo economicus*. London: Pluto.

Fletcher, J. (1997). *Violence and civilization*. Cambridge: Polity.

Frawley, S. (2015). Organizational power and the management of a mega-event: The case of Sydney 2000. *Event Management*, 19, 247–260.

Freud, S. (1961 [1923]). The ego and the id. In J. Strachey (ed.) *The complete collected psychological works of Sigmund Freud, Vol XIX (1923–1925): The ego and the id and other works* (pp. 1–66). London: Hogarth Press.

Goudsblom, J. (1977). *Sociology in the balance*. Oxford: Basil Blackwell.

Gourdin, G., & Meul, I. (2013). Emergence and development of medical unionism in Belgium: An Eliasian perspective. *Management & Organizational History*, 8(3), 306–321.

Jacoby, H. (1973). *The bureaucratization of the world*. Berkeley, CA: University of California Press.

Kaspersen, L. B., & Gabriel, N. (2008). The importance of survival units for Norbert Elias's figurational perspective. *Sociological Review*, 56(3), 370–387.

Kieser, A. (1998). From freemasons to industrious partiots. Organizing and disciplining in 18th century Germany. *Organization Studies*, 19(1), 47–71.

Kuipers, G. (2018). Communicative figurations: Towards a new paradigm for the media age? In A. Hepp, A. Breiter, & U. Hasebrink (eds) *Communicative figurations* (pp. 425–436). London and New York: Palgrave Macmillan.

Latour, B. (1993). *We have never been modern*. Cambridge, MA: Harvard University Press.

Law, J. (1994). *Organizing modernity*. Oxford: Blackwell.

Lesjo, J. H. (2000). Lillehammer 1994: Planning, figurations and the 'Green' Winter Games. *International Review for the Sociology of Sport*, 35(3), 282–293.

Lever, J. (2011). Urban regeneration partnerships: A figurational critique of governmentality theory. *Sociology*, 45(1), 86–101.

Lever, J., & Swailes, S. (2017). Ballet for the Sun King: Power, talent and organisation. In J. Connolly, & P. Dolan (eds) *The social organisation of marketing* (pp. 143–169). London and New York: Palgrave Macmillan.

Loyal, S., & Quilley, S. (2004). *The sociology of Norbert Elias*. Cambridge: Cambridge University Press.

Lukács, G. (1971). *History and class consciousness*. London: Merlin.

Maguire, J. S. (2017). Wine and China: Making sense of an emerging market with figurational sociology. In J. Connolly, & P. Dolan (eds) *The social organisation of marketing* (pp. 31–59). London and New York: Palgrave Macmillan.

Mastenbroek, W. (1993). *Conflict management and organization development.* Chichester: John Wiley & Sons.

Mastenbroek, W. (1996). Organizational innovation in historical perspective: Change as duality management. *Business Horizons, 39*(4), 5–14.

Mastenbroek, W. (2000). Organizational behavior as emotion management. In N. M. Ashkanasy, C. E. J. Härtel, & W. J. Zerbe (eds) *Emotions in the workplace* (pp. 19–35). Westport, CT: Quorum.

Mastenbroek, W. (2002a). Norbert Elias as organizational sociologist. In A. van Iterson, W. Mastenbroek, T. Newton, & D. Smith (eds) *The civilized organization* (pp. 173–188). Amsterdam: John Benjamins.

Mastenbroek, W. (2002b). Management and organization: Does Elias give us something to hold on to? In A. van Iterson, W. Mastenbroek, T. Newton, & D. Smith (eds) *The civilized organization* (pp. 205–218). Amsterdam: John Benjamins.

Mastenbroek, W. (2005). Organizational behavior in historical perspective: Part 2: Emotion management, status competition and power play. *Management Site.* http://www.managementsite. com/content/articles/491/491.asp.

Mennell, S. (1990). Decivilizing processes: Theoretical significance and some lines of research. *International Sociology, 5*(2), 205–223.

Mennell, S. (1999). *Norbert Elias: An introduction.* Dublin: UCD Press.

Mouzelis, N. (1995). *Sociological theory: What went wrong?* London: Routledge.

Newton, T. (1999). Power, subjectivity and British industrial and organisational sociology: The relevance of the work of Norbert Elias. *Sociology, 33*(2), 411–440.

Newton, T. (2001). Organization: The relevance and the limitations of Elias. *Organization, 8*(3), 467–495.

Newton, T., & Smith, D. (2002). Introduction: Norbert Elias and the civilized organization. In A. van Iterson, W. Mastenbroek, T. Newton, & D. Smith (eds) *The civilized organization* (pp. vii–xxviii). Amsterdam: John Benjamins.

Rao, H., Monin, P., & Durand, R. (2003). Institutional change in Toque Ville: Nouvelle cuisine as an identity movement in French gastronomy. *American Journal of Sociology, 108*(4), 795–843.

Reed, M. I. (1997). In praise of duality and dualism: Rethinking agency and structure in organizational analysis. *Organization Studies, 18*(1),21–42.

Reed, M. I. (2005). The agency/structure dilemma in organization theory: Open doors and brick walls. In C. Knudsen, & H. Tsoukas (eds) *The Oxford handbook of organization theory* (pp. 289–309). Oxford: Oxford University Press.

Ritzer, G. (2013). *The McDonaldization of society,* 5th edn. Thousand Oaks, CA: Sage.

Simmel, G. (1896). Superiority and Subordination as Subject-matter of Sociology. *American Journal of Sociology, 2*(2), 167–189.

Simmel, G. (1971 [1908]). *Individuality and social forms.* Chicago, IL: University of Chicago Press.

Smith, D. (2001). Organizations and humiliation: Looking beyond Elias. *Organization, 8*(3),537–560.

Smith, D. (2002). The humiliating organization: The functions and dysfunctions of degradation. In A. van Iterson, W. Mastenbroek, T. Newton, & D. Smith (eds) *The civilized organization* (pp. 41–58). Amsterdam: John Benjamins.

Soeters, J., & van Iterson, A. (2002). Blame and praise gossip in organizations: Established, outsiders and the civilising process. In A. van Iterson, W. Mastenbroek, T. Newton, & D. Smith (eds) *The civilized organization* (pp. 25–40). Amsterdam: John Benjamins.

Stacey, R. (2003). Learning as an activity of interdependent people. *The Learning Organization*, 10(6), 325–331.

Stacey, R. (2007). The challenge of human interdependence. Consequences for thinking about the day to day practice of management in organizations. *European Business Review*, 19(4), 292–302.

Stacey, R. (2012). *Tools and techniques of leadership and management*. London: Routledge.

Stokvis, R. (2002). Figurational sociology, monopolization and corporate governance. In A. van Iterson, W. Mastenbroek, T. Newton, & D. Smith (eds) *The civilized organization* (pp. 85–98). Amsterdam: John Benjamins.

Suddaby, R. (2010). Challenges for institutional theory. *Journal of Management Inquiry*, 19(1), 14–20.

Tsoukas, H., & Chia, R. (2002). On organizational becoming: Rethinking organizational change. *Organization Science*, 13(5), 567–582.

van Iterson, A. (2009). Norbert Elias's impact on organization studies. In P. S. Adler (ed.) *The Oxford handbook of sociology and organization studies: Classical foundations* (pp. 327–347). Oxford: Oxford University Press.

van Iterson, A., Mastenbroek, W., & Soeters, J. (2001). Civilizing and informalizing: Organizations in an Eliasian context. *Organization*, 8(3), 497–514.

van Iterson, A., & Richter, J. (2017). 'Friends and followers': The social organisation of firms' online communities. In J. Connolly, & P. Dolan (eds) *The social organisation of marketing* (pp. 171–192). London and New York: Palgrave Macmillan.

van Krieken, R. (1990). The organization of the soul: Elias and Foucault on discipline and the self. *Archives Europeénnes de Sociologie*, 31(2), 353–371.

van Krieken, R. (1996). Proto-governmentalization and the historical formation of organizational subjectivity. *Economy & Society*, 25(2), 195–221.

van Krieken, R. (1998). *Norbert Elias*. London: Routledge.

van Krieken, R. (1999). The barbarism of civilization: Cultural genocide and the 'Stolen Generations'. *British Journal of Sociology*, 50(2), 297–315.

van Vree, W. (1999). *Meetings, manners, and civilization*. London: Leicester University Press.

van Vree, W. (2002). The development of meeting behaviour in modern organizations and the rise of an upper class of professional chairpersons. In A. van Iterson, W. Mastenbroek, T. Newton, & D. Smith (eds) *The civilized organization: Norbert Elias and the future of organization studies* (pp. 3–24). Amsterdam: John Benjamins.

van Vree, W. (2011). Meetings: The frontline of civilization. *Sociological Review*, 59(S1), 241–262.

van Vree, W., & Bos, G. (1989). Vergaderen, verhoofsing en parlementarisering. *Amsterdams Sociologisch Tijdschrift*, 16(3), 52–75.

Vertigans, S. (2017). Unintentional social consequences of disorganised marketing of corporate social responsibility: Figurational insights into the oil and gas sector in Africa. In J. Connolly, & P. Dolan (eds) *The social organisation of marketing* (pp. 93–118). London and New York: Palgrave Macmillan.

Weick, K. (1969). *The social psychology of organizing*. Reading, MA: Addison-Wesley.

Weick, K. (1995). *Sensemaking*. Thousand Oaks, CA: Sage.

Weick, K. (2012). *Making sense of the organization*. Chichester: Wiley.

Whorf, B. L. (1956). *Language, thought and reality*. Cambridge, MA: MIT Press.

Whyte, W. H. (1956). *The organization man*. New York: Simon & Schuster.

Wouters, C. (1977). Informalisation and the civilising process. In P.R. Gleichman, J. Goudsblom, & H. Korte (eds) *Human figurations* (pp. 437–453). Amsterdam: Amsterdams Sociologisch Tijdschrift.

Wouters, C. (1986). Formalization and informalization: Changing tension balances in civilizing processes. *Theory, Culture & Society*, 3(2), 1–18.

Wouters, C. (1999). Changing patterns of social controls and self-controls – on the rise of crime since the 1950s and the sociogenesis of a 'third nature'. *British Journal of Criminology*, 39(3), 416–432.

Wouters, C. (2004). Changing regimes of manners and emotions: From disciplining to informalizing. In S. Loyal, & S. Quillet (eds) *The sociology of Norbert Elias* (pp. 193–211). Cambridge: Cambridge University Press.

Wouters, C. (2007). *Informalization: Manners and emotions since 1890*. London: Sage.

Wouters, C. (2011). How civilizing processes continued: Towards an informalization of manners and a third nature personality. *Sociological Review*, 59(S1), 140–159.

Zelko, H. P. (1969 [1957]). *The business conference*. New York: McGraw-Hill.

10 Niklas Luhmann and organizations as social systems

Xavier Deroy

Chapter objectives

This chapter highlights how communication structurally changes modern societies and develops the main contributions of German sociologist Niklas Luhmann to the field of management and organization studies.

The chapter discusses how:

- Communication builds a fragmented society of social systems centred on their inherent practices
- Communication operations of social systems are structured by their respective codes
- Communication networks with no centre systematically make up the complexity of modern societies, which may generate unexpected social evolutions
- Organizations constitute stable units in modern societies and are characterized by decisions, designed as communication operations
- The structures and rules communicated by organizations to their members reduce unexpected decisions
- Risk is an inherent element of organizational systemic functioning based on communication operations

Introduction

Born in 1927 into a middle-class family, Niklas Luhmann studied in Freiburg for three years from 1946 and on graduation joined the civil service, where he worked for ten years. He took a sabbatical year in 1962 to study in the USA with Talcott Parsons at Harvard. When he returned to Germany, he obtained a doctorate under the direction of the sociologist Helmut Schelsky. He worked at the University of Munster, and in 1968 was appointed professor of Sociology at the University of Bielefeld. There, he elaborated his social systems theory. After a while, he turned to sociology, with a focus on topics such as trust, love, power and art. He examined those different subjects from a systemic perspective.

With the publication of *Social Systems* (Luhmann, 1995a), his thought became more consistent and his scientific project more coherent. He showed how complex societies could reduce their complexity thanks to their systemic differentiation. Interested in theoretical reflexion, he orientated his theory to a more abstract, deliberately meta-theoretical path. His work includes an impressive number of publications, consisting of 40 books, 350 articles and nearly 14,000 pages of writing. Luhmann often revised and nourished his theory, doing so in a book devoted entirely to organizations. In 1997, a year before he died, his book *Theory of Society* offered a comprehensive view of his social theory.

Recognized and widely discussed in sociology and law, Luhmann remains more marginal in organization studies, though several books and articles highlight his theoretical contribution (Bakken & Hernes, 2003; Seidl & Becker, 2006; Seidl, 2006; Becker & Seidl, 2007; Schoeneborn, 2011). Some early texts by Luhmann himself about the organizations of the system of law (Luhmann, 1995b; Luhmann, 2001) have pointed out empirical implications of his concepts. Nevertheless, only few have yet been inspired by a Luhmannian framework in organization studies despite noticeable exceptions (see Bakken & Hernes, 2003; Becker & Seidl, 2007).

Perhaps because of his highly contentious theory and its intellectual radicalness, something denoted by several authors, including Moeller (2006) and Brunczel (2010), he doesn't appear in major American journals in organization studies. Many reasons may explain this relative marginalization in organization studies. First, Luhmann is very abstract. Sometimes considered as a conservative after his fierce opposition to the Frankfurt School, he is also viewed by others as a postmodernist because of his analysis of complex societies. Another explanation was advanced by Luhmann himself, who observed that his social systems theory has been reduced to the criticism of structural-functionalism advocated by Parsons, his professor at Harvard (Luhmann, 2017a, pp. 2–5). Even if he borrowed a number of important notions from Parsons, Luhmann, by considering that communication is systematically present in modern societies and at the core of their fragmented social systems, set his own theoretical framework. The first part of this chapter deals with the main features of his theoretical framework. These are the concepts of social systems, autopoiesis, codes and other key elements, including the role of communication, which is the omnipresent theme of his analysis of social systems. In his systemic approach, individuals are conceived of as psychic systems embedded in communication networks.

In his work, Luhmann shows that organizations play a crucial part in preventing social disorder. Organizations reduce the contingency of operations of communication and absorb uncertainty derived from these operations, through hierarchies, decision premises and membership. The second part of this chapter deals with the role of organizations in achieving this partial reduction of uncertainty. With his social systems theory, Luhmann provides an approach in which event and contingency are at the centre of modern societies based on communication. Paradoxically, organizational decisions can also reintroduce unexpected and worrying social evolutions, especially when they take decisions about the management of risks.

Main features of Luhmann's theoretical framework

The role of communication

Luhmann stresses the key role of communication in the increasing complexity of modern societies. Communication is the central component of a theory of society characterized by its recursivity. Any operation of communication cognitively and temporarily follows another operation of communication. The recursivity of intertwined networks of communications leads to the autonomy of communication. The autonomization of communication is decisive in Luhmann's theory. Indeed, any 'substance' of other systems (social systems, psychic systems) remains unknown for observers. Only operations of communication are observed and given a meaning. Knowledge of other systems does not exist in itself but is always mediatized by communication.

Communication differentiates social systems composing society. Contrary to well-known sociologists like Durkheim, Weber or even Bourdieu who left the door open for coordination to preserve some social order and control, Luhmann signals his radicalism by this denial of any solid social coordination between social systems. In spite of the fact that communication is systematically present, paradoxically, this omnipresence coexists with a fragmentation in social systems. Social systems have a specific way to communicate, as they represent different universes of meaning. Their functional specialization makes the differentiated problems that modern societies have to cope with manageable. However, modern societies remain fragmented.

For Luhmann, social differentiation is constantly constructing a society composed of loosely coupled social systems making coordination difficult. Such a systemic fragmentation clearly sets the issue of diverse social evolution, as the very idea of mechanisms allowing global control seems quite remote. According to Luhmann, the possibility of an unexpected evolution is endogenous to such a fragmented society and can endanger it. Consequently, his main preoccupation is to understand if there are any mechanisms to limit or stabilize these unexpected social and potentially dangerous evolutions.

Communication networks: the advent of a flat ontology

Communication is the ontological basis for Luhmann's theoretical system (Luhmann, 1995a). Endorsing Husserl's phenomenology (Husserl, 1970), Luhmann points out that meaning is essential in communication operations. Social systems differently observe the factuality of the world, thus giving a distinct meaning to observed facts and communicating in that way their autopoietic difference. Communication defines ontology without transcendence. Discursive networks have discourses as their only perspective and do not refer to any transcendental value. Communication's future as well as its past are yet another aspect of communication. As Luhmann states: 'The problems of communication feed back into communication' (Luhmann, 2012b, p. 127). Flat ontology makes the distinction between the micro and macro levels or between the centre and the periphery irrelevant. Flat ontology develops through the recursivity connecting the infinite succession of interlinked communication operations. Individuals are embedded in networks of communication. The evolution of society and of each social system depends on communication.

Events as units of communication

Events are temporal units of communication that bear meaning (Luhmann, 2012b, pp. 35–36). Past communication events are the basis of present and future communication events. Networks of recursively linked events of communication construct modern societies. Events follow on from and refer to other events. By definition, events are contingent, as they are neither necessary nor stable. Their contingency can engender unexpected evolutions in society.

Intertwined events shape the history and complexity of contemporary societies. With temporal chains of contingent and recursively intertwined events of communication, evolutions of social systems cannot be monitored. For instance, environmental damages occur despite the measures that ecological parties have been proposing for many years to protect the environment. In a fragmented society composed of uncoordinated social systems, the consequences of measures adopted in the political system cannot be predicted. In modern societies there is no longer established causality between systems whose cognitive and discursive rules are different (Luhmann, 2012b, pp. 75–76).

According to Luhmann, the system's internal functioning mechanisms remains (almost) inaccessible and meaningless for other systems located in its environment. Any attempt to get overall control of society must therefore be discarded. For example, an event in the political system (a change of power and the passing of new laws) will affect its internal evolution. Recursively, other systems in its environment, such as the legal system, will also be affected and will, in their turn, produce legal communication events (legal decisions). Yet, in such a context, anticipation and prior control of the respective evolutions of each system endowed with its own cognitive and communication rules remains arbitrary, since they are subject to the very same succession of contingent communication events.

The place of the individuals

Luhmann pushes away individuals to the periphery of society and substitutes operations of communication for agentic action. For Luhmann a theory of action systematically locks the researcher into the circularity of two mutually dependent theories: a theory of society (which defines the social conditions of action) and a theory of agency (which defines the components of agentic behaviour). To build a sociological theory requires giving up the theory of action and to focus exclusively on communication.

As 'psychic systems', individuals are located in the environment of society embedded in communication networks. Nonetheless, similarly to other social systems, individuals observe and construct communication events. Human agents (psychic systems) lack free will (Luhmann, 1995a; Luhmann, 2012b, pp. 271–277; Moeller, 2006) because they are incorporated in communication networks of which they lack overall intelligence. They observe organized social systems and other psychic systems that surround them and construct, over the course of their interactions with them, a network of communication events (Luhmann, 1995a; Seidl, 2003, p. 127). While within stratified societies individuals occupy a predetermined position, in complex modern societies, fragmented into distinct social systems, they can henceforth over a day or a week hold a variety of roles and statuses in different social systems as members of economic organizations (economic social system), of political parties (political social system), of scientific congresses (scientific social system) or also as artists or visitors to museums (social system of art). Against what some of Luhmann's critics claim, individuals, as psychic systems, interact with society from its periphery in attributing meaning to the communication operations of its social systems. As summarized above, these interactions are necessary for the reproduction of social systems and for the very notion of society. Symmetrically, individuals, assimilated to psychic systems, cannot escape from communication networks on which social systems are based. Luhmann describes a complex whole made up of agents (psychic systems) and social systems, which all observe each other through communication events and recursively produce communication events. This theoretical frame, in which communication is the cornerstone, constitutes the systemic theory of society by Luhmann.

The concept of social systems as autopoietic differences

Luhmann developed his social systems theory in two main books entitled *Social Systems* (1995a), which is probably the best known as well as the most abstract, and *Introduction to Social Systems* (2017a), a collection of conference papers undoubtedly more readable for people unfamiliar with his work. In his social systems theory, Luhmann defines the notion of social systems as one of the most abstract but key elements of his work (Luhmann, 2006). For Luhmann, the systemic approach supporting the notion of social systems constitutes a metatheory. Everything is a system (his theory included), despite the intrinsic differences that separate them. Living systems are biological systems; individual conscience and cognitive capacities are psychic systems (Luhmann, 1995a, p. 2); society is a system made of different social systems.

Luhmann's systems theory derives from what is known as second-order cybernetics or the cybernetics of cybernetics (succeeding to the theory of the open systems or first-order cybernetics by Von Bertalanffy [1975]), which concerns autonomous or closed systems as developed by Ashby (1957; 1958) and Von Foerster (2007). Moreover, Luhmann mentions several times his interest in Simon's concept (1997) of bounded rationality. With his conception of social systems, Luhmann acknowledged his debt to Parsons (2005). Functionalism and the very notion of social systems, as Luhmann (2017a) acknowledges, are concepts used by Parsons. However, the differences are so acute that this initial affiliation quickly faded. Luhmann differs from Parsons in terms of two key issues. Firstly, Luhmann developed a social systems theory relative to system mechanisms of construction, reproduction and evolution, whereas Parsons gave them a quasi-transcendental dimension and a status *sui generis*. Secondly, for Luhmann, communication replaces action: 'It should be remembered that the theory of system differentiation that I have outlined ... deals with communications and not with actions' (Luhmann, 2012b, p. 9).

There are three types of social systems: functional social systems, social systems that constitute organizations, and systems of interactions between individuals (psychic systems). In what follows, particular attention will be paid to functional social systems and then to organizations, conceived as social systems.

Functional social systems operate meaningful distinctions in modern societies through their operations of communication. This functional differentiation into (sub)social systems enables the specialized issues that arise in a complex society to be tackled. Hence, functional systems such as those of law, art, economics, politics and science reduce the complexity of society in solving specialized questions in their respective fields, with their own discourse.

Social systems are autopoietic. Luhmann borrows the concept of *autopoiesis* from the biologists Varela and Maturana to design the process of constructing and reproducing the difference intrinsic to each social system. Yet, the German sociologist insists on the analogic dimension of this borrowing and asserts the specificity of autopoiesis applied to social systems, which can be seen in their operations of communication (Luhmann, 1986, pp. 172–173; Luhmann, 1995a; 2005b; 2017a). Any sociological theory of modern societies is thus *exclusively* a theory of differentiation of autopoietic social systems (Luhmann, 2006). According to Luhmann, only the concept of system itself, in its abstraction, makes the unity.

Communication operations construct this difference:

> Social systems consist of communications. Communication is the autopoietic operation that takes recourse to and anticipates itself, thus generating social systems. There is therefore communication only as social systems and only in social systems. Sociality is not a state of affairs independent of communication (for instance as a property of the human being).
>
> (Luhmann, 2017b, p. 67)

The evolution of social systems can form new distinctions, that is, new functional social systems. For example, during its evolution, the system of law becomes differentiated. With the evolution of the political system and the extension of the state's prerogatives, new durable distinctions emerges from the differentiation of private and public law into distinct legal systems having their own rules and organizations. Thus, the functional distinctions of modern societies become inscribed into social systems that are both the causes and the effects of their complexity. The concepts of code and closure are key elements in the differentiation and evolution process of autopoietic social systems. These concepts condition the distinctness of social systems and maintain their identity.

Code as a media and systemic closure

Systemic closure

The relationship between social systems and their environment made up of other social systems is crucial. By differentiating itself, each social system constructs its environment and, simultaneously, its functional field that shapes its identity. The principle of closure establishes a distinction between social systems and their environment. Closure does not imply being closed to the environment. Closure is a condition for the differentiation of social systems and for the keeping of their identities. Because of their closure, social systems deal with the events of their environment only with regard to their own rules relative to their communication operations. This principle of inclusion/exclusion reduces the complexity and makes it manageable. For a closed social system relying on communication, autopoiesis involves the use of a specific language. This specific discourse contributes to the operational closure of the system, to the maintenance of its identity and its autopoietic reproduction. With the uniqueness of discourses comes the notion of code.

The strategic position of code

The notion of code is strategic in Luhmann's theory and in its application to functional social systems. A code is a *form* strictly associated to a given functional social system. It constitutes its discursive and cognitive norm. It regulates communication operations of systems and defines their cognitive limits.

Codes condition the type of information, the way they are mediatized and thus determine the identity of functional systems (Luhmann, 1995a, p. 142). According to Luhmann, who borrows here from Spencer-Brown's theory of form, this discursive code is a *binary* form. It associates and opposes two sides (0/1 in general), each of which refers to the other. Structurally and logically, the meaning of one is necessarily based on the other. As soon as it is operated as a medium in communication processes, the code requires the selection of one of the sides. The discourse within a system cannot escape from the logic of the code that governs it (Luhmann, 2005a). No solution exists outside the code. Beyond its paradoxical form, the code has to be considered as an '"autological conclusion": the concept also applies to itself, one has to accept that self-exemption is prohibited' (Luhmann, 2017b, p. 51).

A decision is a communication operation, which gives a meaning to an event by selecting one of the two sides of a binary code. A code leaves open possibilities of both reproduction and change, but its grammar is structuring the decision (Luhmann, 2017c, p. 162). Therefore, the code of the legal system and its organizations, such as courts, is legal/illegal; the code of science and its organizations, such as universities, is true/untrue, the code of the economic system and its organizations as firms is based on profit/no profit.

Code is closure

A communication operation necessarily activates the code. Using the code to communicate an observation includes it within the system, whatever side is selected. The system's environment is characterized by what has no meaning for the system and thus cannot be articulated in the language of its code. Excluding the environment from the construction of the system prevails as long as an event does not acquire meaning for the system. For example, the political system is part of the environment of the economic system until a decision of the political system acquires meaning for the monetary code of the economic system, as can be the case when the government decides to set up an embargo against another country. A code defines the unity of the social system and establishes its difference from its environment. A code *is* a discursive closure. A code is used to include *and* to exclude. It is the fulcrum of the distinct communication of different social systems observing each other and communicating in reference to it. The idea that modern societies are organized into fragmented subsystems whose identities are defined by specific codes is a major change introduced by Luhmann. It prevents any single subsystem from representing for itself the whole society, because of the exclusive logic of its code.

Luhmann's theoretical frame raises the question of social order. It implies that each event creates uncertainty, to which meaning has to be given by selecting one of the two sides of a binary code. For example, a court will have to *decide* on the legal or illegal character of a case. Similarly, in the economic system, the meaning of an activity will be communicated in terms of whether or not it is profitable.

On social stratification

Luhmann considers that in modern societies there is a relative decline of traditional stratification, a phenomenon particularly observed since the 17th and 18th centuries. During these ages, the stratification into castes, orders or social classes imposed a universally recognized differentiation. Historically, this relative unanimity to the existing social order took a transcendental value clearly illustrated by the French *Ancien Régime* and traditional Asian, African and Middle Eastern societies. In societies of intensive communication characterizing modernity, unanimity about an objective social order is lost and replaced by differentiated meanings attached to social systems. In modern societies, communication networks only refer self-referentially, that is, to their own operations of communication. As ultimate references disappear, theoretical conceptualization of social stratification has to be revised.

With the historical advent of social systems in complex societies deprived of any transcendence, social classes and other types of social stratification are no longer the normative basis on which society is structured (Luhmann, 2017b, pp. 518–519). Nevertheless, these previous distinctions do subsist. For Luhmann, these social categories still subsist but are less predominant sources of social differentiation. According to Luhmann, exclusion from social systems becomes the main cause of discrimination, to the extent that it would mean the exclusion of society (Luhmann, 2012b, p. 12). Society was formerly vertical and stratified under the regimes of different families of orders and classes, but under the regime of communication it becomes horizontal. Verticality is replaced by the flatness of a society that relies on communication networks. No hierarchy exists between the different social systems.

Due to the principle of closure and the contingency of communication networks, the meaning given by social systems to their operations of communication cannot be foreseen by their environment, thus invoking uncertainty in modern societies. Luhmann examines the role of organizations in this political context in which, in spite of rampant contingency, social order exists. In the following part, we mention the specific characteristics of organizations that reduce uncertainty. Then we explain how organizational decisions could paradoxically be dangerous for the evolution of modern societies.

Organizations and the absorption of uncertainty

The second aim of this chapter is to study the place of the organization in Luhmann's theoretical framework as described above. We will cover the definition of organizations as decision-makers, the specific dimensions of organizations as particular social systems and the stabilizing function of organizations in the more general frame of social systems theory.

Organizations are particular social systems, distinct from functional social systems. Being social systems, they are characterized by a more restricted perimeter than that of the functional system. Organizational social systems are based on concentrated communication operations, strictly framed by programmes, hierarchical structures and membership. Codes are the only structures of functional social systems. The organization establishes its closure by differentiating the communication operations carried out by its members.

The specificity of organizations as social systems

The function of organizations is to reduce uncertainty and to stabilize functional social systems. This aspect is especially important, because functional social systems, as art, economics, politics and the media, occupy whole fields of modern societies. Pictured from the *quasi-territorial* perspective of coded communication, functional social systems occupy a more important position than organizations whose operations of communication are more targeted. Organizations are more concentrated on specific tasks than functional social systems. We must therefore apprehend more precisely the relationship between these two types of social systems, functional and organized, to understand the importance of the function of reducing uncertainty and the processes by which it is carried out: 'No single system can obtain its own unity as organization. In other words, no organization in the domain of a functional system can take on all the operations of the functional system and carry them out as its own.' (Luhmann, 2012b, p. 150)

Through their operations, functional systems define the niches where organizations construct their differentiation. Organizations, even the largest, adopt the rules of the functional system in which they are located. They use the language of its code. The code is used for the functional system's communication operations and for the decisions of the organizations it embraces.

The inclusion of organizations in functional social systems is spatial or cognitive/discursive, but not hierarchical. Organizations belonging to functional systems use their medium, which is their system's specific discursive code. Thus, a court will obviously make reference to a legal logic. Decisions in this social system will be taken using the binary code of the legal functional system, legal/illegal. Similarly, e-commerce firms, museums and television news channels will favour the discursive logics of the functional systems to which their distinctions mostly refer, that is, the codes of profit/not profit, art/not art and information/not information, respectively. However, this inclusion in social systems is relative: an organization predominantly depends on one functional system and its code but also takes into account other discursive logics. Thus, an organization belonging to the functional system of the media is governed primarily by the code information/not information, although the code of the economic system also affects it concerning investment decisions.

Because organizational decisions are labelled in the codes of functional social systems, they contribute not only to their own autopoietic reproduction but also to that of the functional system. The circularity of communication between functional systems and organizational social systems corresponds to an ecology inherent in the communication network constituted by the code. The medium of a code shared by the functional system and the organization makes communication possible without rejecting the axiom of closed systems theory. Organizations in functional systems mainly use their own specific code, but their decisions and their premises distinguish them as closed systems within functional systems: 'Organizations are the only social systems that can communicate with the systems of the environment' (Luhmann, 2012b, p. 150).

By building communicative relationships with functional systems, organizations incorporate social regulation. From this point of view, their function of reducing uncertainty turns out to be decisive, as it interrupts the contingency of the indefinite succession of communication operations occurring in functional social systems. By filtering communication operations, organizations defuse the destabilizing effects of the diffusion of unexpected events. Organizations intercept the formation of risks and their uncontrolled social amplification (Luhmann, 2017b, p. 534). In the latent deconstructionism inherent in a society with an event-based conception of communication, organizational social systems have the power to impose stability by their structure and mechanisms:

> The more a society has, for whatever reason, to rely on decisions to generate a future out of its past, the more it will tend to deconstruct the semantics it draws on for this purpose. The more one tries to re-establish what is necessary, valuable, ethical, and so forth, the more the contingency of precisely these operations becomes apparent. ... Because organizations are social systems that consist only of decisions and are reproduced only through the reproduction of decisions, they survive thanks to the prevention of their own deconstruction. However this happens, they can secure acceptance of decisions through decisions. To this end, they form the necessary structures.
>
> (Luhmann, 2017b, pp. 188–189)

Organizations and decisions

Stabilizing decisions

Decisions, considered as communication events, are specific features of organizations (Luhmann, 2003). For Luhmann (2005a), decisions are paradoxical communications. The paradoxical dimension of decisions as communication events implies a degree of uncertainty. By definition, the very concept of decision implies that the choice expressed by communicating the decision is uncertain beforehand. As mentioned above, inside Luhmann's theoretical frame, a decision, in formal terms, is the selection of one side of a binary code. The status of decisions implies in their contents uncertainty which always results from a selection process mediatized by the choice of one side of the code. Thus, decision simultaneously communicates the existence of two sides of the code (without which there can be no decision) *and* the choice of one side by the decision concerned. The presence of the two sides is indeed a problem in the case of functional systems. As we have observed, the latter have no institutionalized mechanisms liable to avoid being confronted on every occasion with the uncertainty inherent in decision-making. Obviously, such a configuration would prevent the establishment of any social order, particularly in highly complex societies with intertwined communication networks.

Organizations operate in their different ways as social systems essential for the establishment of a lasting social order. The mechanisms shaping decisions stabilize the horizon of expectation and generally align the choices formally made by decisions with expectations (Luhmann, 2012a, pp. 230, 321). Nonetheless, some uncertainty remains because of the status of decisions as events. The absorption of uncertainty does not completely eliminate contingency, meaning that divergent observations can sometimes lead to unexpected decisions. What one decision constructs, another can undo, with deconstruction effects amplified by the recursivity of decisions.

The persisting threat of deconstruction

The status of decisions as events, combined with their recursivity, makes the organization's absorption of uncertainty less certain, due to the potential diffusion and amplification of an unexpected decision. The decision-making process can reinforce the organizational order, but can also challenge it. The recursive sequence of decisions generated by an unexpected decision thus communicates a challenge to the existing order. In other words, the actualization of an event, which had previously been potential, is liable to lead quickly to the complete deconstruction of the organization (Andersen, 2003). Organizations contain their opposite, their own paradox.

The organizational mechanisms of absorption of uncertainty

How then can we preserve an organized order and its autopoietic reproduction, which requires decisions that align with expectations in spite of their intrinsic contingency? Several complementary factors combine here: membership of the organization, organizational structures, including the framing of the decision-making process contained in what Luhmann describes as decision premises, and the division of the decision-making process through the hierarchical structure.

In the following we explain how such factors can reduce uncertainty, since they contribute to reducing complexity, and stabilize the horizon of expectations within organizations and also in functional systems.

Membership

Becoming a member of any organization requires being included as an individual (psychic system) by the organizational social system. Organizations decide to include individuals as members. Although access to the different functional systems is (supposedly) equal, this is not the case for organizations. While functional systems are generally characterized by inclusion, organizations distinguish themselves by exclusion, except for their members (Luhmann, 2012b, pp. 150–152). The members of an organization belong to it as the result of a decision to include them, usually through their recruitment, which alters their status from that of non-member to that of member. For Luhmann, membership of an organization also signifies acceptance of its rules and decision-making processes. The condition for inclusion and membership lies in acceptance of the decisions taken by the organization, including corrections or modifications of previous decisions or of their premises (Luhmann, 2008, p. 188; Luhmann, 2017b, p. 529). Membership status also implies holding a position in the hierarchy.

As the members of organizations are also the guardians of the organization's collective memory, to which they contribute by taking part in its communication operations through their decisions, one may expect their decisions to be in line with expectations. The memorization of past decisions communicates to the organization's members a horizon of expectations that makes the reproduction of an expected decision more likely than the reverse. Moreover, organizational systems structurally constrain their members' decisions as they influence their career.

For Luhmann, at a time when traditional hierarchies are wavering, a professional career is the only differentiating element enabling people to advance in society and evolve within it successfully. Exercising power mediatized by communication (contributing to decisions) in a functional system depends on being included in one of its organizations. Since organizational membership provides the possibility of leading a successful career and being included in modern societies, an organization's members are likely to respect their rules and hierarchy. In this context, decisions of organizations' members rarely contradict the organization's memory encrypted in previous operation of communication or the principles decreed by the hierarchy. While the risk of unexpected decisions remains, such an event is less likely than decisions in line with expectations, which are synonymous with non-events.

Decision premises and hierarchy

Decision premises are specific to each organization. They simultaneously contribute to reducing uncertainty taking into account the context of the decisions. They concern precise programmes enabling the regulation of routinized decisions such as organizing stock in warehouses (Luhmann, 2017b, p. 304). Decision premises can also be more general and constitute general guidelines for complex decisions. These can be procedures, designing the hierarchical decision levels concerned, or procedures for arbitrating between contradictory decisions (Luhmann, 2017b, p. 305). By reducing and regulating the volume of information, decision premises contribute to the efficiency of organizational systems: 'decision premises are the outcome of absorbed uncertainty, or, in other words, the form in which the organization remembers uncertainty absorption' (Luhmann, 2017b, p. 303).

Examining decision premises leads incidentally to us revising the notion of hierarchy. Firstly, Luhmann's notion of the hierarchy concerning organizational members is surprising because it contrasts with the exclusively flat ontology characteristic of functional social systems. Secondly, organizational hierarchy needs to be completed by other arguments advanced by Luhmann. While traditional organization theories conceive the hierarchy as a vertical relationship between superiors and subordinates, Luhmann tackles the hierarchy more from the perspective of temporality and of the communicational unity of the system, yet without denying it its primary role of regulation: 'The principle of hierarchy, understood [...] as a hierarchy that includes parts in a greater whole' (Luhmann, 2017b, p. 416).

The hierarchy is incorporated within the decision chain by appearing in its premises. The circular, recursive nature of decision networks makes the notion of vertically hierarchized organizations insufficient. This notion is structural and relatively static. It neglects the flatness and temporality of communication processes and decision networks. Without rejecting the notions of flat or vertical organization, Luhmann favours the temporality present in the flatness of communication processes and decision networks. The function of hierarchy mainly relies on the structuration of such communication networks.

Beyond the search for efficiency, decision premises are guidelines, which help in preventing the materialization of risk. That is consistent with the function of uncertainty absorption associated with organizations. The concern of organizations facing risk is above all to avoid disasters, and only then to look for efficiency. Decision premises favour risk avoidance by establishing cognitive routines memorized by the members of the system, without any need to refer to the hierarchy in emergency situations (Luhmann, 2017b, p. 334). Conversely, the absence of such memorized premises orientating decision-making in unusual contexts can lead to disasters, as in the case of Mann Gulch (Weick, 1996), or more recently in the case of the Air France flight from Rio de Janeiro to Paris which crashed when the pitot tubes froze, leaving the crew with no clear information to observe and no well-established procedure to follow (BEA, 2009).

Although decision premises fully contribute to uncertainty absorption, they do not strictly encapsulate decisions. By selecting a meaning, decisions imply the passage from a strictly coupled system to a loosely coupled one. The relationship between premises and effective decisions is therefore characterized by loose coupling, which maintains the rare possibility of an unexpected decision. If unexpected decisions occur, they become the premises for future decisions, whose recursivity may amplify the initial variation. Nonetheless, due to the loose coupling itself, an opposing decision can occur once more, returning to the original state. Ultimately, rather than eliminating uncertainty entirely, decision premises act as oscillators, which in general sustain organizational stability (Luhmann, 2017b, p. 303).

Now, we will examine the implications of Luhmann's conception of organizations on the notions of event and of risk management. It is indeed interesting to examine the degree to which these concepts are radically altered by social systems theory and a conception of organizations as characterized by a recursive process of decisions oriented towards the absorption of uncertainty.

Events and risk management

Events and organizations

Luhmann's system focusing on communication offers a theoretical basis to define events, viewed here exclusively as the decision of selecting an unexpected meaning. The contingency of decisions makes events possible. Events become rare decisions deviating from the normative reproduction memorized in social systems. The possibility of the event is at the origin of the decision (Luhmann, 2001). That contributes to a field, which interests researchers in organization studies (Hoffman & Ocasio, 2001; Munir, 2005; Christianson et al., 2009; Nigam & Ocasio, 2010; Deroy & Clegg, 2011; Morgeson, Mitchell & Liu, 2015). By introducing events at the heart of the construction of communication networks, Luhmann gives the concept a systematic dimension, an orientation also expressed by Weick (1988; 1996) in the different theoretical context of agentic action theory. Events are incorporated into networks of decisions generating more or less lasting organizational change. Events broaden the spectrum of available memorized references and make future decisions more uncertain. Hence, the occurrence of an event strengthens the likelihood of future events. Events as communication operations produce effects in reality so they are not pure discursive abstractions. Socially and organizationally actualized, they construct in concrete terms not only the historical evolution of societies and of organizations but also new short-term or long-term social practices, or even modify working contexts. In this vein, deriving from a Luhmannian framework, Deroy and Clegg (2015) have shown how the main organizations of the Soviet Union were unable to prevent the final collapse of the whole system. They argue that recursive contingency encrypted in the network of successive events spurred an evolution, which set the system out of control of the rulers in charge of managing it. Events and contingency turned out to be a core determinant of organizational history as they played a systemic role to break the established codes and allow the emergence of different ones.

In this general context of events, risk management based on a hypothesis model-ling contingency appears to be problematic, even though this issue is one of acute importance to organizations.

The asymmetry of danger and risk

Luhmann distinguishes risk and danger. Danger results from an (unexpected) event triggered by organizational decisions managing risk. It differs from risk because it is supported by the environment of organizations, managing their own risks. Risk is present in the decisions taken by organizations, which calculate the likelihood of future situations. Risk relies on the ability of organizations to make the contingency of events probabilizable. Probabilistic decisions concern the evolution of an organ-ization. Danger concerns its environment and results from probabilistic decisions about risks that occur there.

For systems belonging to this environment that cannot, therefore, 'manage' risk, danger originates in ignorance of or the impossibility of influencing decisions, for lack of the power to do so. The use of data collected by organizations from the Internet illustrates this duality between risk and danger. Data mining allows organ-izations to take decisions that are in fact probability calculations, hence forms of risk management. The case of Facebook and Cambridge Analytica (The Guardian, 2018) shows that such decisions represent a danger capable of threatening private life or democracy.

In turn, danger will lead organizations to implement a management of risk. Adaptation of organizations to danger reactivates danger mediatized by the man-agement of risk. When they manage risk, organizations do not always know what dangers their decisions communicate, for their environment and for themselves. Risk and danger are circular, making it almost impossible to allocate a simple cause to the realization of risk. The control of risk remains an illusion, given that decisions are part of complex and intertwined communication networks that decon-struct the notion of causality: 'The decision maker (whether an individual or an organization) cannot even be identified. The mechanism of attributing risks to deci-sions is a *circular* operation.' (Luhmann, 2008, p. 119)

This asymmetry between risk and danger raises concerns about governance and the long-term stability of societies developing dangerous technologies controlled by just a few organizations. Contrary to Habermas, who asserts the possibility for a social consensus thanks to a society reliant on communication, Luhmann main-tains his pessimism regarding the inability of modern societies to manage risks and dangers (Habermas & Luhmann, 1971; see Leydesdorff, 2000, for a synthesis). Luhmann's whole work demonstrates this paradoxical view of a society of commu-nication in which communication is prevented by the closure of coded systems; hence the impossibility of any consensus.

Conclusion

Even if Luhmann is better known in sociology, he is considered abstract, metatheoretical or even radical, in organization sciences. Yet, he innovates in devel-oping an original representation of modern societies and particularly gives a new analysis about organizations as social systems. The first part of the chapter developed the core concepts of his theory. Communication is at the heart of complex modern societies composed of fragmented social systems which do not really communicate between themselves while communication remains widely spread in each fragmented system; hence his concept of social systems as autopoietic differences. Each system constructs and reproduces its own way of functioning, possessing its own discursive code. Codes are binary and allow the autopoiesis. Codes define cognitive closures of functional social systems and explain the fragmentation of modern societies. In such modern societies, individuals, who are not free but embedded in social networks from which they cannot escape, may observe and construct communication events.

The second part of this chapter considered the role of organizations in the absorption of uncertainty derived from the social fragmentation. Organizations are social systems endowed with specific features. They are characterized by their decisions, which are selections of meaning. Decisions are eventful. However, organizational mechanisms frame their contingency and usually prevent unexpected decisions and social disorder. Paradoxically, in managing risk, organizations may also cause dangers for other social systems composing modern societies.

Luhmann sheds light on the debate around order and disorder that is at the heart of any organizational theory. He shows that while organizations contribute to the maintenance of a degree of stability and the reduction of uncertainty, the event created by an unexpected decision always remains possible since processes are based on the meaning attributed to communication operations.

Because the deconstruction of order is endogenous to the contingency of meaning, it constitutes a constant threat, totally unmanageable in terms of logic, partially manageable in organizational practices. With his conception of a fragmented society dominated by the rule of codes, Luhmann leaves the question of conflict between differentiated social systems open.

End-of-chapter exercises

1. What are the principal characteristics of Luhmann's functional social systems? To what extent does this representation align with your own observations?
2. What are the distinctive features of the organizational social system?
3. What is the function of organizations?
4. Is communication possible between stakeholders and different systems in complex modern societies as represented by Luhmann?
5. Is it possible to manage risk? Why?
6. What are the possible implications of Luhmann's theory for managing the environment?
7. What are the possible implications of Luhmann's theory to control communication by the internet?

Glossary

Autopoietic system A closed system, unlike other systems theories that consider them as open. These closed systems construct and reproduce themselves and evolve by autopoiesis, that is, based on their own unique properties. Initially developed in biology by Maturana and Varela, this notion was taken up by Luhmann.

Code In binary form, the code characterizes a functional social system. It includes the language of the system and defines its space. Any communication operation in a social system is mediatized by the code. In the social system, the law of the code is exclusive, and enables its practical distinctness.

Contingency Characterizes what is not necessary. For Luhmann, contingency results from the fundamental impossibility of ensuring fluid communication between different systems.

Event Is associated with the contingency of communication operations, which each time requires the selection of one side of a binary code via a decision. Usually, the meaning of decisions conform to expectations. Any unexpected decision is an event liable to generate increased differentiation. This differentiation resulting from communication events is endogenous to social systems.

Principle of closure The social systems are closed. Every social system includes or excludes, depending on whether the object of observation can be communicated into the functional field of the social system by using its code.

Social system Society is exclusively made up of social systems. Luhmann rejects any integration between the holistic perspectives initiated by Durkheim and perspectives focusing on the individual initiated by Weber. Luhmann considers that any attempt at integration denies the modernity of an increasing differentiated society. There are three categories of social systems: functional social systems covering the general fields of social activity (art, law, economics, etc.), organizations and interaction systems. Individuals, as psychic systems, are located on the margins of society.

References

Andersen, N. (2003). The undecidability of decision. In T. Bakken, & T. Hernes (eds)*Autopoeitic organization theory* (pp. 235–258). Copenhagen: Liber Copenhagen Business School Press.

Ashby, W. (1957). *An introduction to cybernetics*. London: Chapman & Hall.

Ashby, W. (1958). Requisite variety and its implications for the control of complex systems. *Cybernetica*, 1(2), 83–89.

Bakken, T., & Hernes, T. (2003). *Autopoetic organization theory drawing on Niklas Luhmann's social systems perspective*. Copenhagen: Copenhagen Business School Press.

Becker, K. H., & Seidl, D. (2007). Different kinds of openings of Luhmann's systems theory: A reply to la Cour et al. *Organization*, 14(6), 939–944.

Brunczel, B. (2010). *Disillusioning modernity, Niklas Luhmann's social and political theory*. Frankfurt am Main: Peter Lang.

BEA (2009). Rapport final Accident survenu le 1er juin 2009 à l'Airbus A330-203 immatriculé F-GZCP et exploité par Air France vol AF 447 Rio de Janeiro – Paris.

Christianson, M. K., Farkas, M. T., Sutcliffe, K. M., & Weick, K. E. (2009). Learning through rare events: Significant interruptions at the Baltimore & Ohio Railroad Museum. *Organization Science*, 20(5), 846–860.

Deroy, X., & Clegg, S. (2011). When events interact with business ethics. *Organization*, 18(5), 637–653.

Deroy, X., & Clegg, S. (2015). Back in the USSR: Introducing recursive contingency into institutional theory. *Organization Studies*, 36(1), 73–90.

von Foerster, H. (2007). *Understanding understanding: Essays on cybernetics and cognition.* New York: Springer.

Habermas, J., & Luhmann, N. (1971). *Theorie der gesellschaft oder sozialtechnologie. Was leistet die systemforschung.* Frankfurt/Main: Suhrkamp.

Hoffman, A. J., & Ocasio, W. (2001). Not all events are attended equally: Toward a middle-range theory of industry attention to external events. *Organization Science, 12*(4), 414–434.

Husserl, E. (1970). *The crisis of European sciences and transcendental phenomenology: An introduction to phenomenological philosophy.* Evanston, IL: Northwestern University Press.

Leydesdorff, L. (2000). Luhmann, Habermas and the theory of communication. *Systems Research and Behavioral Science: The Official Journal of the International Federation for Systems Research, 17*(3), 273–288.

Luhmann, N. (1986). The autopoeisis of social systems. In V. d. Zouwen (ed.) *Sociocybernetic paradoxes: Observation, control and evolution of self-steering systems* (pp. 172–192). London: Sage.

Luhmann, N. (1995a). *Social systems.* Stanford, CA: Stanford University Press.

Luhmann, N. (1995b). Legal argumentation: An analysis of its form. *The Modern Law Review, 58*(3), 285–298.

Luhmann, N. (2000). *Art as a social system.* Stanford, CA: Stanford University Press.

Luhmann, N. (2001). *La Légitimation par la procédure.* Quebec: Les Presses de l'Université Laval.

Luhmann, N. (2003). Organization. In T. Bakken, & T. Hernes (eds) *Autopoetic organization theory* (pp. 31–52). Copenhagen: Copenhagen Business School Press.

Luhmann, N. (2005a). The paradox of decision making. In D. Seidl, & K. Becker (eds) *Niklas Luhmann and organization studies* (pp. 85–106). Copenhagen: Copenhagen Business School Press.

Luhmann, N. (2005b). The autopoesis of social systems. In D. Seidl, & K. Becker (eds) *Niklas Luhmann and organization studies* (pp. 64–84). Copenhagen: Copenhagen Business School Press.

Luhmann, N. (2006). System as difference. *Organization, 13*(1), 37–57.

Luhmann, N. (2008). *Risk, a sociological theory.* New Brunswick, NJ: Aldine Transaction.

Luhmann, N. (2012a). *Theory of society* (1). Stanford, CA: Stanford University Press.

Luhmann, N. (2012b). *Theory of society* (2). Stanford, CA: Stanford University Press.

Luhmann, N. (2017a). *Introduction to social systems.* Cambridge: Polity Press.

Luhmann, N. (2017b). *Organization and decision.* Cambridge: Cambridge University Press.

Luhmann, N. (2017c). *Trust and power.* Cambridge: Polity Press.

Munir, K. A. (2005). The social construction of events: A study of institutional change in the photographic field. *Organization Studies, 26*(1), 93–112.

Moeller, H.-G. (2006). *Luhmann explained, from souls to systems.* Chicago, IL: Open Court.

Morgeson, F., Mitchell, T., & Liu, D. (2015). Event system theory: An event-oriented approach to the organizational sciences. *Academy of Management Review, 40*(15), 515–537.

Nigam, A., & Ocasio, W. (2010). Event attention, environmental sensemaking, and change in institutional logics: An inductive analysis of the effects of public attention to Clinton's health care reform initiative. *Organization Science, 21*(4), 823–841.

Parsons, T. (2005). *The social system.* London: Routledge.

Schoeneborn, D. (2011). Organization as communication: A Luhmannian perspective. *Management Communication Quarterly, 25*(4), 663–689.

Seidl, D. (2003). Organizational identity in Luhmann's theory of social systems. In T. Bakken, & T. Hernes (eds) *Autopoeitic organization theory* (pp. 123–150). Copenhagen: Copenhagen Business School Press.

Seidl, D., & Becker, K. (2006). Organizations as distinction generating and processing systems: Niklas Luhmann's contribution to organization studies. *Organization, 13*(1), 9–35.

Seidl, D. (2006). General strategy concepts and the ecology of strategy discourses: A systemic-discursive perspective. *Organization Studies, 28*(2), 197–218.

Simon, H. (1997). *Models of bounded rationality: Empirically grounded economic reason.* Cambridge, MA: The MIT Press.

The Guardian, (2018). The Cambridge Analytica Files. https://www.theguardian.com/news/series/cambridge-analytica-files.

von Bertalanffy, L. (1975). *Perspectives on general system theory: Scientific philosophical studies.* New York: Braziller.

Weick, K. E. (1996). Drop your tools: An allegory for organizational studies. *Administrative Science Quarterly,* 301–313.

Whitehead, A. N. (1978). *Process and reality: An essay in cosmology.* New York: Free Press.

11 Organizing Michel Foucault

Power, knowledge and governmentality

Alan McKinlay and Eric Pezet

Chapter objectives

This chapter aims to:

- Highlight the difference between sovereign power and disciplinary power
- Show how knowledge is articulated with power in different modalities of disciplinary power and governmentality
- Show how Foucault used history to support and develop his thinking about power
- Locate the place of specific topics such as madness and surveillance in Foucault's work about power
- Provide an understanding of neo-liberal government through the concept of governmentality

Introduction

There were already many Foucaults during his life: since his death the number of competing Foucaults has grown exponentially. There is the Foucault of discourse and archaeology; of discipline and genealogy; and of ethics and identity. 'Our' Foucault of choice is the historian-philosopher, the Foucault who works out theoretical matters through historical reflection. 'Power', as Ellen Feder (2007, p. 17) puts it,

> Is for Foucault both a product and a producer of history. In a point Foucault develops from Nietzsche, historical accounts – the telling of stories – are themselves bound up with power: power is operating in the telling and receiving of stories and is bound to the knowledge that our stories and histories give us.

Over the last two decades his annual lecture series at the College de France have been published and these have generated yet more Foucaults. The lectures do much more than foreshadow his books: some raise topics that he never considered at length, such as war and military organization; others introduce new concepts such as governmentality or biopolitics that served as provocations to others to develop what were little more than the germs of an idea. So, some 30 years after his death there is the prospect of yet more Foucaults. In this chapter we shall say something of these other Foucaults, particularly this historical Foucault. We begin by outlining monarchic or sovereign power as a concept that requires further elaboration, not just as an archaic precursor deployed to make us think again about the more familiar nature of modern power and knowledge. We then review Foucault's interrelated concepts of power/knowledge and discipline. Finally, we turn to governmentality, a term that Foucault introduced but did not develop – but that has, nonetheless, triggered research across the social sciences.

Power/knowledge

It is a commonplace that the symbolism of power conceals its 'real' nature. But this is a commonplace that Foucault denies. On the contrary, for Foucault, the spectacle is not a distraction from the realities of power, but rather the very stuff of power, or, at least, a particular form of power: monarchic or sovereign power. Foucault is not alone in this. Clifford Geertz (1980, p. 104), for example, observes that the ceremonies of the archaic, monarchic state were profoundly performative: a form of

> Theatre designed to express a view of the ultimate nature of reality and, at the same time, to shape the existing conditions of life to be consonant with that reality; that is, theatre to present an ontology and, by presenting it, to make it happen – make it actual.

Ceremony does not disguise power so much as it constitutes power. The concept of sovereign power suggests that it represents not just an archaic form of power but also a deeply outmoded and misleading way of thinking about modern power. That is, to see 'the leader', 'the state' or 'the corporation' as a source of power is to restore a version of monarchic power: prohibitive, constraining and extractive, and all in an obvious, public fashion. Disciplinary power is, to the contrary, productive, prosaic and inscribed in everyday practices.

Mediaeval jurists conceived of the monarch as having two bodies: a body natural and corruptible, on the one hand; and a body politic, immortal and infallible, on the other. The fiction of the king's two bodies was essential to succession. Although the two bodies were indivisible, the body politic was always superior to the body natural. Indeed, the Crown embodied 'all sovereign rights ... of the whole body politic, was superior to *all* its individual members, including the king, though not separated from them' (Kantorowicz, 1997, pp. 381–382). Maintaining the integrity and legitimacy of the complex body politic was the sovereign's overriding responsibility. The king's body was both mortal and sublime.

In his 1973 lectures to the College de France, Foucault provides an elaboration of sovereign power. These lectures are both an autocritique of how he had thought of power in the *History of Madness* and an anticipation of *Discipline and Punish*. There are at least four ways in which Foucault's preliminary version of sovereign power in 1973 is richer, or at least more concentrated, than that provided in his prison book. First, he argues that sovereign power is irreducible to the person of the king but signified a type of relationship between the crown and the people. This relationship was between the sovereign and an amorphous multitude that was underpinned by violence, or at least the threat of violence. Second, he argues that the relationship between sovereign and subject was profoundly asymmetrical in terms of tithing and the legitimate royal expectation of service in the form of labour or military. Third, that this relationship is legitimized, in part, with reference to divinity and tradition. Foucault approvingly acknowledged Marc Bloch's work on the sovereign's healing powers in his College de France lectures of 1980–1981. The individual sovereign was understood to be divine to the extent that he exercised power consistent with his sacred status. Healing ceremonies or public executions were public trials of the monarch's claim to transcendence. Fourth, the intangibility of the sovereign's power required it to be dramatized in public rituals of just punishment or healing. In both cases, the reach of sovereign power was demonstrated by its ability to strip the individual down to – and act upon – bare life (Foucault, 2006, p. 43).

The contrast between sovereign and disciplinary power was essential to Foucault's articulation of the latter. Monarchic power served as a comparator, an archaic point of departure for Foucault's articulation of disciplinary power. In this sense, monarchic power can be mistakenly relegated both theoretically and historically (Singer & Weir, 2006, p. 444). But the concept also served as a cautionary tale for analysts of contemporary political power: as Foucault repeatedly warned, political power cannot be collapsed into, or derived solely from, the state or from the interests of a class. Where the sovereign appropriation of the body was sporadic and sometimes indirect, disciplinary power aspired to complete, continuous and direct 'seizure' of the body (Foucault, 2006, p. 46). The asymmetry of sovereign power gives way to the 'total hold' of the body in forms of disciplinary power. Equally, the sovereign's authority relied upon some justification rooted in tradition, whether from a real or an imagined past. Disciplinary power, conversely, drew legitimacy from its aspiration to deliver an improved, impossible future that is always just out of reach. The tantalizing prospect means that disciplinary projects are necessarily incomplete, an incompleteness that paradoxically invests them with legitimacy and dynamism. Further, disciplinary power uses perpetual surveillance, or at least its image, as a means of control but, much more importantly, as a way of creating knowledge of individuals and populations. Surveillance was not, then, an end in itself. Surveillance was necessary to knowledge production rather than all-important in itself. Mundane practices of recording, enumerating, centralizing and ranking are crucial to knowledge production (McKinlay, 2013).

Foucault regards sovereign and disciplinary power as two quite different systems of power, 'two absolutely distinct types of power corresponding to two systems, two different ways of functioning: the macrophysics of sovereignty ... and then the microphysics of disciplinary power' (Foucault, 2006, p. 27). Nevertheless, there was no suggestion that sovereign power is to be dismissed as archaic and arbitrary or that these two systems of power cannot be entangled over many decades. Indeed, even in Foucault's stylized institutional histories, quite the reverse is the case. Each form of power has its own specific history that is irreducible to, say, class interests. Here, as elsewhere, Foucault comes close to a Weberian sense of rationalization as the inescapable fate of Western reason. The analytical value of sovereign power is that its centralized, episodic nature highlights the mundane ubiquity of disciplinary power. Where sovereign power can be read through a single ceremonial moment, disciplines require an ascending reading of the imbrication of power in shaping the experience and possibilities of our everyday lives.

Madness challenges not just rationality of the individual but the social order of things. Madness subverts or inverts power, and so opens monarchy to ridicule and question. The politics of madness was a theme that troubled Foucault for almost three decades from his diploma research in psychology in 1950–1952. Specifically, he returned to the worlds turned upside down represented by carnivals, where costumed revellers celebrated the taming of male power or the inversion of convention. Although the carnival lasted just one day, there were no limits to the ridicule that could be heaped upon all sorts of power. This was the world turned upside down. Foucault witnessed this communal parody of power in Munsterlingen in 1954 (Desveaux, 2015, pp. 91–94). There is seldom an explicit, public contest between these two regimes of power, rather a slow erosion or marginalization of sovereign power. Foucault acknowledged the resilience of monarchic power; his 1976 lecture series, *Society Must Be Defended*, points to another way that it was compromised from within. His reflections upon the dynamic relationship between the monarch and administration hint that bureaucratic innovations were evident even in absolutist states. Or, perhaps, one could read Foucault's version of the madness of King George as a competition between two forms of power. Or, even more ironically, one could read George's experience as also a nascent disciplinary power/knowledge being ushered in by the sovereign to preserve his rule and so monarchic power. The metaphor of George III points to the collapse of a monarch's rule, but not to monarchic power itself. This metaphor suggests a paradox: that monarchic power can only be preserved if George III accepts his subordination to the will and knowledge of another *and* that this subordination profoundly endangers his rule even as it extends it.

The sovereign has to be visible, both benign and fearsome. But, mused Foucault, perhaps the king should also be considered in terms of his self-mastery, his public demonstration of his capacity – or incapacity – to govern himself (Foucault, 2017, pp. 281–282). The treatment of the madness of King George III became a founding myth for the turn to humanistic treatment of insanity in the first half of the 19th century. Foucault first came to George III's experience through the account provided by Phillipe Pinel. Foucault rejects the dramatic imagery of Phillipe Pinel casting aside the shackles of patients at Bicêtre. The singularity of Pinel's act – derived from an abstract ideal of human nature – is replaced by a processual account that moves from the particular to the general, if never to the abstract. King George suffered five lengthy episodes of illness over his adult life before his eventual death from the disease in 1820. Each episode was followed by long periods of remission. Perhaps the most dangerous symptom was that he was struck by severe attacks of confused babbling. Delirium was a passing affliction while madness involved a permanent loss of reason. A delirious sovereign could be expected to recover, but a mad monarch would jeopardize the body politic and would have to be replaced by a regent.

Initially, the royal surgeon, somewhat hindered by deference, treated King George. George turned to a cleric, medical doctor and proprietor of a private madhouse, Francis Willis. Willis demanded that he have absolute control over treatment and through the seniority implied by his advanced years, an unrelenting stare and authoritative tone of voice, so that he could temporarily invert monarchic power: the monarch became Willis' subject (Porter, 1996, pp. 42, 46–48). The king's mortal body was utterly subordinated to his physician. Equally, George was deprived of the access to the reports and personal briefings that allowed him to rule in practice. For Willis, derangement was neither exclusively mental nor physical. The body was, however, understood as the source of mental disorder. The cure must be both medical and moral: 'medical science combined with proper management' (Willis, 1823, pp. 4–5, 212). This was also politically expedient since it staved off the prospect that if George was permanently deranged, then he would be forced to abdicate or be replaced by a long-term regent. Willis pursued a strategy of punishment and reward to tease out the rationality temporarily disturbed by physical illness. Reason was rewarded, madness punished. Willis accepted the post so long as he had the same authority over the monarch as he would any other patient. The doctor's expert authority was signified by the sight and prospect of physical restraint but also by Willis' gestures and authoritative tone when speaking to the king, his patient (French, 1964, pp 96–98). If compliant, the monarch received food, while any erratic behaviour resulted in George's being swaddled in bandages or confined to a strait-chair, which he caustically referred to as his throne (Haslam, 1997, p. 546). There was, then, a utilitarian logic at work in these practices, a logic that drew Foucault to Jeremy Bentham. Jeremy Bentham regarded both pleasure and pain as the 'sovereign master' of all. Rationality dictated that the minimum effort would be expended to achieve pleasure and to avoid pain (Marshall, 1995, p. 207). First, render the patient still; second, restore rational order to his choices by the lure of pleasure and the threat of pain.

Foucault's interpretation of the king's confinement, sometimes brutal restraint and physical treatment by emetics, bleeding and blistering, was that this was not a triumph of reason over barbarity. Rather, the restraint of the filthy, foul-mouthed monarch represented 'a sort of reverse subordination' (Foucault, 2006, p. 20). George III was effectively dethroned whilst in the periodic grip of prolonged manic bouts. But sovereign power was not dethroned by a rival monarch but by a different kind of power entirely: 'the silence of regulation takes over ... the empty place left by the king's dethronement'. The king was to be *managed* during his bouts of illness. Hidden from public view, if not political intrigue, George represents the co-dependence of the two regimes. The monarch was dependent upon discipline, and discipline was made possible by the frailty of the king's body and mind. George's long years of treatment represented a liminal space between care and custody, between monarchic and disciplinary power. Disciplinary power – 'anonymous, multiple, pale colourless' – was installed precisely to restore not just the sovereign's health but monarchic powers (Foucault, 2006, p. 22; Elden, 2017, pp. 115–116). Willis was, then, attending to both of the king's bodies, the real and the metaphysical. This episode is an important marker in the history of psychiatry, but also a more general metaphor of how disciplinary power displaces monarchic power: in private; with innumerable, unremarkable kindnesses; through easing physical restraints; and working on the individual as an individual, increasing their self-awareness and self-control.

We can augment Foucault's schematic outline. George III was treated by Francis Willis, a medical entrepreneur. Or rather George III was treated by Willis' sons and a host of anonymous keepers overseen from afar by Willis. The separation of Willis from George's captivity is important for three reasons. First, the easing of George's restraints speaks of a move towards moral therapy in which the patient is treated as an individual rather than subjected to a battery of physical therapies provided indiscriminately for all those confined. Second, custody becomes care; exclusion becomes rehabilitation. Disciplinary logic becomes embedded – and spread – through a language of humanism and reform (De Certeau, 1986, p. 185). Practice precedes but does not of itself produce knowledge. If monarchic power always carries the threat of violence, then disciplinary power understands and articulates its objectives as uplifting and its operations as benign, to act on all rather than to target an individual body as a warning to all. Third, the patient must be watched and recorded in detail by his keepers so that an intimate knowledge of that individual can be produced. These records were the basis of diagnosis and treatment decided by Willis on his visits. Through the fulsome praise Pinel heaped on his keepers and their records of their interactions with their patients, Foucault was well aware of their importance for knowledge production (Bynum, 1964, p. 323). Of course, there was an inherent tension between abstract, actuarial data and descriptive case notes. The differences between rules and practices were no less numerous and recalcitrant in early 19th-century British asylums than they were in the mid-20th-century Californian clinics studied by Harold Garfinkel (Garfinkel, 1967, p. 196). As a strategic, classificatory device, however, patient files remained deeply flawed and local forms of knowledge, even if they held the promise of extended knowledge of individuals and populations (Reed, 2006, p. 164).

Moral therapy was geared to the specificities of the individual patient. If the moral treatment of madness was to be rational then this was a double process. On the one hand, the patient was to be returned to reason, order and independence through the quiet order of the asylum; while, on the other hand, treatment regimes were to be subject to empirical description and analysis (Digby, 1985, p. 60). If the asylum was to become a sanctuary for the patient then it was also transformed into a space for experimentation, the articulation of expertise, and the formation of expert communities. Patient notes gradually replaced the irregular ledger entries kept by private entrepreneurs of madness. As case notes became more clinical, so mad talk, the patient's expression of their experience, was excluded. Equally, confinement developed a hierarchical labour process that began with keepers, through medical superintendents to physicians that gradually developed standard, if local, descriptive categories (Andrews, 1998, pp. 259–260). Physicians were at least one remove from the patient, a distance that both signified their reliance upon detailed case notes compiled by others and their claim to a detached, impersonal expertise. Judgements – and so treatments – were no longer to be derived from abstract first principles but judged by their effects on individuals and, increasingly, categories of patients. In turn, these detailed records provided the foundation of a specific form of psychological expertise that could be shared, debated and used to demarcate psychiatry from medicine, on the one hand, and unregulated, lay houses of confinement, on the other. It was not that technical knowledge and daily routines were established quickly, but the *terms* of debate – a debate that lasted several decades – about the nature of that knowledge and the efficacy of those rival routines. 'The institution thus opens up a whole field of possible knowledge' (Foucault, 2015, p. 91). There was an explosion of classificatory labour by rival factions of doctors, theologians and psychologists, all drawn from their case notes.

The asylum became a site of observation, experimentation and codification. And so knowledge moved from description of the specific to an aspiration to generalize:

regularity becomes the normal; ideals and abnormality become measurable standards and deviations. The individual becomes an object to be understood in terms of population. Data collection, organization and interrogation become a vital process that allows comparisons across time, forms of treatment and the different categories of individual (Goldstein, 1984, pp. 187–188). In part, the legitimacy of emerging knowledge is established by the effectiveness of its treatments. Legitimacy is dependent upon a series of increasingly codified observations, arranged in records that permit – indeed encourage – tracing and comparing the fate of individuals and populations over time and between different treatment regimes. This is the challenge Foucault makes to historians of knowledge: to set aside the accounts of great innovators and instead investigate the complex, tangled regimes that establish certain facts, that declare certain policies or practices as more effective than others. Sovereign power has to reproduce its singularity, more or less faithfully, through ceremony. Disciplinary power, by contrast, expands exponentially, relentlessly through routines. Where sovereign power extracts its tribute, taxes and service periodically, disciplinary power aims for the continuous production of value or the constant manufacture of new subjects; to understand veridical knowledge through the routines that establish local truths, aspire to prediction and adjudicate between contending practices of treatment, rehabilitation or efficiency. Truth moves from being universal and timeless to local and temporally specific, a fiction verifiable through historically specific regimes of power and knowing. Knowledge is not debased by power: *all* knowledge is entangled with power. Almost at the same moment that disciplinary projects emerged to focus on the individual body, so a related but distinct set of practices emerged to understand populations.

> And that the new technology that is being established is addressed to a multiplicity of men, not to the extent that they are nothing more than their individual bodies, but to the extent that they form, on the contrary, a global mass that is affected by overall characteristics of birth, death, production, illness, and so on. So after a first seizure of power that is not individualizing, but ... massifying, that is directed not as man-as-body but at man-as-species.
>
> (Foucault, 2003, pp. 242–243)

Populations, and the shift from political arithmetic to statistics, become the administrative knowledge of monarchic power, and increasingly distinct from the king and his court. This is the moment that triggers a change in the nature of monarchic power. Absolute monarchy was authoritative to the extent that it successfully projects an image of itself. The monarch's self-awareness that their actions are essential is central to the very idea of the institution of monarchy. Understanding the mass of subjects was secondary to this monarchic project: the mass was nothing more than a volume of individuals, all reduced to the singularity of the subject. Conversely, disciplinary power opens up the possibility of them being known both in their individuality and as a population.

Sovereign power was depicted in Foucault's notoriously graphic, meticulous retelling of the public torture and execution of Damien, a would-be regicide. Public torture, the mortification of the accused's flesh, was only one part of the spectacle. The crowd was not just the backdrop to monarchic spectacle. The crowd was transformed by the spectacle into a unified, singular body that bore witness to the *measured* justice of the pain and understood that although experienced only by Damien, *all* were exposed to the same existential threat to their bare life. Any one of the watching crowd could be Damien but only Louis could be sovereign. The precise form and sequence of Damien's agonies were not arbitrary but were designed to be a just measure of pain. The design was settled with reference to precedent and tradition, and not supplemented by the imaginative suggestions of a public referendum (McKinlay & Smyth, 2005). In fact, although Foucault says little about the king's role in the event, Damien's journey culminates with his death by fire at Louis' feet. The event was choreographed around the sovereign's body just as much as Damien's. There was a calculated risk at the centre of public executions. The spectacle drew huge crowds which was risky in itself and even more so if the sovereign's act was perceived as unjust or excessive in conception or execution (Dreyfus & Rabinow, 1982, p. 146). Damien's halting, excruciating march to his death was watched intently by the mob which in turn was watched discreetly by the cavalry in neighbouring streets. The cavalry and the threat of violence they represented was not part of the spectacle, however, but insurance against disorder. The representation of monarchic power required that violence remained an off-stage possibility. By remaining hidden, the military did not detract from the singularity of Louis as the mortal target of the regicide and the visible sign of his immortal 'body', the author of the solemn horror of Damien's slow mortification and eventual execution. The confined George's treatment was, by contrast, attended by the threat of violence, here in service of a nascent disciplinary power and knowledge embodied in Willis, who enjoyed both freedom of movement and delegation.

The crowd that watched Damien's mortification were, in part, judging the equity and efficacy of the crown and the pain inflicted on the wretched body processed through Paris. Philosophers were rethinking the nature of the monarchy: the sovereign was no longer regarded as a sacred figure but as the leading official of the state. However, French popular belief lagged behind philosophical scepticism and only waned in the second half of the 18th century when the disreputable life of Louis XV debarred him from officiating at religious ceremonies or he simply neglected his responsibility to lay his healing hands – the royal touch – on those afflicted by scrofula (Bloch, 1973, pp. 217, 224–226). The healing ceremony was even more carefully scripted than the public execution. The ill and their families were assembled for a religious service. After touching the afflicted, the king would wash his hands to symbolize the end of the ceremony and the end of his thaumaturgical role. Such was the clamour for the royal touch that ceremonies were almost overwhelmed. Administrative efforts to regulate ceremonies simply increased demand. Administration was made even more difficult by monarchs who acted on whim rather than adhered to the healing schedule (Brogan, 2015, pp. 121–135). Punishment and death marked Damien's body but also transformed it into something spectacular and sacred. In this sense, unremarked by Foucault, execution was not just punitive but also redemptive, and shared this meaning with royal healing. Undeniably, this event spoke of violence, but there was more to it than the crude display of brute force. Damien's broken body became not an offering to a distant deity but an essential element of a collective sacrament that constituted *and* represented sovereign power (Santner, 2011, pp. 7–8). This was the healing gift the sovereign offered to Damien: the sovereign provided him with the opportunity to suffer for his crime but also to receive absolution and so reaffirm the reach *and* redemptive nature of monarchic power. Conversely, in disciplinary power, exemplified in the minutely detailed sequences that regiment military cadets, *only* the individuals that are the objects of power are mobile, and only within the smallest of orbits. Power retreats from public view; knowledge ceases to be something mysteriously visible through ceremony and becomes the currency of expert communities. The possibility of redemption lies not in a moment, however revelatory, but in the discharge of painstaking, never-ending routines.

Discipline

Power can no longer be spoken of in the singular. From the Enlightenment, power became multiple and heterogeneous, each local power with its own specific history, each with its own cadence, contingencies and causalities. These specific histories are neither pale imitations of the central state or of a political philosophy, nor the unfolding of a societal logic. Foucault did not just dismiss the possibility of a grand theory, but insisted that understanding specific power/knowledge regimes was a matter of historical investigation, and never a purely theoretical project. There is nothing to be gained by searching for deep motives: strategies and technologies of power are hidden in plain sight and encountered in everyday lives. It is in his prison book, *Discipline and Punish*, that this argument is most fully developed.

It would be tempting, but mistaken, to dismiss yet another tiresome reprise of Jeremy Bentham's design for the panopticon prison. But Foucault remained convinced that panopticism constituted a turning point in the making of modern power and knowledge: 'an ensemble of mechanisms brought into play in all the clusters of procedures used by power. Panopticism was a technological invention in the order of power, comparable with the steam engine in the order of production.' (Foucault, 1980, p. 67) The analogy between the steam engine and panopticism was carefully chosen. To privilege the steam engine, suggests Foucault, is to neglect a host of other technological innovations, not least those 'political technologies' that combined to create *discipline*.

> Discipline is basically the mechanism of power through which we come to control the social body in its finest elements, through which we arrive at the very atoms of society, which is to say individuals. Techniques of individualization of power. How to oversee someone, how to control their conduct, their behaviour, their aptitudes, how to intensify their performance, multiply their capacities, how to put them in the place where they will be most useful: this is what discipline is, in my sense.
>
> (Foucault, 2007, p. 159)

Foucault made only occasional allusions to manufacturing and management, gestures that spoke of the importance of the factory and of his knowledge of Marx. By the 18th century, growing industrial scale

> Made it necessary simultaneously to oversee and coordinate [a whole series of workers – hundreds of workers –] with one another through the division of labour. The division of labour was, at the same time, the reason for which this new workshop discipline had to be invented; but inversely we can

say that this workshop discipline was the condition for the division of labour being able to take hold. Without this workshop discipline, ...without the hierarchy, without the overseeing, without the supervisors, without their chronometric control of movement, it would not have been possible to obtain the division of labour.

(Foucault 2007, p. 157)

Here Foucault skirts around any suggestion of cause and effect. The relationship between liberty and the disciplines is referred to in terms suggestive of 'base' and 'superstructure' but, like Marx, this is about entanglement and mutual necessity rather than logical or historical primacy of the economic (Sayer, 1979). All of these technologies of power were subject to endless experimentation, innovation, resistance but only rarely reversal. Discipline was, then, an untidy, dynamic assemblage of techniques for understanding and managing individual workers in terms of the social body. Just as there is a logic of entailment in terms of the relationship between the individual and the population, between power and knowledge, so the division of labour and discipline have to be thought of as part of the same assemblage. Just as it would be mistaken to privilege the steam engine or the capitalist in the making of the industrial revolution, so it would be no less misleading to identify the architecture of the panopticon as the cause of panopticism.

Foucault's language clearly echoes classical and structural Marxism, the former explicitly and the latter implicitly (McKinlay & Pezet, 2018). From Althusserian Marxism, Foucault deploys sotto voce, that disciplinary powers are not derived from or defined by, 'the great juridico-political structures of a society' but are first developed in response to crises and then through institutional isomorphism. Or, perhaps, this was simply Foucault's careful way of sidestepping controversy, his studied aversion to any distraction from his objective to look at the hidden history of disciplinary power in the human sciences. Foucault spoke and wrote of the accumulation of men and the accumulation of capital as two parallel but increasingly interdependent processes: both involved administrative techniques that formed nascent forms of disciplinary power and knowledge (Foucault, 1977, pp. 220, 222). There is a certain hesitancy here: 'it might perhaps be said'. Again, Foucault recasts Marx's distinction between the formal, contractual symmetry between labour and capital and the power asymmetries of the factory. In Foucault's terms, the universal subject of liberal individualism is made possible by universal panopticism that creates a much more resilient constellation of disciplinary practices. The factory or, at least, value production, is not privileged as the site where social classes are both created and here, at least potentially, class consciousness developed. Again, he nods to Marx: 'We know, for example, how many real procedures undermine the legal fiction of the work contract: workshop discipline is not the least important'. The employment contract is an example, however important, of power asymmetries masked by legal equality. Workshop discipline is acknowledged as particularly, but not all, important (Foucault, 1977, pp. 223, 225). To the classic Marxist question: did the steam engine create the capitalist or vice-versa, Foucault answered that disciplinary techniques were much lesser innovations when considered in isolation but immeasurably greater overall in terms of their effects. Disciplinary projects produced local forms of knowledge that coalesced into the 'strange sciences' of the social.

Importantly, panopticism was, despite the Bentham brothers' various interventions, not derived from a single source, but developed in parallel in a diverse range of institutions. Nor was surveillance about consolidating a singular, malign gaze, but a means of knowledge production. No matter how penetrating, surveillance could only produce knowledge if it was accompanied by the accumulation of comparable individual records. The ledger, the file and the archive were as important as surveillance in the making of a discipline. Surveillant administration was that which developed the capacity to classify and compare individuals according to a wider population. Over time, knowledge and norms encouraged organization to anticipate deviance, rather than simply to react to disorder.

In terms of factory organization and, indeed, the entire panopticon project, Samuel deserves at least as much credit as his brother Jeremy. Faced with Prince Potemkin's chaotic manufactories, Samuel Bentham redesigned buildings and work flows to allow him constant supervision from a central point. And, as Inspector-General responsible for building British naval ships in Crimea, Bentham completed his first, experimental industrial panopticon:

> From a central chamber, 106 feet diameter, could be distinctly seen to the ends of five radial adjuncts, each of them about 100 feet long, and that two floors could be seen at the same time by the Inspector, who could, by a mechanical contrivance, raise his chair to the upper stories without the inmates knowing it.
> (Bentham, 1856, pp. 45–46, 66; Morriss, 2015, pp. 176–179)

For Samuel Bentham, the initial objective was to maximize the constancy of his *personal* oversight. In Crimea, unskilled peasant labour was separated into very broad functional categories: surveillance remained highly personalized and deployed only broad binary categories of labour. Through practice, Bentham refined his concept so that, using proxies and accounting records, the aim was to render surveillance and record-keeping impersonal, more cost-effective, constant and calculable. Bentham's dockyard reforms during the Napoleonic Wars installed new forms of disciplinary power and knowledge. Bentham radically reduced the scope of skilled labour, tied wages to performance rather than status, and, above all, developed extensive, standardized and centralized forms of management accounting. Labour was allocated to increasingly fine-grained categories based on function and performance against productivity norms. Individual accountability was predicated upon calculability and predictability: production was no longer determined by custom but by economic rationality (Ashworth, 1998).

How, then, did the disciplines spread between institutions? For Foucault, this is a second-order problem, much less important that the observable effects that disciplinary logic had across the social field: as schools came to resemble prisons, so the organization of factories echoed asylums. After all, Jeremy Bentham's panopticon project encompassed prisons, factories and battery farming. Consider Andrew Ure, so often Marx's analytical and political foil, who explicitly tried to link science and the order of the factory. This literature created a new, practical object – the division of labour – to be considered, distinct from specific practices of particular factories (Berg, 1980, p. 181). For Ure, the automated factory was not just infinitely more productive than handicraft production; it also produced docile bodies, bereft of skill and so power, thus social order. Ure's narrow technological definition of the factory as 'a system … continuously impelled by a single source' could be extended, without distortion, to suggest a disciplined hierarchy in which factory operatives were forced to surrender their autonomy and individuality to the organization. Ure, a former professor of natural philosophy whom divorce forced into industrial consultancy, pursued performativity: describing the moral order of the automated factory not as a desideratum but as if it already existed. The exchange between science and manufacturers was not confined to a metropolitan elite but was central to provincial cultures of industrial enlightenment (Jones, 2008). Ure himself had directed the new Glasgow observatory, and participated in the development of standardized astronomical tables. This established a labour process that turned on the distinction between measurement and interpretation, between conscientious low-status computing and interpretation reserved for the scientist (Farrar, 1973, p. 301). This was the proto-industrialization of laboratory work that paralleled and contributed to Ure's philosophy of manufactures (Ashworth, 1994).

The initial purpose of factory record-keeping was to track specific investments and returns for time-limited partnerships (McKinlay & Mutch, 2015). By the late 18th century, however, accounting was acquiring new possibilities. Management accounting does not simply measure labour power but produces it as an object to be observed, statistically interrogated, and governed differently (Guerry & Deleule, 2014, p. 75). As the individual worker is allocated to a specific task so a social body and a labour process is simultaneously constructed. Understanding how better to transform labour power into labour is not merely a matter of economics for Foucault but equally a moral imperative. Each act of soldiering is 'not a breach of the law, but a way of stealing the condition of profit' (Foucault, 2015, p. 173). Efficiency, similarly, conveys complexity – certainly, in the narrow, immediate sense of cost, but also the saving of the costs, the sheer excess, of monarchical ceremonies, with all their risks of failure and public disorder. Where monarchic power itself can be jeopardized by the personal failings of a particular monarch, panopticism is indifferent to who acts as the eye of power, watching, recording and acting; disciplinary power seeks ever greater continuity and intensity and to close down porosity; the logic of disciplinary is easily dispersed and replicated, quite unlike the singularity of monarchic power; the burden on the sovereign to maintain centralized, ritualized power is passed to the disciplined subject who assumes responsibility for ensuring his own active compliance. Where monarchic power relied upon spectacular public displays for its reproduction, disciplinary power aimed to be a nondescript, unremarkable, even dreary part of everyday life, a power that is experienced minutely and so borne lightly (Foucault, 1977, p. 218). Monarchic power fails when it becomes manifestly inefficient, overburdened by corruption, and generates intolerable risks of disorder or resistance. Finally, efficiency is inscribed into panoptic organization itself: the capacity to reflect upon the effectiveness of its own operation, to maximize that organizational reflexivity necessary for its improvement. Vitally, as disciplinary projects spread from moments of crisis and the margins of society, so they acquired an increasingly positive, productive function: from controlling disorderly individuals and groups to producing useful citizens, workers and consumers.

Panoptic geometry – whether in architectural or clerical form – permits surveillance but the capacity to watch – either physically or administratively – is by itself ephemeral. Apart from Bentham's optimism that the impossibility of unbroken surveillance would not diminish those subjected to it, they would also act as if permanently watched. The importance of surveillance is that it was essential to the production of knowledge. Surveillance never occurs in an institutional vacuum. All prison warders had to record the performance and their impressions of those they watched. Ledgers noted only the number of prisoners incarcerated, to be verified by inspection. Inspection carries with it the promise of inspectability: a standard order that is the benchmark for individual behaviour, task performance and collective efficiency. Each form of aggregation allows a new form of individualization and each form of individualization necessarily produces a new population. The grid of abstract spaces represents and produces difference even as it produces interventions designed to reduce or eliminate those very differences. Each new mode of representation makes possible new forms of action. By the mid-19th century, prison records were also capable of searching for relationships between, say, demographics, suicide rates and recidivism. The condemned cell in British Victorian prisons was watched around the clock by four warders in 12-hour shifts. The warders' main task was to record all visitors, all conversations, any scripture read by the condemned, all food consumed – together with bodily functions – and any dreams recounted. Recording the physical and moral effects of incarceration is the first step in creating the data that produces criminality as a social and psychological phenomenon to be known through the human sciences, not derived from absolute moral or theological categories. Knowledge production is inscribed implicitly in the routines of gaolers, nurses and supervisors. For Foucault, 'power comes from below' no less than knowledge: there is no 'general matrix … extending from the top down and reacting on more and more limited groups to the very depths of the social body' (Foucault, 1978, p. 94). Power is to be known not by looking at who benefits but at its effects on institutions and individuals. Foucault is again insisting on the distinctive nature of modern power but also intervening in post-1968 debates about political strategy. Politically, his analysis pointed towards pluralist and specific rather than state-centred politics (McKinlay & Pezet, 2018). Theoretically, his formulations gain from the insistence on the multiple sites of power rather than regarding all forms of power as expressive of the interests of the ruling class. Moreover, the specificities of power and conflict have to be understood in their particular social context, irreducible one to the other. The cost, or certainly risk, in Foucault's formulation of action, conflict and struggle is that it remains unclear whether actors are individuals or collective actors (Honneth, 1993, pp. 154–157).

Benthamite disciplines were not to be stripped of all spectacle. Quite the opposite. Just as in reformed prisons, repeated infractions of the rules would result in the public corporal punishment for the miscreant, so public executions should be both exemplary and saturated with symbolism. Jeremy Bentham was one of the architects of the 1832 Anatomy Act that ensured the necessary supply of cadavers for medical dissection: even the bodies of the executed and the poor were to have a social utility. Executions were no longer events dignified by the sovereign's presence. Nevertheless, the execution was to remain a sombre spectacle, invested with religious and social meaning. And, for Bentham, this entailed that care be taken over the smallest of details: that attendants be dressed in black crepe; that the scaffold be painted black; and symbols of the crime be clearly displayed (Marshall, 1995, p. 66). Where the new disciplines failed then the violence that was its necessary corollary was to be invoked. There was no mistaking the threat. The alternative to submitting to discipline was to risk violence. This was the limit case. Breaches of discipline were to be punished but no agency was to be attributed to the [miscreant] and the rules: no master was to become identified with punishment that derived solely from the impersonal rules that bound all. 'All rigour, all acts of severity, need to be attributed to no one. The hand that acts must be artfully hidden' (Skillen, 1977, p. 142). Agency was, wherever possible, to be anonymous, buried in taken-for-granted routines and daily, unremarkable acts of compliance.

Governing

In February 1978 Foucault delivered his annual lectures around the themes of 'security, territory, population'. This lecture series included one lecture on what Foucault termed 'governmentality' that was tantalizing in several respects. Governmentality has proved one of Foucault's most productive concepts, although he introduced it somewhat apologetically – unfinished, not abandoned – as he turned back to Greek philosophy in his final years (Raffnsoe, Mennicken & Miller, 2017). Governmentality was, then, a road not taken by Foucault. The governmentality lectures had only the most limited circulation. While not exactly samizdat, initially the lectures were only available on cassette, first translated into Italian and from this into English. It was finally made available in French almost two decades later. Governmentality spoke of the proliferation of ideals, strategies and knowledge specific to institutions and social domains. From Machiavelli, the art of governing had centred on how best to protect the power and authority of the monarch and the state, this strategic way of thinking had been dispersed across the social. A consequence of this was that the arts of governing were depoliticized. There are many paradoxes of rendering political questions into neutral technical languages and practices. Rather than placing such issues beyond the reach of politics, executives and ministers become answerable in terms of technical decision-making, administrative efficiency and the equity of outcome. Governmentality, insisted Foucault, entailed the state becoming governmentalized, rather than the statization of society (McKinlay & Pezet, 2017).

It is not so much that the concept of governmentality corrects any sense in which 'discipline' can be read as a synonym for social control. 'Discipline', as we have seen, has a much more specific meaning in Foucault. The theoretical innovation of governmentality is that it inverts the notion of social control. The objective of governmentalist projects is not to control or limit the freedom of individuals but radically to increase their personal autonomy and responsibility. Governmentality speaks of overarching projects that are assessed in terms of population but whose success is predicated on the actions, behaviours and attitudes of individuals. Governmentalist projects are best considered as technologies of freedom. The appeal of governmentality is twofold. First, governmentalist projects seek to balance the maximum administrative efficiency with maximum individual freedom. So, governmentalist projects are consistent with founding liberal tenets of minimal government and maximum individual freedom. It is this stress on individual freedom that gives governmentality such resonance for understanding the experience of contemporary neo-liberal regimes. Foucault is clear that understanding the nature of governmental regimes is not a theoretical question but one that can only approached through painstaking empirical and historical research – tracing the formation of expertise, discourses and institutional routines. Power cannot be derived from the interests of this or that professional group or from a social class. Equally, knowledge is not something abstract and pure that is deformed by being pressed into serving the interests of a group or class. Just as the operation of power and knowledge cannot be deduced from the interests of an elite, neither can it be read from the experiences of those subjected to a specific form of power/knowledge. A governmentalist assemblage is 'a thoroughly heterogeneous ensemble consisting of discourses, institutions, architectural forms, regulatory decisions, administrative measures, scientific statements, philosophical, moral and philanthropic propositions .... The apparatus itself is the system of relations that can be established between these elements' (Foucault, 1980, p. 194). Here Foucault performs an analytical manoeuvre that echoes his refusal to equate 'power' with the interests of an individual, group or class. Just as power is not a weapon to wield, so, from the 18th century, the state is not a source from which power radiates or is projected. Governmentality refused to privilege the state as the cold monster, the foundational institution of the social, of civil society. Again, governmentality is as much a political intervention as a conceptual innovation. To target the state as *the* vehicle for societal change is to reproduce conceptually and strategically a monarchic analysis of disciplinary society. Here, perhaps, we can glimpse Foucault's answer to the vexed question of resistance. Resistance was a necessary part of discipline, something inescapably internal to power and knowledge practices. Indeed, resistance might be thought of as a dynamic that extends rather than confounds disciplines. The political importance of governmentality, however, is that the process of subaltern mobilization – of prisoners or workers – produces two effects. First, the arts of collective action are mobile between domains, time and place. Second, the demand to be governed better does not necessarily disturb existing power asymmetries. But the demand to be governed differently questions the structure of relationships inherent in specific institutions or social domains. Being governed is, for Foucault, inevitable: the political choice is whether to be governed better or differently.

The most important work that falls under the governmentalist label was, in fact, produced before the term gained wide currency. Nik Rose and Peter Miller – central figures in the 'London governmentalists' – were examining the hows of power in diverse social settings, from the factory to the marketplace, without explicitly referencing the governmentality lectures. Rather than attempting to derive legitimacy through their fidelity to Foucault, Rose and Miller have consistently pursued theoretical innovation through their historical and empirical labour. Foucault, specifically his *History of Madness,* was treated as a point of departure, not canonical knowledge. Just as all institutions are experiments in governing and living, so the 'London governmentalists' treated their own theoretical and empirical practice as laboratories for innovation, ready to draw upon an eclectic mix of concepts drawn from the philosophy of science and institutional sociology. Theoretical precision and closure were to be avoided, openness and utility celebrated. Innovation was at the centre of the 'London governmentalist' project. Specifically, they concentrate upon *how* knowledge is created systemically, from management accounting, through scientific management, to various forms of psychology. All of these systems are applied to recurring problems and occasional crises of, say, profitability, productivity and anomie. Although all of these forms of the human sciences aspire to scientific knowledge, they gain social traction when translated and applied to everyday lives. The architects of modernity are, then, not philosophers but the administrators who devise the routines, targets and forms that shape governmentalist projects. Where Marx spoke of the paradoxical relationship between capitalism and its proletarian gravediggers, administrators and social scientists are the unheralded authors of governmentality. It is not enough to identify the reforming zeal of those who would rehabilitate prisoners, empower workers or restore meaning and order to feral families and communities. Rather, it is how some prisoners are identified for rehabilitation; how empowerment is measured and extended; and what statistical measures single out certain families and communities for intervention, preferably by incentives rather sanctions. Put most simply, governmentality begins from the identification of some 'urgent' problem, acknowledging that the analyst's standpoint is decisive in this choice (Foucault, 1980, p. 195). The problem is then defined and rendered knowable in different ways. The moral discourse that legitimizes the urgent need for intervention is overlaid with more technical definitions that increasingly encompass both the initial problem and its solution (Miller & Rose, 1990, p. 5). This is the nascent, idealized form of a governmentalist programme for ordering or reordering social and economic life (Miller & Rose, 1990, p. 14). All of these projects entail the definition of an ideal type of individual to provide a marker against which to define all others and to establish an overall population. This suggests that the production of knowledge is both specific and applied but also open to wider constituencies of policymakers and experts who traverse distinct domains. For the 'London governmentalists', the defining conversations take place at the intersections of local, applied and abstract knowledges, the dialogue between practitioners and theoreticians. These projects are not derived from philosophical first principles nor assumed to flow from the interests of managers, politicians or academics.

The translation of a large-scale social problem into local actions centres on the construction of a network that shares a common understanding of a problem, a common measurement of some aspects of that problem or a common set of practices addressing that problem (Rose & Miller, 1992, p. 184). How a network of diverse actors is formed is an empirical rather than a theoretical problem. But experts and expert knowledge are important vehicles that establish a body of knowledge, measures and practices. One measure of the successful enclosure of expertise is its claim to objectivity, an objectivity that simultaneously depoliticizes. Equally, expertise overflows its boundaries so that governmentalist projects migrate between distinct social domains, from macro policies to technologies of the self used by individuals. The surge – and retreat – of knowledge and practices over time and place can be measured through bibliometrics, the membership of specialist interest groups and their attempted professionalization; for example, training budgets can be used as a proxy measure of the embeddedness of discourses and practices at the organizational level (Shenhav, 2002). Governmentalist programmes are translated into ever-more fine-grained technologies of government. This moves from macro-level aspirations to policies through to the documents and forms that codify and capture the data that specify a field to be governed. The 'London governmentalists' programme is defined by its determination to work the surface of language and administrative protocols, a determination that is consistent with the restless empiricism of Foucault's project.

Governmentality regards institutions, first, as laboratories – as sites of knowledge production – and, second, as machines, sites of reform and self-improvement (McKinlay & Taylor, 2014). Governmentality restates this central tenet of panopticism, that Bentham's design was about much more than surveillance to maximize control:

> The Panopticon was also a laboratory; it could be used as a machine to carry out experiments, to alter behaviour, to train or correct individuals. ... to try out different punishments on prisoners, according to their crimes and character, and to seek the most effective ones.
>
> (Foucault, 1977, pp. 203–204)

The novelty of the 'London governmentalists' is to stress the experimental moment in the practical articulation of disciplines and that, in pursuit of enhanced efficiency, aspirations to improve technologies of freedom should be treated seriously rather than as ideological smoke screens. Central to the 'London governmentalist' project is the argument that the disciplinary Foucault wrote of technologies of normalization, of knowledge, that were too easily read as synonyms of constraint and control. Governmenality, by contrast, is best described as a way of thinking about technologies that simultaneously assess risk at the level of populations and produce individual freedom, always tempered by responsibility. Markets and factories are sites in which consumers and workers are understood in specific ways and provided with techniques to make and remake their identities. And, of course, these governmentalist technologies produce expertise and expert communities who reflect on their own practice and the success of their projects. Nikolas Rose insists that the study of forms of governmentality is not at all the same as offering a sociology of the practices of governing or the experience of being governed. Rather, governmentality refers to the construction of a distinct form of expertise, making specific experts authoritative, and, conversely, delegitimizing other forms of knowledge and dissenting voices (Rose, 1999, p. 19). The logic of governmentalist projects is hidden in plain sight, in the abstract and practical debates held inside and across expert communities. There is no need to seek the hidden motives of the powerful or to accompany Marx's Monsieur Le Capital into the secret world of the factory to understand how the disciplines operate.

Conclusion

Power does not hide behind ritual or routine. Power, argues Foucault, *is* ritual or routine. Foucault requires us to take seriously the surface of things, to understand what is hidden in plain sight. The madness of King George was not the source of a new science of the mind but was the limit case that saw the suspension of sovereign power, but not its subversion. The new disciplines that explored the relationship between mind and body were sketched on the body and soul of the king. Even as monarchy displayed its grandeur and its reach, it was also proclaiming something of its precariousness. The scale of the spectacle spoke of the absence of monarchic power from the minutiae of everyday life. The very anonymity, the bland realities of disciplinary power, on the other hand, spoke of its ubiquity and durability. Risk of disorder was implicit in both forms of power. Monarchic power implicitly acknowledged risk, for instance, by the cavalry stationed just off-stage during Damien's execution: riot would be met not with calibrated but *excessive* force. In disciplinary power, risk is measured, predicted and factored into how it is operationalized. Resistance, deviance or even dull compliance becomes something to be understood rather than overwhelmed by violence. Governmentality extends this formulation by accepting that calculated risk is a necessary cost of maximizing individual freedom through oblique behavioural cues, incentives and sanctions. We should not look for hidden motives but formulate the connections that make knowledge possible and power productive, the better to challenge them and produce alternatives. Power does not create, distort or abuse knowledge; rather the knowledge of the human sciences is laden with the power to make new social objects to be understood and modified. The making of the human sciences is also about the ways that we understand and make ourselves. It is not just the factory, the school or home that becomes an everyday laboratory: the individual also becomes a constant work in progress.

End-of-chapter exercises

1. To what extent was King George subject to discipline, in Foucault's sense?
2. In which ways is discipline productive?
3. How did the warders of British Victorian prisons produce knowledge? Which knowledge was it?
4. Who was Bentham? Why does he matter?
5. Would you call Machiavelli a governmentalist?

Glossary

Biopolitics Refers to a governmental practice based on and oriented by a knowledge about the population behaviour.
Disciplinary power   Power which defines itself by its productivity and which aims to make the individual's everyday life productive.
Governmentality   A practice of power which aims to govern a population through knowledge-informed guidance of spontaneous individual behaviour.
Panopticism   Technical approach of government which consists in elaborating devices for the observation of the individual's behaviour.
Sovereign power   A power which defines itself by its incarnation (king, leader) or its institutionalization (state, corporation).

References

Andrews, J. (1998). Case notes, case histories, and the patient's experience of insanity at Gartnavel Royal Asylum, Glasgow, in the nineteenth century. *Social History of Medicine, 11*(2), 255–281.
Ashworth, W. (1994). The calculating eye: Baily, Herschel, Babbage and the business of astronomy. *British Journal for the History of Science, 27*(4), 409–441.
Ashworth, W. (1998). System of terror: Samuel Bentham, accountability and dockyard reform during the Napoleonic Wars. *Social History, 23*(1), 63–79.

Bentham, M. (1856). Memoirs of the late Brigadier-General Sir Samuel Bentham. In *Papers and practical illustrations of public works of recent construction*. London: John Weale.

Berg, M. (1980). *The machinery question and the making of political economy 1815–1848*. Cambridge: Cambridge University Press.

Bloch, M. (1973). *The royal touch: Sacred monarchy and scrofula in England and France*. London: Routledge & Kegan Paul.

Brogan, S. (2015). *The royal touch in early modern England: Politics, medicine and sin*. Woodbridge: Boydell.

Bynum, W. (1964). Rationales for therapy in British psychiatry: 1780–1835. *Medical History*, *18*, 317–334.

De Certeau, M. (1986). *Heterologies: Discourse on the other*, Minneapolis, MN: University of Minnesota Press.

Desveaux, Y. (2015). La fete des fous de Michel Foucault. In J.-F. Bert, & E. Basso (eds) *Foucault à Münsterlingen: À l'Origine de l'Histoire de la Folie*, Paris: EHESS.

Digby, A. (1985). *Madness, morality and medicine: A study of the York retreat, 1796–1914*. Cambridge: Cambridge University Press.

Dreyfus, H., & Rabinow, P. (1982). *Michel Foucault: Beyond structuralism and hermeneutics*. Brighton: Harvester.

Elden, S. (2017). *Foucault: The birth of power*. Cambridge: Polity.

Farrar, V. (1973). Andrew Ure, FRS, and the philosophy of manufactures. *Notes and Records of the Royal Society of London*, *27*, 299–324.

Feder, E. (2007). *Family bonds: Genealogies of race and gender*. Oxford: Oxford University Press.

Foucault, M. (1977). *Discipline and punish: The birth of the prison*. Harmondswoth: Penguin.

Foucault, M. (1978). *The history of sexuality: The will to knowledge*. Harmondswoth: Penguin.

Foucault, M. (1980). Questions on Geography. In C. Gordon (ed.) *Power/knowledge: Selected interviews and other writings 1972–1977*. New York: Pantheon.

Foucault, M. (2003). *'Society must be defended': Lectures at the College de France, 1975–76*. London: Allen Lane.

Foucault, M. (2006). *Psychiatric power: Lectures at the College de France 1973–1974*, London: Palgrave Macmillan.

Foucault, M. (2007). *Security, territory, population: Lectures at the College de France 1977–78*. London: Palgrave Macmillan.

Foucault, M. (2015). *The punitive society: Lectures at the College de France 1972–73*. London: Palgrave Macmillan.

Foucault, M. (2017). *Subjectivity and truth: Lectures at the College de France 1980–81*. London: Palgrave Macmillan.

French, C. C. (1964). *The royal malady*. London: Longmans.

Garfinkel, H. (1967). *Studies in ethnomethodology*. Englewood Cliffs, NJ: Prentice-Hall.

Geertz, C. (1980). *Negara: The theatre state in nineteenth-century Bali*. Princeton, NJ: Princeton University Press.

Goldstein, J. (1984). Foucault among the sociologists: The 'disciplines' and the history of the professions. *History and Theory*, *23*(2), 170–192.

Guerry, F., & Deleule, D. (2014). *The productive body*. Winchester: Zero.

Haslam, M. (1997). The Willis family and George III. *History of Psychiatry*, *viii*, 539–553.

Honneth, A. (1993). *The critique of power: Reflective stages in a critical social theory*. Cambridge, MA: MIT Press.

Jones, P. (2008). *Industrial enlightenment: Science, technology and culture in Birmingham and the West Midlands 1760–1820*. Manchester: Manchester University Press.

Kantorowicz, E. (1997). *The king's two bodies: A study in mediaeval political theology*. Princeton, NJ: Princeton University Press.

McKinlay, A. (2013). Following Foucault into the archives: Clerks, careers, and cartoons. *Management & Organization History*, 8(2),137–154.

McKinlay, A., & Mutch, A. (2015). Accountable creatures': Scottish Presbyterianism, accountability and managerial capitalism. *Business History*, 57(2), 241–256.

McKinlay, A., & Pezet, E. (2017). Governmentality: The career of a concept. In A. McKinlay, & E. Pezet (eds) *Foucault, governmentality and management: Rethinking the management of populations, organizations and individuals*. London: Routledge.

McKinlay, A., & Pezet, E. (2018). Foucault, governmentality, strategy: From the ear of the sovereign to the multitude. *Critical Perspectives on Accounting*, 53, 57–68.

McKinlay, A., & Smyth, J. (2005). Un spectacle des plus mortifiants': Foucault, le pouvoir et l'échafaud. In A. Hatchuel, E. Pezet, & K. Starkey (eds) *Organiser après Foucault*. Québec: Presses Université Laval.

McKinlay, A., & Taylor, P. (2014). *Foucault, governmentality, organization: Inside the 'factory of the future'*. London: Routledge.

Marshall, T. (1995). *Murdering to dissect: Grave-robbing, Frankenstein and the anatomy literature*. Manchester: Manchester University Press.

Miller, P., & Rose, N. (1990). Governing economic life. *Economy & Society*, 19(1), 1–31.

Morriss, R. (2015). *Science, utility and maritime power: Samuel Bentham in Russia, 1779–1791*. Farnham: Ashgate.

Porter, R. (1996). *A social history of madness: Stories of the insane*. London: Phoenix.

Raffnsoe, S., Mennicken, A., & Miller, P. (2017). The Foucault effect in organization studies. *Organization Studies*, 1–28.

Reed, A. (2006). Documents unfolding. In A. Riles (ed) *Documents: Artifacts of modern knowledge*. Ann Arbor, MI: University of Michigan Press.

Rose, N. (1999). *Powers of freedom: Reframing political thought*. Cambridge: Cambridge University Press.

Rose, N., & Miller, P. (1992). Political power beyond the state: Problematics of government. *British Journal of Sociology*, 43(2), 173–205.

Santner, E. (2011). *The royal remains: The peoples' two bodies and the endgames of sovereignty*. Chicago, IL: University of Chicago Press.

Sayer, D. (1979). *Marx's method: Ideology, science and critique*. Brighton: Harvester.

Shenhav, Y. (2002). *Manufacturing rationality: The engineering foundations of the managerial revolution*. Oxford: Oxford University Press.

Singer, B., & Weir, L. (2006). Politics and sovereign power: Considerations on Foucault. *European Journal of Social Theory*, 9(4), 443–465.

Skillen, A. (1977). *Ruling illusions: Philosophy and the social order*. Brighton: Harvester.

Willis, F. (1823). *A treatise on mental derangement*. London: Longman.

12 The Frankfurt School and critical theory

Edward Granter

Chapter objectives

This chapter discusses:

- The formation of the Frankfurt School
- The relevance of critical theory to today's society
- The influence of Marx on the Frankfurt School
- The approach taken to social analysis by critical theory
- How critical theory can be used in studies of organization and society
- The Frankfurt School critique of mass culture
- How critiques of 'corporate culture' have used critical theory
- Emerging perspectives and future directions in critical theory, organization and society
- Criticisms of the work of the Frankfurt School

Introducing the Frankfurt School

The Frankfurt School is the name given to the scholars associated with the Institute for Social Research which was set up in Frankfurt, Germany in 1923. (Jeffries [2016, p. 67] has it opening in 1924.) Members included: Leo Löwenthal (1900–1993); Henryk Grossman (1881–1950); Friedrich Pollock (1894–1970); Erich Fromm (1900–1980); Theodor Adorno (1903–1969); Max Horkheimer (1895–1973); and Herbert Marcuse (1898–1979). Walter Benjamin (1892–1940), 'whose dizzyingly varied career skirted the edges of the Frankfurt collective' (Ross, 2014) was effectively an associate member of the institute and has been an influential figure in his own right.

By the 1920s, it was obvious to those influenced by the work of Marx – as the Frankfurt School were – that capitalism had more staying power than some gave it credit for. Even the Soviet Union, supposedly founded on the ideas of Marx, was showing itself to be riven with contradictions and distortions. As Stalin's grip tightened following Lenin's death in 1924, these distortions took on an ever more barbaric character. Socialism, communism, freedom from exploitation and degradation, were as far away as ever – and getting more distant by the day. Members of the Frankfurt School faced their own, imminent encounter with barbarism and were forced to leave Germany as Nazism took hold during the 1930s; they were Jewish Marxists and in Hitler's Germany, being either one of these incurred an extreme risk of being killed. Horkheimer, Marcuse and Adorno moved to the USA where Marcuse stayed, while Horkheimer and Adorno returned to Germany in the 1950s.

Critical theory is the name given to the approach to social thought which writers such as Horkheimer, Adorno and Marcuse developed. A key aim of critical theory was to try and explain how Marxism could still be relevant in this new age of barbarism and totalitarianism. Such decisions are always made with a combination of motives, reflecting both pragmatism and bias, but in the present chapter, it is these key members of the Frankfurt School on whom we focus. Similarly, not every topic related to critical theory can be covered. The psychoanalytic standpoint, for example, must wait for another opportunity. This chapter draws much of its material from the work of the critical theorists themselves, but the interested reader will find available a wealth of material on the lives and ideas of the Frankfurt School; indeed, the 'market' for books about the Frankfurt School appears remarkable (Agger, 1998; Agger, 1992; Bottomore, 2002; Clausen, 2008; Granter, 2009; Jay, 1996 [1973]; Jeffries, 2016; Kellner, 1984; Kellner, 1989; Sim, 2014; Walton, 2017; Wheatland, 2009; Wiggershaus, 2007; and see also Thompson, 2013). If further evidence of critical theory's contemporary relevance was needed, in 2012 the Brooklyn Institute of Social Research was founded; a 21st-century research and teaching enterprise inspired by, and named in honour of, the original Frankfurt School (https://thebrooklynin stitute.com).

Critical theory today

One might imagine that a group of 20th-century German intellectuals known for discussions of classical mythology (Adorno & Horkheimer, 1997 [1944]) and the philosophy of Kant, Descartes, Spinoza and Hegel (Horkheimer, 2002 [1968]; Marcuse, 1969) would have little to offer in terms of radical critical perspectives on our 21st-century social reality. Were this true, it would be very problematic for critical theory since as the name suggests, its aim is to provide exactly this – methodological and thematic material for a critique of capitalist society. In this introductory section, the aim is to show how the world as described by the critical theorists is similar to the one we live in today. This sort of comparison could probably take up an entire book, but the following is offered as an illustration. Selected quotes are given but this sketch draws from a reading of the critical theorists across their oeuvre.

Writing in 1937, Horkheimer argued that 'the whole condition of the masses' was characterized by: 'Unemployment, economic crisis, militarization and terrorist regimes' (Horkheimer, 2002 [1937], p. 213). He is likely referring to the Great Depression which saw unemployment in Germany rise to over 6 million in 1932 (official figures, the real figure being much higher; see Petzina, 1969, p. 6). Joblessness, poverty and falling living standards played a pivotal role in the rise of fascism – a key theme in critical theory (see Kellner, 1984, pp. 92–129, inter alia). Struggling to survive on welfare, or under imminent threat thereof, confused and disappointed people were easy prey for those who sought to blame 'outsiders' and use this dynamic to channel political power:

The small minority that is sacrificed, the alleged conspirators, the traitor, the kulaks, the Jews, the foreigners, the communists, the liberals – how little they count, how much fun the masses get out of it, how readily they put up with the horror, how they enjoy it, and how significant the savings in the budget!.

(Horkheimer, 1978 [1961–1962], p. 209)

Nationalism and racism rose to unprecedented levels and societies were militarized for the purposes both of internal 'defence' and external conquest. Regimes such as Nazi Germany and Stalinist Russia set up camps for groups who were deemed to be ethnically, politically or morally problematic; they became, effectively, non-people. Families were broken up – children separated from their parents. Deportation remained a possibility for some (Horkheimer, 1978 [1926–1931], p. 24) and in this context was not perhaps the worst outcome. In such 'terroristic regimes', and indeed around the world, barbarism reached new levels of intensity and scope. Those who rebelled against the regime, be they internal enemies or 'insurgents' in conquered lands, were dealt with unequivocally; they were liquidated. This happened with such regularity and on such a scale that 'a single Jesus of Nazareth would barely cause a ripple of annoyance' (Horkheimer, 1978 [1926–1931], p. 19); just another insurgent being dealt with.

In dark times such as these, new types of leaders rose to power. People who were able to capitalize on the authoritarian desires seething beneath the surface of the public consciousness (Adorno et al., 1950). These demagogues thrived on populist notions of strength, greatness, nation and military might. In political discourse, what rational debate existed was replaced with a newly refined type of propaganda making use of novel communication platforms. Lying became part of the mechanics of populist politics, and the bigger the lie, the better (Jay, 2010). Despite their self-identification as national saviours, the political class under fascism were often people with 'murky connections' (Adorno, 2005 [1951], p. 23) – to corporations, to criminals, or a web of contacts comprised of both. Like Al Capone, leaders such as Hitler and Stalin represented a 'brutal gangster chief who cannot tolerate criticism'. However, their ability to spread terror was much greater – it was 'superhuman' (Horkheimer, 1978 [1950–1955], p. 132).

Society as a whole was subjected to a system of total domination and though fascism and Stalinist totalitarianism served as archetypes, Western democracies appeared to be instituting their own modern systems of social control. Those who were not inoculated against reality through the consumption of mass media propaganda were subject to outright repression by the forces of 'law and order' (Marcuse, 2002 [1964], p. 12). Working life was rationalized on the one hand, and mystified on the other. Social science and studies of organizational life tended to operate in the interests of capital and its managers; 'concepts terminate in methods of improved social control: they become part of the science of management' (Marcuse, 2002 [1964], p. 111). In spite of the fact that the technical means existed for alienated work to be vastly reduced, if not abolished (Granter, 2009), 'standardization and routine' (Marcuse, 2002 [1964], p. 28) became the defining experiences of work for manual and 'immaterial' workers alike. Work organizations, like society at large, operated based on 'technocratic' rationality which fetishizes the concept of efficiency – whatever the human cost.

Readers will have already begun to see the parallels between the Frankfurt view and contemporary society, politics and organization. The Global Financial Crisis which began around 2007 intensified already existing inequalities, worklessness and poverty in Europe, America and beyond. Once more, people feel lost and adrift, and populist politicians have seized the moment – offering simple answers, scapegoats and promises of a return to greatness. For many in Britain, 'Brexit' – the withdrawal from the European Union – is symbolic of a nationalist resurgence. In Europe more widely, strengthening nationalist/fascist movements will be familiar to anyone with an interest in current affairs. Interestingly, Jeffries, in a passage highlighting the contemporary relevance of the Frankfurt School, downplays the significance of nations and nationalism but points out that in today's global marketplace, critical theories of consumerism and commodification attain even greater relevance (Jeffries, 2016, p. 10). In a sense he is right because behind the veil of nationalist and populist rhetoric, the currents of global capitalism provide the 'real' bases for the decisions made by the businessmen (still overwhelmingly men) who profit from them and the politicians who belong to the businessmen (Horkheimer, 1978 [1926–1931], p. 93). At the same time, globalization's terrors (Brennan, 2002) include conflict and displacement, which surge in the global south, leading to flows of immigration that then lead to further intensifications of nationalism.

As a pre-presidential Donald Trump once said, 'when bad times come, I'll get whatever I want' (*Trump: An American Dream*: episode 1; see Peel, Bogado & Zinni, 2017), and it seems this dynamic extends beyond New York real estate. Fascism is once again felt to be on the rise (Watts, 2017; Haque, 2018), and fairly or not, Trump and his brand of apparently 'post-truth' politics (played out in new digital media) are seen as part of this. Most of the major world powers continue to be involved in overseas conflicts which are part of a 'war on terror' and which have a domestic element too. Insurgents are selected for elimination and liquidated by hunter-killer drones controlled remotely. Police and security services have their surveillance and enforcement capabilities upgraded to fight internal enemies.

Internal enemies now include those who make it across borders without dying in the attempt; migrants who sometimes end up in camps. Children are separated from their families: something with its own even more poignant historical echoes. Senior politicians and even heads of state of the world's most powerful countries are now routinely embroiled in allegations of illegality and corruption, even relationships with organized criminals – 'murky links' indeed. Scientists, scholars of society and of organization, continue to serve the interests of capital, prompting some critical scholars to call for the bulldozing of the business school (Parker, 2018). Leading universities in major democracies collaborate with state security agencies, and sign partnership agreements with aerospace (security, military technology) companies. More optimistically perhaps, automation is once again a hot topic and discussions of 'the end of work' proliferate (Kessler, 2017). At the same time, the 'gig economy' sees work become ever more contingent for some, while others face toil and even physical harm in the most advanced of work settings (Evans & Jeong Perry, 2018).

The critical theorists themselves had a sense that the more things change, the more they stay the same: 'Just as the structure of capitalist society forever transforms itself while the basis of that society, economic relationships, are left untouched, so the cultural superstructure also constantly changes, yet certain principal elements persist without significant modification' (Horkheimer, 1978 [1926–1931], p. 27).

Their work is at essence a critique of capitalist society and although they charted its mutations and contradictions, the critical theorists took the relations of production (who owns property and businesses, who works and who commands) as their starting point. This material base of society is in critical theory primus inter pares in a web of relationships linking culture, politics, economy and society, and relations of production have not changed significantly. This is essentially a Marxist approach to analysing society and it is necessary now to summarize some of the key elements of Marxism on which it is based.

Marxist foundations

Marx's work provided critical theory with some fundamental perspectives on the relationships between the social world – social structure (classes, organizations, etc.), the norms and beliefs which frame these (culture) – and the subjectivities of human individuals (consciousness). Of particular importance is the view that people themselves create this social world, but find they are enmeshed within its structures in a way that is hard to understand. As Marx put it: 'Men make their own history, but they do not make it as they please; they do not make it under circumstances chosen by themselves, but under circumstances directly encountered, given and transmitted from the past' (Marx, 2008 [1852], p. 16). This is a moment of indeterminacy; we create the world but also find that it places constraints on us and it is hard to pin down what really determines 'the way things are'. In capitalism, according to Marxist analyses, it is the way we organize production which holds the key to understanding the social structure: 'The materialist conception of history starts from the proposition that the production of the means to support human life and, next to production, the exchange of all things produced, is the basis of all social structure' (Engels, 1908, p. 94).

Under the capitalist system of production (i.e. everywhere), some people own and control businesses and organizations, and other people work for and take orders from this group. Owners and managers control businesses and organizations. Workers/employees are controlled. This establishes patterns of relationships between groups of people. People sharing similar positions in relation to these issues around ownership and control, are called classes. Thus capitalist society is a class society. These classes have, almost by definition, different interests and so they are in conflict. Poverty and unemployment result from the contradictions thrown up by market capitalism, as businesses seek to lower their costs as much as possible. Even within the dominant classes there is competition and conflict, and at an international level, this can lead to war (Gilbert, 1978).

As Engel's quote above relates, once things are produced through work, they are exchanged (sold), and, in capitalist society from Marx's time to the present day, they are sold as a 'commodity'. This creates the market for goods and services which is the basis of the capitalist market economy. In Marx's analysis, the commodity has become 'fetishized' which means that it appears to take on an almost supernatural power of its own. In critical theory, this notion was to be developed (via the work of Lukács [see Granter, 2014, pp. 538–539] into a concept of reification. The essential meaning is similar in that it denotes 'thing-ness' – the tendency for something, often a concept, which is actually socially constructed, to become something that stands over and against people; possessed of its own power. Capitalist society is one where politics, the media, culture, ideas – everything, effectively – revolves around the notion of the commodity in the market; selling, buying, money, deals, savings, business, calculations, investments, budgets, innovation, entrepreneurship, risk, efficiency, career, etc. In Marx's view, however, this is not a 'natural' state of affairs and indeed not a desirable one since the commodity system rests on exploitation at work and misery for many in society.

For Marx, the organization and experience of work is central to 'both the constitution of the human individual qua human, and the historical development of the species' (Granter, 2009, p. 52). We noted already that the production and circulation of commodities was at the heart of Marx's political economy. In Marx's analysis, work, rather than being understood as the expression of human species being – an expression of cooperation and sociality which we shape and organize for ourselves – it is distorted by its crystallization into the commodity form.

A commodity is therefore a mysterious thing, simply because in it the social character of men's labour appears to them as an objective character stamped upon the product of that labour; because the relation of the producers to the sum total of their own labour is presented to them as a social relation, existing not between themselves, but between the products of their labour (Marx, 2007, p. 83).

Faced with this contradiction, and with materially degrading conditions at work in many cases, people are alienated from the work they do. Their working lives are marked by conflict, dissatisfaction and exploitation rather than cooperation and self-expression – the latter elements being central to Marx's ideal notion of working life (Granter, 2009, pp. 51–66).

Marx's work represents an attempt to understand how the multifarious elements which make up social life, relate to each other. He 'insisted that any society ... could only be understood as a totality ... social phenomena are interrelated so that work, politics, law, family have to be analysed in terms of their interconnections' (Hyman, 2006, p. 31). Totality, then, is taken as a defining feature of Marxism and one with particular relevance to research on society and organization. In Marx, individuality, the subject, is fundamentally interconnected with the social system or whole. Operationalizing this sense of interconnection is difficult, however, for two reasons. Firstly, it requires the theorist, not to mention the reader, to be adept at holding in their head multiple concepts operating at multiple levels. Clearly it is difficult also for the everyday person, since the working class has consistently failed to 'crack the code' of capitalism and see that it structures social life and consciousness – in a deeply dysfunctional way.

Following Marx, scholars such as Lukács, Gramsci and the Frankfurt School (Jay, 1984) would maintain Marx's concept of totality, of interconnection. They would work on uncovering more precisely how the different elements of the social world are connected to each other. This would be more than an academic enterprise, however, because the critical theorists would also seek to reveal the way these interconnections were structured not just as part of capitalism but often in a way which serves the interests of the capitalist system. To do this they would turn increasingly towards the analysis of everyday life, consciousness and culture, though they would never abandon the Marxist commitment to political economy. Since they considered the capitalist system to be not working (to put it mildly – see above), this project of revealing capitalism's tactics and strategies of survival would be one oriented towards emancipation; freeing people from exploitation, domination and injustice (Garrick & Clegg, 2001, p. 125).

Critical theories of organization and society: concepts and method

Horkheimer's 1937 essay 'Traditional and critical theory' (Horkheimer, 2002 [1937]) establishes the fundamental Frankfurt School approach to social and organizational analysis. Horkheimer argues that 'traditional' (that is, hitherto existing, mainstream, non-critical) theory takes the status quo as given – it is part of 'the production process with its division of labour' (Horkheimer, 2002 [1937], p. 216). Traditional theory functions within the conceptual framework given by capitalism and takes for granted that the way it is set up is legitimate. It does not question that capitalism is a rational and objectively functioning system. Scientists, including social scientists, are rewarded for their non-oppositional approach and are given the opportunity to build careers and a special social status (Horkheimer, 2002 [1937], p. 216) where they are seen as experts. Traditional theory is all about 'what works' and what is 'practical' and 'productive': 'Theories [...] which are confirmed or disproved on the building of machines, military organizations, even successful motion pictures, look to a clearly distinguishable consumer group' (Horkheimer, 2002 [1937], p. 217).

Critical theory, on the other hand, argues that we should not take anything for granted. Social and organizational dynamics are not neutral expressions of the proper functioning of society. Critical theory does not work within the categories laid down by traditional science or the productivity fetish of contemporary society – categories like 'better, useful, appropriate, productive, and valuable' (Horkheimer, 2002 [1937], p. 207). These categories and concepts have, after all, been defined as part of a deeply unequal and unjust social reality. They are the categories which serve capital because capital and its operatives (owners, managers, politicians, mainstream researchers) define what 'better' or 'useful' mean. Fewer staff is better. Private healthcare is better. The ability to hire and fire staff at will is useful. Tax cuts are useful. Jet fighters are useful.

Critical theorists – or to put it another way, truly critical scholars of organization and society – do not dismiss science and rationality out of hand; whatever their faults, organizations and societies are the product of people working together, on one level at least. However, this 'rational' society is also deeply irrational in that it is riven with hardship, war and oppression. Critical theory asks that when we look at organizational and social processes, we consider: is this really rational (does it make society better for all is the definition of 'rational' which critical theory uses), or is this just something that serves capital? In this context, critical scholars should work towards emancipation:

> The Marxist categories of class, exploitation, surplus value, profit, pauperization, and breakdown are elements in a conceptual whole, and the meaning of this whole is to be sought not in the preservation of contemporary society but in its transformation into the right kind of society.
>
> (Horkheimer, 2002 [1937], p. 218)

Beyond the categories of capital

In the 1960s and 1970s the work of Marcuse, Horkheimer and Adorno played a role in inspiring and providing analytical frameworks for protest and social movements around the world. Radical students and protesters became in turn radical academics and so critical theory emerged as a recognized, though certainly not mainstream, part of the intellectual landscape. Even as some of the utopian hopes of the 1960s faded, scholars of social and organization thought continued to look to critical theory as a source of inspiration. The following discussion is far from exhaustive; instead it gives some examples which illustrate the ways in which this inspiration has produced critical perspectives.

One example from the field of organization and society was J. Kenneth Benson's 1977 piece 'Organizations: A dialectical view' which aimed to highlight the need for organizational analyses that did not take capital's own categories as given. Here, central elements of critical theory such as 'social construction/production, totality, contradiction, praxis' (Benson, 1977, p. 2) were employed, although Adorno, Horkheimer and Marcuse are not referenced directly; however, he draws on Lukács, whose work intersects with Frankfurt perspectives. For Benson, work organizations and everyday life are interconnected, and as scholars of organization we should 'see the intricate ties of organizations to the larger society – not only to macro-structural features such as economic and political systems but also to the everyday activities of people' (Benson, 1977, p. 9). Benson's use of the concept of praxis shows that he belongs to an intellectual grouping who, following in the slipstream of Western Marxism, were seeking to work in a way that was emancipatory as well as explicatory. This recalls Horkheimer's pronouncement: 'The issue, however, is not simply the theory of emancipation; it is the practice of it as well' (Horkheimer, 2002 [1937], p. 233).

Burrell and Morgan's *Sociological Paradigms and Organizational Analysis*, published in 1979, introduced many scholars to Frankfurt School critical theory for the first time. The work of the Frankfurt School was categorized by Burrell and Morgan as part of the 'radical humanist' paradigm (Burrell & Morgan, 2005 [1979], p. 33). By 1985, critical approaches to organization of a distinctly Frankfurt-inspired hue were gaining momentum. Alvesson, for example, remarked that his take on critical organization theory was 'Frankfurt-inspired' (Alvesson, 1985, p. 117). As part of his 'Critical framework for organizational analysis', Alvesson makes use of Benson's four principles of dialectical analysis (social construction/production, totality, contradiction). He argues, following Burrell (1980), that within the totality of social life, the organization can be a special focus of attention since 'this is where capital and labour meet, where the working process takes place, and productive and unproductive work interact' (Alvesson, 1985, p. 120).

In Alvesson's view, organizations are dominated by technological rationality: 'Technological rationality stands for a basic attitude to social life and to Nature – an attitude in which instrumental control, supported by scientific and technical knowledge, is a crucial component' (Alvesson, 1985, p. 122). Notions of technological or technocratic rationality play an important role in the Frankfurt School critique. In Marcuse's work in particular (Marcuse, 1998; Marcuse, 2002 [1964]), this rationality is seen as increasingly dominant in a society which is ever more totally controlled and administered. For Alvesson, as for Marcuse, and as seen in

Horkheimer's analysis of traditional and critical theory, science and the generation of knowledge is viewed as primarily in the service of the economic elite. When research, planning and the 'science' of management are applied to the running of organizations, one tends to find that hiding behind claims to rationality or objectivity, it is the managers and owners who benefit. Technological or technocratic rationality segues easily into economic rationality (Alvesson & Willmott, 1992, p. 458) which often seems to involve calls for greater efficiency, for 'doing more with less', for better 'performance' and so on. Under such circumstances, working conditions tend increasingly towards 'monotony, unqualified tasks, and strict supervision and control' (Alvesson, 1985, p. 125). Work becomes increasingly stressful, generating 'mental disorders and psycho-somatic symptoms' (Alvesson, 1985, p. 126) which render leisure time suitable only for passive consumption. What is taken for, or promoted as, objective rationality under capitalism is instead partial and instrumental rationality, serving the economic elite but harming workers.

Neimark and Tinker (1987) introduce readers to Adorno's concept of 'identity thinking' (Adorno, 2005 [1951], p. 74) and how this might be overcome though 'non-identity thinking' and the related process of 'negative dialectics' (Adorno, 1973a). According to these authors, as was the case with Alvesson, mainstream research on organizations, management and society tends to assume that a concept used routinely by businesses, and other mainstream writers, is ideologically neutral. That is, that the word means exactly what they say it means, and the concept therefore requires no further interrogation as to who benefits from the way the concept plays out in practice. Neimark and Tinker illustrate this with the transaction cost theory of the modern corporation and the concepts employed by writers such as Chandler and Williamson. One such concept, and one which speaks to a wide spectrum of writing on business, is the (employment) contract. This is often seen as a 'gentleman's agreement' between employees and employers, a reciprocal 'exchange that is satisfactory to both parties and is not a victory (whether total or partial) of one antagonist over another' (Neimark & Tinker, 1987, p. 669). Neimark and Tinker point out that in fact the employment relationship under capitalism is the result of 'a series of on-going conflicts' (Neimark & Tinker, 1987, p. 669). This reflects the notion of a 'frontier of control' that became the focus of writing on the labour process from the late 1970s; for example, the influential account of Edwards (1979) referred to working life not as characterized by accommodation and agreement, but a dynamic 'contested terrain' where conflicts continually arise. In the present day, employers and employees find themselves in conflict on a regular basis, and this is the case even for professional knowledge workers (Perraudin, 2017).

Another concept Neimark and Tinker draw our attention to is efficiency, which we have already mentioned – it is one of the defining principles, or concepts, of contemporary capitalism (Neimark & Tinker, 1987, p. 666). In contemporary society, the meaning of the word 'efficient' is scarcely questioned by organizations, or in mainstream writing on organization and management. Many of us will have experienced first-hand life in an organization which is seeking to become more efficient. This could be expressed in other ways, such as 'high performing'. It might involve having 'high-performing individuals and teams', and this can be encouraged through a 'performance-orientated culture' and being 'not afraid to make and follow through difficult decisions' (The University of

Manchester, 2015, p. 23). Experience of, and scholarship on, life in organizations who dedicate themselves to the concepts of efficiency and performance indicate that behind the rhetoric of efficiency and/or performance, the interests of 'employees, consumers, and other social constituencies' (Neimark & Tinker, 1987, p. 670) are rarely well served and in fact, conditions for these groups become worse. High performance, like efficiency, is usually defined by managers according to their own interests, whether this is saving on staffing costs, or fitting in with their own self-serving strategic discourse (Clegg, Carter & Kornberger, 2004). Organizations supposedly 'perform' better, but work in them becomes more oppressive and demeaning. Crucially, then, the concepts which managers and mainstream management scholars use as if they were neutral are anything but. Behind them lie inequality, power struggles and the oppression of workers by management. Neimark and Tinker propose that we adopt Adorno's approach and use 'negative dialectics' to unmask the 'fictions' which seem to be inherent in organizational and management thought (Neimark & Tinker, 1987, p. 664). This is a frame of mind, a consciousness, a way of doing social research, which remains open to the possibility that words and concepts must not be taken at face value (see also Giustiniano, Cunha & Clegg, 2016). On one hand, there is a recognition that 'the observer/scientist embodies theories, beliefs and social ideologies' (Neimark & Tinker, 1987, p. 663). On another, there is a sense that we are not 'entirely subjugated by social conditions' (Neimark & Tinker, 1987, p. 664) and so there is space for a critical consciousness to emerge.

The universal in the particular

The Frankfurt School understanding of the different elements of social life as inter-connected led them to utilize an analytical technique which is not unfamiliar to those of a literary bent. James Joyce wrote: 'I always write about Dublin, because if I can get to the heart of Dublin I can get to the heart of all the cities of the world. In the particular is contained the universal.' (Tymoczko, 1997, p. 260; see also Aroles, Clegg & Granter, 2019 for a discussion of organization and literary form) To show the universal in the particular often meant that the critical theorists looked (as novelists do) to everyday life as a source of analytical material. Although it can be found across their work, collections of 'aphorisms' such as *Minima Moralia* (Adorno, 2005 [1951]) and *Dawn and Decline* (Horkheimer, 1978 [1926–1969]) showcase this technique to great effect. Everyday objects, for example, have modes of behaviour 'inscribed in them'. Slippers, for example, are 'monuments to the hatred of bending down'. Teenagers 'owe no-one respect, they put their hands in their trouser pockets. But their elbows, stuck outwards, are ready to barge anyone who gets in their way.' (Adorno, 2005 [1951], p. 110) Such insolence is only permissible because these teenagers are not yet trapped by the world of work and organizations, the capitalist social relations behind which defer-ence hides – they don't sell their labour, and so they owe no one respect. Else-where, Adorno gives us an altogether darker, and more direct, analysis of the relationship between war and business:

> The old exaggeration of sceptical Liberals, that war was a business, has come
> true: ... Every laudatory mention of the chief contractor in the destruction of

cities, helps to earn it the good name that will secure it the best commission in their rebuilding.

(Adorno, 2005 [1951], pp. 53–54)

Jermier created a whole narrative of alternative organizational scenarios for his article 'When the sleeper wakes' (Jermier, 1985) which sought to illustrate the irrationalities contained in organizational life. Here, Jermier uses 'typical cases to illustrate positions' (Jermier, 1985, p. 74) and does so by imagining the inner thought processes of a worker confronted by alienation and dysfunction at work. In doing this, he combines the notion of the universal in the particular, with negative dialectics. Jermier gives a scenario where we see the corporate justification for practices that harm employees and the environment; 'Engineers have studied this and you know they have to design the process to run as efficiently as possible' (Jermier, 1985, p. 69), as well as the critical reflections of an employee: '"Being rational doesn't just mean following production logic," thought Mike ...' (Jermier, 1985, p. 73). The negativity (as in negative dialectics) in Jermier's article functions through using an innovative academic writing form to open up a way of looking at organizations which highlights their hidden dynamics – the way concepts such as efficiency, once again, are not questioned, despite the problems associated with the way they actually play out at work.

Into the 21st century, the aphoristic use of the universal in the particular continues in critical studies of management. Contu, as part of the lively debate around employee resistance in organizations (Contu, 2008), refers to Adorno's Philemon and Baucis, one of the vignettes in *Minima Moralia*. Here, a wife helps her husband put on his coat – he seems to struggle with such simple things, he's 'only a man' (Adorno, 2005 [1951], p. 173). She rolls her eyes; he may think he's the boss, but look how inadequate he really is. Thus the patriarchal power of the man is subtly undermined. But in this 'battle of the sexes', both opponents are wrong. The woman's actions only serve to highlight the fact that where it really matters – not in the parlour, but in the realm of the economy – men remain in control. For men, this is a pyrrhic victory since this this speaks to a society which confuses money earning with human worth. Contu uses Adorno's sketch to make a similar point about subtle, ironic, humorous forms of resistance in organizations. How subversive they seem; how ineffectual they really are – the very fact that they are seen as a form of resistance shows how crushed people are by organizational life under capitalism. Contu's calls for more active forms of resistance (Contu, 2008) seem to chime with Adorno's sign off to Philemon and Baucis: 'No emancipation without that of society' (Adorno, 2005 [1951], p. 173).

Although there has been debate over whether the two are compatible (Putnam et al., 1993), some contemporary writers on organization have sought to use critical theory alongside ethnographic research methods. Hyde, Granter and Hassard (2016), for example, combine action theory with critical theory to form critical-action theory, a combination that they locate in a tradition that includes Beynon's *Working for Ford* (Beynon, 1973), Clegg's *Power, Rule and Domination* (Clegg, 1975) and Willis' *Learning to Labour* (Willis, 1977) (Hyde, Granter & Hassard, 2016, p. 36). From action theory they take an emphasis on social reality as being 'socially constructed, sustained and changed' (Hyde, Granter & Hassard, 2016, p. 34). In fact, this is not dissimilar to the position taken by the critical theorists, but from critical theory, in this context, comes a distinctive commitment to examine; social action and the symbols of society in order to understand the ways in which social groups are ideologically dominated. For critical theory, knowledge is power – it asks questions about the ways in which competing interests clash and the manner in which conflicts are resolved in favour of particular groups (Hyde, Granter & Hassard, 2016, p. 35).

Taking seriously the notion of totality and the interconnection between the individual, organization and society, Hyde, Granter and Hassard spent time with healthcare professionals and uncovered links between their subjective experiences of work and identity, and organizational and politico-economic dynamics. Hospital nurse managers, for example, often spoke of how they were increasingly expected to speak 'the language of business' and how those who could successfully master the discourses of the private sector were those most likely to get ahead. This left some nurse managers with something of an identity conflict – were they nurses or business people, or both? The authors found that discourses of private sector business, and new business systems such as 'lean', modelled on the private sector, seemed to flow from the senior management level of the hospital, through corporate communications, meetings and training programmes. In turn, these discourses evidenced an ideological move at the level of national policy towards private provision of healthcare, and so they were generated at the intersection of politics and corporate domination. There was a sense of language and imagery as something which was not 'happening' accidentally but was being actively shaped by elites in business and politics with the goal of softening up socialized healthcare for privatization. If the culture of healthcare organizations can be infused with the ideology of private sector business, then taking the step of actually privatizing healthcare can be accomplished with less resistance: this is the implication (Hyde, Granter & Hassard, 2016). Rather than assuming that concepts such as 'business-line management' and 'lean' were neutral elements of organizational life, Hyde, Granter and Hassard applied non-identity thinking to interrogate the real meaning of the language of new public management (Hyde, Granter & Hassard, 2016, pp. 9–12).

From mass culture to organizational culture

The Frankfurt School are perhaps best known for their work on the culture industry or 'mass culture' (Adorno, 1991; Adorno & Horkheimer, 1997 [1944]). They were highly critical of the mass media and what they considered to be an industrialized form of leisure in modern society. They argued that films, pop music and so on are pre-formatted and standardized as with any other product and as well as bearing the imprint of capitalism in their form, the products of the culture industry act on the consciousness of those who consume them. They function almost as 'psychoanalysis in reverse' (Adorno, 2002, p. 50) in that they distort, rather than liberate or help make sense of, people's inner thoughts and feelings. The media has in essence a propaganda function and serves both as a form of escapism and also to transmit messages which associate capitalism with heroism (Adorno & Horkheimer, 1997 [1944], p. 151) and the notion that 'anyone can make it' in capitalist societies (Adorno & Horkheimer, 1997 [1944], p. 145). In the face of the misery which capitalism creates, people turn to 'candy floss' (Adorno & Horkheimer, 1997 [1944], p. xv) entertainment for some kind of relief: 'Now, the horror of one's own city is submerged in the general suffering, and people turn their attention to the marital problems of movie stars' (Horkheimer, 1978 [1926–1969], p. 90).

During the 1980s, commentators on management and organization turned increasingly to look at the culture of organizations (Peters & Waterman, 1982; Deal & Kennedy, 1988). The topic of organizational or corporate culture expanded dramatically. Other scholars of management and organization have drawn on critical theory (Gabriel, 1999, p. 181) as part of a more sceptical view of organizational culture. Although, clearly, organizational culture and mass media/leisure culture are different things, what critical perspectives on organizational culture tend to share with the Frankfurt School is a sense of how culture is part of a totality. That is, it is in something of a dialectical relationship with the sphere of production – it is interrelated to questions of who owns and who controls organizations. Further, both the Frankfurt School and critical scholars of organization point to the tendency for culture to be used as part of a system of control. Willmott, for example, views corporate culture as part of a system which aspires to an almost totalitarian form of control. Referencing *The Dialectic of Enlightenment* directly, he sees corporate culture programs as the very antithesis of organizational rationality – rather than seek to work on the flaws in organizational life that make it antithetical to human flourishing, they attempt to establish tighter control over thought and emotion instead, representing part of a 'continuing downward spiral of the Enlightenment project' (Willmott, 1993).

Casey's 1995 book on how organizations seek to 'design' the subjectivities of their employees (Casey, 1995) draws on critical theory throughout, including some of its more psychoanalytical currents. Casey argues that 'The family metaphor – that is, the bourgeois family – is the everyday shop floor organizing principle. It is the family that ensures that everyday organizational procedures are adhered to, that authority is obeyed, and that people carry out their assigned tasks' (Casey, 1995, p. 193). This analysis contains parallels with Horkheimer's 'Authority and the family' (Horkheimer, 2002 [1949]) which also positions the family as a 'key functional element in the development of modern systems of corporate and political authority' (Granter, 2014, p. 552). Casey also appears to combine a sense of totality with the Frankfurt theme of manufactured culture as a new form of mythology. She argues that corporate cultures are an attempt to 're-enchant' social life for workers who have now moved beyond even industrialism's notion of community or belonging. This echoes the Frankfurt School notion of the decline of reason under modernity, where mass culture – films, love songs, horoscopes (Adorno, 2002 [1957]), etc. – provides a 'haven in a heartless world' (Lasch, 1976); a simulation of warmth and authenticity in a world of total administration (Marcuse, 2002 [1964]).

Fleming had already drawn on the 'Freudo-Marxist framework' developed by Herbert Marcuse in *Eros and Civilization* in a 2005 paper on workplace memory (Fleming, 2005), and his use of critical theory continued through his analysis of so-called 'authenticity' in workplace cultures. Fleming finds that organizations increasingly adopt a 'be yourself' culture, meaning that they encourage people to dress, look and behave how they would normally do outside of work (Fleming, 2009). For the organization, this has the advantage of capturing the individuality and 'attitude' which is increasingly prized in the digital service economy. For the worker, however, the call to 'be yourself' is undermined by the organization's continuing use of traditional forms of control, and its attempts to circumscribe what sort of authenticity is permitted. More theoretically, Fleming uses Adorno to show how a 'cult' or 'jargon' of authenticity serves to undermine the understanding of workers as part of a social totality. Here, the 'authentic' individual can be made responsible for their fortunes at work; it is their attitude which is the problem, not the organizational or social structure; 'The social relation, which seals itself off in the identity of the subject, is de-socialized into an in-itself' (Adorno, 1973b, p. 95, cited in Fleming, 2009, p. 141).

Interestingly, and characteristically, Adorno and Horkheimer anticipated even more directly some of the critical dynamics around corporate culture nearly four decades earlier. Possibly influenced by a reading of the emerging field of human resource management connected with the Hawthorne studies (see Parker, 2000), they point to the growing tendency for organizations to promote 'a friendly atmosphere as advised by management experts and adopted by every factory to increase output' (Adorno & Horkheimer, 1997, p. 151). This friendly atmosphere is further enhanced, perhaps, by an air of informality (something emphasized in mainstream corporate culture up to the present day) and so people 'call one another "Bob" and "Harry"' (Adorno & Horkheimer, 1997 [1944], p. 165). This is the culture of the 'sporting analogy' and 'team members' (Adorno & Horkheimer, 1997 [1944], p. 165) where bureaucracy is a 'taboo term' (Adorno & Horkheimer, 1997 [1944], p. 164). All this, of course, masks the continuance of, on the one hand, standardization and interchangeability at work, and on the other, winner takes all competition between nations, organizations and individuals. What we might call corporate culture, in the Frankfurt analysis, 'Brings even the last private impulse under social control precisely because it seems to relate men's circumstances directly to production, and to reprivatize them' (Adorno & Horkheimer, 1997 [1944], p. 151).

Discussion and conclusion

There are many other contemporary currents in critical theory and not all can be included here. Some writers on work and organization, and the future of both, have drawn particularly on Marcuse's writings on the 'end of work'. Granter (2009), for example, draws on the wide-ranging critiques of *One Dimensional Man* – particularly with regard to automation – and also the mix of utopian and psychoanalytic perspectives that informed Marcuse's *Eros and Civilization* (Marcuse, 1987 [1955]). Similarly, Fleming uses Marcuse's notion of 'surplus repression' to help frame his call for resistance against new forms of control at work (Fleming, 2015, p. 37). Frayne has given a useful summary of how critical theory is relevant for radical critiques of work (Frayne, 2016) and his book on the topic has introduced this dynamic to a wider audience (Frayne, 2015). In a related field, Gunderson has used critical theory extensively in his exploration of 'de-growth', and to think through alternative, more peaceful and less environmentally harmful futures (Gunderson, 2018). In the field of criminology, Shulte-Bockholt has drawn on the Frankfurt notion of a 'society of rackets' to help reveal intersections between economic, political and criminal elites (Schulte-Bockholt, 2006; 2013; see also Heins, 2007; 2011 for a critical perspective on racket theory). This concept of intersection between business and organized crime has been explored by writers on organization such as Parker (2012), and Gond, Palazzo and Basu (2009), and the explicit link with critical theory has been made recently by Granter (2017). In his article on racket theory, Granter uses three cases to illustrate the occlusion of business and crime, financial deregulation, global conflict and public policy reform. Thus, the methodology of 'the universal in the particular' is once again brought into use.

There have, of course, been criticisms of the Frankfurt perspective. Some writers from the field of cultural studies have criticized critical theory's take on mass culture, arguing that there are in fact liberatory impulses within consumer culture (Nava, 1991; see also Granter, 2009, pp. 156–161). Even some proponents of critical theory have admitted that the work of the Frankfurt School can seem 'monolithic and puritanical' (Kellner, 1984, p. 159, cited in Granter, 2014, p. 553). Born into a privileged bourgeois elite, the critical theorists were perhaps influenced by their own cultural context in terms of their critique of mass culture – which even today we sometimes refer to as 'low' culture. For sure, not all consumers of handbags, films and pop songs are 'duped' into thinking that these products will make their lives better. At the same time, in an age where products such as *Pop Idol* and *Love Island* exist alongside continued social misery and genocidal global conflict, the notion of 'candy floss' escapism is hard to ignore. That their work was monolithic is also hard to deny, although once again one might point to their social and historical context – does not the repression and barbarity of Nazism stand even today as an historical monolith, a monument to total hate, total destruction, domination and oblivion? Does not total capitalism call for a totalizing critique? On a related point, it is possible to criticize the Frankfurt School for being overly pessimistic, an accusation which lies behind the notion of the 'Grand Hotel Abyss' (Jeffries, 2016, pp. 1–2). Gunderson has provided a detailed rebuttal to this criticism, concluding that 'Those dedicated to improving society must adjust their views in accordance with today's social misery and allow ethical-political visions to be regulated by real social conditions and trends in order to circumvent utopianism, false promises, and [...] ideal theory' (Gunderson, 2015, p. 35). That is, we should base our critique on reality, not speculation. At the risk of contradicting the foregoing point, it should also be noted that there were utopian elements in critical theory, particularly the later work of Marcuse. In works such as *An Essay on Liberation* (Marcuse, 1972), he explores the potentialities for radical change, although notably this would likely involve a 'great refusal' of the capitalist status quo (see the discussion in Granter, 2009, pp. 69–91). Although more prominent in the USA than elsewhere, there is also the concept of 'cultural Marxism' to contend with (see Jamin, 2018 for a survey and analysis). This concept appears to have originated in a 1992 article by Michael Minnicino (1992) which equates the Frankfurt School with political correctness. Ultimately, the goal of critical theory is 'to destroy Western traditions and values' (Jamin, 2018, p. 1). The 'cultural Marxism' analysis appears to suggest that part of this destruction is to be facilitated through turning the mass media into a form of propagandistic mind control: 'The technique of mass media and advertising developed by the Frankfurt School now effectively controls American political campaigning' (Minnicino, 1992, p. 15). One does not have to be an expert in critical theory to understand that this argument represents an inversion of reality, in that the Frankfurt School did not 'develop' mass media and advertising but were highly critical of the tendency for 'entertainment' to crowd out the space for rational thought, and for political language to become distorted and instrumental (see Granter, 2014, pp. 543–544; Jeffries, 2016, pp. 6–8).

We have examined some of the ways critical theory has influenced work on organizations and society. This influence can be seen to coalesce around the sub-discipline of critical management studies, or CMS (Granter, 2014, p. 550). Some have questioned the extent to which CMS stays true to the radical intent of critical theory (Klikauer, 2015) but this area remains fertile ground for new critical directions on work, organizations, management and society. Some scholars working in this field have found their careers disrupted for reasons that remain opaque (Burrell, 2018). Of course, any concrete link between institutional unpopularity and scholars' critical research on business and management is elusive. Even in the comparative safety of Western democracies, it wasn't easy for critical theorists in the 20th century to maintain both a critical approach to capitalism and a professional career; 'one has to fight for socialism, in other words' (Horkheimer, 1978 [1926–1969], p. 36). Perhaps that is one more parallel with the world we live in today.

End-of-chapter exercises

1. The second section of this chapter (critical theory today) considers some similarities between the world described by the Frankfurt School and the world of today. Are these similarities that you recognize? Are there others that could be included?
2. Thinking about the concept of 'the universal in the particular', is there a particular experience that you have had, or something that you have observed, that made you reflect on how society works?
3. Does the mass media really act as a form of mass hypnosis? Would this analysis be any different had the critical theorists been writing in the age of social media?
4. Do we live in a 'society of rackets'? If so, what can we do about it?

Glossary

Emancipation　The freeing of people. This is sometimes related to actual slavery but in the present context means the freeing of people who are dominated in various ways. In the view of critical theory, people are dominated by the ideological (see below) and material elements of capitalism in that they are exploited at work and duped into believing their situation is 'as good as it gets' by the media which serves those they work for. Emancipation means doing away with capitalism but this can only be achieved if people's thinking is also emancipated; hence the Frankfurt School emphasis on rationality and ideology.

Ideology　In common parlance, relating to ideas or beliefs. In the context of critical theory, slightly more specific. Like Marx, the Frankfurt School used ideology to refer to belief systems which capitalism holds up as rational and 'natural', but which are in fact socially constructed. Ideology permeates the whole of life and is transmitted through the media and institutions such as church and family, but also through discourse/language. This is part of the reason critical organization scholars are interested in culture – in organizations, for example, it is 'organizational culture', often most obvious at the discursive level, which serves to transmit the ideology of the company to the employees. Corporate ideology tends to relate closely to the wider ideologies of capitalism such as free choice, risk and productivity. Note that capitalists do not accept that these concepts are constructed mainly for the benefit of capitalists; for them, capitalism is not an ideology.

Marxist Ideas and forms of analysis developed by the political economist Karl Marx (1818–1883) are said to be Marxist. The label Marxist can also be applied to people who use Marx's ideas, in turn, to analyse the world in their own era. Key elements of Marxism include the notion of contemporary society as a distinctly capitalist society, comprised of different and unequal classes, where some are exploited and others benefit from this exploitation. Central to Marxism is the idea that this form of society can be transcended by socialism and communism. The Frankfurt School were Marxists.

Racket A conspiracy which often involves collusion between 'legitimate' business people, politicians and outright criminals. A racket allows those who run it to control prices, competition and markets by forcing people to buy something from them – be it security or material goods. Competition is stifled through relationships with police and politicians who enforce the rules for groups other than the racketeers but give the latter a free hand. For the Frankfurt writers, capitalism increasingly resembles a racket. Here, 'the market', which supposedly operates as an objective mechanism for distributing resources, is corrupted through hidden relationships and agreements. In the same way, 'democracy' is subverted and becomes a scramble for power between competing cliques who have beneficial relationships both with businesses and with criminals.

Rationality Relating to what is reasonable; an opinion or system which is formed through a search for the truth, rather than prejudice or guesswork. Rationality is a term closely associated with science in that scientific methods and ways of seeing the world call for truth to be proven through evidence. For critical theory, the concept of rationality is a battleground because adherents see it as socially constructed, to a great degree. Rationality under capitalism tends to coincide with systems which serve the interests of capitalists. Thus it is not 'real' rationality; it is distorted and ideological. It is the task of critical theory to work to establish a form of rationality that serves the interests of everyone. The Frankfurt School drew heavily on philosophical traditions, from Aristotle to Hegel and many in between.

Totality The totality is the whole and in critical theory means the whole of society, both material and cultural. It encompasses institutions, emotions, everyday life, high culture, low culture, science, philosophy … the full list would be almost infinitely long because totality is 'everything' which makes up society. No one, not even Adorno, Horkheimer and Marcuse, can work out a way for readers to understand all at once how all of these things are connected (although that didn't stop them from trying, one could argue!). According to critical theory, social thought can only really be successful and get to the reality of what is going on if it understands that everything is connected as part of a totality. Often, connected elements are understood dialectically in that they appear to be opposites, but in fact rely on each other for existence. One example of this would be work and leisure in critical theory.

References

Adorno, T. (1973a). *Negative dialectics*, B. Ashton (trans.). New York: Seabury Press.

Adorno, T. (1973b). *The jargon of authenticity*, K. Tarnowski, & F. Will (trans.). London: Routledge.

Adorno, T. (1991). *The culture industry: Selected essays on mass culture*. London: Verso.

Adorno, T. (2002). *Essays on music*, R. Leppert (ed.), S. H. Gillespie (trans.). Berkeley, CA: University of California Press.

Adorno, T. (2005 [1951]). *Minima moralia*. London: Verso.

Adorno, T. (2002 [1957]). *The stars down to earth*. London: Routledge.

Adorno, T., Frenkel-Brunswick, E., Levinson, D. J., & Nevitt Sanford, R. (1950). *The authoritarian personality*. New York: Harper and Brothers.

Adorno, T., & Horkheimer, M. (1997 [1944]). *Dialectic of enlightenment*, J. Cumming (trans.). London: Verso.

Agger, B. (1992). *The discourse of domination*. Evanston, IL: Northwestern University Press.

Agger, B. (1998). *Critical social theories*. Oxford: Westview Press.

Alvesson, M. (1985). A critical framework for organizational analysis. *Organization Studies*, 6 (2), 117–138.

Alvesson, M., & Willmott, H. (1992). On the idea of emancipation in management and organization Studies. *The Academy of Management Review*, 17(3), 432–464.

Aroles, J., Clegg, S., & Granter, E. (2019). Death and the penguin: Modularity, alienation and organising. *Culture and Organization*, 25(2), 104–117.

Benson, K. (1977). Organizations: A dialectical view. *Administrative Science Quarterly*, 22(1), 1–21.

Beynon, H. (1973). *Working for Ford*. London: Penguin.

Bottomore, T. (2002). *The Frankfurt School and its critics*. London: Routledge.

Brennan, T. (2002). *Globalization and its terrors*. London: Routledge.

Burrell, G. (1980). Radical organization theory. In D. Dunkerley, & G. Salaman (eds) *The international yearbook of organization studies 1979* (pp. 90–107). London: Routledge & Kegan Paul.

Burrell, G. (2018, March 25). The attack on organization studies in UK universities – an open letter by Gibson Burrell. (Y. Gabriel, ed.). Retrieved August 8, 2018 from Yiannis Gabriel (blog). http://www.yiannisgabriel.com/2018/03/the-attack-on-organization-studies-in.html.

Burrell, G., & Morgan, G. (2005 [1979]). *Sociological paradigms and organizational analysis*. Aldershot: Ashgate.

Casey, C. (1995). *Work, self and society: After industrialism*. London: Routledge.

Clausen, D. (2008). *Theodor W. Adorno: One last genius*. Cambridge, MA: Harvard University Press.

Clegg, S. (1975). *Power, rule and domination*. London: Routledge and Kegan Paul.

Clegg, S., Carter, C., & Kornberger, M. (2004). Get up, I feel like being a strategy machine. *European Management Review*, 1, 21–28.

Contu, A. (2008). Decaf resistance. *Management Communication Quarterly*, 21(3), 364–379.

Deal, T., & Kennedy, A. (1988). *Corporate cultures: The rites and rituals of corporate life*. London: Penguin.

Edwards, R. (1979). *Contested terrain*. London: Heinemann.

Engels, F. (1908). *Socialism, utopian and scientific*. Chicago, IL: C. H. Kerr.

EPSRC. (2013, March 21). UK's second Cyber Research Institute launched. Retrieved August 8, 2018 from https://epsrc.ukri.org/newsevents/news/secondcyberresearchinstitute/.

Evans, W., & Jeong Perry, A. (2018, April 16). Tesla says its factory is safer. But it left injuries off the books. Retrieved August 2, 2018 from Reveal News. https://www.revealnews.org/article/tesla-says-its-factory-is-safer-but-it-left-injuries-off-the-books/.

Fleming, P. (2005). Marcuse, memory and the psychoanalysis of workplace resistance. Critical Management Studies Conference.

Fleming, P. (2009). *Authenticity and the cultural politics of work: New forms of informal control*. Oxford: Oxford University Press.

Fleming, P. (2015). *Resisting work*. Philadelphia, PA: Temple University Press.

Frayne, D. (2015). *The refusal of work*. London: Sage.

Frayne, D. (2016). Critiques of work. In S. Egdell, H. Gottfried, & E. Granter (eds) *The Sage handbook of the sociology of work and employment* (pp. 616–633). London: Sage.

Gabriel, Y. (1999). Beyond happy families. *Human Relations*, 52(2), 179–203.

Garrick, J., & Clegg, S. (2001). Stressed out knowledge workers in performative times: A postmodern take on project based learning. *Management Learning*, 32(1), 119–134.

Gilbert, A. (1978). Marx on internationalism and war. *Philosophy & Public Affairs*, 7(4), 346–369.

Giustiniano, L., Cunha, M. P., & Clegg, S. (2016). Organizational zemblanity. *European Management Journal*, 34, 7–21.

Gond, J. P., Palazzo, G. G., & Basu, K. (2009). Reconsidering instrumental corporate social responsibility through the mafia metaphor. *Business Ethics Quarterly*, 19(1), 57–85.

Granter, E. (2009). *Critical social theory and the end of work*. London: Routledge.

Granter, E. (2014). Critical theory and organization studies. In P. Adler, P. Du Gay, G. Morgan, & M. Reed (eds) *The Oxford handbook of sociology, social theory & organization studies; contemporary currents* (pp. 534–560). Oxford: Oxford University Press.

Granter, E. (2017). Strictly business: Critical theory and the society of rackets. *Competition & Change*, 21(2), 94–113.

Gunderson, R. (2015). A defense of the 'Grand Hotel Abyss'. *Acta Sociologica*, 58(1), 25–38.

Gunderson, R. (2018). Degrowth and other quiescent futures. *Journal of Cleaner Production*, 198, 1574–1582.

Haque, U. (2018, August 2). Why fascism has the power to seduce the broken. Retrieved August 7, 2018 from https://eand.co/fascism-promises-people-heaven-on-earth-how-do-you-compete-with-that-6e00bc6f48fe.

Heins, V. (2007). Critical theory and the traps of conspiracy thinking. *Philosophy and Social Criticism*, 33(7), 787–801.

Heins, V. (2011). Seduction, alienation, racketeering. *Distinktion*, 7(1), 59–73.

Horkheimer, M. (1978 [1926–1969]). *Dawn and decline*, M. Shaw (trans.). New York: The Seabury Press.

Horkheimer, M. (2002 [1937]). Traditional and critical theory. In M. Horkheimer (ed.) *Critical theory; selected essays* (pp. 188–243). New York: Continuum.

Horkheimer, M. (2002 [1949]). Authority and the family. In M. Horkheimer (ed.) *Selected Essays* (pp. 47–128). New York: Continuum.

Horkheimer, M. (2002 [1968]). *Critical theory: selected essays*, M. J. O'Connel (trans.). New York: Continuum.

Hyde, P., Granter, E., & Hassard, M. (2016). *Deconstructing the welfare state*. Abingdon: Routledge.

Hyman, R. (2006). Marxist thought and the analysis of work. In M. Korkzynski, R. Hodson, & P. Edwards (eds) *Social theory at work*. Oxford: Oxford University Press.

Jamin, J. (2018). Cultural Marxism: A survey. *Religion Compass*, 12(1–2), 1–12.

Jay, M. (1984). *Marxism and totality*. Berkeley, CA: University of California Press.

Jay, M. (1996 [1973]). *The dialectical imagination: A history of the Frankfurt School and the Institute of Social Research 1923–1950*. London: University of California Press.

Jay, M. (2010). *The virtues of mendacity: On lying in politics*. London: University of Virginia Press.

Jeffries, S. (2016). *Grand Hotel Abyss: The lives of the Frankfurt School*, 1st edn. London: Verso.

Jermier, J. M. (1985). 'When the sleeper wakes': A short story extending themes in radical organizational theory. *Journal of Management, 11*(2), 67–80.

Kellner, D. (1984). *Herbert Marcuse and the crisis of Marxism.* London: Macmillan.

Kellner, D. (1989). *Critical theory, Marxism and modernity.* Baltimore, MD: Johns Hopkins.

Kessler, S. (2017, July 3). We've been worrying about the end of work for 500 years. Retrieved from Quartz. https://qz.com/1019145/weve-been-worrying-about-the-end-of-work-for-500-years/.

Klikauer, T. (2015). Critical management studies and critical theory: A review. *Capital and Class, 39*(2), 197–220.

Lasch, C. (1976). The family as a haven in a heartless world. *Salmagundi, 35*, 42–55.

Marcuse, H. (1969). *Reason and revolution; Hegel and the rise of social theory,* 2nd edn. London: Routledge & Kegan Paul.

Marcuse, H. (1972). *An essay on liberation.* London: Penguin.

Marcuse, H. (1987 [1955]). *Eros and civilization.* London: Ark.

Marcuse, H. (1998). Some social implications of modern technology. In D. Kellner (ed.) *Herbert Marcuse: Technology, war and fascism* (Collected Papers of Herbert Marcuse) (Vol.1, pp. 40–65). London: Routledge.

Marcuse, H. (2002 [1964]). *One dimensional man: Studies in the ideology of advanced industrial society.* London: Routledge.

Marx, K. (2007). *Capital: A critique of political economy – the process of capitalist production.* New York: Cosimo.

Marx, K. (2008 [1852]). *The eighteenth Brumaire of Louis Bonaparte.* Rockville, MD: Wildside.

Minnicino, M. (1992). The Frankfurt School and 'political correctness'. *Fidelio,* Winter, 1–24.

Nava, M. (1991). Consumerism reconsidered. *Cultural Studies, 5*(2), 157–173.

Neimark, M., & Tinker, T. (1987). Identity and non-identity thinking: A dialectical critique of the transaction cost theory of the modern corporation. *Journal of Management, 13*(4), 661–673.

Parker, M. (2000). The sociology of organizations and the organization of sociology: Some reflections on the making of a division of labour. *The Sociological Review, 48*(1), 124–146.

Parker, M. (2012). *Alternative business.* London: Routledge.

Parker, M. (2018). *Shut down the business school: What's wrong with management education.* London: Pluto.

Peel, B., Bogado, D., & Zinni, N. (Directors) (2017). *Trump: An American dream* [Motion Picture].

Perraudin, F. (2017, October 4). Manchester University staff vote to strike over academic job cuts. *The Guardian.*

Peters, T., & Waterman, R. (1982). *In search of excellence: Lessons from America's best-run companies.* London: Harper and Row.

Petzina, D. (1969). Germany and the Great Depression. *Journal of Contemporary History, 4* (4), 59–74.

Putnam, L. L., Bentz, C., Deetz, S., Mumby, D., & Van Maanen, J. (1993). Ethnography versus critical theory. *Journal of Management Inquiry, 2*(3), 221–235.

Ross, A. (2014, September 14). The naysayers: Walter Benjamin, Theodor Adorno, and the critique of pop culture. *The New Yorker.*

Schulte-Bockholt, A. (2006). *The politics of organized crime and the organized crime of politics.* Lanham, MD: Lexington.

Schulte-Bockholt, A. (2013). *Corruption as power.* Bern: Peter Lang.

Sim, S. (2014). *Introducing critical theory: A graphic guide.* London: Icon.

The University of Manchester (2015). Manchester 2020: The University of Manchester's strategic plan. Manchester: The University of Manchester.

Thompson, P. (2013). The Frankfurt School [series]. *The Guardian*.

Tymoczko, M. (1997). *The Irish Ulysses*. Berkeley, CA: University of California Press.

Walton, S. (2017). *Neglected or misunderstood: Introducing Theodor Adorno*. London: Zero.

Watts, J. (2017, July 1). British people fear fascism is spreading across the world in wake of Donald Trump victory, poll finds. *The Independent*.

Wheatland, T. P. (2009). *The Frankfurt School in exile*. Minneapolis, MN: University of Minnesota Press.

Wiggershaus, R. (2007). *The Frankfurt School*. Oxford: Polity.

Willis, P. (1977). *Learning to labour*. Farnborough: Saxon House.

Willmott, H. (1993). Strength is ignorance, slavery is freedom: Managing culture in modern organizations. *Journal of Management Studies*, 30(4), 515–552.

13 Judith Butler and performativity

Kate Kenny

Chapter objectives

This chapter discusses:

- How Butler's early work examining discourses of gender and sexuality gave rise to her theories of identification and subjection
- Butler's practical relevance as an influential thinker and a social activist
- Affective recognition and its location relative to other post-structural and psychoanalytic thinking, including that of Foucault and Lacan
- An overview of this approach including its relevance for debates about the relation between self and other, and agency and structure, within organization studies
- The concept of performativity and its implications for studies of networks of power and discourse
- The effects of subjection, including dynamics of exclusion and violence

Examples from organization studies are provided to illustrate each of these points.

Introduction

> Unwilled proximity and unchosen cohabitation are preconditions of our political existence (Judith Butler, *Notes Towards a Performative Theory of Assembly*).

> I felt overwhelmed with pride and gratitude that someone with the integrity to be so out as a lesbian was taking the leadership that the rest of us needed, not just emotionally but practically. It had been a long time since I felt real leadership before me that I could rely on. I experienced a great feeling of relief to see and hear that other voice, that other face literally creating a context one day, for me, whereas the day before there was none (Sarah Schulman [artist-activist and Distinguished Professor of English at the City University of New York]).

Judith Butler holds the Hannah Arendt Chair at the European Graduate School and is the Maxine Elliot Professor in the Department of Comparative Literature and the Program of Critical Theory at the University of California, Berkeley. She is a philosopher and one of the most challenging thinkers of our time. The rich and nuanced theory of identification and subjection she develops encompasses an understanding of the productive, positive side of these processes along with their darker, more hurtful aspects. At the same time her account emphasizes the inescapable unpredictability of the ways in which we identify with dominant aspects of our social world, including our organizations.

This project began in one of her earlier works, *Gender Trouble* (1990), in which she examines discourses of gender and sexuality and how these play out in social life, including how they interact with each other. In theorizing new directions for understanding identification, her work follows on directly from the examination of subjection to power that Foucault was pursuing towards the end of his life – to do with how and why individuals identify with, and contribute to the maintenance of, dominant discourses (see chapter on Foucault, this volume). Butler (1990; 1993) takes up the challenges that he left unanswered by combining ideas from his version of post-structural thought, with insights from her reading of Hegel, along with gender and psychoanalytic theorists including Irigaray, Kristeva, Freud and Lacan. Like Foucault (1991), she is always questioning the things we take for granted; her project is a similar exercise in 'continuous problematization'.

Students interested in questions of how and why networks of power persist, and how we are each involved in these processes, will therefore be fascinated by her ideas. A growing number of scholars in the field of business and management studies have already been inspired (Harding, 2003; 2007; 2013; Fotaki, 2013; Kenny, 2009; 2010; 2018; Roberts, 2005; Riach, Rumens & Tyler, 2014; 2016). As yet a relatively small area of work on organizational recognition, identity and subjectivity (Kenny, Whittle & Willmott, 2011), Butler's ideas are ideally placed to answer some of the most pressing issues facing theorists of organization today who puzzle the ways in which we become invested in and reproduce power (Fotaki, Metcalfe & Harding, 2014; Kenny & Euchler, 2012; Pullen & Knights, 2007; Pullen et al., 2016; Hancock & Tyler, 2007; Ford, 2010; Parker, 2001; 2002; Ford & Harding, 2004; Fotaki, 2014; Hodgson, 2005; Varman & Al-Amoudi, 2016). In social theory, feminist and cultural studies, beyond business and management, she has long been celebrated for offering one of the more valuable explorations of this question (Hall, 2000, p. 28; Lloyd, 2007).

More than many social theorists, Butler puts her ideas into practice. Having been involved in protest movements since the age of 16, she is a hero among activists, including feminist, gay, transgender and transsexual communities, and AIDS activism. This has led to the emergence of a fanzine *Judy* dedicated to her and her ideas. More recently she has been hailed as an inspiration by pro-Palestinian activists for her stance on the academic boycott of Israel – a complex position given that she is a Jewish anti-Zionist, and an outspoken one. This activism has not been well received by all parties, as the protests that accompanied her arrival in Frankfurt to collect the 2012 *Adorno Prize* show. Even so, she remains undeterred in her commitment not only to her theoretical work but also to the necessity of living her intellectual thought through practice and activism. This sets her apart from professorial colleagues at Berkeley, and from other social theorists included in this book. Butler's life, as well as her ideas, have inspired many people and continue to do so.

Affective recognition and organization studies

It is helpful to think of her overall approach as a theory of recognition that describes how we are compelled, affectively and often without our knowledge or will, into subjection to powerful discourses, which can sometimes be harmful. This search for recognition as a 'valid subject' – or a person who is considered legitimate in a given social sphere – powerfully influences life in organizations and institutions. While Butler herself does not tend to use the term 'affective recognition', it usefully brings together some key ideas from her 25 years of theoretical development around questions of subjectivity and power.

One of the most valuable aspects of this approach is that it emphasizes neither the micro-level of the subject, nor the macro-level of structure, at the expense of the other. Instead it offers a way to iterate between these levels, each vital for understanding the enactment of power. She adds a further layer from her readings of Freud and especially Lacan: that of the psyche, arguing that power has a 'psychic life' (Butler, 1997b). Others have provided fuller accounts of the nuances of Butler's theory, including Sarah Salih's *Judith Butler* (2002) as well as Butler's own reflections on her work in, for example, her collections of essays: *Undoing Gender* and *Senses of the Subject*, each of which provides fascinating insights into different facets of her thinking. In this chapter, I present aspects that have proved particularly influential for scholars of organization, with relevant examples given.

Affective recognition is a term that brings together insights from theories of gender, post-structuralism and psychoanalysis to explore how, as subjects, we are formed by and formative of power. To start, it is helpful to recap Foucault's ideas on how power operates through discursive networks that have no centre, or 'locus' (Foucault, 1990), but rather are upheld through the day-to-day practice of many people, in many places. Power persists because lots of people support the discursive networks of which it consists. This occurs both through the operation of power/ knowledge, a term referring to the ways in which power imbues what is taken for granted to be acceptable 'knowledge' in a given social setting, and through the social practices that emerge as a result (Foucault, 1990, pp. 94–95). The overall idea is that power 'works' through networks of discourse, with discourse referring to: 'ways of constituting knowledge, together with the social practices, forms of subjectivity and power relations that support these' (Weedon, 1997, p 105).

Butler's early work focuses on the ways in which gender and sexuality are constituted by such networks. She specifically examines the 'forms of subjectivity' that emerge, and the matrix of power relations that support this. We all contribute to the maintenance of gender as a primary, important category in society, she notes. For example, we tend to ask, first, whether a newborn baby is a boy or a girl, before asking anything else about them. Why would this be our first question, she wonders? What forms of power are in place upholding this binary distinction between male and female, granting it such importance? Butler looks to wider power relations, including those relating to the economic well-being of a state dependent on increasing its population of citizens. She examines norms of patriarchy and the 'compulsory heterosexuality' that effectively upholds this. She concludes that it is the repeated acts of subjection of people everywhere, to these discourses of gender and sexuality, which end up reinforcing the status quo. For Brewis, Hampton & Linstead (1997), in one of the earliest examples of Butler's thought making its way into management and organization studies, it is powerful discourses around binary ideas of gender that constitute subjects in today's work-places as gendered. They instill the impression of a stark difference between male and female subjects. It is not that these differences reflect innate features of people who have particular biological traits; rather the male–female distinction is falsely entrenched and amplified through the emphasis on differences that contemporary workplaces tend to uphold (see also Fotaki & Harding, 2013; 2018). Taking these ideas into the sphere of management, Harding studies norms around what it is to be an acceptable 'manager' and describes the compulsion experienced by profes-sionals to subject themselves to particular ideals that are themselves upheld by a discursive network influenced by law, rationality and modernity (Harding, 2003, p. 7). These become manifest in the subject themselves – the manager – as they struggle to see themselves, and have others see them, as professional managers.

Processes of subjection and the self-other divide

For Butler, the real question is why and how these subject positions are adopted; what is the drive underlying this compulsion? What is the force that operates 'upon' or 'within', for example, Harding's manager? What is it that keeps people subjected to forms of power? While Foucault became increasingly interested in sub-jects and subject positions towards the end of his life (1990), he tended to avoid this particular issue, but Butler declared in *Gender Trouble* that she was going to address it directly through an analysis of post-structural thought via psychoanalysis and gender theory (1997b, p. 18). Subjection, she argues, must be 'traced in the turns of psychic life' (1997b, p. 18). The subject emerges through the positions offered to it in language; one cannot exist outside of these and therefore outside the categories of identity that offer us a valid and recognizable position in the world. We are constituted by these very norms with which we identify because we are compelled to seek recognition from them. In order to be considered and to con-sider oneself as a valid subject, one must be legitimized by the normative identities on offer. Power relations and their manifestations as normative categories therefore dictate the very 'terms through which subjects are recognized' (Butler, 2009, p. 3). Our compulsion to be recognized can be productive in many cases and, for example, leads to the formation of solidarity groups. Butler (1993) describes the 'names project' emerging in the context of AIDS activism; here a community was formed around a sense of collective pain. Also in her book *Bodies that Matter* (1993), she describes how the film *Paris is Burning* evokes forms of alternative kin-ship that can emerge when bodies are bound together in a shared acknowledgement of the subjectivity of the other.

But identification can also cause hurt – sometimes we desire norms that ultim-ately are painful (think of a person subscribing to a particular set of gender norms around being 'female', for example, in order to be recognized as a 'proper woman', and then experiencing these norms as both restrictive and discriminatory) – there is a darker side to subjection. We cannot opt out unfortunately because '… our lives, our very persistence, depend upon such norms, or, at least, on the possibility that we will be able to negotiate within them' (Butler, 2004, p. 32). 'Called by an injuri-ous name, I come into social being … I am led to embrace the terms that injure me because they constitute me socially' (Butler, 1997b, p. 104), a situation that leads

Harding, for example, to describe subjectivity as an ongoing 'tug of war' of desires for subjection and the acknowledged pain it can bring. In many cases, because we cannot do otherwise, it is better to 'exist in subordination' than not to exist at all (Butler, 1997b, p. 7). Affective forces bind the subject to discourse (Braunmühl, 2012; Stavrakakis, 2008).

Butler's ek-static self

These ideas on identification and subjection do not suggest the presence of an 'inner self' in Butler's account, as this is anathema to post-structural thinking. Rather, her psyche is a Lacanian one, structured by the social – the symbolic order, or the world of language. On this view, the idea of an 'inner' psyche is problematized as an illusion informed by a wider social and political context that emphasizes and valorizes the individual (Butler, 1997b, p. 19). Reading Foucault's ideas on discursive power via Lacan, Butler is inspired by the latter's refusal of the persistent 'ontological dualism' whereby the 'inner' psyche and 'outer' world are seen as separate. The subject is constituted through language – through discourse – and thus the psyche and the political are mutually constitutive (see, for example, Lacan, 2006). This implies an 'ek-static' view on what the 'self' is – it is radically outside; 'the terms that make up one's own gender are, from the start, outside oneself, beyond oneself in a sociality that has no single author' (Butler, 2004, p. 1). This turns our commonly accepted view of what it is to be a self, to have an inner life that is somehow our own, on its head. We are radically external, always other to ourselves (Butler, 2004, p. 148; 1997b). This perspective goes beyond other theories of the mutual recognition of self and other,[1] even those proposing that these entities are necessarily mutually constitutive.[2] Butler's approach moves us towards a more radically 'external' concept of the subject, which is different because it eschews the idea of false harmony between the self and the other upon which it depends for existence, instead seeing the condition of 'being in relation' as imbued with tension, 'struggle around abjection and continual iteration' (2004, p. 19; Kenny & Fotaki, 2015). The radically external self-other is at once complex, ambiguous and in a relation that is always in danger of rupturing, for reasons described further on. Moreover, in contrast to other theories of recognition, Butler places power at centre stage.[3] Even though we are constituted as subjects through the presence of wider contextual forces, this does not mean that we as subjects, or the norms to which we find ourselves subjectified, are static or determined, and Butler's concept of performativity illuminates this.

Agency, structure, performativity

In *Gender Trouble*, performativity is developed to problematize the idea that the norms influencing categories of identity to which people find themselves subscribing, even unwillingly, are somehow determined. Performativity shows us that norms are not static but contingent. In search of a valued sense of stability, wholeness and 'coherence' that is always eluding us, we look to powerful norms and discourses in social life, seeking recognition from these. This is not straightforward, however. While many critiques of post-structural thought point out that it offers little room for what they call 'agency', Butler is at pains to show that the reproduction of discourse, by the actions of the subject, is by no means determined. Neither does this imply that the subject is somehow agentic and able to choose her attachments at will. Again, Butler invokes the psyche to complexify this traditional debate around the agency-structure dualism, problematizing both sides as she does so. For her the psyche develops through years of layered identifications and losses, desires that have been variably met or denied, and this unique 'congealment' of attachments affords an unknowingness to any process of subjection (Butler, 1997b, p. 169). In addition, the subject is never self-identical at two consecutive moments in time, but rather exists in an ongoing condition of transformation (Butler, 2004); Derrida's concept of *différance* is drawn upon to describe the subtle time lag between one iteration of a given signifier and the next (Butler, 1990, p. 179). The self that is constituted through signification is thus always 'at a temporal remove from its former appearance' (Butler, 2004, p. 148). These insights represent vital contributions to an organizational scholarship that can become mired in 'either–or' debates around agency and structure that, at best, sees them as mutually constitutive, but even so struggles to theorize the nature of this constitution and what it means both for subjects and relations of power (Kenny, 2012).

Performativity begins with the idea that there is no 'fixed' essence to any phenomena within the social – there is always, as Lacan notes, a lack at the heart of any signification. The ideal subject that is invoked by a particular set of discourses therefore does not exist, but rather is upheld by fantasy. For example, the ideal of 'woman' implied by discourses around gender is an illusion. Instead, each time the label is 'taken up' or appropriated by a subject, it shifts and alters slightly because of accompanying intersections with various other norms around, for example, race and class, but also because of the different psychic landscapes of those involved in the enactment of subject positions, and the temporal subversion inherent to these (Butler, 1990). The impact of this idea has been profound for scholars and people outside of universities alike, because it defuses the power of normative ideals (Borgerson, 2005). It says to people who feel trapped into toxic attachments with labels, just so that they can retain a sense of validity as humans, that these are not determined, and nor does the ideal evoked by the discourse even exist. Attempts to identify with such an ideal are therefore futile. The process of subjection, of 'becoming' a subject in the terms offered by a particular norm, is 'uneasy', unpredictable and overdetermined (Butler, 1997b, p. 30).

Importantly this means that norms can be subverted because of their very unpredictability – and identities can be taken in radical new directions. In a well-known example, Butler uses a drag queen to show how such performances symbolize the 'troubling' of gender. A drag show is a setting that amplifies the realization, on the part of the observer, that there is clearly no substance to the idea of an 'ideal woman' because of the various ways in which this ideal is performed and perceived. This has been one of the more popular of Butler's ideas for organization scholars to date, with the performativity of gender informing studies of how TV comedy shows can disrupt and parody idealized gender positions in the workplace (Tyler & Cohen, 2008), or relations of power and domination in transnational trade organizations under contemporary capitalism (Kenny, 2009). Within organization studies these ideas have been used to show how employees negotiate organizational norms, finding ways of 'doing' new subject positions even as they are injured or 'undone' by expectations of how they should be and act (Thanem &

Wallenberg, 2014; Linstead & Pullen, 2006). Tyler's (2012) account of 'dirty work' in sex shops is an exemplar of these dynamics at play in the context of an organization; she describes how workers absorb the experience of stigma and devalued status because the industry is seen as morally tainted. At the same time they find ways to survive this subjective positioning as 'sex shop workers', including through subverting accepted norms around what this kind of work might look like. Others have described these dynamics in the context of older workers (Riach, Rumens & Tyler, 2014), employees (Harding, 2007), managers (Harding, 2003; Roberts, 2005) and workers in non-profit organizations (Kenny, 2010).

Subjection and exclusion

Subjection causes hurt when we create boundaries around categories of identification – dictating who is 'in' and who is 'out' of what is considered to be normal. This can cause pain to those left outside. Examples from Butler's work include people who do not subscribe to either side of a gender binary but experience themselves as occupying a more complex, fluid gender position. Such individuals can find themselves excluded and punished in certain social settings and also betrayed by an unwilled and yet felt desire to be seen as a normal, 'valid' subject. This can be catastrophic, with people cast as 'impossible beings', outside of the norm and therefore unrecognizable (Butler, 1990; 2004, p. 31). Such exclusions can then be turned in upon the self, in a painful form of self-beratement. Butler valuably works with ideas from Mary Douglas (see also chapter on Douglas in this volume) and Julia Kristeva to develop her account of this darker side to the psychic life of power (1990, p. 168), drawing on the Freudian notion of melancholia to illustrate how this exclusion operates (1997b, p. 139). The point is that these processes of abjection are part of how a sense of subjectivity is constructed: boundaries rely upon that which is outside them in order to come into being and to persist. Repudiated, excluded others are therefore the condition of possibility for the subject herself to exist; they 'form the constitutive outside to the domain of the subject' (Butler, 1993, p. 3). She describes how:

> If construction produces the 'domain of intelligible bodies', must it not also produce as well a domain of unthinkable, abject, unliveable bodies? This latter domain is not the opposite of the former, for oppositions are, after all, part of intelligibility; the latter is the excluded and illegible domain that haunts the former domain as the spectre of its own impossibility, the very limit to intelligibility, its constitutive outside.
>
> (1993, p. ix)

Again, the idea of the autonomy and sovereignty of the 'self' is problematized – it is constituted through and emerges because of such exclusion. The other that has become abject is therefore part of the self (1997a, p. 50); this can yield a strange preoccupation or fascination with the excluded other who must paradoxically be kept close. For Butler, however, this ambivalence that surrounds the ways in which selves are constructed means that we must acknowledge and temper the harm that our own self-constructions might do to others, as she elaborates in *Giving an Account of Oneself*.

On a practical level, this framing is useful for the analysis of contemporary racism and exclusions of vulnerable groups in her recent work. It has also informed her thinking on public acts of speaking; for example, in *Excitable Speech*, these ideas are extended to why some kinds of speech are acceptable and others not. For her the perceived legitimacy of a statement is tied up in the subject position of the person doing the uttering. Certain kinds of speech fall within acceptable norms, with those issuing them considered viable subjects. Others speak outside of what is seen as normal and they can be excluded (Butler, 1997a, p. 133). Her work is aimed at problematizing understandings of hate speech, querying the ways in which gay and lesbian soldiers in the US army were censored in how and when they might articulate their sexuality: speech was regulated through regulating the subject positions held by the speakers. How speech is received depends on how the speaker is framed. In organization studies, scholars have drawn on these ideas to understand legitimate leadership rhetoric (Harding et al., 2011), and illegitimate statements by whistleblowers (Kenny, 2018). In an explication of how this plays out in the context of organization theory and scholarship, Fotaki and Harding (2018) engage with Butler alongside other gender theorists to explain how women occupy a place of exclusion, being subordinated and considered inferior as a result; their analysis also offers suggestions for how this might be overturned.

Organization, violence and precarity

Constructing these kinds of boundaries can be a precursor to violence, as Butler discusses in the compelling account of the US 'war on terror', and the ways in which certain subjects are represented in the media, in *Frames of War* (2010). Her ideas shed light on how the dynamics of recognition within a certain society, in this case the United States, mean that in order for this polity to define itself (as Western, enlightened, civilized and under threat), it must reject and expel a repugnant other (as Middle-Eastern, Muslim, backward, aggressive). Certain discursive 'frames' circulate in which these notions are reinforced, through photographs, stories and even the construction of space, including Abu Ghraib and Guantánamo Bay. These frames appeal to people on an affective level, inciting fear in some, a sense of national pride in others, and ultimately drawing on a felt, emotive force on the part of the person experiencing them. This affective force effectively ensures the construction and continued maintenance of the frame.

Butler's point here is that normative violence – the construction of certain persons as 'abject', other and therefore deserving of exclusion – can be a precursor to actual physical, structural and institutional violence. Framing can rob certain kinds of human of any subjectivity at all, which is a different condition to oppression. As she explains elsewhere: 'to be oppressed means that you already exist as a subject of some kind ... but to be unreal is something else again. To be oppressed you must first become intelligible' (2004, p. 30). It is easy to exert and to defend acts of violence against a population of 'unreal' people – who have never been subjects – because this does not evoke the kind of empathy or rage that violence against sympathetic groups of people would bring. Ultimately 'there have been no lives, and no losses', where violence of this nature takes place, because, from the perspective of the viewer, there is 'no common physical condition, no vulnerability that serves as the basis for an apprehension of our commonality' (Butler, 2004, p. 25). Framing can militate against the formation of any empathetic fellow feeling, or impulse to protect the other against the vulnerability that is the common condition of humanity. It is, she argues in *Precarious Life*, this shared vulnerability that might provide the basis for a sense of solidarity between states and societies that are ostensibly very different, albeit that opportunities to foster this seem to be lessening.

In organization theory, there is a growing albeit very limited scholarship on the role played by organizations in the enactment of violence, and Butler's work on normative violence stands to make a valued contribution to this essential project (Kenny, 2018; Varman & Al-Amoudi, 2016). Indeed, while it has not been a primary focus of her work, organization has increasingly featured in her later writings in which she reflects upon the precarity of working life under contemporary conditions of capitalism, and its subtle structural violences. In conversation with Athena Athanasiou (2013, p. 148), she describes the 'violent rhythms of being instrumentalised as disposable labor' as new forms of work bring new forms of vulnerability and suffering: 'Never knowing the future, being subjected to arbitrary hirings and firings, having one's labor intensively utilized and exploited' all lead to a condition of 'radical helplessness' for many in work today. In addition to this focus on precarious labour, she is also interested in how social movement organizations emerge and are sustained, and specifically how bodies – physical and material presences that can effect change by simply 'showing up' – continue to represent essential sites of protest but also solidarity, even in a world where communication and social commentary increasingly move into the virtual.

Conclusion

Overall, affective recognition offers a rich and evocative theory for scholars wishing to explore processes of identification and subjection, including those relating to organizations. It encompasses the pleasure and warmth of identification and belonging – essential aspects of being human – but also the potential for pain and indeed violence both to ourselves and to others around us, that are inherent to these dynamics. Affective recognition is, like life itself, ultimately ambivalent; the norms that hold such power over our lives are neither determined nor monolithic but always open to being subverted. The 'game' goes on.

End-of-chapter exercises

1. Butler is widely recognized for putting theory into practice. Think about the social theories that most appeal to you, including those learned in this book. How might you practise these in everyday life?
2. Think about one of the 'identity categories' that you occupy. Is it, as Butler suggests, performative in how it operates?
3. Are the social norms that inform this category changing, and if so, how?
4. What kinds of attachments do you experience in relation to this category: are they affective and if so, do you experience this as positive, negative or otherwise?
5. For Butler and other gender theorists, the body is central to effective organizing, including organizing of social protest. Can you think of ways in which bodies are important to other kinds of organizing we encounter in everyday life?

Glossary

Affective recognition   In search of a valued sense of stability, wholeness and 'coherence' that is always eluding us, we look to powerful norms and discourses in social life, seeking recognition from the subject positions on offer from these, albeit often unconsciously. We thus subject ourselves to such norms. This recognition is experienced affectively, through psychic attachments to the process.

Exclusions   Exclusion can emerge when, in the process of subject construction, boundaries are created around categories of subject, determining who is included and who is left out. This can cause hurt and pain to those outside the limits of what is seen to be a normal, 'valid' subject, an experience in which violence directed at the self by others can turn inward. Exclusions are part of the way in which a sense of subjectivity is constructed: boundaries rely upon that which is outside them in order for categories of subject to come into being and to persist. Repudiated, excluded others are therefore the condition of possibility for the subject herself to exist.

Performativity   Performativity explains how there is no 'fixed' essence to any category of identity. The norms that influence these categories are not static but contingent, and open to change. These norms are performed over time and therefore are always being produced, and altered, by those who adopt them. Norms of gender, for example, while having significant influence over us, are not determined.

Notes

1 See critiques of Charles Taylor and Axel Honneth's work, for example in McQueen (2015); McNay (2008).
2 See, for example, Levinas (1969); Merleau-Ponty (2002)
3 In addition to Foucault and Butler described here, see also Haraway (1991); Lloyd (2005); McNay (2008) on this point.

References

Borgerson, J. (2005). Judith Butler: On organizing subjectivities. *Sociological Review*, *53*(1), 63–79.

Braunmühl, C. (2012). Theorizing emotions with Judith Butler: Within and beyond the courtroom. *Rethinking History*, *16*, 221–240.

Brewis, J., Hampton, M. P., & Linstead, S. (1997). Unpacking Priscilla: Subjectivity and identity in the organization of gendered appearance. *Human Relations*, *50*, 1275–1304.

Butler, J. (1990). *Gender trouble: Feminism and the subversion of identity*. London: Routledge.

Butler, J. (1993). *Bodies that matter: On the discursive limits of 'sex'*. London: Routledge.

Butler, J. (1997a). *Excitable speech*. New York: Routledge.

Butler, J. (1997b). *The psychic life of power: Theories in subjection*. London: Routledge.

Butler, J. (2004). *Undoing gender*. New York: Routledge.

Butler, J. (2009). *Frames of war*. New York: Verso.

Butler, J., & Athanasiou, A. (2013). *Dispossession: The performative in the political*. Cambridge: Polity Press.

Ford, J. (2010). Studying leadership critically: A psychosocial lens on leadership identities. *Leadership*, *6*(1), 1–19.

Ford, J., & Harding, N. (2004). We went looking for an organisation but could find only the metaphysics of its presence. *Sociology*, *38*(4), 815–830.

Fotaki, M. (2013). No woman is like a man (in academia): The masculine symbolic order and the unwanted female body. *Organization Studies, 34*(9), 1251–1275.

Fotaki, M. (2014). Can consumer choice replace trust in the National Health Service in England? Towards developing an affective psychosocial conception of trust in health care. *Sociology of Health & Illness, 36*(8), 1276–1294.

Fotaki, M., & Harding, N. (2013). Lacan and sexual difference in organization and management theory: Towards a hysterical academy? *Organization, 20*(2), 153–172.

Fotaki, M., & Harding, N. (2018). *Gender and the organization: Women at work in the 21st century*. London: Routledge.

Fotaki, M., Metcalfe, B., & Harding, N. (2014). Writing materiality into organisation theory. *Human Relations, 67*(10), 1239–1263.

Foucault, M. (1990). *The history of sexuality, Volume I, an introduction*, R. Hurley (trans.). London: Penguin.

Foucault, M. (1991). Polemics politics and problematizations. In P. Rabinow (ed.) *The Foucault reader* (pp. 381–390). London: Penguin.

Hall, S. (2000). Who needs 'identity'? In P. du Gay, J. Evans, & P. Redman (eds.) *Identity: a reader* (pp. 15–31). London: Sage/The Open University.

Hancock, P., & Tyler, M. (2007). Un/doing gender and the aesthetics of organizational performance. *Gender, Work and Organization, 14*(6), 512–533.

Haraway, D. (1991). *Simians, cyborgs, and women: The reinvention of nature*. London: Free Association Books.

Harding, N. (2003). *The social construction of management: Texts and identities*. London: Routledge.

Harding, N. (2007). On Lacan and the 'becoming-ness' of organizations/selves. *Organization Studies, 28*(11), 1761–1773.

Harding, N. (2013). *On being at work: The social construction of the employee*. New York: Routledge.

Harding, N., Lee, H., Ford, J., & Learmonth, M. (2011). Leadership and charisma: A desire that cannot speak its name? *Human Relations, 64*(7), 927–950.

Hodgson, D. (2005). Putting on a Professional performance: Performativity, subversion and project management. *Organization, 12*(1), 51–68.

Kenny, K. (2009). The performative surprise: Parody, documentary and critique. *Culture and Organization, 15*(2), 221–235.

Kenny, K. (2010). Beyond ourselves: Passion and the dark side of identification in an ethical organization. *Human Relations, 63*(6), 857–873.

Kenny, K. (2012). Someone big and important: Identification and affect in an international development organization. *Organization Studies, 33*(9), 1175–1193.

Kenny, K. (2018). Censored: Whistleblowers and impossible speech. *Human Relations, 71*(8), 1025–1048.

Kenny, K., & Euchler, G. (2012). 'Some good clean fun': Humour, control and subversion in an advertising agency. *Gender, Work and Organisation, 19*(3), 306–323.

Kenny, K., & Fotaki, M. (2015). From gendered organizations to compassionate borderspaces: Reading corporeal ethics with Bracha Ettinger. *Organization 22*(2), 183–199.

Kenny, K., Whittle, W., & Willmott, H. (2011). *Understanding identity and organization*. London: Sage.

Lacan, J. (2006). Seminar on 'The purloined letter'. In B. Fink, H. Fink, & R. Grigg (eds) *Ecrits: The first complete edition in English* (pp. 6–48). New York: Norton.

Levinas, E. (1969). *Totality and infinity: An essay on exteriority*. Pittsburgh, PA: Duquesne University Press.

Linstead, S., & Pullen, A. (2006). Gender as multiplicity: Desire, displacement, difference and dispersion. *Human Relations, 59*(9), 1287–1310.

Lloyd, M. (2005). *Beyond Identity Politics: Feminism, Power and Politics*. London: Sage.

Lloyd, M. (2007). *Judith Butler: From norms to politics.* Cambridge: Polity.

McNay, L. (2008). *Against recognition.* Cambridge: Polity.

McQueen, P. (2015). *Subjectivity, gender and the struggle for recognition.* London: Palgrave Macmillan.

Merleau-Ponty, M. (2002). *Phenomenology of perception*, C. Smith (trans.). Oxford: Routledge.

Parker, M. (2001). Fucking management: Queer theory and reflexivity. *Ephemera, 1*(1), 36–53.

Parker, M. (2002). Queering management and organization. *Gender, Work & Organisation, 9* (2), 146–166.

Pullen, A., & Knights, D. (2007). Editorial: Organizing and disorganizing performance. *Gender, Work and Organization, 14*(6), 506–511.

Pullen, A., Thanem, T., Tyler, M., & Wallenberg, L. (2016). Sexual politics, organizational practices: Interrogating queer theory, work and organization. *Gender, Work and Organization, 23*(1), 1–6.

Riach, K., Rumens, N., & Tyler, M. (2014). Un/doing chrononormativity: Negotiating ageing, gender and sexuality in organizational life. *Organization Studies, 35*(11), 1677–1698.

Riach, K., Rumens, N., & Tyler, M. (2016). Towards a Butlerian methodology: Undoing organizational performativity through anti-narrative research. *Human Relations, 69*(11), 2069–2089.

Roberts, J. (2005). The power of the 'imaginary' in disciplinary processes. *Organization, 12* (5), 619–642.

Stavrakakis, Y. (2008). Subjectivity and the organized other: Between symbolic authority and fantasmatic enjoyment. *Organization Studies, 29*(7), 1037–1059.

Thanem, T., & Wallenberg, L. (2014). Just doing gender? Transvestism and the power of underdoing gender in everyday life and work. *Organization, 23*(2), 250–271.

Tyler, M. (2012). Glamour girls, macho men and everything in between. In R. Simpson, N. Slutskaya, P. Lewis, & H. Höpfl (eds) *Dirty work* (pp. 65–90). Basingstoke: Palgrave.

Tyler, M., & Cohen, L. (2008). Management in/as comic relief: Queer theory and gender performativity in 'The Office'. *Gender, Work and Organization, 15*(2), 113–132.

Varman, R., & Al-Amoudi, I. (2016). Accumulation through derealization: How corporate violence remains unchecked. *Human Relations, 69*(10), 1909–1935.

Weedon, C. (1997). *Feminist practice and poststructuralist theory*, 2nd edn. Oxford: Blackwell.

14 Manuel Castells and informationalism[1]

Cátia Miriam Costa, Tiago Lima Quintanilha and Sandro Mendonça

> I turned my attention, from my new vantage point in Berkeley, to a major structural transformation in the making: the emergence of a new social structure, identified by some as postindustrial, that I gradually conceptualized as a global network society.
>
> (Castells, 2016, p. 5)

Chapter objectives

This chapter refers to the work of the Paris-trained, US-tenured, world-travelled Catalan sociologist Manuel Castells and explore his interests and concerns about a social world empowered by/dependent on information and communication technologies to reveal how his concepts and insights can be of help in understanding and steering organizations and institutions.

The chapter discusses:

- The development of Manuel Castells' thought, its influences and framings contexts
- How a society increasingly intensive in information and communication technologies was deemed suitable for autonomous theorizing work
- How the logic of networks became globally pervasive and the defining logic of our historical time
- Cities and technopoles were early informational phenomena in which the rise of the network society could be perceived
- How the dynamics of domination and rebellion in an internet-based age are co-evolutionary forces of a networked nature and global reach

Introduction

Manuel Castells evolved into one of the leading social theorists charting the defining character of our times and spaces. It is difficult to think of a sociologist who has engaged as early and as thoroughly with the global transformation associated with the information and communication technologies (ICTs) as did Castells. Indeed, to discuss Castells' work makes one immediately engage with his hallmark concept, the 'network society', which in 1996 was introduced in the first volume of a now-famous trilogy (afterwards republished and re-edited) on the economic, societal and cultural aspects of *The Information Age*. But this idea is just a node in an expanding cluster of other issues that have characterized his work, such as urban-regional development, informational economy, social movements and mass self-communication.

The writings of Manuel Castells display a number of features that make them an enduring source for inspiration and guidance. They came of age during a period of intense and intriguing change. They combine a desire to describe technology seriously as a point of departure with an aspiration to make insights capable of understanding the ultimate guideposts of organized life in society. They synthesize myriad empirical observations over several decades (in the form of statistics, interviews, case studies, etc.) and a number of long-lasting research programmes (from sociology, economics, communication studies, development studies, etc.). They reflect a mosaic of contemporary experiences while integrating an open and adaptive mode of enquiry. That, is Castells' work is itself multidimensional and multimodal: it is the end product of many sources; it is an analysis of many kinds; it is the initial material from which many other intellectual outcomes are to be made.

Castells in space and time

Manuel Castells was born in 1942 and grew up in and around Catalonia under the regime of Franco. He took part in demonstrations and polemicized in writing against the dictatorship, was censored and had to interrupt his studies in law and economics at the Universitat de Barcelona, becoming an exile at the age of 20. He went on to enrol at the Université de Paris, where he would obtain a doctorate in sociology. He was teaching when the events of 1968 occurred. His activism got him expelled from France, but not for long thanks to the intervention of Alain Touraine, his thesis supervisor (Hoogvelt, Kenny & Germain, 1999; Scott, 2007).

In his university career Castells had an early stint in North America when he spent the academic year of 1969–1970 at the University of Montreal, Canada. He would move to the United States later in the decade, in 1979, where he was made Professor of City and Regional Planning at the University of California, Berkeley. In 2003 he took up a position at the University of Southern California, with a double appointment in the School of Communication and the School of International Relations. His North American base made him able to accommodate a number of visiting fellowships and extended lectureships, including, among others, Japan, Hong Kong, Taiwan, Singapore, Russia, South Africa, Bolivia and Mexico. He also become a member of various Academy of Sciences (Britain, Spain, Mexico and the United States) and won a number of prizes, medals and honorary degrees from academic institutions in many other parts of the world.

Castells has always been active policy-wise and as a public intellectual. The CV available on his personal website (www.manuelcastells.info, supported partially by Fundación Telefónica) lists a number of advisory roles to several governments (Chile, China, Brazil, Ecuador, Finland, Portugal, among others) and consultancy experience at international organizations (the European Commission, OECD, UNESCO, UNDP, USAID, World Bank, among others). He has also maintained a weekly column in the *La Vanguardia* newspaper and is regularly interviewed by the mainstream media (including radio and television). His continued impact as a well-known figure can be grasped by a couple of quick illustrations, as Castells is sometimes evoked as a symbol of the fields he contributed to reshape. He has been dubbed one of 'the high priests of new media studies' and the inventor of 'the idea of the network society' in the *Financial Times* (January 6, 2006). When asked to enlighten a topical social problem, *The Economist* (February 26, 2015) quoted his views regarding how the fluidity of smartphone-based apps is changing the experience of time by teenagers – whereas elders would perceive events in a timeline dictated by proverbial mechanical clocks, teenagers' lives play out in 'timeless time' as activities and exchanges happen in parallel or a criss-crossed way. That is, Castells and his work communicate beyond the borders of scholarly circles and carry their influence onto national and international policy arenas while spilling over into the public sphere via both local and global media.

The intellectual roots of Manuel Castells

In a recent interview, Manuel Castells looks back on his time in the 1960s and 1970s: 'Paris was the most creative intellectual and thinking place in the world, and exerted an enormous influence. The thinkers of that time are still the reference in today's world.' (interview, *La Vanguardia*, February 26, 2018) For Castells, a leading light among these *maîtres à penser* was Alain Touraine. His doctoral supervisor had been one of the first to theorize (from a historicist angle) about the birth of a new society, the *post-industrial society* (1969). In this scenario the major cleavages ceased to be between capital and labour but rather between those in conditions to influence the political-economic decision-making apparatus (the technocrats) and those unable to escape a dependent mode of participation.

Touraine's view was echoed in the Anglo-American world by the follow-up work of Daniel Bell (1973). Bell postulated the rise of a 'scientific knowledge class' and a trend toward the 'intellectualization of technology' at the heart of the economy accompanied by 'renewed communalism in politics' and growing acrimony at the cultural level. Manuel Castells thanks both these sociologists in his own major instalment on *The Rise of the Network Society* and emphasizes that the post-manufacturing shift is accompanied by new types of inequality: both inside advanced economies (a consequence of the change in occupational structures) and between countries (given the uneven capacity of their economies to replace goods production with higher-margin information-processing activities and informational institutions) (see Castells, 2010, pp. 14, 232).

In his own reflections regarding the lineages of his thinking, in addition to Touraine, whom he credits as 'original mentor and intellectual father', Castells (2016, pp. 15–16) recognizes some distinct sources of intellectual debt. His structural Marxian heritage came from his friend and colleague Nicos Poulantzas, becoming a latent factor in his work despite being methodologically inapplicable for much of it. Thanks to his links to Latin America, and his exposure to thinkers such as Fernando Henrique Cardoso,[2] Castells confesses to having learned to appreciate the unbalanced and unequal nature of globalization, especially through mechanisms such as technology dependency and the political history of paths of development. Finally, Anthony Giddens provided crucial keys in terms of formulating social theory. Giddens' answer to the structure-agency problem (a type of chicken-and-egg riddle in social theory) has influenced Castells' own approach to networking social practices and communication power.

Learning from the streets and the territory

It seems fair, however, to list two other sources of inspiration: the *crowd* and the *ground*.

First, Manuel Castells refers often to a specific year, 1968, as providing 'particularly formative experience' (Hoogvelt, Kenny & Germain, 1999, p. 382). For Castells, in spite of all the radical left-wing jargon, the crowd on the streets were more engaged in anarchical practices than in a Marxist-led insurrection. These were *proactive* (rather than *reactive*) social movements animated by different values than those derived from industrial society: they resonated with access to learning, environmental issues and women's liberation, thus very different from proletarian calls to arms. With the benefit of hindsight, for Castells, these movements were in fact precursors of the nascent networked society and they were all the rage (in terms of entrepreneurialism as well as counterculture) when he came to California ten years later. Castells participated throughout in his own way. He has been consciously and critically embedded in society; less interested in producing pure social theory than in advancing genuine empirical research while putting urges for social reform into perspective.

Second, Castells seeks to provide a bridge between old-style *grand* theorizing and *grounded* theorizing. This deliberate methodological choice meant that he would always start from a few theoretical constructs only to use them in the midst of live empirical materials as *un*-finished *re*-search tools that could be modified as long as they would be useful to explore an evolving, diverse and multidimensional reality (Castells, 2016, p. 3). True theory is actually repositioned as open theorizing. That is to say, analytical tools only earn their epistemological legitimacy while asserting their power of discovery on the social terrain. The critique of '*technological* determinism' and the critique of '*theoretical* determinism' go hand in hand in Castells. For instance, an awareness of both business models and social movements is fundamental to make sense of the network society as a whole. Thus, 'interthematicity' is the ability to orchestrate different specialist themes (such as technology and organization), each one with its own specialist knowledge (such as engineering and philosophy), to explain socio-technical complexity (Rantanen, 2005, p. 139).

By the time Castells migrated to Berkeley he was committed to being as pragmatic about interpretation as he was hands-on about evidence. Substantive detail matters, while theory is disposable (Scott, 2007). As he put it in an interview:

> I was no longer interested in correct answers but in relevant questions. I became more political when I left Marxism. I left the Parisian salons with wonderful categories that had nothing to do with reality and started relying on my own observations.
>
> (Rantanen, 2005, p. 137)

From the city to the globe

For a sociologist such as Manuel Castells, interested in the generation of new social forms and norms, the city presented itself as a lively laboratory, a locus of experimentation. Creative urban processes, such as those driven by social movements, overturn given models of interaction and constitute innovative pattern-breakers of the established order. Social movements are, indeed, new relationships in the making. And what happens in cities does *not* stay in cities: it diffuses fast and wide.

Initially, Castells focused on urban sociology. His work helped to bring the Marxist approach closer to the phenomenon of urbanization (see Castells, 1977; 1978). Civic activism played a key role in bringing about 'urban spaces' (as his commentator, Howard [2011, p. 12], emphasizes). Local and trans-local resources, like transportation systems, housing and libraries, were the product of social struggle. These special sites, in turn, shaped social processes since they brought together people from a variety of backgrounds and became the basis for new shared experiences in large modern agglomerations. The development of large cities was the outcome of the interplay between the production and the collective consumption of public goods, activities that happen to be mediated by the state and local governments. But cities, the prime geographical points of accumulation of capitalism vis-à-vis the rural world, were also a place of integration of emigrants and of patterning new shared cultures.

The urban context is eventful by definition and perpetually ambiguous in reality. It did not conform easily to neat and static regional divisions of labour. Moreover, change was not simply originating from a class struggle that could be resolved once the housing question was settled. There was conflict and protest. There was also culture and creation. Cities became the wellspring of social change, not just the non-countryside. Moreover, fast-changing cities were not simple targets for social engineering. In this way, the city changed from within and carried the whole society with it. The notion of class failed to account for this wellspring of novelty. The dynamic and many-splintered nature of cities only became more visible with the student revolts in Paris in the late 1960s or the gay liberation campaign in San Francisco Bay in the late 1970s (Castells, 1983). The same goes for the identity differences that erupted in many places in 1980s and 1990s, such as those involved in nationalities and languages. Place mattered; place was people on the move.

Framework, know thyself

The first time Castells seems to have adopted the term 'informational' was as a qualifier for the city. In Castells' book *The Informational City* (1989) the major themes of technology and organization are fleshed out and clearly at play. Here, Castells sets out to understand the process of transformation and the global reach of those post-industrial cities in which science and technology coalesced with new behaviours and norms ('social innovations'). Moreover, as demonstrated by the experiences of city-states (such as Hong Kong and Singapore) and urban regions (like Silicon Valley), developmental policy was possible. Not only that: restructuring places could re-structure the whole world economy. All this is discussed in a plethora of institutional variations: there is no cultural determinism at play either.

The book's opening reverberates with the later Castells (1989, p. 1): 'A technological revolution of historical proportions is transforming the fundamental dimensions of human life: time and space'. It went on to state that social organization was what made the difference between the potential and the actuality of technologies, that firms were freed in their operation by new information systems, that families could be open to interactive communication flows and still be quietly at home. It referred to an 'information age' that came out as a non-linear response to the twin events of structural crises and the electronic innovations of the previous decade. The restructuring of socio-technical organization could now be recognized as the 'informational mode of development'. Importantly, given the date of writing, the new historical interaction between social changes and technological changes was represented as taking place within (not replacing) the capitalist system.

Technologies such as micro-electronics, computer-aided design and optical fibres enabled the augmentation of capacity to generate, process, exchange and store information. ICTs had a dramatic impact on industry (flexible manufacturing) and services (office automation). Moreover, by facilitating the reprogramming of information embodied in materials (ceramics, alloys) and living organisms (genetic engineering), these innovations paved the way for new general pattern of changes in production and in management. These changes converged into a new (techno-economic) 'paradigm' (Castells, 1989, pp. 12–13).

As one can read in the book's notes, this representation was heavily influenced by a number of economic theorists and historians. Indeed, mention is made of Schumpeter's 'creative destruction', whereas the broad notion of *paradigm* is harvested from neo-Schumpeterian thought (namely Peréz, 1983, but also from the closely related, but institutionalist in bent, French 'régulation' school, e.g. Boyer & Coriat, 1986). The influence of history-friendly, comparison-sensitive, organization-inspired American economists is also notable (Nathan Rosenberg and David Mowery being in the bibliography). Years later, this economic undercurrent would become even more explicit: in Castells' *The Rise of the Network Society*, the celebrated first volume of his *Information Age*, Christopher Freeman[3] and Richard Nelson even came to figure directly in the acknowledgements.

In line with these authors' own macro perspective, Castells' research on the 'informational city' as an important new phenomenon would soon be scaled up to the level of the entire economy:

> Thus, with the revolution in information technology as the material basis of the emerging system, the various features of structural economic transformation that we have identified relate closely to each other. In fact, they join together to form a new type of economy that I, along with a growing number of economists and sociologists propose to call the *'informational economy'* because, at its core, the fundamental source of wealth generation lies in an ability to create new knowledge and apply it to every realm of human activity by means of enhanced technological and organizational procedures of information processing. The informational economy tends to be, in its essence, a global economy; and its structure and logic define, within the emerging world order, a new international division of labor.
>
> (Castells, 1993, p. 20, emphasis added)

As was already abundantly clear, countries and territories were already positioning themselves on a global chessboard in which science and intangibles were the key strategic bets. Locked into interregional competition in a world in which the borders of the nation-state were increasingly fluid, some degree of intra-regional cooperation complemented by flexible planning was involved. The dynamic mixed economy outlook steered urban areas vying for prosperity in an uncertain world on the back of the innovation ticket. The most interesting of these emerging 'spaces of flows' (such as 'technopoles', 'science parks', etc.) were, thus, instances of collective agency. They were observed to contain combinations of public and private sectors involved in partnership schemes, the geometry of which varyied in time and space, often in association with anchoring institutions (like universities) and other actors linked to trans-border knowledge networks (such as flagship firms in global value chains). In these technology-seeking complexes the basic resources of the 'informational economy' of the 21st century endogenously came into existence (Castells & Hall, 1994; see also Saxenian, 1994; Bresnahan & Gambardella, 2004).

The fully fledged 'network society' concept

It is easy to realize that the very rise of the *network society*, both the idea and the phenomenon, is a network story.

Castells' framework is the product of a networked intellectual (see Howard, 2011, p. 16). His account was gradually built from first-hand inputs (including extensive travelling and extended stays in and out from his base in the Bay Area, California), from big ideas in the secondary literature (from Freud to Foucault), and from several long-standing descriptive-analytic traditions (from political economy to evolutionary economics) (see Castells, 2010, p. 25). Books and theories, as 'intellectual products are, to a large extent, collective enterprises synthesized in the solitude of authoring' (Castells, 1989, p. vii).

The emergence of computer-powered and internet-based networks was itself also a triumph of geographically based social networking. Both in terms of hardware and software, the success of the microelectronics technological wave rested in the hands of US West Coast youngsters (like Bill Gates and Steve Jobs) who were famously described as making millions, battling global competition, while still unable to get a date (Stephens, 1996). Theirs was a densely connected world, in which entrepreneurs and engineers accepted that they could learn from others and then trial their own technological solutions on economically valuable problems, this being a process that von Hippel (1988) described as 'informal know-how trading' and 'knowledge-bartering'. Groups of 'hackers, geniuses and geeks' were instrumental in advancing the ICTs that transformed, and keep transforming, the world economy. These were the:

> Social and cultural forces that provide the atmosphere for innovation. For the birth of the digital age, this included a research ecosystem that was nurtured by government spending and managed by a military-industrial-academic collaboration. Intersecting with that was a loose alliance of community organizers, communal-mined hippies, do-it-yourself hobbyists, and homebrew hackers, most of whom were suspicious of centralized authority.
>
> (Isaacson, 2014, p. 2)

The momentous changes unleashed by the widespread deployment of the new technologies and correlated governance models has been characterized as the *Third Industrial Revolution* (Freeman & Louçã, 2001), a process leading to the unfolding of the *ICT paradigm* (Freeman, 2007). It is the kind of society which has generated and co-evolved with this new techno-economic template that has been best captured by Manuel Castells. It is this achievement that makes him notable among other social theorists.

The basic unit of economic organization is no longer the 19th-century *entrepreneur* (the atomistic agent of the First Industrial Revolution) nor the *corporation* (the bureaucratic agent of the Second Industrial Revolution), but the *network* (a distributed type of agent of change itself composed of a variety of agents). This network model of organization is the engine of the new economic order and is itself held together by a cultural code

> Informing and enforcing economic decisions at every moment in the life of the network ... The 'spirit of informationalism' is the culture of 'creative destruction' accelerated to the speed of the opto-electronic circuits that process its signals. Schumpeter meets Weber in the cyberspace of the network enterprise.
>
> (Castells, 2010, p. 382)

Castells prefers the term 'network society' to 'post-industrial society', since it gives a substantial answer to what comes next (an informational social structure in a globalizing economy powered by ICTs) (Castells, 2010, p. 219). It also takes issue with the terms 'information society' and 'knowledge economy' because what is new and specific to our age is not just more information or better knowledge (they have been found to be central and growing in all historically known societies): 'What is new is the microelectronics-based, networking technologies that provide new capabilities to an old form of social organization: networks' (Castells, 2005, p. 4). In a nutshell, Castells (2016, p. 8) came to recognize that 'the new society in the making was, in all dimensions, made up of networks'. This is what the new social structure is all about: social, organization, institutional, technological networks.

Communication, media, and all that power

It is with *The Rise of the Network Society* that Castells' perspectives came to bear on the media system (Howard, 2011, p. 14). Access and capabilities to navigate the net are a prerequisite to participate in the contemporary life, thereby determining exclusion of the self (see Scott, 2007) and the nature of inequality in the Informational Age (Mendonça, Crespo & Simões, 2015). The ability to create and govern networks is most demanding in terms of communication skills. This is why Castells invested so much in discussing media and new media:

> I came to the hypothesis that processes of construction of meaning around the realm of communication were central to the formation of power and counter-power, and that communication was undergoing a major process of transformation in the age of digital technologies and the organizational restructuring of business and government.
>
> (Castells, 2016, p. 8)

Given that the church or the state no longer have a monopoly over information, cultural power is perceived to have moved to communication systems (Howard, 2011, p. 23). However, the media itself has gone through structural transformations: the classical broadcasting set-ups of radio, newspaper and television (one-to-many architectures) have been complemented, supplemented and even partially substituted by 'mass self-communication' forms of expression (Castells, 2009). Technical convergence between information technologies and communication technologies have brought about an ever rising 'common digital bitstream representing all forms of digital media' (Mansell & Steinmueller, 2000, p. 335). Indeed, the technical possibilities for interpersonal communication configurations have been expanding in each successive generation of personal and mobile devices and ever accumulating layers of operative systems, software programs and cloud-based apps (see Cardoso, 2008). The internet is no level playing field; rather, it is a constructed, rugged and shifting terrain. There is, in fact, no escape from mediation (Slevin, 2000), as there is no escape from risk, such as the loss of privacy (Mansell & Steinmueller, 2000).

The internet has in itself interactional qualities: its specific instantiations have specific qualities the management of which is non-trivial (emails, blogs, vlogs, wikis, podcasts, chats, instant messaging, massively multiplayer online gaming, etc.) (Castells, 2010, p. xxviii). What is more, the interplay between online and offline activities compounds the implications of the digital communication channels and environments (Mansell et al., 2007, p. 5). The use of any medium involves asymmetries of power. And communicative acts are 'skilled performances', the efficacy of which crucially depend on creativity in using the medium (Slevin, 2000, pp. 63–80).

The change in the mode of production and reproduction of news is an illustration of the consequences of the *Internet Galaxy* (Castells' apt book title, reusing McLuhan's own catch-phrase *Gutenberg Galaxy*). Here, Manuel Castells (2002) noted the accelerated migration to a many-to-many form of communication and the coming into existence of 'networked individualism'. The intensification of this pattern and the democratization of the instruments of symbolic production led, for instance, to further extensions of Castells' ideas, such as 'networked journalism': the merger between users and producers of news content that creates a seamless continuum of data and distraction (van der Haak, Parks & Castells, 2012).

In this context, Manuel Castells came to propose his own 'network theory of power'. In a network society, according to Castells (2009), there is a shifting balance between the elementary forms of *coercive* (exercising control over others through violence or the threat of violence) and *persuasive* (through induced submission to hegemonic interests and values) types of power. The discursive production of power becomes dominant, which happens through communication. Both those holding power and those trying to mobilize countervailing power play a network game. Network forms of organization either in the media business or in the political business (both realms themselves converging) are becoming the most efficient ways to leverage resources and solve problems of collective action (Howard, 2011, pp. 23–23). As Castells (2016, p. 12) puts it:

> In a world of networks, the capacity for social actors to exercise control over others depends on two basic mechanisms: (a) the ability to constitute network(s) and to program/reprogram the network(s) in terms of the goals assigned to the network, and (b) the ability to connect and ensure the cooperation of different networks by sharing common goals and combining resources while fending off competition from other networks by setting up strategic cooperation. I call holders of the first power position *programmers*; holders of the second power position are *switchers*.

In open democracy settings the social mobilization *through* networks, or *of* networks, creates turbulence (Castells, 2012). The internet cannot be overestimated in terms of elevating the quality and transparency of a genuinely participatory political processes (Sey & Castells, 2004). Meanwhile, platforms such as Facebook and Twitter may produce decisive and irreversible effects by combining virality with an exponentially enhanced power to fragment debate and algorithmically manipulate information (see Castells 2012, p. 229; see also von Humbolt, 2018).

Extensions, concerns, further potential

Over the years Manuel Castells has made efforts to update the application of his views, either as single author or in the company of colleagues. In the 2010 edition of his *Rise of The Network Society*, Castells referred to a number of topical events and structural developments. A few major themes are worth noticing: the Global Financial Crisis that unfolded since 2008 he sees as the result of a global automated sector powered by electronic network infrastructures; work restructuring was also seen as a major force behind income polarization; the arrival of China to informationalism.

The work of Castells is, nonetheless, not without is critics. In a number of passages in many books, Castells (2012, p. 6) contends that 'technology does not determine society: it embodies it. But neither does society determine technological innovation: it uses it.' Many critics, however, have remained unconvinced and still claim that Castells' oeuvre displays too much technology euphoria. Fuchs (2012), for instance, insists that Castells' reasoning is far too simplistic: the internet surely mediates but the intricate set of ongoing struggles and protests have greater bearing on transformation than techno-discontinuities. Goodwin (2018), in turn, questions Castells about the overly 'Americanness' of the *network society* notion and its actual usefulness for other audiences (such as, one might think, from small countries in 'old' Europe, from laggard peripheral territories in the global south, or from large non-Western fast-moving insurgent countries such as China that have vast tangible resources and their specific reserves of civilizational identity).

How has Castells' work been received (and used) in the fields of business research, managerial practice, organizational studies and economic theorizing? A search in a bibliometric database such as Scopus for articles and reviews displaying the term 'network society' in the title, abstract and keywords finds 201 published papers between 1998 and 2017. Among the first papers to take up the notion were contributions to journals *Organization, World of Work, Geoforum* and the *Journal of Intellectual Capital* (for the sake of illustration these were the journals in which such papers were published in the year 2000 alone). Perhaps surprisingly, no less than 26 per cent were papers that had something to do with management (a proportion rising to 30.9 per cent if economics is included), whereas only 22.5 per cent in the social sciences (the data are compiled using the journal Scopus classification system). It seems as though the kernel of Castells' work had a real impact on the study of organizational and economic dynamics. The field of strategy has also developed in ways compatible with the network perspective: it is now less exotic to talk about 'complementary forces' (Rugman & D'Cruz, 2003), 'collaborative advantage' (Dyer, 2000), 'relational capabilities' (Dyer & Singh, 1998), the 'community view' of the firm (Lawson, 2015), the ritualistic synoptics of the 'post-it note economy' (Wilf, 2016), 'open innovation' and institutionalized R&D free-riding (Martin, 2016), the shifting 'symbolic boundaries' of markets (Grodal, 2018) and the 're-worlding of post-Western strategizing' (Shih & Hwang, 2018).

More negotiation with existing organizational approaches and economic theories was to occur as Castells' work percolated further but where are the multiple crucial adaptions, synergies and challenges to be expected? There are surely relevant aspects of contemporary experience that Castells does not cover. An exhaustive list is impossible to produce, but one could run through the themes of interest aligned with another key communication scholar to provide a yardstick. Robin Mansell (2012), in her own recent work of synthesis, underscored the importance of regulatory policy, intellectual appropriability mechanisms, the political economic of interfaces in mediated environments, the inclusion and re-skilling of informational stakeholders, the perils of quasi-monopolistic proprietary platforms, the understanding of internet social imaginaries, etc. These could all be areas for fruitful engagement for both researchers and decision-makers.

A final word of encouragement for students and practitioners of change can perhaps be gleaned from an edited book by Castells and one of his many network of colleagues. In a collective work on the constraints and opportunities arising from the crisis of 'triumphant global informational capitalism', Castells, Caraça & Cardoso (2012, p. 13) suggest that we consider *economy as culture*, that is, a complex system forever in transition. We may, we are invited to hope, 'witness the rise of new cultures based on the use value of life as a superior form of human organization'.

Conclusion

The discussion here is a selective and stylized summary of Castells' rich set of contributions to dynamic social theory and to our understanding of the often confusing and contradictory pathways of contemporary structural transformation. Castells studies how communication impacts power. In this chapter, his insights on the importance of ICTs were retained, contextualized and packaged with a view to further use and future creative reusage. Relating one's work to Castells' should be a fascinating (networking) enterprise; this is because his theorizing is open to evolution and unexpected recombinations.

End-of-chapter exercises

1. In what sense does the 'network society' concept help in making sense of the contemporary world? Reconstitute the ways by which Manuel Castells came to develop it?
2. The 'informational economy' was a concept Castells (1993) articulated in the early 1990s as the Soviet Union collapsed and the capitalist system became recognizably more reliant on intangible inputs. Consider how this underpins Castells' broader social theory.
3. Is Castells a 'technological determinist'? Discuss this label in relation to Castells (2005) rejection of the 'information society' and the 'knowledge economy' terminology.

4. Is power a multidimensional phenomenon? In what ways does power take form in a world in which networks are the key mode of operation (Castells 2016, p. 13)?
5. Is drawing on Castells' views on 'communication power' to discuss 'informational democracy' the same as an 'informed democracy' (Sey & Castells, 2004)? In what sense can an internet-augmented democracy be a dystopia?

Glossary

Communication   The process of sharing meaning through the exchange of information (Castells, 2012, p. 6).

Globalization   Globalization is a manifestation of and another way to refer to the network society. It is the transformation that takes place as global networks become the operating unit of many geographies and spheres of human activity, starting with the economy. The network society spreads to the entire world but unevenly so. Inclusion is, notwithstanding, imperfect, although the entire humanity is increasingly influenced by its logic. Forces both promoting (e.g. financial markets) and opposing (social movements) globalization deploy the new, flexible and pervasive information and communication technologies (Castells, 2016).

Informationalism   The paradigm that constitutes the material basis of early 21st-century societies. Informationalism is the result of the complex interaction of technology and society that took shape from the 1970s. It refers to the broad template of patterns and dynamics that defines the current historical time (the Information Age), in much same way that the diffusion and uses of motorization and electrification defined modern industrial times. At its core lies the augmentation of the human capacity of information processing and communication that was made possible by microelectronics, computing, software, internet and other revolutionary technologies (Castells; 1989; 2004, p. 8; 2016, p. 8).

Mass self-communication   The usage by individuals of the tools provided by telecommunications providers and over-the-top platforms, often through accessible mobile devices but at the sacrifice of personal privacy. This digital capacity to autonomously produce and reproduce content through the Internet becomes a distinctive source of power in the Information Age. The overlapping and interactive networks of self-directed mass communication become a 'new media' system (Castells, 2009).

Networks   In formal terms, a network is a set of interconnected nodes. A node is the point where the curve intersects itself. A network has no centre, just nodes. Nodes may be of varying relevance for the network. Nodes increase their importance for the network by absorbing more relevant information, processing it more efficiently, and accumulating knowledge. Networks are open structures that change and grow by adding or removing nodes and links. The digital-based technologies of informational processing and decentralized communication empower this old organization form, making it transcend the domain of private life and assume new coordination roles in the world of production, power and culture. Networks become the operating unit of an increasing number of dimensions of human activity (Castells, 2004; 2010; 2016).

Network society   The 'network society' is the social structure that results from the interaction of new technological infrastructure and social organization. This emerging, expanding and consolidating social structure is one made of networks powered by digital and decentralized information and communication systems. The logic of interconnectivity is its multidimensionality as linkages are built across technologies and individuals, communities, companies, industries, states, and all objects and actors that become alive in digital environments (Castells, 2004; van den Bulck, Donders & Lowe, 2018, p. 12).

Networked individualism   This is the dominant form of sociability provided by the evolving informational platforms and systems. The internet is a space where individuals can interact and build their networks, online and offline, on the basis of their interests, values, affinities and projects (Castells, 2002, pp. 130–131; Sey & Castells, 2004).

Networked social movements   A new species of social movements in the digital age based on multimodal, digital networks of horizontal communication that are faster and more autonomous, interactive and decentralized, reprogrammable and less hierarchical (Castells, 2012, p. 15).

Power   Power relations are the most fundamental of social relationships, as they define the institutions that regulate social life. There are two main forms of power: coercion (e.g. law) and persuasion (e.g. values). Power over bodies (coercion) is a weak form of exercising power, whereas power over minds (persuasion) is more lasting. To understand the discursive production of power in the 'Information Age', it is important to understand the organizational and technological transformation of communication systems (Castells, 2009; 2016).

Social movements   Social movements are the producers of new meanings and goals around which the institutions of society emerge or are transformed to represent these values by introducing new norms to organize social life. Social movements arise as counter-power by constructing themselves through a process of autonomous communication, free from the control of the incumbents and institutionalized forms of power (Castells, 2012, p. 9).

Technology   Technology is material culture. Technological change is socially embedded. Technology *is* society (Castells, 2005, p. 3; 2010, p. 5).

Notes

1 The authors acknowledge the support of FCT (the Portuguese Science and Technology Foundation) through the grants UID/GES/00315/2013, SFRH/BD/131338/2017, the strategic project UID/GES/00315/2013, and BDP/113289/2015.
2 Sociologist, President of the International Sociological Association, later President of Brazil.
3 To one of this chapter's authors Chris Freeman mentioned Castells as being the new Weber (personal conversation, circa 2000)

References

Bell, D. (1973). *The coming of post-industrial society: A venture in social forecasting.* New York: Basic Books.

Boyer, R. & Coriat, B. (1986). Technical flexibility and macrostabilisation. Paper presented at the Venice Conference on 'Innovation Diffusion', Venice, April 2–4.

Bresnahan, T., & Gambardella, A. (eds) (2004). *Building high-tech clusters: Silicon Valley and beyond.* Cambridge: Cambridge University Press.

Cardoso, G. (2008). From *mass* to *networked* communication: Communicational models and the Informational Society. *International Journal of Communication*, 2, 587–630.

Castells, M. (1977). *The urban question: A Marxist approach*. Cambridge, MA: MIT Press.

Castells, M. (1978). *City, class and power*. London: Palgrave.

Castells, M. (1983). *The city and the grassroots: A cross-cultural theory of urban social movements*. Berkeley, CA: University of California Press.

Castells, M. (1989). *The informational city: Information technology, economic restructuring, and the urban-regional process*. Oxford: Blackwell.

Castells, M. (1993). The informational economy and the new international division of labor. In M. Carnoy, M. Castells, S. S. Cohen, & F. H. Cardoso (eds) *The new global economy in the Information Age: Reflections on our changing world* (pp. 15–43). University Park, PA: Penn State University Press.

Castells, M. (2002). *The internet galaxy: Reflections on the internet, business and society*. Oxford: Oxford University Press.

Castells, M. (2005). The network society: From knowledge to policy. In M. Castells and G. Cardoso (eds) *The network society: From knowledge to policy* (pp. 3–21). Washington, DC: Brookings Institution Press.

Castells, M. (2009). *Communication power*. Oxford: Oxford University Press.

Castells M. (2010). *The Information Age: Economy, society, and culture, Vol.1: The rise of the network society*, 2nd edn with a new preface. Chichester: John Wiley & Sons.

Castells, M. (2012). *Networks of outrage and hope: Social movements in the internet age*. Cambridge, MA: Polity Press.

Castells, M. (2016). A sociology of power: My intellectual journey. *The Annual Review of Sociology*, 42(1), 1–19.

Castells, M., Caraça, J., & Cardoso, G. (eds) (2012). *Aftermath: The cultures of the economic crisis*. Oxford: Oxford University Press.

Castells, M., & Hall, P. (1994). *Technopoles of the world: The making of twenty-first century industrial complexes*. London: Routledge.

Dyer, J. H. (2000). *Collaborative advantage: Winning through extended enterprise supplier networks*. Oxford: Oxford University Press.

Dyer, J. H., & Singh, H. (1998). The relational view: Cooperative strategy and sources of interorganizational competitive advantage. *Academy of Management Review*, 23(4), 660–679.

Freeman, C. (2007). The ICT paradigm. In R. Mansell, C. Avgerou, R. Silverstone, & D. Quah (eds) *The Oxford handbook of information and communication technologies* (pp. 34–54). Oxford: Oxford University Press.

Freeman, C., & Louçã, F. (2001). *As time goes by: From the industrial revolutions to the information revolution*. Oxford: Oxford University Press.

Fuchs, C. (2012). Some reflections on Manuel Castells' book 'Networks of Outrage and Hope: Social Movements in the Internet Age'. *tripleC: Communication, Capitalism & Critique*, 10(2), 775–797.

Goodwin, P. (2018). An impossible challenge for public service media? The intellectual context of the networked society. In L. G. Lowe, H. van den Bulck, & K. Donders (eds) *Public service media in the networked society* (pp. 29–41). Gothenburg: Nordicom.

Grodal, S. (2018). Field expansion and contraction: How communities shape social and symbolic boundaries. *Administrative Science Quarterly*, 63(4), 783–818.

Hoogvelt, A., Kenny, M., & Germain, R. (1999). The millennium symposium. Conversations with Manuel Castells, Robert Cox and Immanuel Wallerstein. *New Political Economy*, 4(3), 379–408.

Howard, P. N. (2011). *Castells and the media*. London: Polity Press.

Isaacson, W. (2014). *The innovators: How a group of hackers, geniuses, and geeks created the digital revolution*. New York: Simon and Schuster.

Lawson, T. (2015). The nature of the firm and peculiarities of the corporation. *Cambridge Journal of Economics, 39*(1), 1–32,

Mansell, R. (2012). *Imagining the internet: Communication, innovation, and governance.* Oxford: Oxford University Press.

Mansell, R., Avgerou, C., Silverstone, R., & Quah, D. (2007). The challenges of ICTS. In R. Mansell, C. Avgerou, R. Silverstone, & D. Quah (eds) *The Oxford handbook of information and communication technologies* (pp. 1–28). Oxford: Oxford University Press.

Mansell, R., & Steinmueller, W. E. (2000). *Mobilizing the information society: Strategies for growth and opportunity.* Oxford: Oxford University Press.

Martin, B. R. (2016). Twenty challenges for innovation studies. *Science and Public Policy, 43* (3), 432–450.

Mendonça, S., Crespo, N., & Simões, N. (2015). Inequality in the network society: An integrated approach to ICT access, basic skills, and complex capabilities. *Telecommunications Policy, 39*(3–4), 192–207.

Peréz, C. (1983). Structural change and assimilation of new technologies in the economic and social systems. *Futures, 15*(4), 357–375.

Rantanen, T. (2005). The message is the medium: An interview with Manuel Castells. *Global Media and Communication, 1*(2), 135–147.

Rugman, A. M., & D'Cruz, J. R. (2003). *Multinationals as flagship firms.* Oxford: Oxford University Press.

Saxenian, A. (1994). *Regional advantage: Culture and competition in Silicon Valley and Route 128.* Cambridge, MA: Harvard University Press.

Scott, J. (2007). *Fifty key sociologists: The contemporary theorists.* London: Routledge.

Sey, A., & Castells, M. (2004). From media politics to networked politics: The internet and the political process. In M. Castells (ed.) *The network society: A cross-cultural perspective* (pp. 363–381). Cheltenham: Edward Elgar.

Shih, C. Y., & Hwang, Y. J. (2018). Re-worlding the 'West' in post-Western IR: The reception of Sun Zi's the Art of War in the Anglosphere. *International Relations of the Asia-Pacific, 18*(3), 421–448.

Slevin, J. (2000). *The internet and society.* London: John Wiley & Sons.

Stephens, M. (1996). *Accidental empires: How the boys of Silicon Valley make their millions, battle foreign competition, and still can't get a date.* New York: Penguin.

Touraine, A. (1969). *La Société Post-industrielle: Maissance d'une Société.* Paris: Denoël.

van den Bulck, H., Donders, K., & Lowe, G. F. (2018). Public service media in the networked society. What society? What network? What role? In G. F. Lowe, H. van den Bulck, & K. Donders (eds) *Public service media in the networked society* (pp. 11–26). Gothenburg: Nordicom.

van der Haak, B., Parks, M., & Castells, M. (2012). The future of journalism: Networked journalism. *International Journal of Communication, 6,* 2923–2938.

von Hippel, E. (1988). *The sources of innovation.* New York: Oxford University Press.

von Humbolt, A. (2018). Power and counter-power in the Digital Society. Interview with Manuel Castells. *Encore: The Annual Magazine on Internet and Society Research, 2017,* 49–53.

Wilf, E. (2016). The Post-it Note economy: Understanding post-Fordist business innovation through one of its key semiotic technologies. *Current Anthropology, 57*(6), 73.

15 Liquefying modernity

Zygmunt Bauman as organization theorist[1]

Stewart Clegg and Miguel Pina e Cunha

Chapter objectives

This chapter presents the contours of an era characterized by volatility, relentless change and fuzzy boundaries. It does so through the work of Zygmunt Bauman who calls such a world one of 'liquid modernity'.

The chapter discusses how:

- New digital technologies are erasing the boundaries between public and private, organization and environment, entity and process
- The liquefying of the world changes processes of leadership and organizing
- The meaning of work and career is altered by liquid modernity
- Traditional bureaucracy is replaced by new forms of distributed power and organizational control

Introduction

In this chapter we discuss organizing in our digital age in terms of liquidly modern times, whose birth was announced by Zygmunt Bauman. There is a view, represented in Clegg et al. (2016), which sees the world of organizations changing radically in ever more liquid ways: new media generate business innovations, collaborative idea creations and new forms of participation, exploitation and criticism. Distinctions between organizations and their environments as objective determinants fade into irrelevance as strategy increasingly focuses on creating new environments rather than adapting to existing ones. The boundaries of the firm dissolve as Coase's (1937) explanation for the existence of firms is revisited. In these new contexts strategy, it is argued, morphs into a co-produced socio-technical phenomenon where local practices transform globally available resources and professionals move between projects in a world that is post-organizational in at least two ways: first it is one that deviates from the norms of an organizational society premised on Weberian characteristics such as organizational careers, transforming into a society where experts use organizations as temporary platforms, in which, second, the organization, as a specific unit defined by those activities it envelops, is decomposing, fragmenting, reforming and deforming, globally. Control, once vested firmly within organizational pyramids, becomes distributed across a network of actors, including new media and their users. The private sphere of management control as a peak activity enveloped in a tangible and specifically modernist form is dissolving. Workers are becoming globally sub-contracted, matrixed and fragmented. Boundaries, choices and control are all shifting in the direction of increasing fluidity and plurality. The times may be changing. The research question that this paper addresses is the nature of the contours of these changes and their import for organization analysis. This exploration is supported by the work of Zygment Bauman's *oeuvre*.

Bauman's corpus

Zygmunt Bauman is the author that best guides our explorations of the liquid world. We will discuss the reception of Bauman's work in organization studies with a special focus on the notion of liquid times. We will focus on three liquid themes: liquid selves, liquid organizations and liquid aesthetics. Zygmunt Bauman is a link to an older, classical concept of sociology as social theory, one that has almost died out. By social theory we mean the capacity to range theoretically across a wide scope of social issues and questions rather than being a narrow specialist. As a social theorist Bauman stands as one of the major intellectual figures of the 20th and 21st centuries.

Born to Jewish parents in Poland in 1925, in his youth a committed Marxist who fought as an anti-fascist with the Russians in the Polish First Army in the Second World War, Bauman worked with the Communist authorities in Poland in the early years after the war. He suffered from anti-Semitic persecution from the communist authorities during the period of the 1967 Arab-Israeli war as a part of the Cold War alliance of the Soviet Union with the Arab states. In the aftermath of the war, in 1968, as a result of a power struggle within the Polish Communist Party, related to events in Czechoslovakia's Prague Spring, there were purges resulting in an expulsion of 15,000 Poles of Jewish origin between 1968 and 1972. Bauman was one of the purged intellectuals and was obliged to give up both his Chair at the University of Warsaw and his Polish citizenship. Initially, he migrated to Israel and taught at the University of Tel-Aviv, as well as spending a period as a Visiting Professor in Canberra at the Australian National University.

In 1972 Bauman was appointed to the Chair of Sociology at the University of Leeds. At this time the appointment was surprising to many British sociologists who were not aware of the 14 books that he had already published in Polish. Prior to 1972, when a version of his 1960 London School of Economics PhD thesis was published as *Between Class and Elite: The Evolution of the British Labour Movement – a Sociological Study* by Manchester University Press, he had written little in English. At Leeds, Bauman built a solid sociological department whose seminars were legendary for the plethora of top sociologists and social scientists who were invited to speak at them and for the quiet way in which Bauman, after others had asked their questions of the visiting speaker, would remove his pipe and ask a question that invariably cut to the core of the presentation.

From 1972 his publications in English bloomed. The period between 1972 and 1983 was marked by a focus on issues of class, Marxist analysis, culture and hermeneutic methods. One of these early works, *Culture as Praxis*, from 1973, introduced the concept of structuration that subsequent theorists such as Giddens (1984) were to popularize. In the period bookmarked by *Memories of Class* (1982) and *In Search of Politics* (1999), the predominant themes were those of modernity and postmodernity, ethics and globalization. In 2000, however, he published the first of his subsequent studies into *liquid modernity*, which have continued to the present day. Past themes of ethics, culture and inequality were joined by a new focus on consumerism as the hallmark of liquidly modern societies, societies in which class was increasingly only a memory.

Bauman's reception in organization studies

Despite his widespread reception across the social sciences, Bauman's address of liquid themes has not been greatly influential in organization studies. Most references to his work are only in passing (Dale, 2005; Knox et al., 2008; Jensen, Sandström & Helin, 2009; Jensen, 2010; Hensby, Sibthorpe & Driver, 2012; Ekman, 2014; Weiskopf & Munro, 2012; Hancock & Rehn, 2011; Johnsen & Gudmand-Høyer, 2010). Ybema et al. (2009) see one of the symptoms of individualism in liquid modernity to be the search for 'identity', while Hollinshead and Maclean (2007) see signs of liquid modernity in Serbian enterprise. The most extensive use of Bauman's theme of liquidity in the journals is the work of Clegg and Baumeler (2010), who argue that the 'crucial space in which the liquidly modern organizational self works is in project teams'. As Clegg and Baumeler suggest, liquid organizations are those in which investments in people are highly liquid and easily liquidated, with no long-term investment implications. These authors explore the ethical, political, identity and organizational consequences of increasing liquidity. Ethically, liquidly modern leaders are forever reassembling the pieces of their own identity as the liquid state changes. Politically, power relations become marked by a new lightness of synoptical power relations augmenting and supplementing the more traditional panoptical power (also see Lancione & Clegg, 2014). In terms of identity, liquidity is marked by the immediateness of the self in the moment. Organizationally, liquidity predisposes its leaders to improvisation over heavy scripting.

Power et al. (2009, p. 301) briefly cite Bauman (2007) in relation to themes of 'increased ambiguity and uncertainty at the level of individuals and a problematization of trust in, and legitimacy of, institutions and experts in an interconnected world'. The themes that Power and his colleagues address are those of how specific social, organizational and managerial processes occur that enable the recognition of risk and attempts at risk management. Pelzer (2014) deepens this analysis by more explicitly linking the discussion of risk to Bauman's theory of liquid society. For Pelzer (2014), the financial markets function as a prototype for studying the effect of increasing liquidity. Liquidity is seen as the essence of risk management within financial markets. In organizational terms, as Clegg and Baumeler (2010) argue, leaders, as well as employees in general and their organizations, are becoming more liquid. Employees increasingly are employed on short-term or highly contingent contracts, accordingly reducing their commitment and loyalty to organizations, subject to changing personnel policies. These policies place them at more risk by lessening employment certainty in the name of a freedom of choice that, for its recipients, is essentially limited.

Increasingly, those who assume the role of leaders are less likely to be positional experts solidly grounded in organizational hierarchies and technical expertise so much as managerial expertise in 'leadership' as a practice of shared, dispersed and mutually constituted influence gained in successful steering of projects despite the irreducible contingency of unforeseen events. In reality, suggests Bauman (2007;

2000), there is little in the way of central control that is steering events. Deregulation, individualization, weakened human bonds, increased fluidity of solidarities, and the drift from normative regulation to seduction are all key features of the liquid condition identified by Bauman (in Jacobsen & Tester, 2007, p. 313).

Liquid themes

The major treatment of Bauman's implications for organizations and, implicitly, for leadership and strategy is to be found in *Liquid Organization: Zygmunt Bauman and Organization Theory*, edited by Kociatkiewicz and Kostera (2014), who characterize Bauman's later work as focusing on three main themes: the *dynamics of modernity*, the *possibilities of radical social change*, and the *ethics of compassion* – which they term 'sociological compassion'.

In terms of the *dynamics of modernity*, elements of these themes were prefigured in earlier works, such as the 1993 books *Modernity and Ambivalence* and *Postmodern Ethics* and the 1998 book *Work, Consumerism and the New Poor*. In the period before 2000, Bauman's reflections were cast in binary terms, influenced, suggests Jensen (2014), by Tönnies' famous distinctions between *Gemeinschaft* (embedded and constraining community) and *Gesellschaft* (disembedded and liberating society), drawing contrasts between 'modernity' and 'postmodernity'.

The apex of modernity, for Bauman (1989), was reached in the death camps that delivered the Holocaust, where the strengths of normal organization in delivering efficient terminal mass production was exemplified.[2] The thesis has been widely discussed (see Clegg, Courpasson & Phillips, 2006) and also criticized by scholars who have argued that the Holocaust was not organized by practices of bureaucracy (du Gay, 2000). The critics, such as du Gay, have sought to preserve the notion of Weberian bureaucracy, arguing that what occurred in the camps was organization's corruption by fascism rather than an example of bureaucracy's ethos.

Posing a dualism between one state, modernity, and another, post modernity, is inherently problematic. It leads to a problem of transition: how does one move from one state of existence to the other and how does one know that the transition has occurred? Such historical breaks are the exception rather than the rule, which is not to say that change does not occur, for it surely does, but more continuously, as a process of everyday life and living. The solidities of one time morph slowly into history, into something else, as they die of neglect or are extinguished. It is these moments of unfolding that are captured by the notion of postmodernism as a moment in the unfolding of history (Clegg & Kornberger, 2003). As Lyotard (1993) says, postmodernism is not the end of modernism, but its birth and rebirth, its constant coming into being. Modernity is a constantly shifting edge, struggles over the meaning of which define both modernism that seeks to condense its meaning and postmodernism that seeks to liquidate rather than consolidate.

More recently, Bauman distinguishes between solid and liquid modernity. Solid modernity represents the world of conventional organization and management theory. Its hallmarks are a concern with objective structure, rational strategy and normal equilibrium. It is a world stalked by uncertainty and equivocality – the evils to be minimized and avoided as best as is possible by formulating appropriate strategies and structures. Stable bureaucracies, rational systems, orderly routines, formal leadership, long-range planning – these are the devices used to ward off evils.

The dominance of solid modernity defined much of the post-war era. Large bureaucratic organizations, characterized by rational planning and long-term careers for their cadres, were the norm, in both the state and civil society. But events conspired to unmake this solidity. On the one hand, from the early 1970s onwards, fuelled by the costs of maintaining the US warfare state, initially in Vietnam, the US state began to experience a fiscal crisis as it became more and more indebted due to deficit financing (Gamble & Walton, 1976). On the other hand, inspired by the political economy of economic neo-liberalism (Harvey, 2005), organizations became increasingly global in their decomposition and recomposition (see Clegg, Harris & Hopfl, 2011), through strategies of outsourcing, offshoring and alliancing.

The idea of a process, of a transition from one state to the other, still accompanies the very idea of there being a dualism, which is why, perhaps, in his later work, Bauman abandons the juxtaposition that served him well in the 1990s for a formulation that much better captures this sense of an edge of uncertainty and introduces instead the idea of there being a liquid modernity. Liquid spreads, seeps, leaches and moves by osmosis. Liquid modernity's other is not post but solid: being solid it does not melt or fade away but becomes a container, here more effectively, there less so, of a liquid edge that is forever seeping beyond its containment. The solid and liquid phases of modernity are implicated together: the one contains but that which it contains is never constrained by the form of the historical container; it shifts shape, it trickles off in new directions and new containers develop to try and restrict its viscosity, to discipline its flows, as it seeks to liquidate its containment. However, the very term liquid modernity still invites comparison with its antimony, solid modernity; for this reason, we will stress the verb rather than the noun and write of liquefying modernity.

The world we have lost: the dynamics of liquefying modernity

The organizations that flourished from the end of the Second World War through the 1970s built on the long-range planning that the US Army Chiefs of Staff engaged in when planning the campaign to defeat Hitler, starting with the Normandy landings. A natural ecology for leadership was to be found in the very large firms, such as General Motors, that dominated predictable and secure markets that they sought to control through long-range planning. Ironically, at the time that the Soviet bloc engaged in the same practices of long-range planning – the five-year plans – corporate America, the bastion of private enterprise, sought to do the same – albeit based on corporate as opposed to state planning. In the Soviet case it was the state that sought to plan; in the American case it was left to the corporations. In doing so they were assisted by the facts of post-war corporate life: markets that were largely based in the United States, protection from foreign competition by tariffs, standardization, regulation, subsidies, price supports and government guarantees.

Keynesian demand management was not just a feature of the United States. In Europe, especially in France with its *plannification*, there was a very explicit linking of centralist state and private sector interests by bureaucrats schooled in the Parisian *Grande Ecoles*. Keynesianism was allied with a strong central planning structure in the UK under the Wilson administrations of the 1960s and 1970s. The state, it was believed, could steer the white heat of technological revolution, a belief that died during the terminal stages of the Callaghan administration when the first fluttering of the new 'monetarism' emerged to assume full bloom in the Thatcher era of the 1980s, as Keynes was dismissed and Hayek became the new point of reference.

After 1980, with the rise of a new economic liberalism under the sponsorship of President Reagan and Prime Minister Thatcher, new competition was unleashed by the joint forces of creative destruction and liberal economic deregulation, liquidating the solidities of the modernist high-water mark. The emergence of a new class of managers from the 1980s onward saw them greatly enriched in remuneration relative to all other wage and salary earners, in part, by the adoption of agency theory as a strategy in practice widely used in the American corporate world. The corporate organization increasingly came to be assumed as merely an aggregation of individual agents, constituted as a legal personality that contracts real individuals to its purposes, the principal with whom contracts are entered. These contracts are incomplete because of uncertainty that cannot be predicted and covered by contract. Fama and Jensen (1983) presumed that the firm is a nexus of contracts between individuals in which the costs of enforcing contracts that are always incompletely stipulative will be a perennial problem.

Corporations that were quite obviously social institutions, with organizational employees treated in a manner in some respects similar to social democratic citizens, with family healthcare programmes, decent wages, salaries and pensions, were being invited to deconstruct. '[T]he "nexus" imagery served as a useful provocation, a lever to bust up the unwieldy and shareholder-hostile conglomerates built up over the prior decades. This was a theory perfectly designed to legitimate a bust-up takeover wave' (Davis, 2016a, p. 509). Agency theory was an account that spawned in practice on a grand scale what it theorized, increasing the liquidity of organizations financially as well as making life within their frame more liquid because it was less bound by bureaucratic norms.

The growth and application of agency theory to practise over the last 40 years or so, particularly but not exclusively in the financial sector (Mallaby, 2010), has seen agents become rewarded as principals that don't even have to risk their own capital. In tying their agency to that of the principals, they have voted themselves stock options, thus becoming significant principals in their own right. In most companies in the United States the CEO tends to enjoy a considerable imbalance of power compared to the nominal authority of the board that appoints the CEO and to which they are legally accountable. Hence, the growing control of CEOs in governance on company boards has vested them with an ability to set, up to a point, their own salaries as well as nominate stock options. Leadership in this context became a proxy for personal enrichment on a scale unprecedented in prior rational-legal organizations as the euthanasia of bureaucracy was accomplished by the triumph of the *rentiers*. Modern organizations were being liquidated (Davis, 2016a, b).

There were corollaries to these processes of liquidation in terms of organizational changes: careers gave way to project portfolios; leaders give way to dispersed leadership and self-leadership; bureaucracies became leaner as non-core elements of the business were outsourced; their operations became more global as it was realized that enhanced value could be captured in value chains that probed wide and far into production sites and subcontractors in faraway places. The state also decomposed its bureaucracies in search for more efficient privatization of those goods and services once take for granted as within its domain.

In solid modernity the major container was work and the relations of production that this entailed. Successful capitalism, however, successful in fulfilling and perpetually expanding material wants and needs, shifted its register inexorably from a productive container defined primarily by exploitative relations of production that state interventions into the welfare of its labouring citizens modified, to an infinitely plastic container that expanded with the accelerating fetishization of ever more phenomena, including work itself. Work that had equated with a lifelong career, in the sense of an unfolding, a linear progression, of working, often in the same or very similar organizations, saw its meaning liquefied. Liquefying modernity increasingly replaces citizens with consumers.

Solid modernity, at its best, developed a whole programme for citizens around the rights of labour (Abrahamson & Broström, 1980). Liquefying modernity erodes the relations associated with being employees, such that having employment contracts and deploying capital became more fluid, less secure, increasingly unstable. Liquidity was translated in terms of the prevailing political and economic ideologies into increased choice and freedom for the individual. These freedoms dissolved established commitments and sense of obligation and the institutions that supported these, such as mutual societies, trade unions, established religions and political parties. Identities founded in church and chapel, union and community, party allegiance and its tribal oppositions, weakened. The political process became more marketized, such that selling the message was becoming more crucial than what the message might say. Universities weakened their collegial bonds and became increasingly sites for the mass production of knowledge workers and specialist boutique ventures for the creation of intellectual property that could be valorized.

In a cliché, the reality of liquefying modernity is that the only certainty is change; uncertainty becomes the new norm; instability and insecurity the new order; identity a matter of choice, and choice a matter of improvisational ability and access to the resources available to sustain it. Identity became the major arena for struggle: entrepreneurial subjects could propel themselves from being local identities to cosmopolitan personalities, thus setting new norms of identity for others to struggle to emulate or exceed.

Consumption can never be sated when global capital roams. Every day, in every way, new, improved and breakthrough delights for consumption will be tantalizingly available to those who can afford to sample them, disposing of outdated, inferior and unfashionable modes of consumption and of stuff already consumed. No thing is sacred; nothing is secure; every thing can be made redundant, become more liquid – including the leaders of products past. Identity increasingly is posited to reside not in being who one is, defined by the old materialities such as relations of (un)employment and place, so much as in who and what one might become through the consumption of things in the desire for expressing selfhood. The injunction that by one's work(s) one shall be known is replaced by the exhortation to buy now and become what one might be. As the political events associated with Brexit and Trump demonstrate, this breeds a politics of resentment on the part of those who feel themselves excluded from cosmopolitan identities, tastes and consumption.

Life is increasingly being lived in public. What was once private life is routinely displayed on Facebook; what one is thinking in the moment, off the 'top' of one's head, can be tweeted irretrievably without reflection. What were once just tools for talking have become McLuhanite (McLuhan, 1964) extensions of our nervous systems. Using smartphones we create and consume content, with the medium having become a more constant presence than the content it produces on Snapchat, only for it to disappear.

Leading in liquefying times

What does it mean to lead in liquidity? In this section we discuss liquid selves, liquid organizations and liquid aesthetics, as three facets of a post-canonical Baumanian theory of leadership relations.

Liquid selves

Life lived in public increasingly pervades people's experiences in organizations. It does so in two ways: one is through an enhancement of the panoptical tendencies of solid modernity, where the few exercise surveillance over the many; the other is through the development of new forms of synoptical power, where the many watch each other and the ambitious among them watch the few. The two systems of power combine within liquid modernity. Organization studies developed a term to capture this combinatorial effect when it accepted the idea of the 'emotionally intelligent' subject (Salovey & Mayer, 1990; Goleman, 1995).

The emotionally intelligent subject displays emotional competencies (Goleman, 1998), learned capabilities for outstanding work performance. The key competences are in being liquid about innovation, commitments, adaptability and achievement (Clegg & Baumeler, 2014): each of these is viscous, shifting and redefinable – in a word, liquid. Liquid in the sense of being quick to liquidate not only tasks performed but also how they are performed, where they are performed and with whom they are performed. Liquidity requires autonomy, spontaneity, creativity, adaptability, and communicative and relational competence, as well as significant capacities to invest in social and educational capital and a capacity to develop swift trust in switches from project to project, as liquid life in organizations is lived not in a linear career but in a succession of projects experienced in the moment. Being, self and actants are organized in a series of reflexive autopoietic loops, looping round existential anxiety.

The most acute and stubborn worries that haunt liquid leaders are fears of not being in the moment. Organizationally, liquid life is a mess of contradiction: liquidly modern leaders (of the self) have to be perpetually constructing and reconstructing themselves; they are forever reassembling the pieces of their own identity, refining themselves day after day (Bauman, 2005). Inadequacy in this new liquidity involves inability to acquire the desired image to which leaders aspire. Adequacy is having the ability to be simultaneously the plastic subject, sculptor and object of one's self, of becoming both the onlooker of self-work and the teacher of that self, a voyeuristic self, engaged in a process in which watching self watching others watching self becomes the liquid centre of self-existence and leaderly achievement (Clegg & Baumeler, 2014, pp. 51, 52). In short, to succeed in liquid times leaders must become strategists of their portable selves (Petriglieri, Petriglieri & Wood, 2017). Impression management rules (Goffman, 1959), mediated through the media extensions of the self as LinkedIn, Facebooked, tweeted, etc. Jensen (2014, p. 24) suggests a prime fear of the liquid organizational member is to be unseen – especially when one occupies a position of visibility, such as that of a leader (Maravelias, 2009).

Liquid selves are valorized as free selves: free to choose, free to take responsible action for their self, free to construct their own biographies and projections of self. These projections are all self-centred, even as they project synoptically to others. The chief responsibility owed is to and for one's self (Bauman, 2007, p. 92). The organization provides arenas in which scenes may be staged that enable the aesthetic projection of the self. As Clegg and Baumeler (2014, p. 38) suggest, liquidly modern leaders are entrepreneurs of their selves: they must manage with enthusiasm and with passion and expect to share an ethos of immediacy, playfulness, subjectivity and performativity (Hjorth & Kostera, 2007; Bauman, 2008). Between the performance and presentation of self and the reaction of significant others yawns a chasm of uncertainty as the subject, still of surveillance but now also committed to being passionate, must choose how to make the killer presentation – of self – that secures their profile as the kind of subject they anticipate that their significant others expect them to be (Jackall, 1988). Being in the liquid state is an unfolding project in which constant vigilance and perpetual effort must be expended, with no guarantees that the performance will pay off, as Bauman states (2000, p. 8).

Liquid organization

The cornerstone of the liquid organization is an absence of moral concern. Liquid organizations are adiaphoric, that is, subject to *adiaphorization*:

> Making certain actions, or certain objects of action, morally neutral or irrelevant – exempt from the categories of phenomena suitable for moral evaluation. The effect of adiaphorization is achieved by excluding some categories of people from the realm of moral subjects, or through covering up the link between partial action and the ultimate effect of co-ordinated moves, or through enthroning procedural discipline and personal loyalty in the role of the all-overriding criterion of moral performance.
>
> (Bauman, 1995, p. 149)

Adiaphorization will especially characterize the top management team: while each member may ontologically be a moral subject, the organization cannot be. This is the essence of leaderly strategies, as we shall see in due course. Leadership may well be formulated within governance structures, rules, guidelines and policies but it is essentially ethically blank in its representations. As Bauman (2014, p. xvi) expressed it:

> Organizations ... serve the process of adiaphorization – of excising large swathes of human behaviour and human habit from the realm of moral evaluation and ethical obligations and thereby rendering them less sensitive to moral impulses. To put it simply: they serve the process of cutting down moral responsibility to a manageable size; and of recycling it into a form that is amenable to management. Reduction and simplification of moral obligations and ethically inspired emotions in general are viewed as indispensable conditions for a focused, determined, efficient and therefore rational conduct.

Strategic imperatives are seen to flow from this process of adiaphorization: one is not so much responsible for a generalized set of other selves as responsible to the order in which one is employed: its rules, its authorities, its definitions of what is right according to the rules and what the rules make wrong. Necessarily, this invests considerable synoptic power towards the hierarchical ordering of judgements and their expression as imperative commands transmitted through vertical command-obedience sequences; simultaneously, it makes of one a specimen subject to the multitude of panoptical powers used to exercise surveillance over one's self at work. Devices such as audit (Power, 1999), HRM (Townley, 1993), CCTV and those ubiquitous recordings of customer interactions that call centres suggest may be used for training purposes, are all oriented towards the latter.

The combination of synopticism, panopticism and responsibilization pump and transfer the moral responsibility of the executors of commands upwards, as Bauman (2014) suggests, to the command givers. Those who enact, the subordinates, 'are excluded from the authorship of their acts' (Bauman, 2014, p. xvi). Those who command do not enact – that is the responsibility of those subject to the imperative commands. 'As a consequence, neither bears full, undivided responsibility for their acts. Absolute moral responsibility is thereby "deconstructed".' (2014, p. xvi). What remains is the ethical pose of the individual subject, judged only according to the organizational rules. Responsibility floats and ethics are defined largely in terms of the contracts that leaders have entered into with stockholders, such that, in principle, as Bauman says, no leader can be perceived as a moral subject qua organizational membership. Their moral responsibility is to be found in service of organization strategies, strategies turned towards abstractions of the market and their manifestations in analysis and shared values, not their questioning.

In the past, before modernity became so liquid, this was efficient enough when composed wholly within the envelope of an all-encompassing organization that organized itself on classical bureaucratic lines. Members were expected to express a vocation, to display character, respect and ethos. Careers in the service of the organization and its solid composition as a bureaucracy reinforced a sense of disciplined ethical virtue expressed in deference to routines, rules and rationalities. However, as a result of what Bauman (2014, p. xvii) refers to as the 'second managerial revolution', the solid organization has decomposed. It is not that bureaucracy is being superseded but it is becoming embroiled in complex processes of hybridization (du Gay, 2000; Courpasson & Reed, 2004), simultaneously decomposing and recomposing.

Decomposition takes us to the world of supply chains and outsourcing. It also takes us into the world of the others, the undeserving poor, those whose subjectivity is insufficiently *legitimately* entrepreneurial, which is to say that they might well be illegitimately entrepreneurial in an undisciplined mode – perhaps in the local narco-economy. Their marginal existence warns us that apart from consumption there is only deserved misery. Recomposition takes us into the world of new organizational forms. In the former, there are some very familiar politics of surveillance and control; in the latter there are more innovative developments that centre on the replacement of the central figure of the bureaucrat with the project leader, and the central life experience of the occupational career followed largely in one organization being replaced by the individual's leadership achievements in projects. The politics of the project become the testing ground for elite reproduction (see Clegg & Courpasson, 2004; Clegg, 2011).

What is distinctive about leading and working in the contemporary liquid decomposed organization is that the major mechanism of the career has undergone a substantial change. Careers will be increasingly project-based, flowing now like mercury and then reconsolidating in a new plane of activity (Schein & Van Maanen, 2016). The project – whether innovation, R&D, engineering, marketing or whatever, becomes the major vehicle for organization networks and alliances and developmental tasks within specific organizations – although, increasingly these will involve team members from other organizations. In such hybrid and often-unclear situations, conflict and confrontation are inevitable, so managing emotions becomes a crucial skill. Leaders need to create learning environments – via coaching, hands-on teaching and mentoring – to stimulate and develop their employees, and to manage expectations about evolving roles in projects. Employees become sensitive to shifting roles and the signals they send about a person's worth. A popular metaphor for the post-bureaucratic leader is that of a coach trying to build a team out of a group of highly paid free agent talents, networking like crazy. For the committed employee, work spills over into downtime, occupying the wakeful creative moments of the organizational members, travelling with them as they use their portable digital devices, the playing with which is seen as almost 'better than sex' (Trinca & Fox, 2004).

If one follows the direction of decomposition it is clear that in the new margins located on the global shores of modernity, in the electronic panopticon of the call centre or the outsourced production line, bureaucracy is alive and well in a particularly centralized, standardized and routinized form. Here the bureaucratization of the shop floor has proceeded into the heart of the white collar, pink blouse, and colourful, indigenously attired digital factory, policed by the spectre of the reserve army of the unemployed and underemployed, the non-respectable poor. If, on the other hand, one follows the recomposition route into the upper echelons of leaner and more entrepreneurially oriented organizations, a surprising finding emerges. Leaders are no longer responsible subjects – at least not for performance in all its manifestations: ethical, financial, production, etc.

The more they are able to do less of the work of the organization, the more efficient and the less responsible they are. Efficiency is measured in simple terms as value considered only in costs and profits. Responsibility is pushed down and out. Pushed down it is subsidiarized by being constituted as empowerment of the subaltern workforce who become panoptical governors of their employment relations (Barker, 1993). Pushed out it is outsourced, sub-contracted, and embedded in a supply chain whose governing mechanism is invariably contractually expressed in financial terms. Should those financial terms be delivered in ways that seem ethically dubious, where people die, become ill, poisoned or incapacitated, then the responsibility does not reach the top of the chain: the buck stops where the contract remotely resides. Gains flow upwards through the circuits of power, while costs are pushed downwards. Greater responsibilities are no longer attached to higher remuneration:

> Chief executive officers have by now gained a nearly comprehensive insurance against punishment for failure to deliver results, including failures caused by their indolence, incompetence, neglect or downright sloth: the eventual loss of their golden nests would be amply recompensed by golden handshakes, paid for their subordinates in the currency of job and career losses.
>
> (Bauman, 2014, p. xviii)

Leaders self-manage and convince their subordinates to do the same; in doing so they bring to bear all their emotional intelligence and attachment, using digital devices that register their participation in working panoptically as they project their efforts synoptically to their LinkedIn network and Facebook 'friends', interpolating work achievements into life lived outside official confines, outside of the office (Clegg & Baumeler, 2010; 2014). In liquefying modernity, leaders' success is measured by their wealth.

> In 2014, the richest 1% of people in the world owned 48% of global wealth, leaving just 52% to be shared between the other 99% of adults on the planet. Almost all of that 52% is owned by those included in the richest 20%, leaving just 5.5% for the remaining 80% of people in the world. If this trend continues of an increasing wealth share to the richest, the top 1% will have more wealth than the remaining 99% of people in just two years ... with the wealth share of the top 1% exceeding 50% by 2016 ... The very richest of the top 1%, the billionaires on the Forbes list, have seen their wealth accumulate even faster over this period. In 2010, the richest 80 people in the world had a net wealth of $1.3tn. By 2014, the 80 people who top the Forbes rich list had a collective wealth of $1.9tn; an increase of $600bn in just 4 years, or 50% in nominal terms. Meanwhile, between 2002 and 2010 the total wealth of the poorest half of the world in current US$ had been increasing more or less at the same rate as that of billionaires; however, since 2010, it has been decreasing over this time.
>
> (Oxfam, 2015)

The most recent trends from 2015 data reported in 2016 show no shift to a better distribution of incomes in terms of the prospects for growth; in fact, the inequalities are increasing: just 62 people own as much as the poorest half of the world's population, increasing their wealth by more than half a trillion dollars to $1.76 trillion with no positive trickle-down effects.[3] Organizationally, liquid wealth composition occurs largely through tax minimization by transfer pricing increasing the pie and stock options increasing the slices of the pie apportioned to leaders.

Liquid aesthetics

The liquidly modern organization announces itself to be so visually in its style and in the disposition of its internal spaces. Not for it the bland boxes and skyscrapers of solid modernity. There are several ways of being liquidly aesthetic. For early and start-up organizations it is typical that they will rent a funky, slightly distressed space, perhaps part of an old factory or warehouse, preferably with valid heritage features: the location of design companies such as Advanced Digital Institute in the remains of Salt Mill in Saltaire, Bradford, a World Heritage Site, is typical of a liquidly aesthetic workplace statement. The employees sought are those whom Warren (2014, p. 71) terms 'liquid employees' – individuals who choose their jobs as they would a commodity, as a statement, an affirmation, a badge of identity, then the liquid organization seeks to make the workplace one that offers aesthetic fulfilment and proximity to good transport links and housing. Being in a conventional edge of the city industrial park just doesn't cut it in these terms.

More established liquid organizations will prefer a signature architect, preferably a starchitect. To be a starchitect the designer must have achieved celebrity and critical acclaim that has transformed them into major figures in the world of architecture, usually indicated by the award of major prizes and the commissioning of landmark buildings. Those who are best known have a name recognition that extends to a degree of fame amongst the general public. To become a starchitect requires some pretensions to the avant-garde – nothing classical or classically modern will do. The essential feature is the aestheticization of the workplace, whereby 'aspects of objects, places, events, people and experiences of everyday life are made more appealing through the decoration, enhancement or other embellishment of their appearance' (Warren, 2014, p. 71). De rigueur are highly designed spaces and finishes, coupled with laid-back open spaces, bicycle spaces – very important symbolically – and the provision of quality fit-outs in terms of kitchens, cafes, coffee machines, etc. The occasional sculpture or modern art piece also helps, which an art consultancy can supply on lease; occasional musicians, artists, poets or writers in residence can also help create a suitably funky sense of place.

Hancock (2003) suggests that liquid organizations will seek to structure fun, novelty and excitement into the experience of being at work. Above all, the spaces must be flexible: they should not be solidified into structures that cannot adapt and change easily. Open spaces, hot desking, bookable meeting rooms, no anchoring in offices – these are all preferred. Of course, the opportunities for both synoptical and panoptical power increase as visibility and transparency of working conditions increases. Nonetheless, these characteristics signify 'coolness' – the accolade that a liquid organization and liquid leaders must have (see Lancione & Clegg, 2014). The contrast is with the constructions of earlier modes of organization such as factories, modernist towers and desolate warehouse spaces of the industrial park. Aesthetically liquid organizations cannot be authentic if they occupy such spaces. Authenticity has to be signified by style and the style must be cool.

Conclusion

Taking together the characteristics constituting the conditions for increasingly liquid modernity, it is not surprising that projects emerge as the point at which all the contradictions of the new liquidity are concentrated. Looked at from below, from the perspective of the subaltern, contemporary organizations are shape-shifters, project-based, with teams composing and decomposing, locations shifting as projects are completed, key performance indicators (KPIs) changing with projects, and one's individual organizational future uncertain. From the perspective of the leaders the story is quite different. They know that they are over the threshold where the golden chains are evident. The largest problem that they must deal with is using the project shape-shifting that goes on outside the threshold as the basis for competitions and tournaments that will decide who of the subaltern may cross the threshold into leadership. Looked at by the outsiders to liquefying modernity, the rural poor, the underemployed and unemployed, the marginal non-cosmopolitans, their sense of traditional identity rooted in old certainties of relations of production are being eroded, as employing organizations disappear to other states and as newer cosmopolitan identities increasingly fill representational space in the media they consume. Politically, those whose sense of identity is eroding, become increasingly susceptible to 'populist authoritarianism' orchestrated by the 1 per cent, as Weigel (2016) argues.

Organizationally, the hybrid political structure of liquid organizing needs both leadership differentiation to ensure a credible competition among various centres of power (individuals and/or subgroups) and unification to ensure a relative consensus on basic values and on the legitimate rules of the internal political arena. Leaders are differentiated from sub-elites who, in turn, are distinguished from the population of knowledge workers, experts and professionals, with regard to values, demographic characteristics and types of aspirations. Beyond their everyday concern are the distant global margins where the objects of desire are produced, as are the local spaces marginalized by liquefying processes.

Corporate leaders have a direct interest in shaping, grooming and educating selected aspirants, constituting subjects with an appropriate comportment, etiquette and equipage to qualify as disciplined. Running projects with paradoxical criteria of performativity (on time, on budget, on specification, while delivering innovation) successfully hints, in a weak way, that one has been spotted as someone with potential which the elites wish to test out, to see if the project leader can display certain indispensable characteristics for the leadership elite. Mostly, these characteristics pertain to an ability to accept and work creatively with an existing order and existing rules; thus, they go far beyond merely technical and professional expertise. They are the new way of reinvigorating *habitus* when organizational borders have become porous, careers liquid, leadership identities contingent on project success and, for many others, employment is increasingly self-managed and precarious: paradoxically work is increasingly more omnipresent and more precarious, with the Fordist model being replaced by the gig economy, land of the precariat (Mumby et al., 2017).

What the conditions of liquid organization and leadership offer those ostensibly being led is a great propensity for anomie. Anomie is usually taken to mean a state of normlessness, detachment and non-solidarity created by a mismatch between personal or group standards and wider social standards.[4] The gap occurs because of the lack of social ethics integrating individuals into broader moral sentiments. When behavioural norms of leadership practice spread indifference to the fate of others, when the decomposition of the corporation becomes the norm, when social relations become predominantly digitally mediated, anomie will escalate not only as existing corporate ranks are diminished through increasing culls on membership but also as, in the digital 'sharing' economy, the vast majority of people working become self-employed, precarious and marginal employees, or are outsourced subcontractors of the corporate behemoths remaining (Clegg, Cunha & Rego, 2016). The corporation becomes an increasingly remote citadel that few can breach. When there are few people left to lead and many who feel cast asunder by the leaders of the past and present, through increasingly liquid states and organizations, leadership as an ethical claim to significance and difference tends to be an option with diminishing prospects other than leading to an inflation of leadership rhetoric, such as we see with Trump, amongst other leaders.

End-of-chapter exercises

1. Traditionally, organizations relied on planning to regulate their relations with the market and its evolution. How can organizations prepare for the future in liquid times?

2. The career was a progression in a hierarchical system, involving some predictability. How will careers be reimagined in liquid organizations?
3. What challenges confront managers in terms of their leadership roles in liquid organizations?
4. What is the connection between liquid times and post-hierarchical organizations, such as the Holacracy?
5. Put yourself in the position of an 'organizational man' of the 1950s. When facing a liquid organization what could his thoughts be?
6. From the perspective of the employee, what is the promise and peril of working in a liquid organization?
7. Have the politics of consumption now replaced the politics of production in the creation of social identity?

Glossary

Adiaphorization According to Bauman, adiaphorization occurs when 'systems and processes become split off from any consideration of morality'.

Bureaucracy According to Weber, bureaucracy was a legal-rational instrument for organizing. It had three essential clusters of characteristics: those that were *scalar* (hierarchy, discipline, formal authority, rule orientation); those that were *functional* (a defined sphere of competence; selection and advancement on the basis of formal qualifications); those that related to *career* (free selection and contract, separation of the bureaucrat from the means of administration as a rational-legal relation, and appointment to a full-time salaried career with tenure).

Digitalization The use of digital technologies to change a business model and provide new revenue and value-producing opportunities; it is the process of moving to a digital business by enabling, improving and/or transforming business operations and/or business functions and/or business models/processes and/or activities, using digital tools such as the mobile devices and technologies that make them mobile and/or using social collaboration and unified communication platforms, leveraging digital technologies and a broader use and context of digitized data, turned into actionable knowledge, with a specific benefit in mind.

Emotional intelligence The capacity to be aware of, control and express one's emotions and other people's emotions, to be able to discern between different feelings and label them appropriately, to use emotional information to guide thinking and behaviour, and to manage and/or adjust emotions to different environments, contexts or goals.

Liquid organizations Liquefying an organization means disrupting bureaucratic assumptions of rigid structures and making it adaptive, dynamic and resilient. Often based on lean management and open collaboration principles, the liquid organization model is flat, meritocratic and value-driven, enabling indirect coordination, collaboration and organic effectiveness.

Liquid selves The liquid self is an identity shaped by consumption and the gaze of others on the material signs of one's selfhood. Unlike the solid self of industrial society, embedded in class relations, it is fluid, dynamic and highly dependent on a sense of belonging to specific identity categories.

Liquid times In 'liquid' times, social forms and institutions no longer have sufficient time to solidify and cannot serve as frames of reference for human actions and long-term life plans, so individuals have to find other ways to organize their lives. They have to splice together an unending series of short-term projects and episodes that don't add up to the kind of sequence that gave birth to ideas of 'career' and 'progress' – with no long-term investments (Clegg, 2018). Liquid times produce fragmented lives that require individuals to be flexible and adaptable – to be constantly ready and willing to change tactics at short notice, to abandon commitments and loyalties without regret and to pursue opportunities according to their current availability. In liquid times the person becomes a strategist constantly calibrating their self in the face of endemic uncertainty.

Panopticism   Describes a form of secular Protestantism where the self is always the subject not of God's gaze but of an awareness that they are always under surveillance by secular authorities at work, in the street, shopping centres, etc. The important thing is not so much the surveillance *per se* as the inscription of an awareness of being under surveillance in the consciousness of the subject. It creates a form of neurotic self-control, constantly checking on self.

Post-bureaucracy   Literally, after bureaucracy. Usually post-bureaucratic organizations are described in terms of structural design features that are the opposite of those of bureaucracy. They are flatter, more flexible, more informal.

Project-based organizations   These are seen as the increasingly liquid form of organizing where teams of specialists come together for a specific project, be it an innovation project, a design challenge or a major work. They collaborate and disperse after the project is accomplished to reform in other new projects. Project-based organizations often have to juggle complex and contradictory directives: being on time and being on budget; being creative and delivering to specifications, etc.

Projects   Any project, literally, is a forward-throwing projection of an imagined future and the means of attaining it.

Synopticism   A situation in which the many can see the few, in which social media and the internet are altering our perceptions of what is acceptable when it comes to surveillance as we inform the world about ourselves on Facebook or other social media – we become a potential object of the gaze of the many whom we do not know in any face-to-face sense.

Notes

1 This article partly draws on a keynote address prepared by Stewart Clegg for the FORE School of Management, New Delhi Foundation Day International Conference on *Riding the New Tides: Navigating the Future Through Effective People Management*, November 24–25, 2016. In addition, Miguel Pina e Cunha's contribution was funded by National Funds through FCT – Fundação para a Ciência e Tecnologia under the project Ref. UID/ECO/00124/2013 and by POR Lisboa under the project LISBOA-01-0145-FEDER-007722.

2 Bauman's (1989) study *Modernity and the Holocaust* takes seriously Eichmann's plea that he was merely a good bureaucrat, following orders, establishing routines, and processing flows in a system – albeit one in which the throughput was extinction of life for certain bureaucratically defined categories of person. In such a system ethics could be reduced to being a good functionary.

3 http://www.oxfam.org.uk/media-centre/press-releases/2016/01/62-people-own-same-as-half -world-says-oxfam-inequality-report-davos-world-economic-forum

4 The term is ineluctably associated with the sociologist Émile Durkheim but was, in fact, coined by Jean-Marie Guyau (1886; see Orru, 1983).

References

Abrahamson, B., & Broström, A. (1980). *The rights of labor*. Beverly Hills, CA: Sage.

Barker, J. R. (1993). Tightening the iron cage: Concertive control in self-managing teams. Administrative Science Quarterly, *38*, 408–437.

Bauman, Z. (1972). *Between class and elite: The evolution of the British labour movement – a sociological study*. Manchester: Manchester University Press.

Bauman, Z. (1989). *In search of politics*. Palo Alto, CA: Stanford University Press.

Bauman, Z. (1995). *Life in fragments: Essays in postmodern morality*. Oxford: Blackwell.

Bauman, Z. (2000). *Liquid modernity*. Cambridge: Polity Press.

Bauman, Z. (2005). *Liquid life*. Cambridge: Polity.

Bauman, Z. (2007). *Liquid times: Living in an age of uncertainty*. Cambridge: Polity.

Bauman, Z. (2008). Organization for liquid-modern times? Unpublished paper provided by the author.

Bauman, Z. (2014). Preface. In J. Kociatkiewicz, & M. Kostera (eds) *Liquid organization: Zygmunt Bauman and organization theory* (pp. xiv-xix). London: Routledge.

Clegg, S. R. (2011). The futures of bureaucracy? *Insights, 4* (1). http://www.dur.ac.uk/ias/insights/.

Clegg, S. R. (2018). Reading Bauman and *Retrotopia. Scandinavian Journal of Management, 34*(4), 354–363.

Clegg, S. R., & Baumeler, C. (2010). Essai: From iron cages to liquid modernity in organization analysis. *Organization Studies, 31*(12), 1713–1733.

Clegg, S. R., & Baumeler, C. (2014). Liquid modernity, the owl of Minerva and technologies of the emotional self. In J. Kociatkiewicz, & M. Kostera (eds) *Liquid organization: Zygmunt Bauman and organization theory* (pp. 35–57). London: Routledge.

Clegg, S. R., & Courpasson, D. (2004). Political hybrids: Tocquevillean views on project organizations. *Journal of Management Studies, 41*(4), 525–547.

Clegg, S. R., Courpasson, D., & Phillips, N. (2006). *Power and organizations*. Thousand Oaks, CA: Sage.

Clegg, S. R., Cunha, M. P., & Rego, A. (2016). Explaining suicide in organizations. Durkheim revisited. *Business & Society Review, 121*(3), 391–414.

Clegg, S., Harris, M., & Hopfl, H. (eds) (2011). *Managing modernity: Beyond bureaucracy*. Oxford: Oxford University Press.

Clegg, S. R., & Kornberger, M. (2003). Modernism, postmodernism management and organization theory. In E. Locke (ed.) *Postmodernism in organizational thought: Pros, cons and the alternative* (pp. 57–89). Amsterdam: Elsevier.

Clegg, S. R., Schweitzer, J., Pitelis, C., & Whittle, A. (2016). *Strategy: Theory & practice*. London: Sage.

Coase, R. H. (1937). The nature of the firm. *Economica, 4*, 386–405.

Courpasson, D., & Reed, M. (2004). Introduction: Bureaucracy in the age of enterprise. *Organization, 11*(1), 5–12.

Dale, K. (2005). Building a social materiality: Spatial and embodied politics in organizational control. *Organization, 12*(5), 649–678.

Davis, G. F. (2016a). What might replace the modern corporation? Uberization and the web page enterprise. *Seattle University Law Review, 39*, 501–515.

Davis, G. F. (2016b). *The vanishing American corporation*. Oakland, CA: Berrett-Koehler.

du Gay, P. (2000). *In praise of bureaucracy: Weber, organization, ethics*. London: Sage.

Ekman, S. (2014). Is the high-involvement worker precarious or opportunistic? Hierarchical ambiguities in late capitalism. *Organization, 21*(2), 141–158.

Fama, E. F., & Jensen, M. C. (1983). Agency problems and residual claims. *Journal of Law and Economics, 26*, 327–349.

Gamble, A., & Walton, P. (1976) *Capitalism in crisis: Inflation and the state*. London: Macmillan.

Giddens, A. (1984). *The constitution of society: Outline of the theory of structuration*. Cambridge: Polity Press.

Goffman, E. (1959). *The presentation of self in everyday life*. Harmondsworth: Penguin.

Goleman, D. (1995). *Emotional intelligence: Why it can matter more than IQ*. New York: Bantam Books.

Goleman, D. (1998). *Working with emotional intelligence*. New York: Bantam Books.

Hancock, P. (2003). Beautiful untrue things: Aestheticizing the corporate culture industry. In A. Carr, & P. Hancock (eds) *Art and aesthetics at work* (pp. 174–194). Basingstoke: Palgrave Macmillan.

Hancock, P., & Rehn, A. (2011). Organizing Christmas. *Organization, 18*(6), 737–745.

Harvey, D. (2005). *A brief history of neoliberalism*. Oxford: Oxford University Press.

Hensby, A., Sibthorpe, J., & Driver, S. (2012). Resisting the 'protest business': Bureaucracy, post-bureaucracy and active membership in social movement organizations. *Organization, 19*(6), 809–823.

Hjorth, D., & Kostera, M. (eds) (2007). *Entrepreneurship and the experience economy*. Copenhagen: Copenhagen Business School Press.

Hollinshead, G., & Maclean, M. (2007). Transition and organizational dissonance in Serbia. *Human Relations, 60*(10), 1551–1574.

Jackall, R. (1988). *Moral mazes: The world of corporate managers*. New York: Oxford University Press.

Jacobsen, M. H., & Tester, K. (2007). Sociology, nostalgia, utopia and mortality: A conversation with Zygmunt Bauman. *European Journal of Social Theory, 10*(2), 305–325.

Jensen, T. (2010). Beyond good and evil: The adiaphoric company. *Journal of Business Ethics, 96*(3), 425–434.

Jensen, T. (2014). On adiaphoric organizations and adiaphoric organizational members. In J. Kociatkiewicz, & M. Kostera (eds) *Liquid organization: Zygmunt Bauman and organization theory* (pp. 13–34). London: Routledge.

Jensen, T., Sandström, J., & Helin, S. (2009). Corporate codes of ethics and the bending of moral space. *Organization, 16*(4), 529–545.

Johnsen, R., & Gudmand-Høyer, M. (2010). Lacan and the lack of humanity in HRM. *Organization, 17*(3), 331–44.

Knox, H., O'Doherty, D., Vurdubakis, T., & Westrup, C. (2008). Enacting airports: Space, movement and modes of ordering. *Organization, 15*(6), 869–888.

Kociatkiewicz, J., & Kostera, M. (eds) (2014). Towards sociological compassion: An introduction. In *Liquid organization: Zygmunt Bauman and organization theory* (pp. 1–12). London: Routledge.

Lancione, M., & Clegg, S. R. (2014). The lightness of management learning. *Management Learning*, March 24. DOI:10.1177/1350507614526533.

Lyotard, J-F. (1993). *Toward the Postmodern*, R. Harvey and M. S. Roberts (eds). Atlantic Highlands, NJ: Humanities Press.

Mallaby, S. (2010). *More money than God: Hedge funds and the making of a new elite*. London: Bloomsbury.

Maravelias, C. (2009). Make your presence known! Post-bureaucracy, HRM and the fear of being unseen. *Personnel Review, 38*(4), 349–365.

McLuhan, M. (1964). *Understanding media: The extensions of man*. Cambridge, MA: MIT Press.

Mumby, D., Thomas, R., Martí, I., & Seidl, D. (2017). Resistance redux. *Organization Studies, 38*(9), 1157–1183.

Orru, M. (1983). The ethics of anomie: Jean Marie Guyau and Emile Durkheim. *British Journal of Sociology, 34*(4), 499–518.

Oxfam (2015, January 15). Wealth: Having it all and wanting more. Retrieved from Oxfam. https://www.cdn.oxfam.org/s3fs-public/file_attachments/ib-wealth-having-all-wanting-more-190115-en.pdf.

Pelzer, P. A. (2014). Paradoxical attempt to freeze liquid modernity by liquidity: The return of fate. In J. Kociatkiewicz, & M. Kostera (eds) *Liquid Organization: Zygmunt Bauman and Organization Theory* (pp. 204–217). London: Routledge.

Petriglieri, G., Petriglieri, J. L., & Wood, J. D. (2017). Fast tracks and inner journeys: Crafting portable selves for contemporary careers. *Administrative Science Quarterly, 63*(3), 479–525.

Power, M. (1999). *The audit society: Rituals of verification.* London: Sage.

Power, M., Scheytt, T., Soin, K., & Sahlin, K. (2009). Reputational risk as a logic of organizing in late modernity. *Organization Studies, 30*(2/3), 165–188.

Salovey, P., & Mayer, J. D. (1990). Emotional intelligence. *Imagination, cognition, and personality, 9*(3), 185–211.

Schein, E. H., & Van Maanen, J. (2016). Career anchors and job/role planning: Tools for career and talent management. *Organizational Dynamics.* DOI.org/10.1016/j.orgdyn.2016-07.002.

Townley, B. (1993). Foucault, power/knowledge and its relevance for human resource management. *Academy of Management Review, 18*(3), 518–545.

Trinca, H., & Fox, C. (2004). *Better than sex: How a whole generation got hooked on work.* Sydney: Random House.

Warren, S. (2014). Consuming work: Aestheticization and the liquid employee. In J. Kociatkiewicz, & M. Kostera (eds) *Liquid organization: Zygmunt Bauman and organization theory* (pp. 70–84). London: Routledge.

Weigel, M. (2016, November 30). Political correctness: How the right invented a phantom enemy. Retrieved on December 1, 2016 from *The Guardian.* https://www.theguardian.com/us-news/2016/nov/30/political-correctness-how-the-right-invented-phantom-enemy-donald-trump.

Weiskopf, R., & Munro, I. (2012). Management of human capital: Discipline, security and controlled circulation in HRM. *Organization, 19*(6), 685–702.

Ybema, S., Keenoy, T., Oswick C., Beverungen A., Ellis, N., & Sabelis, I. (2009). Articulating identities. *Human Relations, 62*(3),299–322.

16 Management, organizations and contemporary social theory

An index of possibilities[1]

Miguel Pina e Cunha and Stewart Clegg

Organization theory can now be described as a disciplinary field with a venerable history: with robust theories (Miner, 1984), paradigms (Burrell & Morgan, 1979), even heroes (including 'Nobel' prizes awarded by the Sveriges Riksbank to laureates such as Herbert Simon) and myths (Cummings et al., 2017) in the sense of unfounded stories whose constant repetition 'proves' their supposed truth. As a result, its development often occurs within well-defined conceptual and empirical boundaries. This can be considered normal (Kuhn, 1962). Yet in a world in flux, with the constant arrival of new technologies, paradigmatic normalcy can pose serious questions, such as the incapacity of dominant organization theories to explain changes in the organizational world, including the demise of the corporation (Davis, 2016), the advent of the social enterprise (Saebi, Foss & Linder, 2018), the rise of post-bureaucratic forms (Josserand, Teo & Clegg, 2006), digitalization (Westerman, Bonnet & McAfee, 2014), Uberization (Fleming, 2017), etc.

We organize this final chapter in three parts. First, we explore four major change trends that may matter for social and organizational theorists. Next, we present an index of possibilities raised by the discussion in the volume. We conclude with a brief final note.

What is changing?

A number of trends are propelling the need to revise our theories of organization substantially. We briefly consider four: the decline of traditional forms, digitalization with its utopian and dystopian sides, the grand challenges facing humanity and changing workers' expectations.

The decline of traditional forms

Traditional forms of organizations have been challenged by emergent designs. They have been variously called post-bureaucratic (Josserand, Teo & Clegg, 2006), holacratic (Robertson, 2015), flat (Carzo Jr & Yanouzas, 1969), amongst many other suggestions. Regardless of name, empirical evidence shows that organizations are flatter than they used to be. These forms all share a motivation to depart from the dysfunctions of bureaucracy: they aim to be more agile, more participative, less pyramidal. New forms may reflect changing currents in society.

People raised in social democratic societies may aspire to work in more transparent organizations (Birkinshaw & Cable, 2017), more open to scrutiny and more open to their members' agency, wondering why, in many cases, despite the growth of new organizational forms, they must still leave the individual liberty to have contrary opinions and give voice outside the workplace.[2] Yet this movement in the direction of flatter organizations coexists with a decline in the democratic ethos in many societies. As elements of a liberal political economy in which individualism is paramount are promulgated in association with the digital platform economy, leading to Uberization (Fleming, 2017), social, democratically and collectively achieved rights are under threat. The broader patterns of social, political and economic ordering are a contested domain in which the frontiers of power and control, resistance and rights, are the markers. Social theories are necessary to explore these relations between society and organizations. We need to know more about, for example, how political regimes influence the diffusion of organizational forms. Extant work, namely on the varieties of capitalism (Hall & Soskice, 2001) can be helpful in this regard but more work is needed to analyse the mutual constitution of networks, social movements, political regimes, organizational forms and functions.

The promise and threat of digitalization

Current developments in the emergence of digital technologies constitute an important field for social theorists. The current debate is almost dualistic, with some analysts extolling the utopian features of a digital world, where intelligent machines do the boring bits of work, smart tools communicate with equally smart object-peers, humans see their competencies augmented and so on. On the other side of the debate, commentators refer to increasing probabilities of unemployment, the world dominated by artificial intelligence, even a 'robotcalypse'.

For social and organizational theorists alike, the emergence of digitalization offers numerous opportunities for research. Social theory, with its attention to the large and deep societal aspects of this change potentially challenges the more functional focus of organization theorists on what works, how and why. The critical perspective of social theory is central to informing debates in this field, which promises to revolutionize the way human societies are designed, controlled and organized.

Organizations do not change simply because of individual proclivities; they change in concert with the changing times and to focus too unduly on what is happening in specific organizations is to risk missing the larger currents that social theory can highlight. Digitalization is not just a matter of making the material immaterial; it is the spearhead of new ways of being at work; of new ways of contesting the frontiers of work and play, work and non-work; of new ways of consuming as well as producing; of new positioning of old subjectivities such as the identity of the employee, the customer, the retail experience; of new ways of conceptualizing old categories such as the transaction, competition, taxation, network, capitalism and so on. These are not necessarily the characteristics that organization theories will attend to most obviously but they are all aspects of broader social change having major implications for the identity and practice of organizing – putting in question even the category of the organization itself as society becomes more liquid and some established forms of organization dissolve.

Grand challenges

The UN's grand challenges have attracted important research attention (George et al., 2016). These grand challenges are often wicked to tackle and extremely difficult to resolve. Yet they need a share of the attention and energy of social and organizational theorists. In a discipline that is incremental and inward-looking, more attention is needed to explore how organizations can contribute to tackling major problems confronting humanity. These include global problems such as climate change, human exploitation, social inequality in general and gender and ethnic inequality in particular, increasingly autocratic forms of social control in totalitarian regimes, the sources and consequences of involuntary and voluntary human migrations, the impact of new forms of communication and so on.

As we elaborate next, organizational scholars have not been as attentive as one might expect about most of these and other issues. The public seems more attentive to these themes (consider, for example, the success of Harari's books *Sapiens* [2014] and *Homo Deus* [2016]), and it is imperative that organizational researchers should zoom out of their narrow fields to communicate with society at large, framing some of their work as directed to the wider public. One might well ask, where are the public intellectuals in organization theory? There is, we believe, a necessity to reorient organization theory from its narrow academic concerns to meaningful social contributions. In doing so we echo earlier contribution of Hinings and Greenwood (2002) and Clegg and Starbuck (2009) and would urge the field to draw on some of the insights from cognate areas, such as sociology, and the growth of a renewed concern with the role of public intellectuals (Burawoy, 2005; see Braithwaite, 2005 for some counterpoints). Indeed, Zygmunt Bauman, one of our cast of characters, has been mooted as providing pointers for this role (Aidnik, 2015). There are so many public domain debates that represent grand challenges in which organization theorists could and should be intervening – Brexit, austerity and its organizational impact, the organizational chaos of political office run as a family and nepotistic business on the basis of patrimonialism, the erosion of collective rights of labor and so on.

Changing workers' expectations

People's expectations seem also to be changing. Younger generations pay more attention to the social consequences of commerce and organizations than did previous ones. Some of the questions being raised include: are organizations sustainable in their practices? Do they discriminate on the basis of identity attributes or not? What kinds of security and rights do their supply chains afford? Are human and animal rights respected and advanced? What do they invest in the future of humanity and the planet? Young workers seem to be less interested in working in traditional corporate settings such as those populated by the 'organizational man' (Whyte, 1956) of the past. These expectations have resulted in some palpable changes. Some organizations are trying to become more inclusive, more socially inclined, which gives rise to the notion of the social enterprise, more interested in reaching out to those at the base of global political economy and the economic markets that are constructed in their name. Of course, noble ideas, such as that of the organization focused on the base of the pyramid, are in some cases espoused purposes that become countered by a masquerade of exploitative practices. Nonetheless, the trend seems evident: organizations need to consider and accommodate the motivations of generations that do not feel a commitment to traditional organizations and their environments.

These trends give rise to more concrete research avenues, as we explore next.

An index of possibilities

New times require new concepts and a new organizational language (Eisenhardt, 2000). This book offers a rich menu of possibilities for refreshing the theorizing of organizations. In this concluding note we strive to identify some common themes and to open possibilities for advancing management and organization theory through the contributions of general social theorists, as Loscher, Splitter and Seidl aptly call them. These general social theorists advance many powerful ideas that may easily change the way we imagine theories of organization.

Such theories tend to look less at organizations with the mechanistic, rationalist lenses that have dominated in the past; instead favouring the view of organizations as 'the condensation of local cultures of values, power, rules, discretion and paradox' (Clegg, 1994, p. 172). This representation of organization beyond the mechanistic-cognitivist offers a menu of possibilities. With no intention of being exhaustive we explore twelve: becoming, bodies, boundaries, digital, flatness, hyperagency, inequality, (non)human, paradox, power, practice and violence.

Becoming

As many organizations gain more liquid characteristics (see Clegg & Cunha, this volume), organization scholars need to heed becoming. Instead of seeing organizations as mechanistic, scholars are exploring the relation between agency and structure as mutually constituting (Chaterjee, Kunwar & den Hond, this volume) and in permanent flux. Therefore, instead of studying structures as they are, it is critical to consider how structures and agents engage in mutual shape-shifting. Seeing change as the natural state means that even resistance to change reeds to be reframed from a becoming lens: change and resistance as one and the same need to be conceived as attempts to manage the duality of stability and change as parts of the same process. For example, attempts at stability may actually propel change in force. What is especially interesting now is the impact of social media in the triggering and diffusion of change.

Some examples exist at the articulation of organizations, leadership and society. For example, how did Mohamed Bouazizi, a Tunisian street vendor who set himself on fire on December 17, 2010, ignite the sequence of revolution and reaction known as the Arab Spring? How did the military junta in Myanmar neutralize change by bringing its major opponent Aung San Suu Kyi to office and limit her capabilities for change in so doing?

A too narrow focus on corporate leadership is also stifling the capacity to understand the relation between political and corporate regimes beyond cooptation. What are the boundaries of appropriate forms of organization in contemporary times? Where are the many organization theorists reminding the public once again of the ethos and values of liberal bureaucracy once promulgated by Weber and defended in contemporary times by a few, such as du Gay (2000), in the face of its corruption in the highest offices in so many countries, not least the most powerful? What does it mean for the theory of organizations when association with rumours of corruption taints political office and its public administration? Is it possible that transactional leadership in the highest office in the world can become transformational, merely by hingeing on the art of the deal? What has organization theory, as distinct from communication theory (Ott, 2017), to offer?

Other more analytical research questions might include:

- When and how does an excess of stability produce change?
- When and how does an excess of change produce stability?
- How are the previous processes influenced by other societal factors, such as political regimes?
- How does digital media change the process of change?

Bodies

The role of the body and the understanding of the world by embodied individuals features importantly in several chapters (see chapters by Kenny, Mutch and van Krieken, this volume). Yet with few exceptions, the biology of people is still absent from research. Most research topics look at people as cognitive entities, as 'brains': rational decision-makers. We now know that decisions are highly emotional (Schwarz, 2000); that sensemaking involves the body (Cunha et al., 2015); that sexual drives are not neutralized in the workplace (Hearn, 1989); that the workforce is aging and will live longer (Gratton, 2016); that metaphors fuse neural pathways (Castells, 2015). In other words, and in spite of recent efforts in this direction, much more needs to be known about the presence of embodied being in organizations.

Emerging organizational vocabularies such as those brought by the logic of performativity (see Kenny, this volume) may help to illuminate the role of biology and the body in organizations but this is at the early stage of research.

Possible research questions:

- How do organizations deal with bodies? Are there specific types of bodies required by specific professions?
- How has the food industry produced the obesity epidemic that other industries try to tackle?
- Can AI help to overcome prejudice regarding some bodies?
- How do organizations deal with diversely gendered, aged and ethnic bodies?
- Why do some organizations manage to approach bodily differences (such as in the case of people with disabilities) differently?

Boundaries

Social theorists may also inform organization theories by considering boundaries. As Luhmann theorized, 'Differentiating itself, each social system constructs its environment' (quoting Deroy, in this volume). What is especially interesting is that in our liquid societies, boundaries are becoming blurred (see Clegg & Cunha, this volume). The drawing of boundaries is challenging: where are the boundaries between home and work in a society of smartphones and portable computers (Mazmanian, Orlikowski & Yates, 2013)? (Part of this chapter was written by one of the authors away from work and home, in the Algarve, southern Portugal, while on vacation, early in the mornings; the whole book was edited by two authors whose mobilities spanned the globe during the process of writing.) What are the boundaries between digital and non-digital, between human and artificial intelligence, when cyborg bodies are no longer science fiction but science fact? What are the boundaries between the human and the non-human? What are the boundaries between being an insider and an outsider in an economy of gig work?

In the field of politics boundaries are especially complicated as they define identity. The advent of the politics of identity seems particularly troubling in the world of globalization. The definition of politics around identity in a binary and dichotomous way premised on various sorts of 'othering' constitutes a major fact in current world politics. Organizations are sometimes caught in these geopolitical conflicts, such as multinationals in Catalonia, faced with the decision of maintaining their Spanish centres in Barcelona or moving them to Madrid, and in either case being associated with the political consequences of their decisions. The politics of Brexit are another example: 'Should I stay or should I go' (Strummer & Jones, 1982) is an old song that must lurk in the subconsciousness of many CEOs whose organizations and enterprises are presently located in the UK.

Possible research questions:

- How can boundaries be defined?
- How do new digital businesses blur boundaries?
- How should boundaries include and exclude?

Digital

Social theorists need to interpellate the digital. As witnessed by many chapters in this book, they are already doing it. Digital technologies have changed the way societies work and they will certainly continue to do so. Digital technologies are touching and challenging the very core of organization and management: they offer new business models; redesign communication networks; offer new possibilities for redesigning organizational processes. Moreover, they replace old certainties such as the stable employment relation by the 'self-employed' gig worker. Recent evidence shows that states are trying to regain control of their capacity to regulate the economy (*Financial Times*, 2018).

In this context, activities that were fundamentally internal, such as innovation, can now open up and be translated in ideas such as those of the crowd, open innovation in recognition that the sources of innovation are not necessarily inside organizations and that innovations need to be opened rather than protected and hidden (Svahn, Mathiassen & Lindgren, 2017). What happens to the industry associated with patenting in a world of more open innovation? Enormous changes in organizational processes are occurring not only in areas such as innovation but also in routine work, decision-making based on AI, or augmented reality with all its operational implications.

Possible research questions:

- How will AI technologies change human work?
- How will people accept co-working with robots?
- What will the meaning of work be in societies that are increasingly roboticized?
- Will robots and AI aggravate inequality?

Flatness

Some social theory and most of that of management has been marked by the logic of levels of analysis. Levels are so useful as conceptual categorizations that they have become naturalized as normal; yet, they constitute artificial layers. As discussed in this volume, people embrace social reality with no layers. Or as Luhmann observed, there is 'only one single level of social reality' (Loscher, Splitter & Seidl, this volume; see also O'Doherty). This points to the need to consider communication networks as 'the advent of flat ontologies' (see Deroy, this volume).

Organization scholars have defended the need for flatter and taller ontologies (Seidl & Whittington, 2014) and this idea is echoed in several chapters in this book. Flatter ontologies collapse a number of themes considered in several chapters. From a performative perspective, people participate in human–non-human networks in which the separation of the social and the material is useful but ultimately false. As Law (1987) explained in his study of the Portuguese maritime journeys of discovery, people embody knowledge much as tools do. Therefore, to introduce a chasm between the human and the material is just another expression of dualism so pervasive in the social sciences.

Possible research questions:

- How does ordinary materiality render the extraordinary banal?
- How can organizational scholars overcome the logic of layers?
- How does flatness articulate real and empirical domains?

Hyperagency

In a world with fewer corporations some successful entrepreneurs gain the status of hyperagents (Maclean & Harvey, this volume). The role of hyperagents deserves a central position in social theory. Long gone are the times of the faceless executive who was a mere employee (Whyte, 1956). Before organization man, entrepreneurs, the 'robber barons' of early American capitalism, were major identities globally and in their national society. Today, techpreneurs, such as Steve Jobs or Elon Musk, carve out a very special niche in societies, much as the entrepreneurially charismatic figures from the turn of the 20th century. Some of them have amassed incredible amounts of capital (Maclean & Harvey, this volume) and project their power accordingly. The organizations that they create often transcend and confuse boundaries, legal, tax and otherwise, and are some of world's biggest and most global businesses.

States and their representatives court these hyperagents. These hyperagents promulgate rules and practices that challenge the legal rules of national states and that create globally united states of virtuality that minimize tax liabilities and maximize profits in financial operations whose contributions to society are dubious, legitimated through the prevailing ideology of shareholder value (Davis, 2016) that has ruled since the 1980s. Given their liquid nature they are often difficult to scrutinize. As such they pose very real questions at the boundary of (hyper)agency and governance structures for the digital age.

Possible research questions:

- How does the hyperagency of the new elites contribute to reshaping the global powers?
- How do hyperagents interact with nation-states and their representatives?
- What are the impacts of the new, digital hyperagents over systems of governance – in organizations and societies?
- What types of reactions do these hyperagents stimulate? How does digital whistle-blowing play out in the digital age?

Inequality

Inequality is a major threat to stability. Bourdieu's work on the formation of elites (see Maclean & Harvey, this volume) offers an important glimpse of the way the privileged manage to protect their condition. The rise of organizations based on digital capabilities poses new problems in terms of control. On the one hand, they can grow rapidly to become imperial behemoths, such as Google or Microsoft. Being fundamentally immaterial, these companies create problems previously unknown. Inequality is a major social issue globally as is the digital divide, in terms of access to and capabilities with digital platforms. Not much is known about the way digitalization is shaping and having an impact on equality issues in organizations. For instance, in cases where routine and programmable jobs become automated, what will happen to the people who used to perform them? Current discussions around robot taxes, a universal basic minimum income and related issues are clearly of relevance for organization and management theory but are also areas in which the reflections of social theory have been prescient.

In addition to inequality, the fact that organizations are becoming adiaphoric (see Clegg & Cunha, this volume) poses even more stringent challenges to organizations:

> *Adiaphorization* will especially characterize the top management team: while each member may ontologically be a moral subject, the organization cannot be. This is the essence of leaderly strategies ... Leadership may well be formulated within governance structures, rules, guidelines and policies but it is essentially ethically blank in its representations.

Adiaphorization offers a window on a theme for a social theory of organization: how can organizations, their owners and managers rebuild their social contracts? The crisis of confidence in organizations (Child, 2002) has eroded the gap between people and the corporate world and increased inequality in some of its most visible expressions between the many and the few, to coin a phrase. Piketty's book and its impact are indicators of how serious the matter is; the concerns of *Capital* (Marx, 1976) are, once again, salient.

Possible research questions:

- How will digitalization have a future impact on inequality within human societies as AI gathers pace?
- How will digitalization have an impact on inequality between human societies?
- How will moral accountability and tendencies to adiaphorization have an impact on issues such as business ethics and inequality?

(Non-)human

A central theme in social theory refers to the meaning of being human (see Pierides & Sewell, this volume). Another refers to the role of individuals in integrated networks or wholes; they are 'finitely connected into an integrated whole'. A main challenge for social theory refers to the redefinition of the meaning of being human in a society which is increasingly blurring the boundaries of human–non-human. Cobots, artificial intelligence and other digital possibilities are mixing the worlds of human and digital. Possibilities arise for technology to replace parts of human bodies including the brain (Oliveira, 2018). How in this context can being 'human' be defined? Actors are becoming actants as chips are implanted and actants are increasingly central to action as AI and digital devices organize ever more organizational practice. Actor networks and digital networks will be of increasing salience for future organizations (see O'Doherty as well as Costa, Quintanilha & Mendonça, this volume).

The human–non-human nexus also leads to other themes. Organizational scholars have paid fundamental attention to humans as the subjects of organizational research, as if matter did not matter. As the authors in this volume stress, understanding the role of matter is critical for understanding how humans construct their societies and organizations. The new technological developments just mentioned are normalizing the cyborgization of organizational life.

Possible research questions:

- How will the collaboration between people and machines redefine human societies?
- If people incorporate artificial organs and are assisted by intelligent machines, how will the boundaries of the human and non-human, and vice versa, be determined? Is *Blade Runner* the future?
- How will human–non-human systems collaborate in the definition of the organizations of the future?

Paradox

A theme that has gained notoriety in organizations recently is that of paradox. Paradox refers to opposites that define one another and that persist over time in an exercise of constant tension (Clegg, Cunha & Cunha, 2002; Smith & Lewis, 2011). Paradox featured in many occasions throughout this volume. As Deroy summarized, 'Organizations contain their opposite, their own paradox'. Social theory may inform organization studies by contributing to the debate on the paradoxes at the very core of organizing. Organizations are part of society and should strive for the social good, yet they are moved by their own interests that are often at odds with some of those of society as a whole, such as a strong tax base – a tension that is leading some organizations to consider the responsibility of organizations as good citizens (Abbatiello et al., 2018).

A paradox lens may also help to explore the tensions opposing inclusion and exclusion, diversity and homogeneity, identity as fixed and as malleable. A paradox lens can contribute to exploring grand challenges such as those related to environmental sustainability (Hahn et al., 2010) from a both/and perspective (Smith, Lewis & Tushman, 2016). Paradox stretches the way we think by countering dualisms/dichotomies and showing that tensions can indeed be generative and a source of social progress, when framed as dualities (Farjoun, 2010). A major limitation of current debates resides in polarizations that limit the quality of conversations (Jay & Grant, 2017).

Possible research questions:

- How can paradox contribute to the quality of conversations?
- How and when do social actors transform dualisms into dualities?
- How do paradoxical choices confront social actors and decision-makers?

Power

Power is the omnipresent theme throughout the volume. Ultimately the organization of business firms and all other organizations, as well as of society in general, is a matter of the architectonics and arrangements of power relations (Clegg, 1989; Clegg, Courpasson & Phillips, 2006). At the intersection of several themes discussed in this volume, the representation of power is sometimes presented as undergoing a major change: the end of traditional power (Naím, 2013) and the emergence of a 'new power' (Heimans & Timmins, 2017) is said to be on the rise, which is is more fluid, more dispersed, more transparent, symbolized by post-hierarchical organizations, flat designs and holacracies (Robertson, 2015). The nemesis of these forms is the traditional bureaucracy and its organization of societies and citizens (Hamel & Zanini, 2016).

Some authors, on the contrary, maintain that we are still the same (Pfeffer, 2013) or that the new power is possibly more concertative and transparent but no less panoptical. Power relations will continue to attract the imagination of organizational and social theorists alike as new technologies create the conditions for entirely new methods of control. These are sustained in a new dualism: institutions such as the state need to control people for the sake of overall security, but paradoxically, in the name of security, societies will be stripped of civil freedoms as is happening in the 'surveillance state of China', namely in the Xinjiang region. As they put it, there 'the people have sharp eyes' (Lucas & Fang, 2018, p. 16). Sharp eyes can cut like a knife.

Possible research questions:

- Is there really an end of power/new power?
- What are the further adventures of 'veillance' in the contemporary post-panopticon era?
- How do digital possibilities contribute to imposing new forms of power, more transparent but no less intense?

Practice

Organizations are often viewed as reified 'things' independent of people. This volume foregrounded the importance of practice in making organization happen and thus studying organization through the lens of those whose doings enact it (see Whittle & Mueller, this volume) through their everyday practices, discourse and especially conversation. Practices come in bundles, amalgams (Loscher et al., this volume). Yet we tend to separate bundles in order to render them more visible and empirically accessible. Consider paradox: paradox scholars tend to focus on two contradictory demands (e.g. change–stability). This is understandable, but real-world tensions are entangled in complex webs of oppositions (Raisch, Hargrave & Van de Ven, 2018). Therefore, putting practice at the core of organization analysis enables the study of them as they are actually socially organized rather than assuming that they are modelled according to some meta-rationality.

Possible research questions:

- How do the new digital vocabularies influence the happening of new forms of organization?
- How may practices collapse a micro-macro understanding of organizations?
- How can practices inform the design of more inclusive and dignified forms of organization – for example by indicating the tactics people use to protect their dignity as members of hierarchies?

Violence

The interplay of organization and violence has been insufficiently studied. Yet organizations can impose violence, either symbolically (see Chatterjee, Kunwar & den Hond, this volume) or materially (Bauman, 2000). Organization studies has mostly remained silent on this propensity for violence. At one extreme, however, organizations and the supply chains they compose have been associated with necro-capitalist practices (Banerjee, 2008). These practices reach public awareness in episodes such as the disaster at Rana Plaza (Reinecke & Donaghey, 2015) or the waves of suicides in companies such as Foxconn and France Telecom (Clegg, Cunha & Rego, 2016) but such events are the tip of an iceberg that involves exploitation, slavery and workplace violence (e.g. Crane, 2013). Bauman's work on the modern dimension of the Holocaust offers an extreme case of a process that deserves more attention than it has received. As Clegg (2006) pointed out, organization studies have been fundamentally ignorant about genocide. Yet genocide most often involves sophisticated forms of organization and is, ethically, the most evil that organization can achieve. We should not neglect the wrongs and the evil that organization makes possible.

Possible research questions:

- How are the conceptual tools of everyday organization used to produce violence?
- How does such violence escape public scrutiny?
- What is the relationship between utopia and dystopia?

Closing the curtain

In this chapter we offered, without any pretense at completeness, an index of possibilities for research at the intersection of social theory and organization studies. The volume can be read as an invitation for organizational scholars to think more often in engagement with social theorists and to zoom out of their narrow fields of specialization. Of course, the challenge goes against some of the professional rules of the discipline with its pressure for zooming in over narrow issues, but a measure of resistance against pressures for conformity will contribute to refreshing the discipline and to increasing its appeal beyond disciplinary frontiers. If the price of specialization is practical irrelevance in terms of the big issues and grand questions of the day, then we, as authors and editors, and our contributors, would want no part of such a prognosis. Once again, we invoke not only the major social theorists analysed herein but a tradition that stretches back to the giants of the 19th century on whose shoulders we stand. We hope the volume stimulates the imagination and the curiosity of our readers. The ideas expressed herein are rich enough to fertilize research in numerous sub-disciplinary fields. In this sense, we see the book as an homage to some intellectual giants of modernity and as an invitation to follow in their footsteps and to stretch the boundaries of our thinking in the pursuit of an engaged social science aimed at the creation of more inclusive and humane societies.

Let us close with a couple of remarks that we extract directly from Pierides and Sewell: first, the book is not intended to offer a series of précis on central authors of social theory; second, the books and the authors discussed herein should be 'consulted directly'. In fact, we hope that the book serves as an aperitif, an invitation for something of more substance than what is on offer here: the rich oeuvres of the authors explored. We are sure all the authors in this volume will be aligned with this invitation. As such, as we close we invite you to continue your exploration, perhaps starting the project with the mapping offered here. Bon voyage.

Notes

1 The subtitle borrows from David Sylvian, an artist in constant transformation himself.
2 In the autocracies, such as the People's Republic of China, these aspirations are more brutally repressed.

References

Abbatiello, A., Agarwal, D., Bersin, J., Lahiri, G., Schwartz, J., & Volini, E. (2018). *The rise of the social enterprise*. Bersin: Deloitte Consulting.

Aidnik, M. (2015). A sociology for the 21st century? An enquiry into public sociology reading Zygmunt Bauman. *Studies of Transition States and Societies*, 7(2), 7–18.

Banerjee, B. S. (2008). Necrocapitalism. *Organization Studies*, 29(12), 1541–1563.

Bauman, Z. (2000). *Modernity and the Holocaust*. Ithaca, NY: Cornell University Press.

Birkinshaw, J., & Cable, D. (2017). The dark side of transparency. *McKinsey Quarterly*.

Braithwaite, J. (2005). For public social science 1. *The British Journal of Sociology*, 56(3), 345–353.

Burawoy, M. (2005). For public sociology. *American Sociological Review*, 70(1), 4–28.

Burrell, G., & Morgan, G. (1979). *Sociological paradigms and organisational analysis: Elements of the sociology of corporate life*. London: Routledge.

Carzo Jr, R., & Yanouzas, J. N. (1969). Effects of flat and tall organization structure. *Administrative Science Quarterly*, 178–191.

Castells, M. (2015). *Networks of outrage and hope*. Cambridge: Polity Press.

Child, J. (2002). The international crisis of confidence in corporations. *Academy of Management Executive*, 16(3), 142–144.

Clegg, S. R. (1989). *Frameworks of power*. London: Sage.

Clegg, S. R. (1994). Weber and Foucault: Social theory for the study of organizations. *Organization*, 1(1), 149–178.

Clegg, S. R. (2006). Why is organization theory so ignorant? The neglect of total institutions. *Journal of Management Inquiry*, 15(4), 426–430.

Clegg, S., Courpasson, D., & Phillips, N. (2006). *Power and organizations*. London: Sage.

Clegg, S. R., Cunha, J. V., & Cunha, M. P. (2002). Management paradoxes: A relational view. *Human Relations*, 55(5), 483–503.

Clegg, S., Cunha, M. P., & Rego, A. (2016). Explaining suicide in organizations. Durkheim revisited. *Business & Society Review*, 121(3), 391–414.

Clegg, S. R., & Starbuck, W. H. (2009). Can we still fix M@n@gement? The narrow path towards a brighter future in organizing practices. *M@n@gement*, 12(5), 332–358.

Crane, A. (2013). Modern slavery as a management practice: Exploring the conditions and capabilities for human exploitation. *Academy of Management Review*, 38(1), 49–69.

Cummings, S., Bridgman, T., Hassard, J., & Rowlinson, M. (2017). *A new history of management*. Cambridge: Cambridge University Press.

Cunha, M. P., Clegg, S., Rego, A., & Gomes, J. F. S. (2015). Embodying sensemaking: Learning from the extreme case of Vann Nath, prisoner at S-21. *European Management Review*, 12(1), 41–58.

Davis, G. F. (2016). Can an economy survive without corporations? Technology and robust organizational alternatives. *Academy of Management Perspectives*, 30(2), 129–140.

du Gay, P. (2000). *In praise of bureaucracy: Weber-organization-ethics*. London: Sage.

Eisenhardt, K.M. (2000). Paradox, spirals, ambivalence: The new language of change and pluralism. *Academy of Management Review*, 25, 703–705.

Farjoun, M. (2010). Beyond dualism: Stability and change as duality. *Academy of Management Review*, 35, 202–225.

Financial Times (2018, June 13). Gig workers need better employment protections. https://www.ft.com/content/411047c4-6ef9-11e8-852d-d8b934ff5ffa.

Fleming, P. (2017). The human capital hoax: Work, debt and insecurity in the era of Uberization. *Organization Studies*, 38(5), 691–709.

George, G., Howard-Grenville, J., Joshi, A., & Tihanyi, L. (2016). Understanding and tackling societal grand challenges through management research. *Academy of Management Journal*, 59(6), 1880–1895.

Gratton, L. (2016). *The 100-year life: Living and working in an age of longevity*. London: Bloomsbury Publishing.

Hahn, T., Figge, F., Pinkse, J., & Preuss, L. (2010). Trade-offs in corporate sustainability: You can't have your cake and eat it. *Business Strategy and the Environment*, 19(4), 217–229.

Hall, P. A., & Soskice, D. (2001). *Varieties of capitalism: The institutional foundations of comparative advantage*. Oxford: Oxford University Press.

Hamel, G., & Zanini, M. (2016). *The $3 trillion prize for busting bureaucracy (and how to claim it)*. London: The Management Lab.

Harari, Y. N. (2014). *Sapiens: A brief history of humankind*. New York: Random House.

Harari, Y. N. (2016). *Homo Deus: A brief history of tomorrow*. New York: Random House.

Hearn, J. (1989). *The sexuality of organization*. London: Sage.

Heimans, J., & Timmins, H. (2017). *New power*. London: Macmillan.

Hinings, C. R., & Greenwood, R. (2002). ASQ forum: Disconnects and consequences in organization theory? *Administrative Science Quarterly*, 47(3), 411–421.

Jay, J., & Grant G. (2017). *Breaking through gridlock*. San Francisco: Berrett Koehler.

Josserand, E., Teo, S., & Clegg, S. (2006). From bureaucratic to post-bureaucratic: The difficulties of transition. *Journal of Organizational Change Management*, 19(1), 54–64.

Kuhn, T. S. (1962). *The structure of scientific revolutions*. Chicago: University of Chicago Press.

Law, J. (1987). Technology and heterogeneous engineering: The case of Portuguese expansion. In W. E. Bijker, T. P. Hughes, & T. J. Pinch (eds) *The social construction of technological systems: New directions in the sociology and history of technology* (111–134). Cambridge, MA: MIT Press.

Lucas, L., & Fang, E. (2018). Inside Chain's surveillance state. *Financial Times Life & Arts*, July 21–22,16–17.

Marx, K. (1976). *Capital*. London: Penguin.

Mazmanian, M., Orlikowski, W. J., & Yates, J. (2013). The autonomy paradox: The implications of mobile email devices for knowledge professionals. *Organization Science*, 24(5), 1337–1357.

Miner, J. B. (1984). The validity and usefulness of theories in an emerging organizational science. *Academy of Management Review*, 9(2), 296–306.

Naím, M. (2013). *The end of power*. New York: Basic Books.

Oliveira, A. (2018). *The digital mind*. Boston, MA: MIT Press.

Ott, B. L. (2017). The age of Twitter: Donald J. Trump and the politics of debasement. *Critical Studies in Media Communication*, 34(1), 59–68.

Pfeffer, J. (2013). You're still the same: Why theories of power hold over time and across contexts. *Academy of Management Perspectives*, 27(4), 269–280.

Picketty, T. (2014). *Capital in the 21st century*. Boston, MA: Harvard University Press.

Raisch, S., Hargrave, T. J., & Van de Ven, A. H. (2018). The learning spiral: A process perspective on paradox. *Journal of Management Studies*. https://doi.org/10.1111/joms.12397.

Reinecke, J., & Donaghey, J. (2015). After Rana Plaza: Building coalitional power for labour rights between unions and (consumption-based) social movement organisations. *Organization*, 22(5), 720–740.

Robertson, B. J. (2015). *Holacracy: The revolutionary management system that abolishes hierarchy*. London: Penguin.

Saebi, T., Foss, N. J., & Linder, S. (2018). Social entrepreneurship research: Past achievements and future promises. *Journal of Management*. https://doi.org/10.1177%2F0149206318793196.

Schwarz, N. (2000). Emotion, cognition, and decision making. *Cognition & Emotion*, 14(4), 433–440.

Seidl, D., & Whittington, R. (2014). Enlarging the strategy-as-practice research agenda: Towards taller and flatter ontologies. *Organization Studies*, 35(10), 1407–1421.

Smith, W. K., & Lewis, M. W. (2011). Toward a theory of paradox: A dynamic equilibrium model of organizing. *Academy of Management Review*, 36(2), 381–403.

Smith, W.K., Lewis, M. & Tushman, M. (2016). 'Both/and' leadership. *Harvard Business Review*, May, 63–70.

Strummer, J. and Jones, M. (1982) Should I stay or should I go. *Combat Rock*. New York: Epic.

Svahn, F., Mathiassen, L., & Lindgren, R. (2017). Embracing digital innovation in incumbent firms: How Volvo cars managed competing concerns. *MIS Quarterly*, 41(1),239–253.

Westerman, G., Bonnet, D., & McAfee, A. (2014). *Leading digital: Turning technology into business transformation*. Boston, MA: Harvard Business Press.

Whyte, W. H. (1956). *The organization man*. New York: Simon and Schuster.

Index

Locators in *italics* refer to figures, those followed by the letter 'g' relate to glossary entries.

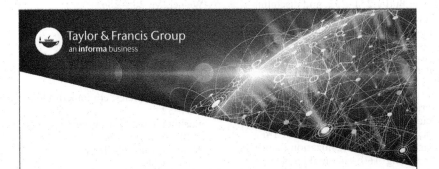